essentia

Access 2000
advanced

John Preston
Eastern Michigan University
Sally Preston
Washtenaw Community College
Robert Ferret
Eastern Michigan University

Prentice Hall
A division of Pearson Education
Upper Saddle River, NJ 07458

Access 2000 Essentials Advanced

International Standard Book Number: 1-58076-302-2

Library of Congress Catalog Card Number: 99-60070

Printed in the United States of America

First Printing: *June 1999*

03 02 01 4 3 2

Interpretation of the printing code: the rightmost double-digit number is the year of the book's printing: the rightmost single-digit number, the number of the book's printing. For example, a printing code of 00-1 shows that the first printing of the book occurred in 2000.

Trademark Acknowledgments

Screens reproduced in the book were created using Collage Plus from Inner Media, Inc., Hollis, NH.

Access 2000 Essentials Advanced is based on Microsoft Access 2000.

Publisher:
Robert Linsky

Executive Editor:
Sunthar Visuvalingam

Series Editors:
Marianne Fox and
Larry Metzelaar

Annotated Instructor's Manual (AIM) Series Editor:
Linda Bird

Operations Manager:
Christine Moos

Director of Product Marketing:
Susan Kindel

Acquisitions Editor:
Sunthar Visuvalingam

Development Editor:
Jan Snyder

Technical Editor:
Debra Griggs

Software Specialist:
Angela Denny

Book Designer:
Louisa Klucznik

Design Usability Consultant:
Elizabeth Keyes

Project Editor:
Sherri Fugit

Copy Editor:
Melody Layne

Proofreader:
Debbie Williams

Indexer:
Brad Herriman

Layout Technicians:
Juli Cook
Liz Johnston

Team Coordinator:
Melody Layne

Usability Testers:
Sarah Ann Margulies J.D., University of Michigan Law School
Lakshmy Sivaratnam M.S., University of Missouri at Kansas City
Cathy Gillmore, Shell Chemical Company

About the Authors

Robert Ferrett is the Director of the Center for Instructional Computing at Eastern Michigan University. His center provides computer training and support to faculty at the university. He has authored or co-authored more than thirty books on Access, PowerPoint, Excel, Word, and Word Perfect and was the editor of the *1994 ACM SIGUCCS Conference Proceedings*. He is a series editor for the *Learn 97* and *Learn 2000* books, and has been designing, developing, and delivering computer workshops for nearly two decades. He has a BA in Psychology, an MS in Geography, and an MS in Interdisciplinary Technology from Eastern Michigan University. He is ABD in the Ph.D. program in Instructional Technology at Wayne State University.

John Preston is an Associate Professor at Eastern Michigan University in the College of Technology, where he teaches microcomputer application courses at the undergraduate and graduate levels. He has been teaching, writing, and designing computer training courses since the advent of PCs, and has authored and co-authored more than two dozen books on Microsoft Word, Excel, Access, and PowerPoint. He is a series editor for the *Learn 97* and *Learn 2000* books. He has received grants from the Detroit Edison Institute and the Department of Energy to develop Web sites for energy education and alternative fuels. He has also developed one of the first Internet-based microcomputer applications courses at an accredited university. He has a BS from the University of Michigan in Physics, Mathematics, and Education, and an MS from Eastern Michigan University in Physics Education. He is ABD in the Ph.D. program in Instructional Technology at Wayne State University.

Sally Preston is President of Preston & Associates, a computer software-training firm. She utilizes her extensive business experience as a bank vice president in charge of branch operations. She provides corporate training through Preston & Associates and through the Institute for Workforce Development at Washtenaw Community College, where she also teaches computer courses part time. She has co-authored nearly 20 books on Access, Excel, PowerPoint, Word, and Word Perfect, including the *Learn 97*, *Learn 2000*, *Office 2000 Essentials*, and *Access 2000 Essentials* books. She has an MBA from Eastern Michigan University.

Acknowledgments

Although the authors are solely responsible for its content, this book and the *Essentials* series as a whole have been shaped by the combined experience, perspectives, and input of the entire authoring, editorial, and design team. We are grateful to the Series Editors, **Larry Metzelaar** and **Marianne Fox**, and to the College of Business Administration at Butler University for hosting the listserv on which the implications and value of every series element were thoroughly discussed and finalized even as this book was being written. They also hosted a November 1998 seminar for the AIM authors and coordinated much of the usability testing at the Butler campus. We acknowledge **Robert Linsky** (Publisher, Que Education and Training) for having provided the initial direction and for having allowed the Essentials 2000 team to shape this edition as we saw fit. You, the reader, are the greatest beneficiary of this ongoing online collaborative effort.

Chuck Stewart adapted the original Que E&T *Essentials* series for corporate training. In early 1998, however, he began revamping the *Office 2000 Essentials* pedagogy to better serve academic needs exclusively. He enlisted the services of Series Editors Metzelaar and Fox because of their extensive background in courseware development, many years of classroom teaching, and innovative pedagogy. Early discussion with the Series Editors revealed the need for the three new types of end-of-chapter exercises you find in the *Office 2000 Essentials*. Chuck continued to provide ideas and feedback on the listserv long after handing over the executive editorship to Sunthar. Together, they completely overhauled the *Essentials* series, paying particular attention to pedagogy, content, and design issues.

Sunthar Visuvalingam took over as Executive Editor for the *Essentials* series in October 1998. He stepped into a process already in full swing and moved quickly to ensure "a level of collaboration rarely seen in academic publishing." He performed admirably the daunting task of coordinating an army of widely dispersed authors, editors, designers, and usability testers. Among the keywords that characterize his crucial role in forging a well-knit "learning team" are decisive leadership, effective communication, shared vision, continuous pedagogical and procedural innovation, infectious enthusiasm, dogged project and quality management, active solicitation of feedback, collective problem-solving, transparent decision making, developmental mentoring, reliability, flexibility and dedication. Having made his indelible mark on the *Essentials* series, he stayed on to shepherd the transition of the series to Alex von Rosenberg.

Linda Bird (AIM Series Editor and author of both *PowerPoint Essentials* books) and **Robert Ferrett** (co-author of *Office Essentials*, all three *Access Essentials* books, and of the related *Learn* series) made significant contributions to enhancing the concept and details of the new series. A newcomer to the series but not to educational publishing, **Keith Mulbery** seized increasing ownership of *Essentials* and undertook the initiative of presenting the series at the April 1999 National Business Education Association Convention.

Alex von Rosenberg, Executive Editor, manages the Computer Applications publishing program at Prentice Hall (PH). The PH team has been instrumental in ensuring a smooth transition of the *Essentials* series. Alex has been ably assisted in this transition by **Susan Rifkin**, Managing Editor; **Leanne Nieglos**, Assistant Editor; **Jennifer Surich**, Editorial Assistant; **Nancy Evans**, Director of Strategic Marketing; **Kris King**, Senior Marketing Manager; and **Nancy Welcher**, Media Project Manager.

Operations Manager **Christine Moos** and Senior Editor **Karen Walsh** worked hard with Sunthar and Alex to allow authors maximum flexibility to produce a quality product, while trying to maintain a tight editorial and production schedule. They had the unenviable task of keeping the book processes rolling while managing the complex process of transitioning the series to Prentice Hall. Book Designer **Louisa Klucznik** and Consultant **Elizabeth Keyes** spared no efforts in making every detail of the new design attractive, usable, consistent, and appropriate to the *Essentials* pedagogy. **Joyce Nielsen**, **Jan Snyder**, **Asit Patel**, **Nancy Sixsmith**, and **Susan Hobbs**—freelancers who had worked on earlier editions of the *Essentials* and the related ***Learn*** series in various editorial capacities—helped ensure continuity in procedures and conventions. **Tim Tate**, **Sherri Fugit**, **Melody Layne**, and **Cindy Fields** also asked sharp questions along the way and thereby helped us refine and crystallize the editorial conventions for the *Essentials*.

Debra Griggs, who has been teaching out of the *Access 97 Essentials* books at Bellevue Community College, offered many excellent comments and suggestions, and provided great technical expertise throughout the beta-testing stage. **Sarah Ann Margulies**, a retired lawyer and continuing learner, greatly enhanced this book by providing exceptional assistance during the usability-testing phase.

Finally, the authors would like to thank **Debra Griggs** for her great technical editing, and **Jan Snyder** for seeing this book through development during particularly trying times. **Melody Layne** did her usual excellent job of copy editing, and Project Editor **Sherri Fugit** pulled everything together on a very tight schedule. Also, thanks to **Marianne Fox** and **Larry Metzelaar** for taking on the series editorship and doing a great job, even though it must have been far more work than they could ever have imagined. Our particular thanks go to **Sunthar Visuvalingam**, for having a vision of what this series should be, and then seeing it through.

Contents at a Glance

	Introduction	xi
Project 1	Designing a Complex Database	1
Project 2	Making the Input Form More User-Friendly	41
Project 3	Managing Changing Data	69
Project 4	Using Access Tools	95
Project 5	Analyzing and Reporting Data	123
Project 6	Filtering Data in a Linked Table Using Parameters and Form Filters	165
Project 7	Sharing a Database with Others	187
	Task Guide	213
	Glossary	221
	Index	223

Table of Contents

Introduction xi

Project 1 Designing a Complex Database 1

Lesson 1: Defining Desired Output 2
Lesson 2: Organizing the Fields into Several Tables 6
Lesson 3: Relating Tables Using One-to-One and One-to-Many Relationships 9
Lesson 4: Relating Two Tables Using a Third Table 13
Lesson 5: Refining the Design to Eliminate Redundant Fields 16
Lesson 6: Creating Queries and Testing the Design 21
Lesson 7: Documenting the Design 25
Summary 26
Checking Concepts and Terms 27
True/False 27
Multiple Choice 27
Screen ID 29
Discussion Questions 29
Skill Drill 30
1. Selecting Fields for an Emergency Contact List Report 30
2. Selecting Fields and Modifying the Design to Allow Reporting on Employee Specialty 31
3. Selecting Fields and Modifying the Design to Allow Reporting on Employee Parking 32
4. Selecting Fields and Modifying the Design to Allow Reporting on Clients 33
5. Selecting Fields and Modifying the Design for Producing a Form Used to Look Up Project Information 33
6. Selecting Fields and Modifying the Design to Be Able to Produce a Form to Look Up Non-Sensitive Employee Information 34
Challenge 35
1. Determining if the Design Will Support Summary Reports 35
2. Modifying the Design to Do a Report for the Client 35
3. Examining the Design to See if a Form with a Subform Can Be Used to Look Up Information About the Clients and Projects 37
4. Examining the Design to See if a Form with a Subform Can Be Used to Look Up Information About the Projects and Employees 37
Discovery Zone 38
1. Create a Form Letter and Connect It to a Query in the Company Database 38
2. Publish a Current List of Clients and Projects on the Company Intranet 39

Project 2 Making the Input Form More User Friendly 41

Lesson 1: Changing the Color of Text, Backgrounds, and Borders Using Buttons 43
Lesson 2: Using the Format Painter to Copy Formats Between Controls 46
Lesson 3: Formatting More Than One Control at a Time 48
Lesson 4: Changing Colors Using Properties 50
Lesson 5: Adding Status Bar Instructions in the Form View 52
Lesson 6: Adding Customized ControlTips to Controls 54

Lesson 7: Creating a Custom Toolbar 57
Checking Concepts and Terms 60
True/False 60
Multiple Choice 60
Screen ID 61
Discussion Questions 62
Skill Drill 62
1. Changing the Title Color and Background 62
2. Changing Multiple Controls 62
3. Creating Visual Cues for Special Fields 63
4. Adding Status Bar Instructions to a Field 63
5. Adding a ControlTip to a Field 63
6. Adding Buttons to a Toolbar 64
Challenge 65
1. Adding Instructions to a Form 65
2. Changing the Look of the Text Control Box 66
3. Hiding Controls on a Form 66
4. Setting Up a Toolbar for Form Design 66
5. Changing Toolbar Properties 67
Discovery Zone 67
1. Creating a Custom Toolbar and Adding a Macro as a Button 67
2. Editing a Button on a Toolbar 68

Project 3 Managing Changing Data 69
Lesson 1: Replacing Data in a Table Using an Update Query 70
Lesson 2: Replacing Portions of Fields Using an Update Query 74
Lesson 3: Updating Tables Using a Calculated Expression 76
Lesson 4: Updating a Table Based on Values in Another Table 79
Lesson 5: Updating Linked Tables Automatically 82
Summary 85
Checking Concepts and Terms 85
True/False 85
Multiple Choice 86
Screen ID 87
Discussion Questions 88
Skill Drill 88
1. Updating a Table with a New Category 88
2. Updating a Table with a New Company Label 89
3. Identifying Multiple Disk Sets by Analyzing the Serial Number 89
4. Using a Cascade Update 89
5. Using a Cascade Delete 90
Challenge 90
1. Using Multiple Criteria in an Update Query 90
2. Adding Text to Fields Using an Update Query 91
3. Updating Salaries Based on Department 91
4. Creating a Calculated Field to Update a Table Field in Another Table 92
5. Creating a Calculated Field Using More Than One Field 92
Discovery Zone 93
1. Creating Update Queries to Update a Second Table 93
2. Updating a Field Based on Several Other Fields 94

Project 4 Using Access Tools **95**

Lesson 1: Correcting Spelling with the Spelling Checker **97**
Lesson 2: Customizing Data Entry Using AutoCorrect **99**
Lesson 3: Analyzing a Table **102**
Lesson 4: Analyzing Database Performance **107**
Lesson 5: Updating the Database Using Name AutoCorrect **109**
Lesson 6: Using Office Links to Analyze Data with Excel **112**
Summary **115**
Checking Concepts and Terms **115**
True/False **115**
Multiple Choice **116**
Discussion Questions **117**
Skill Drill **117**
1. Using the Table Analyzer **117**
2. Checking the Spelling **118**
3. Adding an AutoCorrect Entry **118**
4. Analyzing Database Performance **118**
5. Updating Field Names Using Name AutoCorrect **119**
6. Using Office Links to Analyze Data **119**
Challenge **119**
1. Publishing Access Data with MS Word **120**
2. Using the Documenter to Get Detailed Information About an Object **120**
3. Changing the Default Field Settings **120**
4. Changing the Way the Program Works **121**
Discovery Zone **121**
1. Creating a Mail Merge Document Based on an Access Table **121**
2. Changing the Look of the Access Screen **122**

Project 5 Analyzing and Reporting Data **123**

Lesson 1: Using the Totals Tool in a Query **126**
Lesson 2: Creating Crosstab Queries and Reports **129**
Lesson 3: Creating Crosstab Queries with Conditions and Total Columns **131**
Lesson 4: Analyzing Data Using PivotTables **135**
Lesson 5: Adding a Subform to an Existing Form **139**
Lesson 6: Inserting Subreports into Reports Using the Subform/Subreport Wizard **142**
Lesson 7: Creating Reports Using the Chart Wizard **147**
Summary **151**
Checking Concepts and Terms **151**
True/False **151**
Multiple Choice **152**
Screen ID **153**
Discussion Questions **154**
Skill Drill **154**
1. Using the Totals Feature in a Query **154**
2. Creating a Crosstab Query **155**
3. Creating a Crosstab Query with Conditions **155**
4. Creating a PivotTable Form **156**
5. Creating a Chart **157**
6. Adding a Subreport to an Existing Report **158**

Challenge 159
1. Adding Conditions to the Totals Feature in a Query 159
2. Creating a Crosstab Query Using the Crosstab Query Wizard 160
3. Creating a Crosstab Query with Two Levels of Row Headers 160
4. Creating a Query That Displays More Than One Function 160
Discovery Zone 161
1. Creating a PivotTable with a Third Subgroup 161
2. Using Access Data to Create an Excel Chart 162

Project 6 **Filtering Data in a Linked Table Using Parameters and Form Filters** 165
Lesson 1: Linking to a Large Table in Another Database 167
Lesson 2: Selecting Records Using Filter by Selection 172
Lesson 3: Selecting Records Using Filter by Form 173
Lesson 4: Using Parameters as Matching Criteria in a Query 175
Lesson 5: Using Parameters with Comparison Operators in a Query 176
Lesson 6: Using Parameters with Wildcards as Criteria in a Query 177
Summary 178
Checking Concepts and Terms 178
True/False 178
Multiple Choice 179
Screen ID 181
Discussion Questions 182
Skill Drill 182
1. Using Filter by Selection to Find All the Books Published in 1992 182
2. Creating a Filter Based on a Form Using the Between Operator 182
3. Using a Parameter with the Like Operator for Partial Matches 182
4. Use the Between Operator with Two Parameters 183
Challenge 183
1. Use a Parameter to Provide User Input in a Calculation 183
2. Use the Like Operator with Two Asterisks to Match Any Part of the Field 184
3. Use the Not Null Operator to Remove Irrelevant Records 184
4. Using the Shortcut Menu to Filter by Exclusion 185
5. Use the Shortcut Menu to Create a Compound Filter 185
Discovery Zone 185
1. Using the Concatenation Operator 185
2. Use a Parameter to Find Matches Between Fields 186
3. To Filter a Database to Answer Specific Questions 186

Project 7 **Sharing a Database with Others** 187
Lesson 1: Assigning a Password to Your Database 188
Lesson 2: Changing or Removing a Database Password 190
Lesson 3: Encrypting a Database 191
Lesson 4: Creating a Switchboard 194
Lesson 5: Setting Startup Parameters 198
Lesson 6: Setting Access Defaults 201

Summary 204
Checking Concepts and Terms 204
True/False 204
Multiple Choice 204
Discussion Questions 205
Skill Drill 206
1. Adding a Password to a Database 206
2. Removing a Password from a Database 206
3. Adding a Switchboard and Running It Automatically Whenever the Database Is Opened 206
4. Opening a Switchboard Automatically Whenever the Database Is Opened 207
5. Encrypt a Database 207
Challenge 207
1. Prevent Change to Data in One Field 208
2. Hide and Unhide Columns in a Table 208
3. Hide a Table, a Relationship, and a Form in a Database 209
Discovery Zone 209
1. Print Help Pages About Workgroups 209
2. Print Help Documents About User and Group Accounts 210
3. Planning to Implement User-Level Security 210
Task Guide 213
Glossary 221
Index 223

Introduction

Essentials courseware from Prentice Hall is anchored in the practical and professional needs of all types of students. This edition of the *Office 2000 Essentials* has been completely revamped as the result of painstaking usability research by the publisher, authors, editors, and students. Practically every detail—by way of pedagogy, content, presentation, and design—was the object of continuous online (and offline) discussion among the entire team.

The *Essentials* series has been conceived around a "learning-by-doing" approach, which encourages you to grasp application-related concepts as you expand your skills through hands-on tutorials. As such, it consists of modular lessons that are built around a series of numbered step-by-step procedures that are clear, concise, and easy to review. Explicatory material is interwoven before each lesson and between the steps. Additional features, tips, pitfalls and other related information are provided at exactly the place that you'd most expect them. They are easily recognizable elements that stand out from the main flow of the tutorial. We've even designed our icons to match the Microsoft Office theme. The end-of-chapter exercises have likewise been carefully graded from the routine Checking Concepts and Terms to tasks in the Discovery Zone that gently prod you into extending what you've learned into areas beyond the explicit scope of the lessons proper. Below, you'll find out more about the rationale behind each book element and how to use each to your maximum benefit.

How to Use This Book

Typically, each *Essentials* book is divided into seven or eight projects, concerning topics such as managing changing data, filtering data using parameters, and using advanced reports. A project covers one area (or a few closely related areas) of application functionality. Each project is then divided into seven to nine lessons related to that topic. For example, a project on designing a complex database is divided into lessons explaining how to organize the fields into more efficient tables, refine the design to eliminate redundant fields, and test and document the database design. Each lesson presents a specific task or closely related set of tasks in a manageable chunk that's easy to assimilate and retain.

Each element in *Access 2000 Essentials Advanced* is designed to maximize your learning experience. Here's a list of the *Essentials* project elements and a description of how each element can help you:

- **Project Objectives.** Starting with an objective gives you short-term, attainable goals. Using project objectives that closely match the titles of the step-by-step tutorials breaks down the possibly overwhelming prospect of learning several new features of Access into small, attainable, bite-sized tasks. Look over the objectives on the opening page of the project before you begin and review them after completing the project to identify the main goals for each project.
- **Key Terms.** This book includes a limited number of useful vocabulary words and definitions, such as ControlTip, cascade update, normalize, and crosstab. Key terms introduced in each project are listed in alphabetical order immediately after the objectives on the opening page of the project. These key terms are shown in bold italic and defined during their first use within the text. Definitions of key terms are also included in the Glossary.
- **Why Would I Do This?** You are studying Access so you can accomplish useful tasks in the real world. This brief section tells you why these tasks or procedures are important. What can you do with the knowledge? How can these application features be applied to everyday tasks?

- **Visual Summary.** This opening section graphically illustrates the concepts and features you will learn in the project. One or more figures, with ample callouts, show the final result of completing the project. This road map to your destination keeps you motivated as you work through the individual steps of each task.
- **Lessons.** Each lesson contains one or more tasks that correspond to an objective on the opening page of the project. A lesson consists of step-by-step tutorials, their associated data files, screenshots, and the special notes described below. Though each lesson often builds on the previous one, the lessons (and the exercises) have been made as modular as possible. For example, you can skip tasks that you've already mastered, and begin a later lesson using a data file provided specifically for its task(s).
- **Step-by-Step Tutorial.** The lessons consist of numbered and bold step-by-step instructions that show you how to perform the procedures in a clear, concise, and direct manner. These hands-on tutorials, which are the "essentials" of each project, let you "learn by doing." Regular paragraphs between the steps clarify the results of each step. Also, screenshots are introduced after key steps for you to check against the results on your monitor. To review the lesson, you can easily scan the bold numbered steps. Quick (or impatient!) learners may likewise ignore the intervening paragraphs.
- **Need to Know.** These sidebars provide essential tips for performing the task and using the application more effectively. You can easily recognize them by their distinctive icon and bold headings. It's well worth the effort to review these crucial notes again after completing the project.
- **Nice to Know.** Nice to Know comments provide extra tips, shortcuts, alternative ways to complete a process, and special hints about using the software. You may safely ignore these for the moment to focus on the main task at hand; or you may pause to learn and appreciate these tidbits. Here you'll find neat tricks and special insights to impress your friends and co-workers with!
- **If You Have Problems...** These short troubleshooting notes help you anticipate or solve common problems quickly and effectively. Even if you don't encounter the problem at this time, make a mental note of it so that you know where to look when you find yourself (or others) in the same difficulty.
- **Summary.** This provides a brief recap of the tasks learned in the project. The summary will guide you to places where you can expand your knowledge, which may include references to specific Help topics or the Prentice Hall *Essentials* Web site (http://www.prenhall.com/essentials).
- **Checking Concepts and Terms.** This section offers optional True/False, Multiple Choice, Screen ID, and Discussion Questions designed to check your comprehension and assess retention. If you need to refresh your memory, the relevant lesson number is provided after each True/False and Multiple Choice question. For example, [L5] directs you to review lesson five for the answer. Lesson numbers may be provided, but only where relevant, for other types of exercises as well.
- **Skill Drill Exercises.** This section enables you to check your comprehension, evaluate your progress, and practice what you've learned. The exercises in this section build on and reinforce what has been learned in each project. Generally, the Skill Drill exercises include step-by-step instructions.
- **Challenge Exercises.** This section provides exercises that expand on or relate to the skills practiced in the project. Each exercise provides a brief narrative introduction followed by instructions. Although the instructions are often written in a step-by-step format, the steps are not as detailed as those in the Skill Drill section. Providing less specific steps helps you learn to think on your own. These exercices foster "near transfer" of learning.

- **Discovery Zone Exercises.** These exercises require advanced knowledge of project topics or application of skills from multiple lessons. Additionally, these exercises may require you to research topics in Help or on the Web to complete them. This self-directed method of learning new skills emulates real-world experience. We provide the cues; you do the exploring!
- **Learning to Learn.** Throughout this book you'll find lessons, exercises, and other elements highlighted by this icon. For the most part, they involve using or exploring the built-in Help system or Web-based Help also accessible from the application. However, their significance is much deeper. Microsoft Office has become so rich in features catering to such diverse needs that it's no longer possible to anticipate and teach you everything you might need to know. It's becoming increasingly important that, as you learn from this book, you also "learn to learn" on your own. These elements help you identify related, perhaps more specialized, tasks or questions and show you how to discover the right procedures or answers by exploiting the many resources already within the application.
- **Task Guide.** The Task Guide that follows the last project lists all the procedures and shortcuts you've learned in this book. It can be used in two complementary ways to enhance your learning experience. You can refer to it, while progressing through the book, in order to refresh your memory on procedures learned in a previous lesson. Or you can keep it as a handy real-world reference while using the application for your daily work.
- **Glossary.** Here you'll find the definitions—collected in one place—of all the key terms defined throughout the book and listed on the opening page of each project. Use it to refresh your memory.

Typeface Conventions Used in This Book

We have used the following conventions throughout this book to make it easier for you to understand the material:

- Key terms appear in ***italic and bold*** the first time they are defined in a project.
- Text that you type, as well as text that appears on your computer screen as a warning, confirmation, or general information, appears in a special `monospace` typeface.
- Hotkeys, the underlined keys onscreen that activate commands and options, are also underlined in this book. Hotkeys offer a quick way to bring up frequently used commands.

How to Use the CD-ROM

The CD-ROM accompanying this book contains all the data files for you to use as you work through the step-by-step tutorials, Skill Drill, Challenge, and Discovery Zone exercises provided at the end of each textbook project. The CD contains separate parallel folders for each project. The filenames correspond to the filenames called for in the textbook. Here's how the files are named: The first three characters represent the software and the book level (such as AC3 for *Access 2000 Essentials Advanced*). The last four digits indicate the project number and the file number within the project. For example, the first file used in Project 1 would be 0101. Therefore, the complete name for the first file in the *Access Advanced* book is AC3-0101.

Files on a CD-ROM are read-only; they cannot be modified in any way. In order to use the provided data files while working through this book, they must first be transferred to a read-write medium where you may modify them. Since classroom and lab rules governing the use of storage media vary from school to school, this book assumes the standard procedure of working with the file(s) on a 3.5-inch floppy.

A word of caution about using floppy disks. As you use a data file, it will increase in size or automatically generate temporary work files, so you should make sure your disk remains at least one-third empty to provide the needed extra space. Moreover, using a floppy for your work disk is slower than working off a hard drive; also, you'll need several floppies to hold all the files on the CD.

- **Saving to a 3.5-inch floppy disk.** For security or space reasons, many labs do not allow you to transfer files to the hard drive at all. The only way you can transfer Microsoft Access databases to a floppy disk is by manually copying the files. Unlike the other Office applications, Access does not have a Save As command for databases. This means that you cannot open and save each data file individually with a different name as you may have done while working with Word, Excel, or PowerPoint.

  First, select the files on the CD that you want to copy and ensure that their combined size (shown on the status bar of the Explorer window) will fit onto a 1.44MB floppy. Right-click on the selection with your mouse; choose Send To on the context menu that appears; then choose 3 1/2 Floppy on the submenu. After copying, select the copied files on the floppy and right-click the selection with the mouse again. This time, choose Properties and choose the General tab on the Properties dialog box that appears; then uncheck the Read-Only attribute at the bottom of this page. Because the original files on the CD-ROM were read-only, the files were copied with this attribute turned on. You can rename files copied in this manner after you have turned off the read-only attribute.

  Though you can use the same method to copy the entire CD contents to a large capacity drive, it is much simpler to use the installation routine in the CD-ROM for the purpose. This will automatically remove the read-only attribute while transferring the files.

- **Installing to a hard drive or Zip drive.** The CD-ROM contains an installation routine that automatically copies all the contents to a local or networked hard drive, or to a removable large-capacity drive (for example, an Iomega Zip drive). If you are working in the classroom, your instructor has probably already installed the files to the hard drive and can tell you where the files are located. You'll be asked to save or copy the file(s) you need to your personal work area on the hard drive or to a floppy disk.

  Otherwise, run the installation routine yourself to transfer all the files to the hard drive (for example, if you are working at home) or to your personal Zip drive. You may then work directly and more efficiently off these high-capacity drives.

CD-ROM Installation Routine

If you have been instructed to install the files on a lab computer or, if you are installing them on your home computer, simply insert the CD-ROM into the CD-ROM drive. When the installation screen appears, follow these steps:

1. From the installation screen, click the Install button.
2. The Welcome dialog box is displayed. Click the Next button.

3. The Readme.txt appears. The Readme.txt gives you important information regarding the installation. Make sure you use the scrollbar to view the entire Readme.txt file. When you are finished reading the Readme.txt file, click the Next button.
4. The Select Destination Directory is displayed. Unless indicated otherwise by your instructor, the default location is recommended. Click Next.
5. The Ready to Install screen appears. Click Next to begin the installation.

   A directory will be created on your hard drive where the student files will be installed.
6. A dialog box appears confirming that the installation is complete.

The installation of the student data files enables you to access the data files from the Start menu programs. To access the student data files from the Start menu, click Start, click Programs, and then click the Essentials title you installed from the list of Programs. The student data files are in sub-folders arranged by project.

Uninstalling the Student Data Files

After you complete the course, you may decide that you do not need the student data files anymore. If that is the case, you have the capability to uninstall them. The following steps walk you through the process:

1. Click on the Start menu, and then click Programs.
2. Click the *Essentials* module that you wish to uninstall.
3. Click Uninstall.
4. Click one of the Uninstall methods listed:
   - Automatic—This method deletes all files in the directory and all shortcuts created.
   - Custom—This method allows you to select the files that you want to delete.
5. Click Next.
6. The Perform Uninstall dialog box appears. Click Finish. The Student data files and their folders are deleted.

The *Annotated Instructor's Manual*

The *Annotated Instructor's Manual* (*AIM*) is a printed copy of the student workbook complete with marginal annotations and detailed guidelines, including a curriculum guide, that helps the instructor use this book and teach the software more effectively. The *AIM* also includes a Resource CD-ROM with additional support files for the instructor. These include suggested solution files that show how students' files should look at the end of a tutorial, answers to test questions, PowerPoint presentations to augment instruction, additional test questions and answers, and additional Skill Drill, Challenge, and Discovery Zone exercises. Instructors should contact Prentice Hall for their complimentary copy of the *AIM*. Prentice Hall can be reached via phone at 1-800-333-7945 or via the internet at `http://www.prenhall.com`.

Project 1

Project 1

Designing a Complex Database

Objectives

In this project, you learn how to

- **Define Desired Output**
- **Organize the Fields into Several Tables**
- **Relate Tables Using One-to-One and One-to-Many Relationships**
- **Relate Two Tables Using a Third Table**
- **Refine the Design to Eliminate Redundant Fields**
- **Create Queries and Test the Design**
- **Document the Design**

Key terms introduced in this project include

- Document a design
- Equi-join
- Fifth Normal Form
- First Normal Form
- Foreign key field
- Fourth Normal Form
- Inner join
- Intersection table
- Join
- Key
- Left outer join
- Many-to-many
- Normalization
- One-to-many
- One-to-one
- Referential Integrity
- Right outer join
- Second Normal Form
- Third Normal Form

Why Would I Do This?

There is a big difference between creating a database by following directions in a book and designing one yourself. There are errors that are easy to make when you are setting up tables that will not be immediately apparent but that will cause major problems later when you try to create reports and analyze data. You may have entered hundreds or thousands of records before you realize that you cannot produce the reports you want, given your table structure.

If you follow a few basic guidelines when creating your tables and setting up the relations between them, you can save yourself a lot of trouble later. Also, if you are working with an existing database that seems to be very difficult to use, you may be able to recognize its design flaws from the things you learn in this project.

This project teaches a method of setting up a database that assumes you have a good idea of the types of reports you want to produce.

Visual Summary

When you have completed this project, you will have designed a database whose tables are related in the following manner:

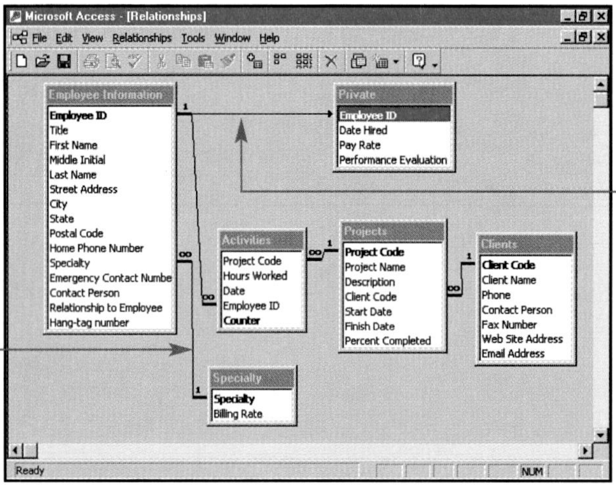

One-to-one relationship using a left outer join

One-to-many relationship with referential integrity enforced

Figure 1.1
You learn how to design complex databases to produce desired reports and forms.

Lesson 1: Defining Desired Output

Designing a database takes planning, a knowledge of what the program can do, and its intended use. This design method assumes that you can determine what type of reports are desired, how the forms will be used to look up individual records, what form letters you need to send, and what content should be posted to a Web site. As a person who is familiar with what Access can do, you must talk to the intended users and elicit from them a general description of what the reports, forms, documents, and Web pages must accomplish.

In this project, you use a case study to simulate this process.

The greatest temptation, and your biggest mistake, is to launch the Access program at this point. If you do, it is likely that you will concentrate on the details before you have a master plan. For that reason, the exercises in the first lesson are done using planning aids, not Microsoft Access.

In this project, we assume that you are designing a database for a small construction management company. This company has about twenty-five employees whose time is allocated to various projects. Each employee keeps a record of the time they spend on each project. This is done on a paper form that is turned in each week. The manager has come to you with a request that you put these records into a database so that various reports can be generated quickly and easily.

Select a partner to play the role of the company manager. He or she will use the case study information and sample documents that are provided while you conduct the interview. This person does not need to be familiar with databases or Access. It might even be better if they are not.

Begin this project by conducting an interview with the manager to determine how to produce a report and a form that the manager would like to see. You are guided through a description of the first report. Try to answer each question before you refer to the acceptable answers that are provided.

To Define the Fields Needed to Create a Report

1. **Launch Microsoft Word.**

2. **Open the file, AC3-0101 in the student/Project01 folder on your CD-ROM and print it. Close the file. Provide the person who will play the role of company manager with these pages. Find the AC3-0102 file on your CD-ROM, open it, and save it on your floppy disk as `Report Design`. Read the first two paragraphs. If you prefer to work on paper, print out the document. Otherwise, fill out the form on the screen.**
   This form is a guide to conducting an interview with a person who wants to use the reports generated by the database. You can use it to identify the fields that would be necessary to produce a report and how they should be arranged. If you are working by yourself, read the case study description along with the interview guide.

3. **Ask the manager to describe one of the reports that he or she must prepare. Make up a title for this report and enter it in the first item's blank on the interview document.**
   Agree upon a title. Use this as an icebreaker to establish a cooperative dialog. An example of an acceptable answer would be: A Report of Worker Activity by Project.

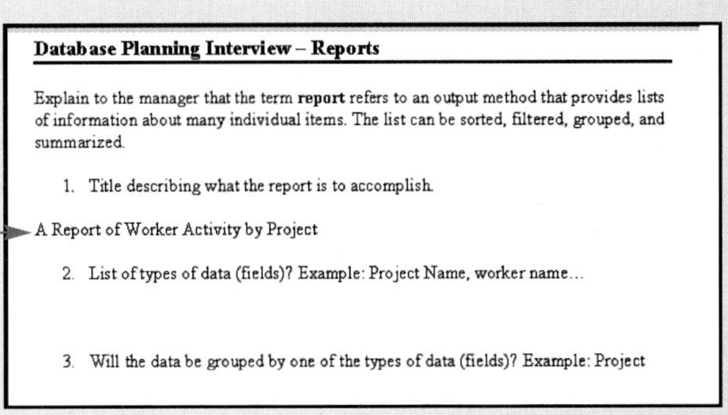

Database Planning Interview – Reports

Explain to the manager that the term **report** refers to an output method that provides lists of information about many individual items. The list can be sorted, filtered, grouped, and summarized.

1. Title describing what the report is to accomplish.

A Report of Worker Activity by Project

2. List of types of data (fields)? Example: Project Name, worker name...

3. Will the data be grouped by one of the types of data (fields)? Example: Project

Figure 1.2
Translate the description into a title for the report.

continues ▶

To Define the Fields Needed to Create a Report (continued)

4. **Determine what fields you would need to produce this report. Refer to the sample provided by the manager. Determine if any of the fields would qualify as a primary *key field* (unique value for each record). List the fields under item number 2. Put an asterisk next to the field that might be used as a primary key field, if any.**

   An acceptable list of fields would be: Project Name, Worker Name, Date of work, and Hours Worked. These may not be the final field names you use. They are a starting point.

5. **Determine what fields are used to group the records by project. Enter the field names under item 3.**

   If additional fields will be used to subgroup the records, list them in order from left to right.

6. **Discuss what fields will be used to filter the report. Determine if the manager needs several variations on the same report. Will it need to be restricted by date, project, customer, or some other factor? Enter the names of the fields under item 4.**

7. **Determine how the records will be sorted. If the records are grouped, the sorting will apply within the group. Enter the fields that will be used for sorting under item 5.**

8. **Determine which of the fields in the report will contain numeric data. Determine if these fields should be summarized using sum, average, minimum, or maximum functions. Enter the fields and the summary function that will be used under item 6.**

9. **Transfer the results of your discussion of the first report to the first empty row in the Planning Reports table provided. If the same field is listed in more than one place, make sure you use the same name. This table may be used to describe the other reports at a later time.**

   Your list of fields should resemble those in Figure 1.3.

Figure 1.3
Use the table to record the fields used in the first report.

Attachment A – Planning Reports

Report Title	Fields (indicate primary key field with an *)	Group on what fields (list in order if subgroups are used)	Filter on what fields (provide criteria)	Field(s) used for sorting - use A for ascending, D for descending	Totals or subtotals on which fields?
1) A Report of Worker Activity by Project	Project Name, Worker Name*, Date, Hours Worked	Worker Name, Project Name, Date	Date, Worker Name	Sorted first by Worker Name - A, then by Project Name - A, then by Date - A	Hours Worked - summed

The asterisk indicates primary key field

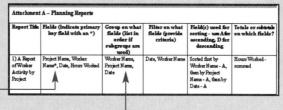

Sequence indicates grouping hierarchy

Keep the document open for use in the next section in which you conduct an interview about the use of forms.

Another method of getting information out of the database is to view it onscreen. Forms are best for this purpose if you are looking at one record at a time, because they can display a large number of fields on each screen. The following section guides you through an interview process to determine what fields are necessary to display the information the manager wants to see about each employee.

To Define the Fields Needed to Create a Form

1. **Scroll down to the section of the Report Design document titled Database Planning Interview: Forms Used to Find Individual Records.**
   Read the introductory paragraph and the questions following it.

2. **Ask the manager if he or she would like to be able to look up all the information about a particular employee or project and view it on the screen. Record the type of information desired under item 1.**
   An example of an acceptable answer would be Employee information. It is possible to do this with tables or queries; however, the fields are represented in a single row and the row is often too long to fit on the screen. Using a form for this purpose allows you to display a lot of data about a single individual or item at one time in a useable format.

3. **Ask the manager to describe what items of information should be displayed on the screen. List the field names under item 2.**

4. **Ask what piece of information they would like to type in to find this person or item. Record the field name under item 3.**

5. **Check the field names to see if you have used a different name for the same field. Check this list against the field names used in the report table. Make sure that you have used the same field name wherever it occurs in the design. Transfer the results of your discussion of the first form to the first empty row in the Planning Forms table that is provided as Attachment B.**
   This table may be used to describe other forms at a later time. Your list of fields should resemble those in Figure 1.4.

Attachment B – Planning Forms

Name of Form (base the form name on the answer to step 1)	List of fields to be displayed	Field used to find individual records
Employee Information	Worker Name, Address, Specialty, Home Phone, Employee ID, Pay Rate*	Worker Name

Figure 1.4
Use the table to record the fields used in the first form.

Print the two tables and close the Design document. Save your changes.

Some of the information in this database should not be available to all of the employees who may use it. This is a good time to ask the manager what types of data deserve extra security.

To Determine Which Fields Need Extra Security

1. **Review the types of information that the manager wants in the forms and reports. Ask if any of these fields contain sensitive information that may need to be password protected.**
2. **Underline the field names that require extra protection; for example: Date Hired, Pay Rate, Performance Evaluation.**
3. **If you are working onscreen, print attachments A and B and close the Report Design document. Close Word.**

Lesson 2: Organizing the Fields into Several Tables

The records in a table should be about one thing. Each record should contain data describing one employee, one project, one activity, or one of whatever the table is about. The first step in organizing the fields into tables is to separate them into common groups according to the thing they describe.

Once you have separated the fields into common groups, you examine each field that you have defined to see if it is really two or more pieces of information that should be stored in separate fields. The Employee Name field is a good example. Is that just one field or should it be broken up into two or more fields?

You also check to see if any of the fields are calculated from other fields. For example, you may have a field for Hours worked and another for Rate of Pay. If so, you do not need to store the product of these two numbers (wages) in the table. The value can be calculated each time it is needed from the other two fields. In general, it is better to calculate numbers each time you need them than it is to store them in the table.

Finally, you look for a field that may be used as the primary key field. It must contain a unique value for each record. If none of the fields qualifies, use a counter field for the primary key field.

An examination of the fields listed in the Planning Reports and Planning Forms tables reveals that several of the fields are about employees. Now it is time to launch Access and start designing the tables. The first table created will be the Employee Information table.

Refer to the figures in Lesson 1. These fields are used in the following steps.

To Organize Fields into an Employee Information Table

1. **Launch Access. Select the Blank Access Database option, and click OK. Select your floppy disk in drive A and name the database `Consulting`. Click the Create button.**
   The database will be created on your floppy disk in drive A.
2. **Choose the Tables object button, if necessary. Double click the Create table in Design view option in the Database window.**
   The table design view is displayed.
3. **The most obvious field that should go in this table is Employee Name. Enter `Worker Name` in the first Field name box.**

4 Look at the other fields in the Planning Reports table. Decide which ones, if any, directly relate to a worker and add them to the table design.

If you are not sure, include the field.

5 Look at the Planning Forms table. Decide which fields relate directly to the employee. Add those fields to the table design.

If you are not sure, include the field. After you have made your selection, refer to Figure 1.5.

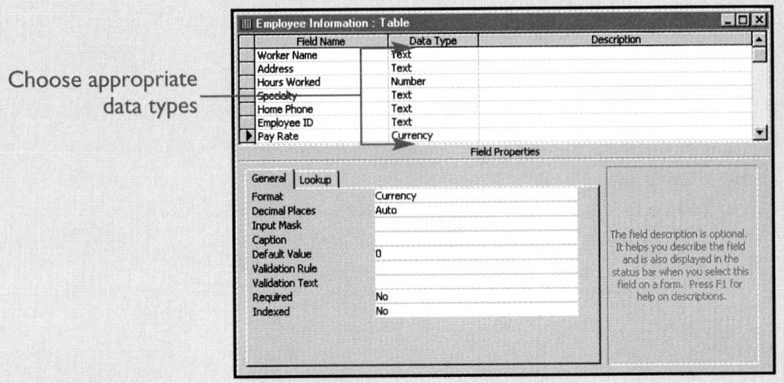

Figure 1.5
Fields that describe the employee are added to the table.

6 Close the table. Save the table as `Employee Information`. Do not choose a primary key at this time.

7 Double-click the Create table in Design view option to create a second table.

This table will be used for the rest of the fields, which have something to do with projects.

8 Enter the fields related to projects in this table. Make sure that all the fields are used in one table or the other.

Since this table is about projects, the project name should be unique.

9 Select the Project Name field and click the Primary Key button (see Figure 1.6).

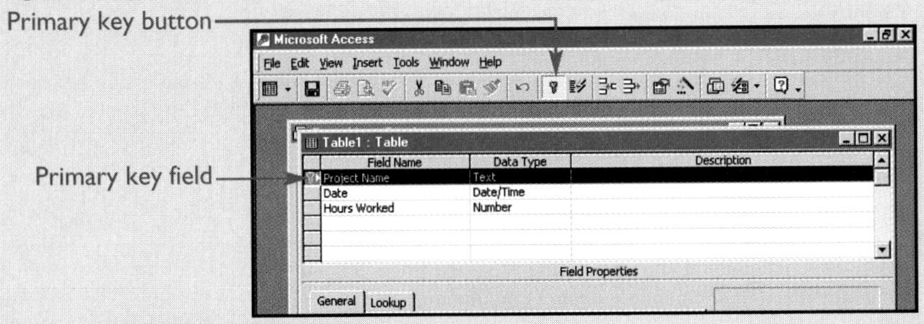

Figure 1.6
Fields that describe the project are used in the Projects table.

10 Close the table and save it as `Projects`.

This is not the final configuration of these tables but it is a good place to start.

It is also necessary to examine each field to determine if it is the smallest practical unit of information. If the field contains two or more individual pieces of information, it is a candidate for further division.

To Make Each Field into the Smallest Practical Unit of Information

1. **Select the Employee Information table and click the Design button.**
The Design view is displayed. The employee's name actually consists of several parts; Title, First Name, Middle Initial, and Last Name. The Title field can be used to store titles such as Mr., Mrs., Ms., and Dr. The title and Middle initial fields are important if you ever use this information in a form letter.

2. **Click in the row below the Worker Name field and click the Insert Rows button four times to insert four new rows. Enter the following field names: `Title`, `First Name`, `Middle Initial`, and `Last Name` (see Figure 1.7).**
These four text fields replace the Employee Name field.

Figure 1.7
The Employee Name field should be divided into four new fields.

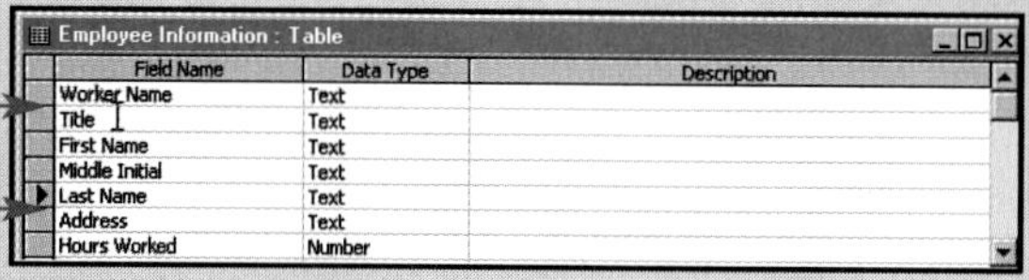

3. **Click anywhere in the Worker Name field and click the Delete Rows button.**

4. **Use this method to replace the Address field with the fields; `Street Address`, `City`, `State`, `Postal Code`.**

5. **Select the Employee ID field and click the Primary Key button (see Figure 1.8).**

Figure 1.8
Smaller units of information have replaced the Address field.

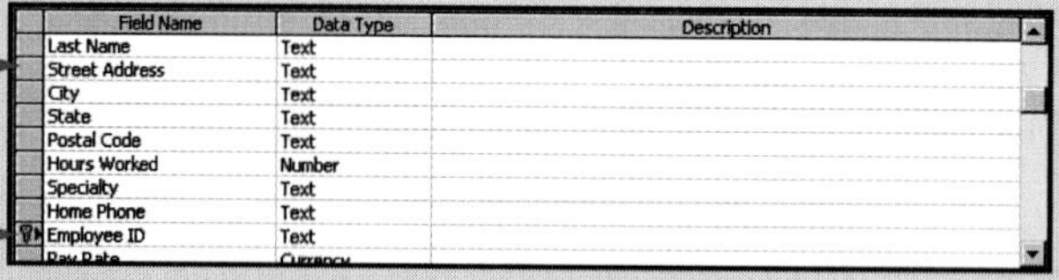

6. **Close the table and save the changes.**
The smaller units of information provide many more options for sorting, filtering, and grouping the data in reports.

This is a good time to consider security needs. In the last section of the interview, you asked the manager if any of the information is of a sensitive nature and should not be available to most of the people who would use the database. One way to handle this situation is to split a table into two tables—one table that contains the employee information that can be viewed by other employees, and the other table that should not be easily accessible.

To Create a New Table for Sensitive Information

1. **Right-click on the Employee Information table and choose Copy from the shortcut menu.**

2. **Right-click on an empty space in the database window and select Paste from the shortcut menu.**
   The Paste Table As dialog box is displayed.

3. **Enter `Private` in the Table Name box and select the Structure Only option. Click OK.**
   A copy of the table that contains the field names, but no data, is created.

4. **Select the Private table and click the Design button. Delete all of the fields except Employee ID and Pay Rate. Add the fields Date Hired and Performance Evaluation. Choose Date and Memo as the data types for these two fields.**
   The Employee ID field is left because it is the primary key field, not because it is private information. It will be used later to connect this table with the others (see Figure 1.9).

The Employee ID field will be used to join tables

Field Name
Data Type
Description
Employee ID
Text
Pay Rate
Currency
Date Hired
Date/Time
Performance Evaluation
Memo

Figure 1.9
The Private table will be used to store sensitive information.

5. **Close the table and save the changes.**

6. **Select the Employee Information table and click the Design button.**

7. **Scroll to the bottom of the list of fields and delete the Pay Rate field. Click on the row header for the Employee ID field. Click and drag the field to the top of the list of fields (see Figure 1.10).**
   It helps if the primary key field is listed first. It makes it easier to find if it is always in the same place in the field list.

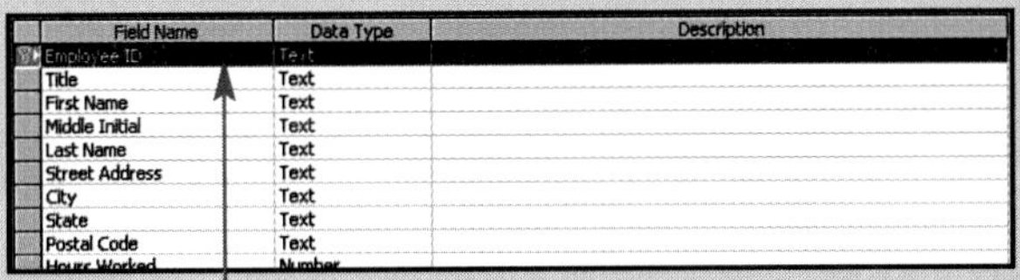

Field Name
Data Type
Description
Employee ID
Text
Title
Text
First Name
Text
Middle Initial
Text
Last Name
Text
Street Address
Text
City
Text
State
Text
Postal Code
Text

Move the primary key field to the first row

Figure 1.10
The Employee Information table will be used for non-sensitive information only.

8. **Close the table and save the changes.**
   Leave the database open for use in the next lesson.

Lesson 3: Relating Tables Using One-to-One and One-to-Many Relationships

The strength of a relational database such as Access is the ability to divide the data into several specialized tables. If this is done correctly, it minimizes the amount of data that needs to be stored. If you enter a person's address into the database once, there is no need to do it again. Storing each fact only once in a single location makes it much easier to change it.

The challenge to using multiple tables is that each table must be designed correctly and the tables must be linked together according to certain rules.

In this lesson, you establish two kinds of ***relationships*** between the tables.

To Link Two Tables Using a One-to-One Relationship

1 Click the Relationships button. Select the Employee Information table and click the Add button. Repeat this process to add the Private table to the Relationships window, then click Close. Adjust the size of each field list box to display the entire list of names (see Figure 1.11).

The Relationships window is used to create and view the links between tables. The primary key field in each table is indicated in boldface type.

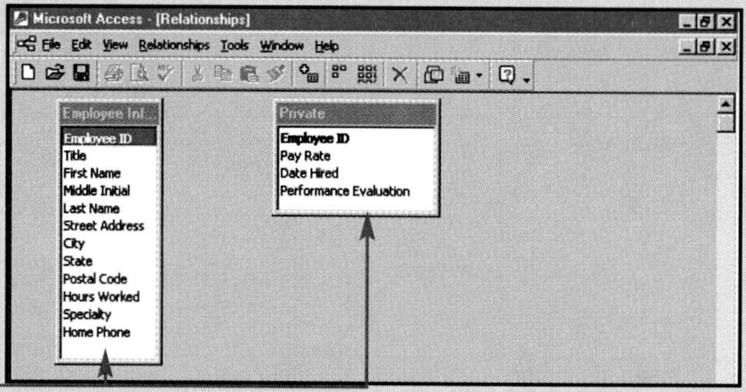

Figure 1.11
The Relationships window displays the fields in each table and any relationships.

The field list boxes may be enlarged to display all the field names

2 Move the pointer onto the Employee ID field in the Employee Information field list. Click and drag the pointer onto the Employee ID field in the Private field list. Release the mouse button, and the Edit Relationships dialog box opens.

The program examines the tables and determines what relationship is possible between the two tables using these two fields. In this case, there is one record per employee. This is an example of a ***one-to-one*** relationship (see Figure 1.12).

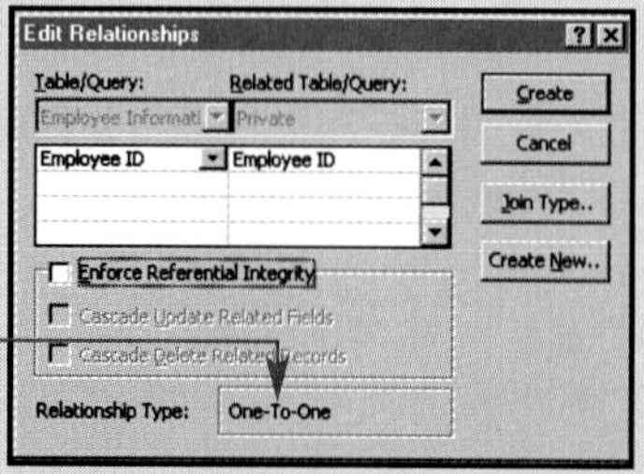

Figure 1.12
The Edit Relationships dialog box displays several relationship options.

There is one record per employee in each table

3 Click the Join Type button.

You want to make sure that all the records in the Employee Information table are displayed whether there is a corresponding record in the Private table or not.

Three Types of Joins

There are three types of ***joins*** to handle the situation where one table may have records that do not have a corresponding record in the other table. For example, if temporary employees are listed in the Employee Information table but nobody bothers to keep sensitive information about them in the Private table, you need to choose join number 2. If you used the first type, the temporary workers would not be included because they do not have matching records in the Private table. An example of a situation where you might use the third type of join would be if you had some performance evaluation records for employees who were involuntarily out-placed (fired). They would no longer be in the Employee Information table but you would want to keep their performance evaluations. The third join would include all the records in the Private table and any corresponding records in the Employee Information table.

4 Select option 2 and click OK. Click Create.

A line between the tables indicates which fields are used to join the tables and the type of join (the arrow points from the table whose records are all included to the table from which only matching records are included). See Figure 1.13.

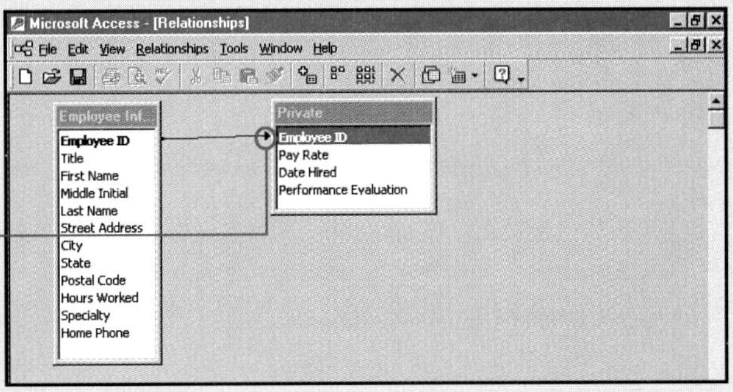

Figure 1.13
Relationships are represented by join lines.

5 Close the Relationships window and save the changes.

The most common type of relationship is where one record in a table is related to many records in another table. In this example, one person may work on many projects. For each person in the Employee Information table (the "one" side of the relationship), there will be several records (the "many" side) in the Projects table. The way to establish a relationship between the two tables is to connect the primary key of the "one" table to a field in the "many" table that contains the same data.

We can establish this type of relationship between the Employee Information table and the Projects table if we add another field to the Projects table.

In this section, you add a field named Employee ID to the Projects table. This field will contain the identification number of the employee who worked on the project. This field can be used to establish a ***one-to-many*** relationship.

One-to-many relationships occur between the primary key field in one table and a matching field in another table. The matching field is called the ***foreign key field***.

To Join Two Tables Using a One-to-Many Relationship

1 Select the Projects table. Click the Design button to open the Design view. Add a field named `Employee ID` (see Figure 1.14).

Tables may be joined if the two fields contain the same type of data. In this case, both fields must be text fields.

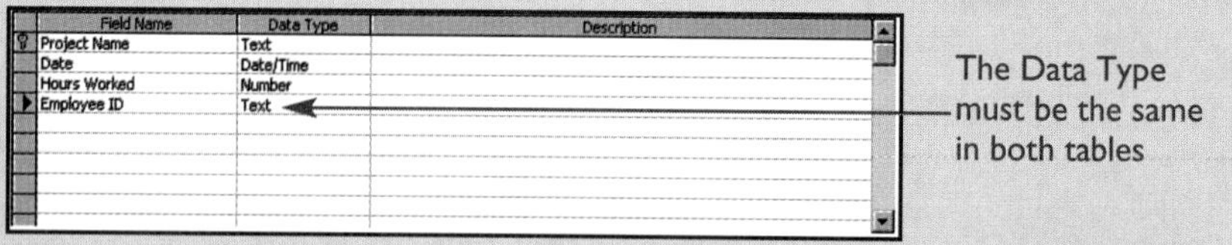

Figure 1.14
The Employee ID field is added to support a one-to-many join.

2 Close the table Design view and save the changes. Click the Relationships button. Click the Show Table button and add the Projects field list to the Edit Relationships window. Close the Show Table dialog box. Move the Projects table to a position below the Private table.

Notice that the Employee ID field in the Projects table is not displayed in boldface, because it is not the primary key field in that table.

3 Move the pointer to the Employee ID field in the Employee Information table. Click and drag a join to the Employee ID field in the Projects table.

The Edit Relationships dialog box opens. The program recognizes that one of the fields in the relationship is a primary key field and the other is not. It displays the relationship as one-to-many (see Figure 1.15).

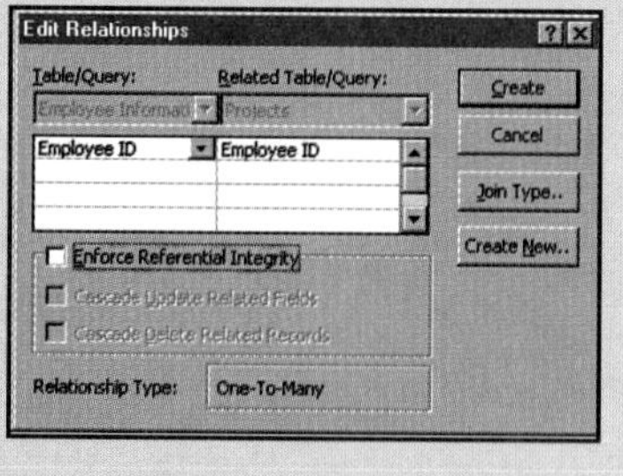

Figure 1.15
The relationship between the Employee Information table and the Projects table is one-to-many.

4 Click the Join Type button.

The three join types are displayed. In this case, we only want to see the records of employees who worked on projects. This is an example of a good time to use the first type of join.

Names of Joins in a One-to-Many Relationship

The three types of joins in a one-to-many relationship have their own names. The first type of join that includes only the records that have corresponding records in both tables is called an ***inner join***. It is also referred to as an ***equi-join***. The other two joins assume that the table that uses its primary key field (the "one" table) is on the left and the other table (the "many" table) is on the right. The join that uses all the records from the table on the left (the "one" table) is called a ***left outer join***. The join that uses all the records on the right (the "many" table) is called a ***right outer join***.

These terms make more sense, and are easier to remember, if you envision two circles that overlap. Each circle represents all the items in one table. The overlapping area represents the items that are common to both tables (an inner join). If you want all the items from the left circle and only the items from the right circle that are in the overlapping area, it is a left outer join. If you want all the items in the right circle and only the items from the left circle that are in the overlapping area, it is a right outer join.

5. **Confirm that option 1 is selected (the inner join) and click OK. Click Create.**

   A one-to-many relationship is displayed between the two tables.

6. **Close the Relationships window and save the changes.**

Lesson 4: Relating Two Tables Using a Third Table

Upon further examination, you realize that there is a problem relating the Employee Information and Project tables. Each person's time sheet will list the project name many times. Since the Project Name field is the primary key field, it will not allow duplicate entries. The problem in this case is that there are many employees who work on the same project, and a project could have many different people working on it. This table cannot be used to record the timesheet data.

This is an example of a ***many-to-many*** relationship between Employees and Projects. Access does not have a direct way to join two tables together in a many-to-many relationship. Instead, you create a third table of individual activities, known as an ***intersection table***, and join the Employee table to it with a one-to-many relationship and then join a new Projects table to it with another one-to-many relationship.

In this lesson, you rename the Project table and call it Activity. You use it to record individual activities from the time sheet. You also create a new table named Projects that has general information about the project. The Projects and Activity tables are joined using the Project Code field.

To Create a Many-to-Many Relationship by Creating Two, One-to-Many Relationships

1 Right-click on the Project table and choose Rename from the shortcut menu. Change the name to `Activities`.

2 Click the Design button. Select the Project Name field name. Click the Primary Key button on the toolbar to deselect the field as the primary key. Change the field name from Project Name to `Project Code`.
The Activities table does not have a primary key because all of the fields in it may contain duplicate data.

3 Insert a new row and enter a new field named `Counter`. Make its Data Type AutoNumber.
You can use the Employee ID field to join to the Employee Information table and the Project Code field to join to a new table that has general information about the project (see Figure 1.16).

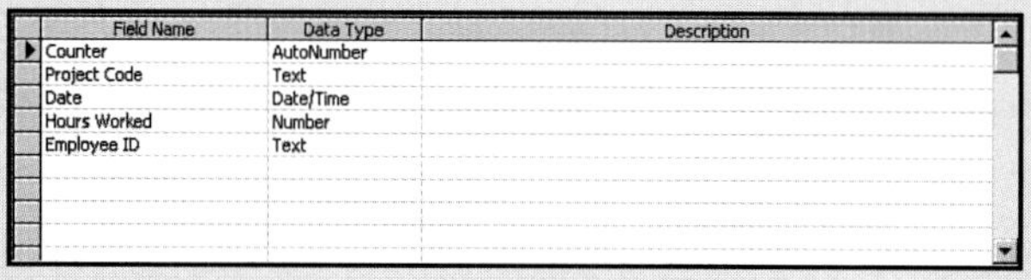

Field Name
Data Type
Description
Counter
AutoNumber
Project Code
Text
Date
Date/Time
Hours Worked
Number
Employee ID
Text

Figure 1.16
The Activities table can be used to join the Employee Information table and the new Projects table.

4 Close the table design and save the changes.

5 Click the New button. Select the Design View option and click OK. Enter the following field names and data types:

Project Code	Text
Project Name	Text
Description	Text
Start Date	Date/Time
Finish Date	Date/Time
Client Code	Text
Client Name	Text

These fields may be used to describe the project. The Project Code field may be used to join this table to the Activities table.

6 Select the Project Code field. Click the Primary Key button on the toolbar to mark this field as the Primary Key field.
The project code will be entered many times in two tables. It is better to use a short code instead of a long name. Your design should look like the example (see Figure 1.17).

The Project Code field will be used to join to the Activities table.

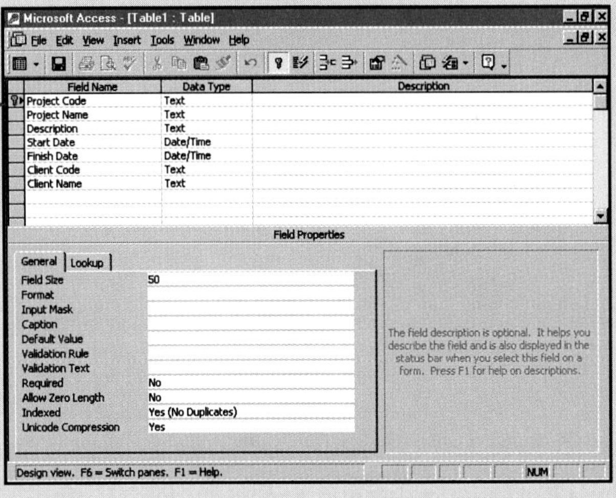

Figure 1.17
The new table will be used to store information about the project.

7. **Close the table and name it `Projects`.**
There are now four tables in the database.

8. **Click the Relationships button on the toolbar.**
The Relationships window opens. Notice that we have to reestablish the connections to the Projects table.

9. **Click the Show Table button. Add the Activities table, then close the Show Table window. Adjust the location and size of the tables to resemble the arrangement shown (see Figure 1.18).**

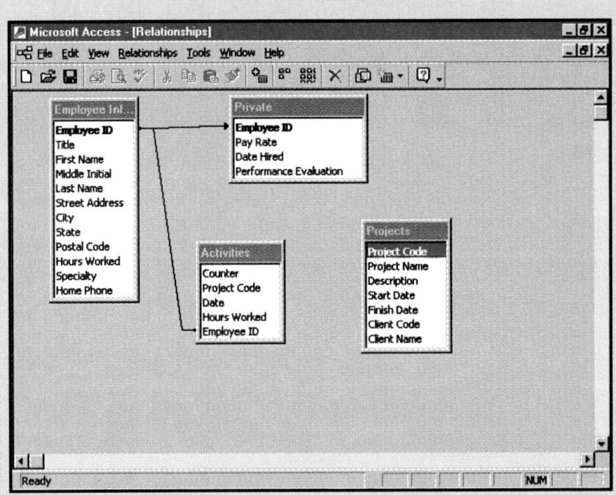

Figure 1.18
The Activities and Projects tables are ready to be joined.

10. **Right-click on the join line between the Employee Information table and the Activities table and select Edit Relationships from the shortcut menu.**
The Edit window opens. In the next step, you ensure that an activity can be performed only by an individual who first exists in the Employee Information table.

11. **Select the Enforce Referential Integrity option.**
When you select to enforce ***referential integrity***, a matching field is required to exist in the joined table.

continues ▶

To Create a Many-to-Many Relationship by Creating Two, One-to-Many Relationships (continued)

Attempting to Enter Data Without Corresponding Records
If you attempt to enter an Employee ID number in the Activities table that does not have a corresponding record in the Employee Information table, an error message will be displayed and the entry will not be allowed.

12. **Click OK. A one-to-many join line is displayed between the tables.**
13. **Drag a join from the Project Code field in the Projects table to the Project Code field in the Activities table. Select the Enforce Referential Integrity option for this join as well. Click Create.**
    The Employee Information table and the Projects table are both joined to the Activities table in one-to-many relationships (see Figure 1.19).

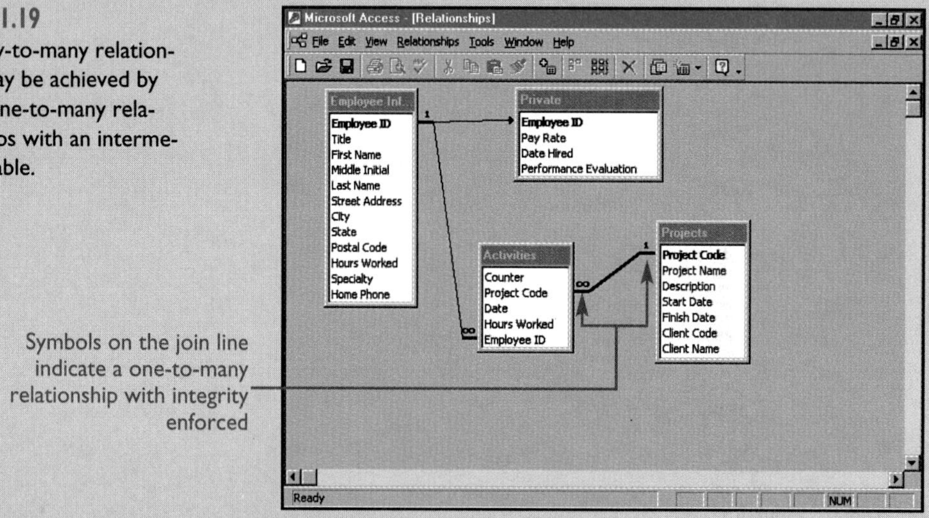

Figure 1.19
A many-to-many relationship may be achieved by using one-to-many relationships with an intermediate table.

14. **Close the window and save the changes. Close the database but leave Access open.**

Lesson 5: Refining the Design to Eliminate Redundant Fields

Before you enter data, it is important to make a final check of the design. Database experts have devised standards that you should use to design tables for a relational database. These standards use terms that are familiar to mathematicians. For example, applying one of these standards is called ***normalization***. These standards were created to avoid problems when data is inserted or deleted from a table.

You already applied one of the rules when you divided the fields into their smallest practical unit of information. Once this is done, the table is in ***First Normal Form***. Refer to the Glossary for a more complete definition.

In this lesson, you learn how to evaluate the tables and their relationships to see if they conform to three of these normalization rules plus check for duplication of fields. There are four normal forms that are not included. They are the ***Second Normal Form***, the Boyce-Codd Normal Form, the ***Fifth Normal Form***, and the Domain/Key Normal Form. The Second Normal Form and the Boyce-Codd Normal Form deal with tables that use two or more fields in combination to form key fields that we have chosen not to cover in this book. The last two types are advanced concepts that are not often used.

The rules are:

First Normal Form	Each field contains the smallest meaningful unit of information and there are no repeating field names such as project1, project2, project3.
Third Normal Form	The table is in First Normal Form (and Second Normal form if combined key fields are used) and each field in the table that is not a foreign key relates directly to the primary key.
Fourth Normal Form	No one-to-many relationships are allowed between the primary key field and another field in the same table.

In addition to these rules about individual table design, also make sure that fields that are not primary or foreign keys only occur in one table.

If you have a design that violates any of these three rules, the solution is to create additional tables and move the problem fields to their own table. If you find the same field in two tables, and it is not being used as a primary or foreign key, remove the field from one of the tables.

At this point in the process, you discover that someone else tried to design a database to manage these projects but did not finish because they could not figure out how to get the reports they wanted. They spent a lot of time trying to get the reports to work, but the problem was really the design of their tables. In the next section, you examine the design that they used.

To Check for Design Errors in Another Database

1. **Click the Open button and locate the AC3-0103 database file in the Student/Project01 folder on the CD-ROM that came with the book. Open the file directly from the CD.**
   You do not need to make changes to this database so you may open it in read-only mode.

2. **Click the Relationships button on the toolbar.**
   The Relationships window opens, displaying the fields in the database's two tables and the one-to-many relationship between those tables (see Figure 1.20).

continues ▶

To Check for Design Errors in Another Database (continued)

Figure 1.20
Examine these tables to see if they conform to the rules for table relationships.

This table was based on the Employee Time Sheet

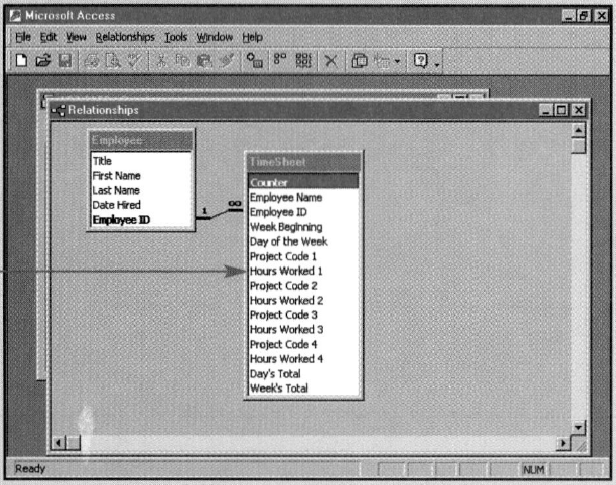

3 Examine the two tables to see if any of the fields could be reduced to a smaller meaningful unit.
The Employee Name field in the TimeSheet table could be separated into Title, First Name, and Last Name fields (see First Normal Form). The Day's Total and Week's Total may be calculated from the other fields. They should not be in the table at all (see Third Normal Form).

4 Examine the TimeSheet table to see if there are repeating field names.
The project code and hours worked information has been recorded in four different fields (see First Normal form). One of the reasons that this approach was abandoned was that the designer found out that some of the workers actually did five or six different jobs each day and wrote the work in the margin of the time sheet. The designer would have had to add more fields to the table and all the reports and forms that had already been designed.

5 Examine the TimeSheet table to see if each field in the table (except the foreign key, Employee ID) relates to the primary key field (Counter) and not one of the other fields.
The counter displays a different number for each row in the time sheet. One row of the time sheet is a day's work on one project. The Week Beginning field and the Day of the Week field have their own one-to-many relationship (see Third Normal Form). These two fields should be replaced by a single Date field that relates directly to the project's task.

6 Examine the TimeSheet table to see if there are any one-to-many relationships between the primary key (Counter) and any of the other fields.
The table does not seem to have this problem. The Day's Total and Week's Total fields have a one-to-many relationship to the Counter but in the other direction. They would be removed due to other rule violations anyway.

7 Examine the tables to see if any fields that are not primary or foreign keys are duplicated.

The Employee Name field in the TimeSheet table contains the same data as the Title, First Name, and Last Name fields in the Employee table. It should be removed (see Rule #5). Consider what would happen if an employee changed her/his name? If the name occurs in one location you only have to change it once. In this example, it would need to be changed in every record in the TimeSheet table.

8 Close the Relationships window and close the database. Leave Access open.
It is no surprise that this project ended in failure. The designer thought that he could just use the fields in the time sheet and then figure out the reports later. The data went in easily, but the reporting proved to be impossibly difficult.

The Consulting database that you have designed does not have as many problems as the database you just examined, but you are not done with the design until you check for these types of problems.

To Check for Design Errors in the Consulting Database

1 Open the Consulting database and click the Relationships button.
We have already removed any repeating fields and divided the data into its smallest meaningful units so we are confident that the tables are in the First Normal Form (see Figure 1.21).

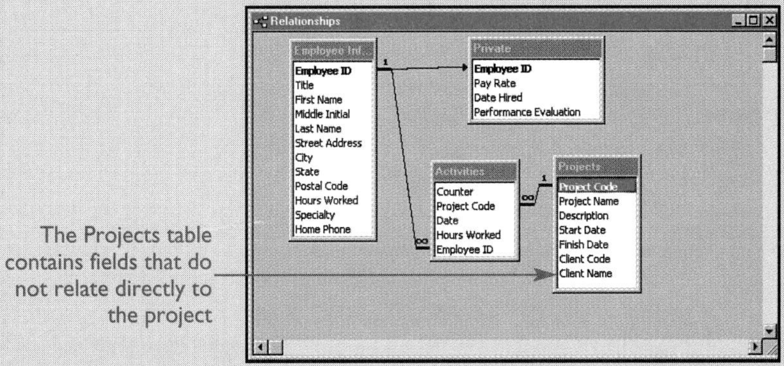

Figure 1.21
Examine these tables to see if they conform to the rules for table relationships.

2 Examine the tables to see if any of the non-key fields do not provide information about the primary key.
The Projects table contains two fields, Client Code and Client Name, that do not relate directly to the individual project. It would be valuable to know who the client is, but it is not appropriate to have both of these fields in this table. The solution is to create a separate table for client information.

3 Close the Relationships window. Click New to create a new table, select Design View, and click OK. Add the fields: `Client Code`, `Client Name`, `Phone`, `Contact Person`. Make the Client Code field the primary key. Close the table design and name it `Clients`.

continues ▶

To Check for Design Errors in the Consulting Database

4 Open the Design view of the Projects table. Delete the Client Name field. Close the table design view and save the changes.

5 Click the Relationships button to open the Relationships window. Click the Show Table button and add the Clients table. Create a one-to-many relationship between the Client Code fields in the Clients table and the Projects table. Enforce referential integrity. Adjust the positions of the tables as shown in Figure 1.22.

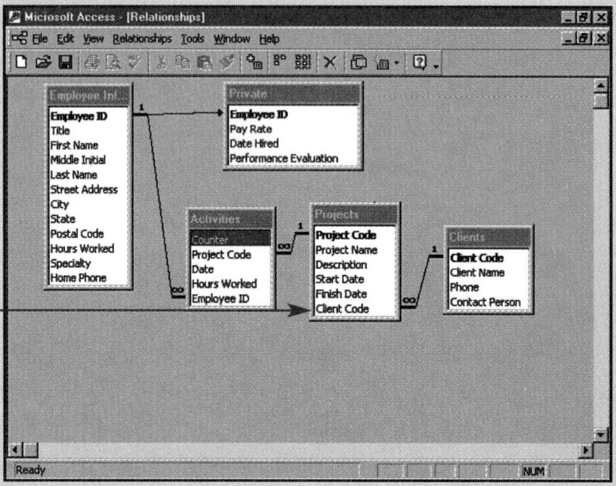

Foreign key field

Figure 1.22
These tables are in Third Normal Form

6 Examine the tables to see if there are any examples of a one-to-many relationship between the primary key field and any of the fields in the same table that are not foreign keys.

None of the tables have this problem.

7 Examine the tables to see if any of the non-key fields are duplicated in more than one table.

The fields that are used to join the tables are duplicated but that does not violate this rule. The Phone field in the Clients table and the Home Phone field in the Employee Information table look suspicious, but they contain different information. The Hours Worked field exists in the Employee Information table and the Activities table. The Hours Worked field should be removed from the Employee Information table.

8 Close the Relationships window and save the changes. Open the design view of the Employee Information table and delete the Hours Worked field.

The tables are now ready to receive sample data.

9 Close the design window and save the changes. Close the Consulting database. Leave Access open.

The entire design process to this point could have been done without using a computer, and it may have been faster to do it on paper. Consider all the changes that were made to the table designs. If you had invested time entering data prior to this point, it would have been wasted effort.

Lesson 6: Creating Queries and Testing the Design

The next step is to enter enough data in each table to enable you to test the design and then create the queries that are needed. In general, you want to enter enough records, with enough variety, to test the searching, sorting, filtering, and grouping described in the report and form designs. Then, you create queries that use the same fields that the reports or forms will use and see if you can sort and limit the data in the same way that is required by the report or form.

If your report or form design requires that you restrict the output by specifying criteria, you can test this by creating a query with the fields needed for the report or form.

If no restrictions are specified, you can create the report directly from the tables to test the design. Forms that use fields from several tables are often based on queries. Forms may also incorporate subforms to include fields from additional tables.

To save time, some data has been entered for you in a database on your CD-ROM. Information on the employee's specialty has also been added.

The report description requires that the user be able to restrict the output of the report to one month. If a report or form has such a restriction, create a query that contains the fields used in the report or form and use the criteria boxes in the query design to limit the output as desired.

To Create a Query to Test the Reporting Criteria

1. **Click the Open button. In the Open dialog box, locate AC3-0104 in the Student/Project01 folder on your CD-ROM. Right-click the file and select Send To, 3 1/2 Floppy (A) from the shortcut menu. Change the Look in box to 3 1/2 Floppy (A:).**
   The file on the floppy disk is displayed. This file has a Read-only property that occurred when it was written to the CD-ROM. It needs to be removed before you can make changes or add objects.

2. **Right-click AC3-0104, select Properties, and remove the Read-only property. Right-click AC3-0104 again and select Rename. Change the name of the file to `Consulting2` and press ↵Enter. Select `Consulting2` and click Open.**
   The name is changed and the Consulting2 database is opened for use. Confirm that you opened Consulting2 and not Consulting.

continues ▶

To Create a Query to Test the Reporting Criteria (continued)

3. **Click the Queries button in the Objects pane and double-click the Create query in Design view shortcut.**
   The Query1: Select Query window opens and the Show Table window opens in front of it.

4. **Add the field lists for the Projects, Activities, and Employee Information tables. Close the Show Table window. Check the report design to confirm that the required fields are present in at least one of these tables.**
   The field lists for the three tables are displayed (see Figure 1.23).

Figure 1.23
These tables contain the fields needed to produce the report.

Join lines represent relationships

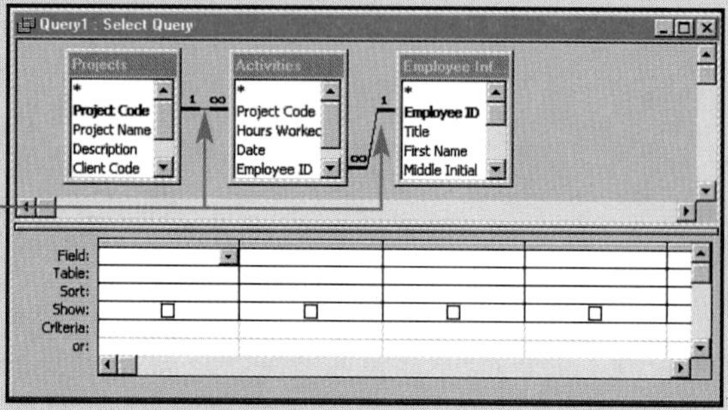

5. **Refer to the grouping requirements for the report. Add Last Name and First Name to the design grid from the Employee Information table. Add Project Name from the Projects table. Add Date and Hours Worked from the Activities table. Maximize the window, if necessary.**
   The fields necessary to create the report have been added to the design grid (see Figure 1.24).

Figure 1.24
The design grid contains the fields needed to produce the report.

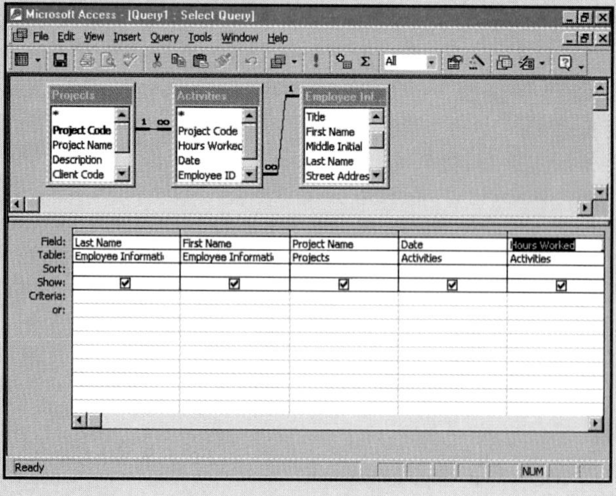

6 Set the Sort option to Ascending for the Last Name, First Name, Project Name, and Date fields.

The fields will be sorted from left to right to simulate the sorting required by the report.

7 To restrict the records to those between two dates, select the Criteria box in the Date column and type `Between 4/1/00 and 4/30/00` (see Figure 1.25).

The criteria box is not wide enough to display the entire criteria

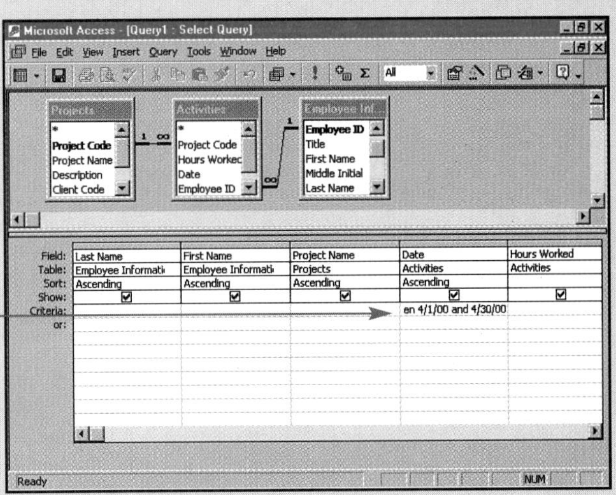

Figure 1.25
The first four fields are sorted and the Date field has a criteria limiting output to dates in April.

Using the Zoom Property to Edit Criteria

The criteria box is too small to view any complex criteria such as the one used in this lesson. You can right-click on the criteria box in the query design grid and a shortcut menu opens. Click on Zoom to open the Zoom window. You may use this window to write or edit a criteria that is too long to be displayed in the grid box. You can also open the Zoom window using Shift + F2.

8 Click the Run button to view the query in Datasheet view, sorted and limited to the records in April.

This method of using a criterion will be replaced by a more advanced method, called a parameter query, in a later project. That method allows the user to enter a beginning and ending date each time the query is run.

9 Close the query and name it `Employee Projects`. Leave the database open.

If a form uses fields from several tables, you can base the form on a query that contains those fields. To test the data to see if you can produce the proper form at a later time, create a query with all of the required fields and then see if you can locate the desired record using a form filter.

To Create a Query to Test a Form

1. **Double click the Create query in Design view option. Refer to the list of field names that should be in the form. Add the tables that contain those fields. Close the Show Tables window.**
   The necessary fields are found in the Employee Information and Private tables.

2. **Select all of the fields in the Employee Information table, then select the Date Hired, Pay Rate, and Performance Evaluation fields from the Private table.**
   The Employee ID field does not need to be listed twice.

3. **Click the Run button. Maximize the screen. Scroll across the datasheet to confirm that it can display all the required fields from both tables.**
   The fields that were added last are on the right.

4. **Click the Save button. Enter the name `Test Form` in the Query Name box and click OK.**
   The query is saved. It may be used for reports or forms that need to display all of the fields from both tables.

5. **Click the drop-down arrow next to the New Objects button on the toolbar and select AutoForm.**
   The fields of the query are placed in a simple form, and they are arranged in a single column. This simple form may be modified later or deleted when the testing is finished.

6. **Click the Filter by Form button and click in the Last Name field.**
   The form is displayed without data. A drop-down arrow is displayed next to the Last Name field to make it easy to choose from the list of existing names.

7. **Click the drop-down arrow next to the Last Name field and select Adams.**
   This name will be used as a criterion for filtering the records displayed in the form.

8. **Click the Apply Filter button.**
   All the records matching that criteria are displayed from the Employee Information and Private tables. This form meets the basic requirements for the form (see Figure 1.26).

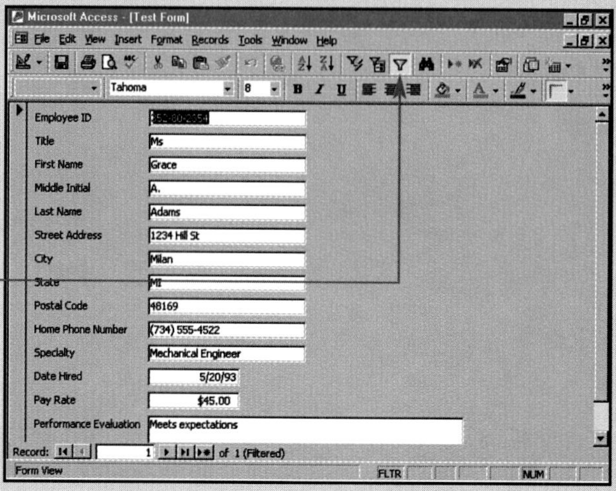

Use this button to remove the filter

Figure 1.26
The form contains all the required information and is searchable by individual name.

9 Click the Remove Filter button. Click the Save button and save the changes. Close the form and the query. Leave the Consulting2 database open.

Lesson 7: Documenting the Design

The database design is adequate to produce the report and form that are required. It is likely that some additional fields will be required to produce other reports, forms, documents, or Web pages, and you may need to add another table or two, but the basic design is sound.

This is a good time to ***document the design***. Documenting the database design is a process of recording the design of each of the database objects and the relationships between them. Fortunately, this process is automated with Access.

In this lesson, you select which database objects to include in the documentation and let Access do the rest.

To Document the Database Design

1 Choose Tools, Analyze, Documenter from the menu.
The Documenter window opens.

> If the Documenter Wizard has never been used on your computer before, you may be prompted to install it. If you are working at home, you will need to insert the Office 2000 CD in your machine. If you are in a laboratory, see your instructor or the lab manager.

2 Click the All Object Types tab.
The Documenter dialog box is displayed (see Figure 1.27).

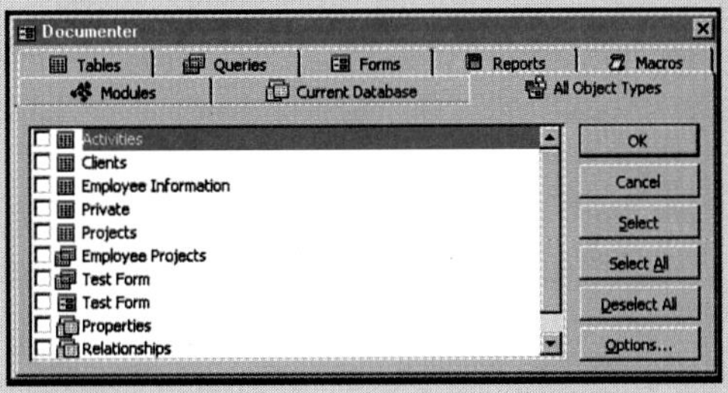

Figure 1.27
You can choose which objects to document.

3 Click the Select All button, then click on the two Test Form objects and the Properties option to deselect them.
The Test Form is temporary and does not need to be included. The properties option documents all the settings for elements within each table, query, form, or report.

4 Click OK.
This process takes about three minutes on a 233-megahertz computer using the A drive and produces a nine-page report documenting the database design. The document is displayed in the Print Preview mode.

continues ▶

To Document the Database Design (continued)

5 Click the Last Page button on the navigation bar and look at the last page of the report that displays the relationships. Note the page number in the navigation bar (see Figure 1.28). Your page number may differ from the one shown.

You can print selected pages of the report if you know their page numbers.

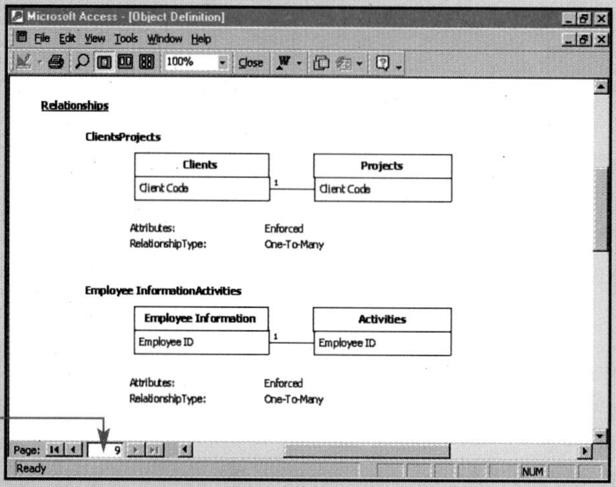

Figures 1.28
The relationships between the tables are documented.

Page number

6 Choose File, Print from the menu. Enter the page number (9) in both the From and To boxes in the Print Range section, then click OK.

The relationships page is printed.

7 Close the report document. Close the database and leave Access open for use in the following exercises.

Summary

Proper design of the tables and the relationships between them is critical to the success of a database. This project used a method that starts with the desired results and designs the necessary database to produce them. A case study was used to simulate an interview process by which the designer can determine the desired output of the database.

After the interview process determined the characteristics of the desired report and form, you were guided through the process of reorganizing the fields and tables and defining relationships between them so that they conform to rules for proper database design.

When the design was established, a similar database with test data already entered was used to evaluate the design to see if it could produce queries that have the same desired characteristics as the report and form. Once the queries demonstrated that the data could be recalled, as specified, the database design was documented for future reference.

Checking Concepts and Terms

True/False

For each of the following, check *T* or *F* to indicate whether the statement is true or false.

__T __F **1.** The best way to design a new database is to set one up on the computer before you talk to the end user so that you can tell them what they should do to reach their goal. [L1]

__T __F **2.** In the first interview, pay particular attention to the layout of the reports that are currently produced so that you can reproduce them exactly. [L1]

__T __F **3.** Fields should be grouped into the same table if they all describe one thing, event, or person. [L2]

__T __F **4.** If a field is selected as the primary key field, it must contain a unique value for each record in the table. [L2]

__T __F **5.** To create a many-to-many relationship between two tables, you drag a join between the primary key fields of each table. [L4]

__T __F **6.** A one-to-one relationship is used if some of the fields that relate to the primary key field have special characteristics, such as privacy requirements. [L3]

__T __F **7.** All the fields in a table should describe or relate to the primary key field, not another field in the table. [L5]

__T __F **8.** There should be no one-to-many relationships between the primary key field and another field in the same table. [L5]

__T __F **9.** A one-to-many relationship has a join between the primary key in the "one" table and the foreign key field in the "many" table. [L3]

__T __F **10.** Non-key fields should exist in only one table to avoid duplication. [L5]

Multiple Choice

Circle the letter of the correct answer for each of the following questions.

1. For what purpose are reports used? [L1]

a. To display all the fields, one record at a time

b. To print many records

c. To enter new data into tables

d. To search for data with interactive questions

2. How can forms be used to provide information quickly? [L1]

a. A form can show all the fields in a record. The user can scroll through the records one at a time using the navigation buttons.

b. The user can open a form and use the sort button.

c. The user can switch from Form view to Datasheet view to see more records at once and then scroll through them.

d. The user can use the Filter by Form button to enter matching criteria in a blank form then apply the filter.

3. A one-to-many relationship is made between what two fields? [L3]

a. the primary key field in each table

b. the primary key in the "one" table and the foreign key in the "many" table

c. the foreign key in the "one" table and the primary key in the "many" table

d. the foreign key in each table

4. Two tables can have a many-to-many relationship under what conditions? [L4]

a. One-to-many relationships are created between each table and a third table where the third table is on the "many" side of both relationships.

b. The join is created between the primary key fields of each table.

c. It is impossible.

d. The join is created between the foreign key fields of each table.

5. If you enforce referential integrity between two tables that have a one-to-many relationship, what will happen if you try to add a new record to the "many" table that does not have a matching record in the "one" table? [L3]

a. A view of the "one" table will open automatically, and you will be prompted to add a matching record.

b. The record will appear to be recorded but it is not saved when you close the table.

c. Access automatically adds a record to the "one" table that includes the matching value in its primary key field. The rest of the record is left empty.

d. A warning messages displays, and it will not allow you to enter the record.

6. Which of the following is ***not*** an example of repeating field names? [L6]

a. Project1, Project2, Project3

b. First Quarter, Second Quarter, Third Quarter, Fourth Quarter

c. City, State, Postal Code, Phone

d. Year1, Year2, Year3

7. If the primary key field of a table is Employee ID, which of the following fields would violate the rule against having a field that does not relate directly to the primary key field if it were in the same table? [L6]

a. Date Hired

b. Name of Spouse

c. Name of Supervisor

d. Phone Number of Supervisor

8. If the primary key field of a table is Employee ID, which of the following fields would violate the rule against having a one-to-many relationship with another field in the same table? [L6]

a. Projects

b. Parking Space

c. Birthday

d. Home Phone

9. When you enter test data into the tables, how do you decide how much data to enter? [L6]

a. Transfer all the data that currently exists in electronic form. Save the hand-entered data until later.

b. Enter ten records in each table.

c. Consider the grouping, sorting, and filtering that needs to be done. Enter enough data of sufficient variety to be able to see if these features work.

d. Enter ten records for each feature.

10. What does it mean to "document" a design? [L7]

a. Print out an example of each report, form, or table.

b. Use the Documenter feature to produce a detailed printout of the design of each database object and their relationships.

c. Capture an image of each table, report, or form from the monitor.

d. Write a detailed description of the process you used to arrive at the current design. Save this as a Word document.

Screen ID

Label each element of the Access screen shown in Figure 1.29.

Figure 1.29

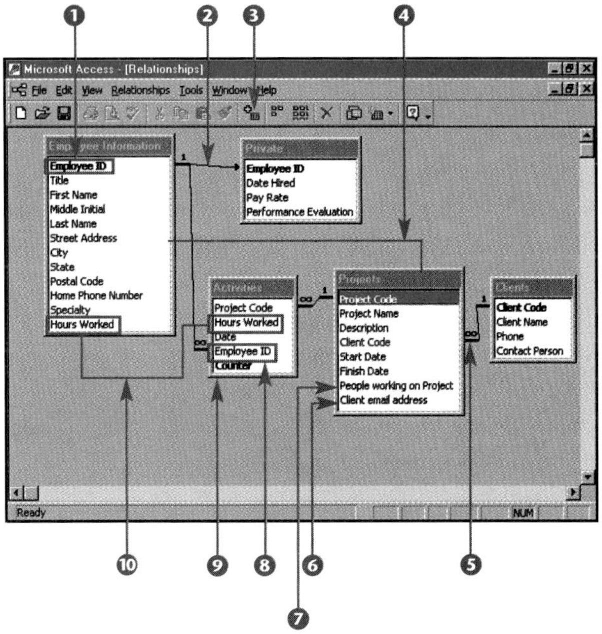

- **A.** Show Table button
- **B.** Duplicate non-key fields
- **C.** Field not related to the primary key in that table
- **D.** Primary Key Field
- **E.** Join indicating a one-to-many relationship
- **F.** Foreign key field
- **G.** Field with a one-to-many relationship to the primary key in the same table
- **H.** Type 2 join in a one-to-one relationship
- **I.** Intermediate table used to facilitate a many-to-many relationship
- **J.** Tables in a many-to-many relationship through an intermediate table

1. ____________________
2. ____________________
3. ____________________
4. ____________________
5. ____________________
6. ____________________
7. ____________________
8. ____________________
9. ____________________
10. ____________________

Discussion Questions

1. Open the database file, AC3-0103, and look at the effort that was made to create a query to display GM-125 project entries. Does it work? What would happen to this design if people worked on more than four projects? Could you find out the total amount of time that was spent on this project?
2. What is an example of a table that has a one-to-many relationship between its primary key field and another field in the same table?
3. What is an example of a table that has a field that is not directly related to its primary key field?
4. What is an example of a many-to-many relationship? What kind of intermediate table could you create to make two one-to-many relationships possible?
5. What changes would you make to the interview form that was used in the first lesson? What changes would you make to the interview process to make it work better for you?

Skill Drill

Skill Drill exercises reinforce project skills. Each skill reinforced is the same, or nearly the same, as a skill presented in the project. Each exercise includes a brief narrative introduction, followed by detailed instructions in a step-by-step format.

In the following exercises, you use a database that is essentially the same as the one you just created. (Some records have been changed to make it possible to distinguish the two databases.)

1. Selecting Fields for an Emergency Contact List Report

After your initial interview, the manager sends you a note describing another report that she would like to produce. You need to evaluate this report to see what fields must be added and in which table they belong. The note reads as follows:

`The secretary would like a printout that displays a list of employee's names, an emergency contact phone number, the person to contact in case of an emergency, and that person's relationship to the employee. The list should be sorted by the employee's name.`

To change the design to accommodate a new report that lists emergency contact information, complete the following steps:

1. Launch Access, if necessary. Click the Open button. In the Open dialog box, locate AC3-0105 in the Student/Project01 folder on your CD-ROM. Right-click the file and select Send To, 3 1/2 Floppy (A) from the shortcut menu. Change the Look in box to 3 1/2 Floppy (A:).
2. Right-click AC3-0105, select Properties, and remove the Read-only property. Right-click AC3-0105 again and select Rename. Change the name of the file to `Ex0101` and press Enter.
3. Select Ex0101 and click Open.
4. Fill out the second line of Attachment A, Planning Reports. Use `Emergency Call List` as the title. Refer to the requirements specified above and write in the field names that you think are necessary to produce this report.
5. Click the Relationships button to view the field lists for the tables.
6. Compare the list of field names that you wrote down in step 4 to the lists of fields that already exist. If you have chosen a different name for a field that already exists, change the name to match the existing field.
7. Determine which fields do not exist in any of the tables.
8. Create a new table named `Emergency Contacts`. Include the Employee ID field as a foreign key and the new fields. Let the program create a primary key when you save the table.
9. Open the Relationships window. Add the Emergency Contacts table and create a one-to-many relationship between the Employee Information table and the Emergency Contacts table. Compare the field lists in your tables with those shown (see Figure 1.30).

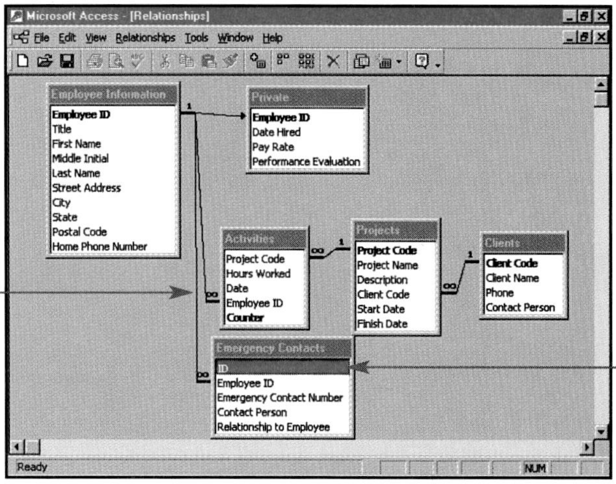

Figure 1.30

10. Close the Relationships window and save your changes.

Your answers may differ somewhat from those shown. For example, you may use several fields for the Contact Person's name. The definition of "smallest practical unit of information" depends on how the table will be used. If your answers differ from those shown, consider how you would justify your choices.

2. Selecting Fields and Modifying the Design to Allow Reporting on Employee Specialty

Another memo arrives on your desk from the manager stating that he or she wants to be able to produce a list of employees that is sorted by their specialty. The list should include their name, specialty, and the date they were hired. The list should be sub-sorted by date hired within each specialty.

To evaluate your design to see if it needs additional fields to produce this report, complete the following steps:

1. Fill out the third line of Attachment A, Planning Reports. Use `Employee Specialties` as the title. Refer to the requirements specified above and write in the field names that you think are necessary to produce this report.
2. Click the Relationships button to view the field lists for the tables.
3. Compare the list of field names that you wrote down in step 1 to the lists of fields that already exist. If you have chosen a different name for a field that already exists, change the name to match the existing field.
4. Determine which fields do not exist in any of the tables.
5. Add the field(s) to the Employee Information table.
6. Open the Relationships window. Compare the field lists in your tables with those shown (see Figure 1.31).
7. Close the Relationships window. Leave the database open for use in the next exercise.

Figure 1.31

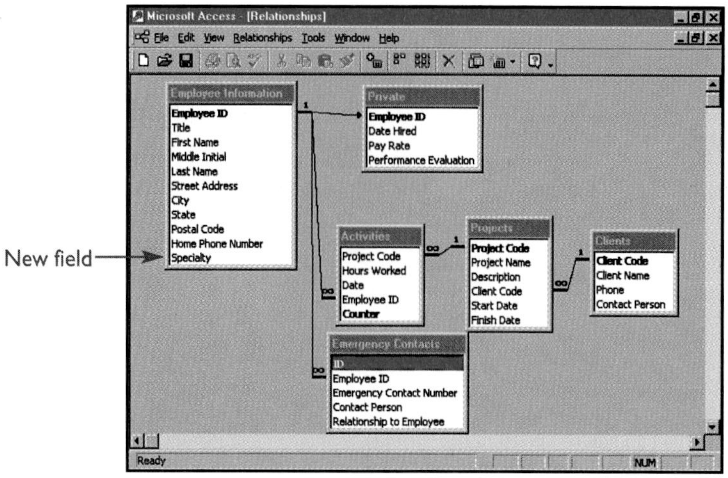

3. Selecting Fields and Modifying the Design to Allow Reporting on Employee Parking

The building manager had lunch with your manager and found out about this project. He would like to have a list of each employee's name and parking permit number so that he can check on cars that are parking in restricted areas. The list should include the employee's name and parking permit number. The list should be sorted by the parking permit number. A typical number is SC-3459.

To evaluate your design to see if it needs additional fields to produce this report, complete the following steps:

1. Fill out the fourth line of Attachment A, Planning Reports (use additional pages as needed). Use `Parking` as the title. Refer to the requirements specified above and write in the field names that you think are necessary to produce this report.
2. Click the Relationships button to view the field lists for the tables.
3. Compare the list of field names that you wrote down in step 1 to the lists of fields that already exist. If you have chosen a different name for a field that already exists, change the name to match the existing field.
4. Determine which fields do not exist in any of the tables.
5. Add the field(s) to the Employee Information table.
6. Open the Relationships window. Compare the field lists in your tables with these shown (see Figure 1.32).

Figure 1.32

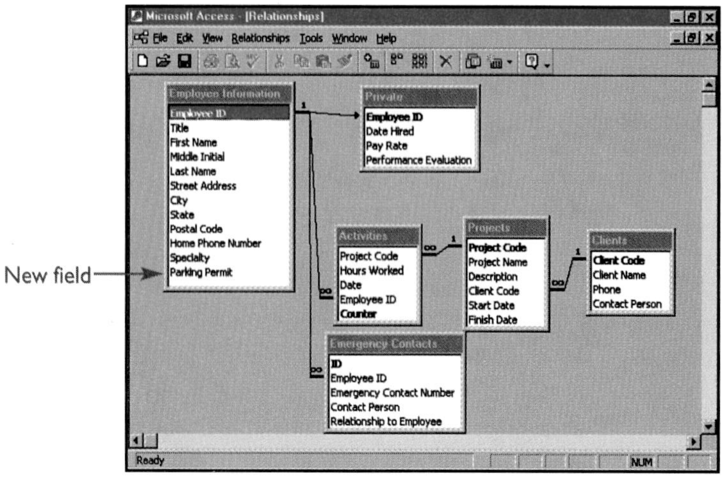

7. Close the Relationships window. Leave the database open for use in the next exercise.

4. Selecting Fields and Modifying the Design to Allow Reporting on Clients

The manager sees you in the hallway on your way to the parking lot and says that she would like to be able to print a list of client information. It should include the client's name, identification code, contact person, phone number, fax number, Web site address, and email address. It should be sorted on the client's name.

To evaluate your design to see if it needs additional fields to produce this report, complete the following steps:

1. Fill out the fifth line of Attachment A, Planning Reports. Use `Client Information` as the title. Refer to the requirements specified above and write in the field names that you think are necessary to produce this report.
2. Click the Relationships button to view the field lists for the tables.
3. Compare the list of field names that you wrote down in step 1 to the lists of fields that already exist. If you have chosen a different name for a field that already exists, change the name to match the existing field.
4. Determine which fields do not exist in any of the tables.
5. Add the field(s) to the Clients table.
6. When you add the field for Web Site Address, use Hyperlink as the Data Type.
7. Open the Relationships window. Compare the field lists in your tables with those shown (see Figure 1.33).
8. Close the Relationships window. Leave the database open for use in the next exercise.

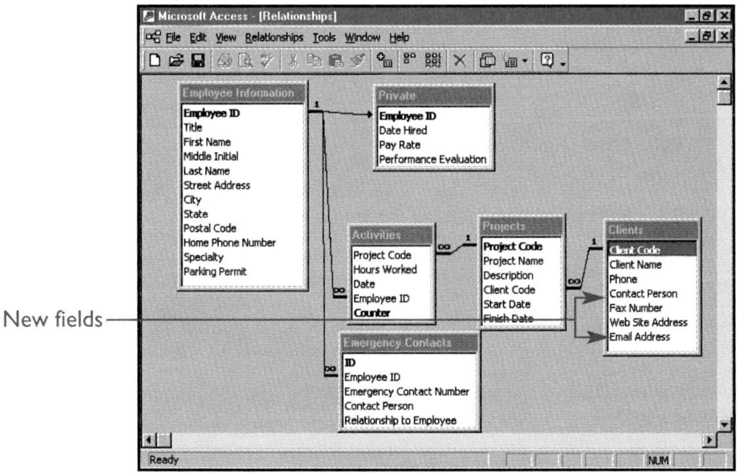

Figure 1.33

5. Selecting Fields and Modifying the Design for Producing a Form Used to Look Up Project Information

At the company picnic, the manager sees you and mentions that it would be nice to be able to call up (on the screen) information about a single project by entering the project name. He or she would like to be able to quickly determine what the start and finish dates are and what percentage of the project is completed.

To evaluate your design to see if it needs additional fields to produce this form, complete the following steps:

1. Fill out the second line of Attachment B, Planning Forms. Use `Project Information` as the title. Refer to the requirements specified above and write in the field names that you think are necessary to produce this form.
2. Click the Relationships button to view the field lists for the tables.
3. Compare the list of field names that you wrote down in step 1 to the lists of fields that already exist. If you have chosen a different name for a field that already exists, change the name to match the existing field.
4. Determine which fields do not exist in any of the tables.
5. Add the field(s) to the Projects table. Format the new fields to display numbers as percentages.
6. Open the Relationships window. Compare the field lists in your tables with those shown (see Figure 1.34).
7. Close the Relationships window. Leave the database open for use in the next exercise.

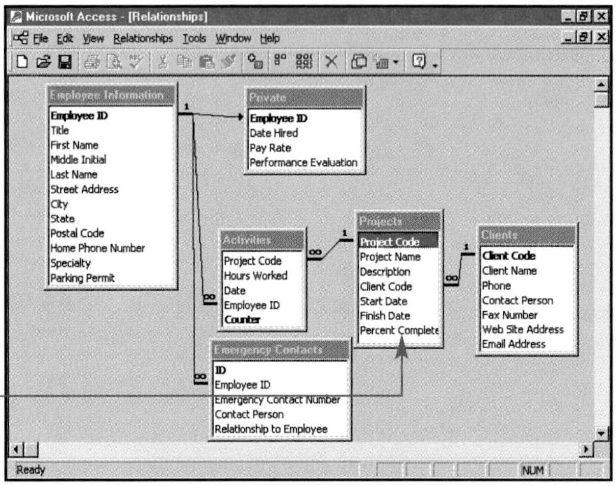

Figure 1.34

6. Selecting Fields and Modifying the Design to Be Able to Produce a Form to Look Up Non-Sensitive Employee Information

The manager's secretary calls you and says that they are planning to hire an intern to help with some of the routine office tasks such as updating the personnel files. He would like to have a form that could be used to bring up information about employees but it should not include any of the sensitive information. When an employee submits an information update form, the intern would enter the employee's ID number to bring up the specific record and then edit the information that is displayed. The Date Hired, Pay Rate, and the Performance Evaluation information should not be included.

To evaluate your design to see if it needs additional fields to produce this form, complete the following steps:

1. Click the Relationships button to view the field lists for the tables.
2. Fill out the third line of Attachment B, Planning Forms. Use `Non-sensitive Employee Information` as the title.
3. Refer to the requirements specified above and write in the field names that you think should be included in this form.
4. Close the Relationships window and leave the database open for use in the following exercises.

Challenge

Challenge exercises expand on or are somewhat related to skills presented in the lessons. Each exercise provides a brief narrative introduction followed by instructions in a numbered step or bulleted list format that are not as detailed as those in the Skill Drill section.

These exercises use the same database that was used to do the Skill Drill exercises. If you did not do those exercises, follow the instructions in the first Skill Drill exercise to copy the AC3-0105 file, rename it as Ex0101, and remove the Read-only property.

1. Determining if the Design Will Support Summary Reports

The manager sends you another message that describes a report that would be very valuable to her. Each month, she has to submit a report to the owner that shows a list of employees and how many hours each of them spent on projects that could be billed to clients. This report does not show any details other than a list of employees, sorted by last name, the total number of billable hours for each one, and the time period covered by the report. It would be ideal if the secretary could generate that report each month by simply entering the starting and ending date of the month. He or she would like to know if you could do this.

You will learn the details of how this type of report is done in a later project. Sometimes, you need to decide if something is possible, even if you do not know how to do it yet. At this point, it is enough to know that Access can produce reports that summarize numeric fields using either the Sum, Average, Minimum, or Maximum functions.

To determine if the database can produce summary reports, complete the following steps:

1. Determine which fields are needed to print and sort the report.
2. Click the relationships button to view the list of fields and their relationships. Determine which fields should be added to the design, if any, and where they should go. (Hint: no new fields are needed.)
3. Determine which field(s) would be summarized (summed in this case).
4. Open the table(s) that contain(s) the field(s) to be summarized. Check the data type to make sure that it is either Number or Currency.
5. If the database contains all the necessary fields and the field that needs to be summarized is a number or currency data type, this report is possible. Fill out a row of the Planning Reports table with the information describing this report. If you conclude that it is not possible, fill out the row and make a note to that effect. Use `Billable Hours` as the title.
6. Leave the database open for use in the next exercise.

2. Modifying the Design to Do a Report for the Client

The accountant stops by your office to talk about the monthly invoices she has to prepare for each client. To assist in this process, she would like a report that has two levels. The first level would show an alphabetical list of projects. The second level would show a list of people who worked on each project and the total hours they worked.

This level of the report should also look up and display the person's specialty and billing rate. (The client is billed at a set rate per hour for each specialty.) It should then calculate the cost to the customer for that person's time. The report should have a subtotal of the cost per project and a grand total of the cost for the month. You would like to be able to print this report in its entirety or for an individual client, and she would like to be able to specify any time period so she can choose between specifying the start and end date for the project or any other range of dates to prepare monthly or annual reports. She provides you with an outline of what the report might look like as shown below:

Project Cost to Client

For the period starting: 4/1/00 and ending: 4/30/00

Client: General Mechanics

Project: Paint Factory – safety inspection and action plan

Baker	64 hrs	at $95/hr	$6,080
		Total	$6,080

Project: Warehouse renovation

Adams	2 hrs	at $105/hr	$210
Baker	43 hrs	at $95/hr	$4,085
		Total	$4,295
		Total for General Mechanics	$10,375

To modify the design to create a client billing report, complete the following steps:

1. Determine what fields are needed to produce this report. (Hint: The billing rate is not the same as the pay rate in the Private table. It is based on the specialty.)
2. Determine what report values are calculated and which ones are fields. Add the new field(s) to the existing tables or create a new table, if necessary. (Hint: It is necessary.) Name the new table `Specialty`.
3. Enter the following billing rates for the existing specialties as shown below:

Architect	100
Civil Engineer	95
Draftsperson	35
Mechanical Engineer	105

4. Create a one-to-many relationship between the primary key field of the new, Specialty table and the corresponding field in the Employee Information table. Enforce referential integrity (the four specialty names shown previously must be spelled exactly as shown or it will not work).
5. Create a query that contains the field that is used to limit the scope of the report by date and the field that is used to limit the report by client. Add the other fields used in the report to the new query.
6. Create a calculated field in the query to determine the product of the hours worked and the billing rate. Use the caption, `Billed Amount`, for the field.
7. Use the sorting options in the query design to sort the fields to match the report requirements.
8. Use the criteria option in the Client field to limit the report to a particular client.
9. Use the Between function in the criteria box for the Date field to limit the report to dates between two specified dates. (Hint: use Help to look up "between criteria".)

10. Test the query to see if it can display the data as specified for the report. You should be able to match the sorting and filtering requirements and display the calculated amount for each worker's billing amount. It is not necessary to calculate the totals and subtotals at this time. They will be added in the final report.
11. Save the query as `Cost to Client`.
12. Fill out a row of the Planning Reports table with the information describing this report. Use `Cost to Client` as the title.

3. Examining the Design to See if a Form with a Subform Can Be Used to Look Up Information About the Clients and Projects

The secretary mentions to you that she often gets calls from the clients asking for a situation report. She would like to be able to call up a form on the screen that would display the client's name, contact person, phone number, fax number, and email address. The client's projects should also be displayed, including the project name, description, start date, finish date, and percent completed.

To determine if a form for client information and a subform for project information is possible, complete the following steps:

1. Open the Relationships window and examine the field lists of tables.
2. Determine if all the fields needed for the client portion of the form exist in the Clients table.
3. Determine if all the fields needed to display the desired project information are present in the Project table.
4. If the desired fields are contained in the two tables, and they are joined in a one-to-many relationship, record a description of this form in a row of the Planning Forms table. Use `Client and Project Information` as the title. If the tables do not meet the requirements above, record a description and make note of how it does not meet the requirements.

4. Examining the Design to See if a Form with a Subform Can Be Used to Look Up Information About the Projects and Employees

The manager calls and tells you that she would like to be able to determine quickly who is working on which project. It would be nice if she could enter the project name and bring up the project name, description, start date, finish date, and percent completed onto the screen and also see a list of the names of people who are working on the project.

To determine if a form for project information and a subform for Employee information is possible, complete the following steps:

1. Open the Relationships window and examine the field lists of tables.
2. Determine if all the fields needed for the project portion of the form exist in the Projects table.
3. Determine if all the fields needed to display the desired Employee information are present in the Employee Information table.
4. Determine if the two tables are joined in a one-to-many relationship. If they are not, a Form/subform will not provide the desired results.

5. If the desired fields are contained in the two tables, and they are joined in a one-to-many relationship, record a description of this form in a row of the Planning Forms table. If not, record a description of the desired form but explain that the subform would display a separate row for each employee activity.
6. Use `Projects and Employees` as the title. Print the Report Design table and the Form Design table if you have been using them onscreen. Close the Report Design document, if necessary. Close the Relationships window but leave the database open for use in the next exercise.

Discovery Zone

Discovery Zone exercises help you gain advanced knowledge of project topics and/or application of skills. These exercises focus on enhancing your problem-solving skills. Numbered steps are not provided, but you are given hints, reminders, screen shots, and/or references to help you reach your goal for each exercise.

These exercises use the same database that was used to do the Skill Drill and Challenge exercises. If you did not do those exercises, follow the instructions in the first Skill Drill exercise to copy the AC3-0105 file, rename is as Ex0101, and remove the Read-only property.

1. Create a Form Letter and Connect It to a Query in the Company Database

The manager's secretary calls and says that she is supposed to send out a letter to all the employees who are eligible for an increase in benefits. To be eligible, the employee must have worked for the company more than five years. The form letter must include the employee's name, mailing address, a salutation that includes the employee's title (for example, Dear Mr. Jones), and their date of employment.

Goal: Create a query that contains the fields necessary for the form letter. Enter a criterion that will limit the records to those whose hiring date is more than five years (1,826 days) ago.

You may use the computer's clock to determine today's date and then use that date in a calculation to determine the number of days difference between the value in a date field and the current date.

To create the form letter and its associated query:

- Create a query that contains the required fields. Be sure to include the Date Hired field from the Private table.
- Sort the records alphabetically by last name and by first name.
- Add a calculated field that subtracts the Date Hired field from the Date().

  Hint #1: For example, if you enter Date()-[Date Hired] in a field box in the query, the program will subtract the Date hired value from today's date. The result is the number of days separating the two dates.
- Enter a criterion in the calculated field to limit the records to those where the difference between today's date and the hire date is greater than the number of days in five years.
- Save the query using the name `Benefits`. Close the query.

- Merge the query with a Word document that informs the employee that they are eligible for a new benefit. The letter should start with the employee's name, ID number, and mailing address. Insert the date hired somewhere in the body of the letter.
- Save the letter on the floppy disk. Name it `Benefits Notice`.

2. Publish a Current List of Clients and Projects on the Company Intranet

The manager's secretary says a lot of employees do not enter the correct code for the project on their time sheet and others would like to know how far along a project is. He would like to make the project information available on the company intranet and set it up so that it is always current.

Goal: Create a data access page that contains the Project Name, Project Code, Description, Client Name, Start Date, Finish Date, and Percent Completed.

The data access page may be created if all of the desired fields are present in tables that are properly related. Use the following guidelines:

- Open the relationships window to see if all of the required fields are present in one or more related tables.
- Click the Pages button and use the wizard to create a data access page. Select the fields in the sequence described in the goal statement above. Sort it on Project Name. Title it `Project Information`.

  Hint: You need to look in more than one table to find all the fields you need.
- Close the page and save it on your floppy disk as `Project Information`.
- After you create the data access page, launch Internet Explorer 5.0. (You do not need to be connected to the Internet for this step.) Type `A:\Project Information` in the Address box, press ↵Enter to view the page.
- Close the browser, close the database, and close Access.

Project 2

Project 2

Making the Input Form More User Friendly

Objectives

In this project, you learn how to

- Change the Color of Text, Backgrounds, and Borders Using Buttons
- Use the Format Painter to Copy Formats Between Controls
- Format More Than One Control at a Time
- Change Colors Using Properties
- Add Status Bar Instructions in the Form View
- Add Customized ControlTips to Controls
- Create a Custom Toolbar

Key terms introduced in this project include

- Control
- ControlTip
- Format Painter

Why Would I Do This?

Customizing the appearance and functions of Access helps you to personalize the database, making it more interesting, informative, and easier to use. Effective use of colors, buttons, and help features can make the difference between a boring database and a professional-looking product.

Most data entry is done in the Form view. Changing the color of the text, background, and border colors can improve the look of the form and can also be used to provide important information to the user. You can use colors, for example, to warn the user of required fields.

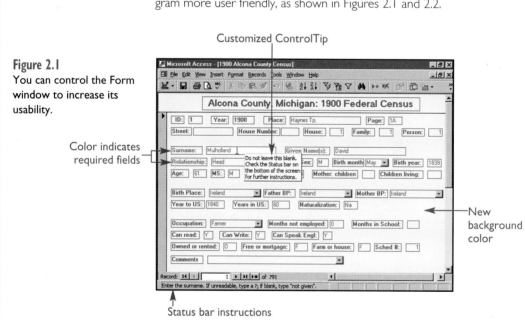

Changing the format or adding new features to each ***control*** on a form can be time consuming. Access has a rapid format feature that can save you a great deal of time.

Access gives you the option of adding customized help for the user. You can place instructions on the status bar, and you can even add ControlTips to the controls on a form.

You can also improve the functionality of a form by customizing the toolbars. You can add predefined buttons that are included with Access to any toolbar and remove seldom-used buttons. The order of the buttons can even be rearranged.

In this project, you learn how to change the appearance of various form controls to give the user more information and to make the database look professional.

Visual Summary

When you have completed this project, you will have made a form and the Access program more user friendly, as shown in Figures 2.1 and 2.2.

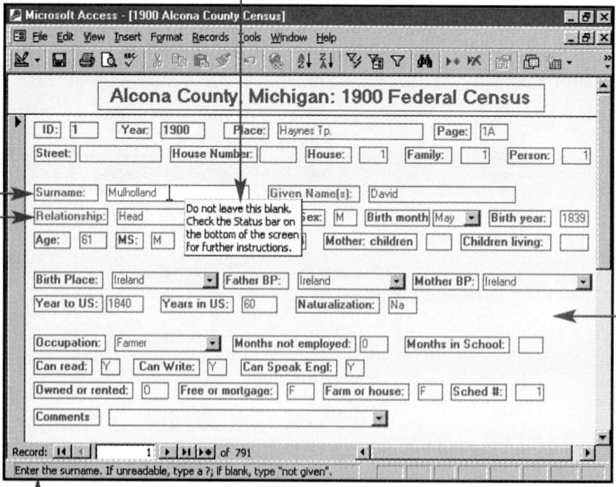

Figure 2.1
You can control the Form window to increase its usability.

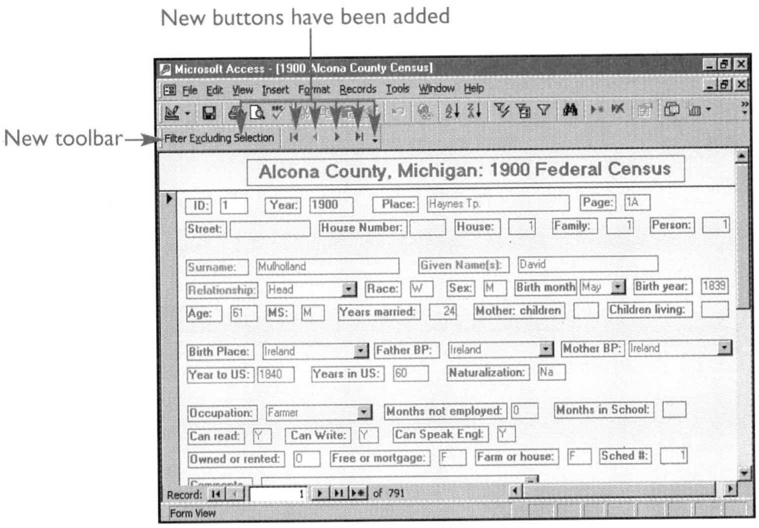

Figure 2.2
You can customize the Access toolbars.

Lesson 1: Changing the Color of Text, Backgrounds, and Borders Using Buttons

You can make the form easier to read through a restrained use of color. Try not to overdo the use of colors. Too many different colors on a screen can be distracting, and bright colors with high contrast can be hard on the eyes. You can also use colors as cues for the user.

In this lesson, you learn how to change the colors of the text (foreground), background, and control borders in a form using buttons on the Formatting (Form/Report) toolbar.

To Change the Color of Text, Backgrounds, and Borders Using Buttons

1. **Find the AC3-0201 database file from your CD-ROM and send it to drive A. Right click the filename; select Properties from the shortcut menu, and then remove the Read-only status. Use the shortcut menu to rename the file `Federal Census`, and then open the database.**
The Database window should now be open to the Tables area (see Figure 2.3).

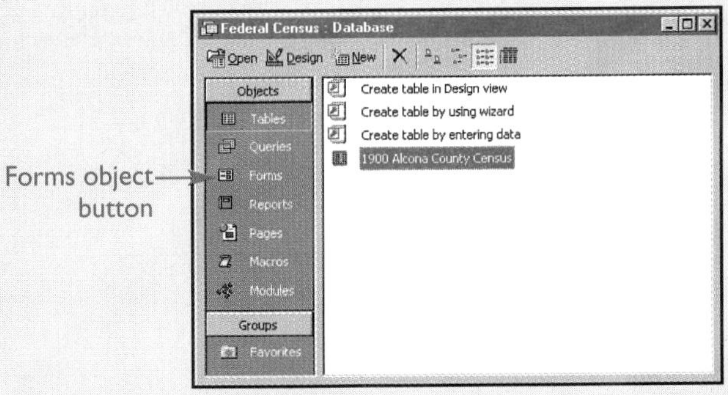

Figure 2.3
The Database window displays the Tables area of the Federal Census database.

2. **Click the Forms object button.**
The 1900 Alcona County Census form should be highlighted. The table accessed by this form contains only the data collected from one township during

continues ▶

To Change the Color of Text, Backgrounds, and Borders Using Buttons (continued)

that census. Because it is a subset of a much larger table, some of the fields may seem unnecessary. This table contains empty fields that do contain information in some of the records that were eliminated in this example.

3 Click the Design button. Maximize the Design window and the Access window, if necessary.

The 1900 Alcona County Census form is ready for design changes.

4 Click the title `Alcona County, Michigan: 1900 Federal Census` to select it.

Handles are displayed around the title (see Figure 2.4).

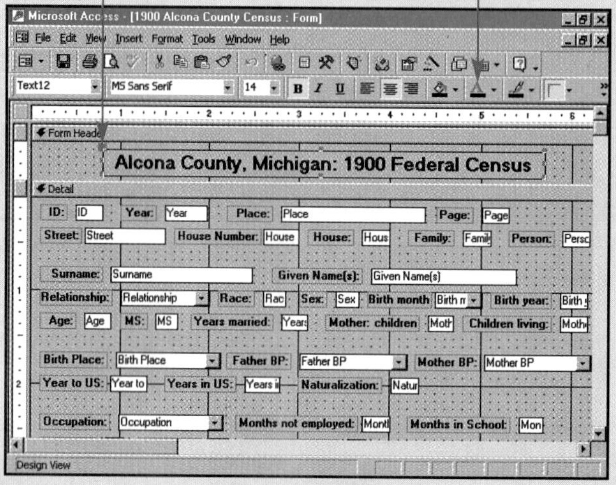

Figure 2.4
The title is in the Form Header of the form Design area.

5 Click the down arrow on the Font/Fore Color button on the Formatting (Form/Report) toolbar.

The Font/Fore Color drop-down box is displayed. The Font/Fore Color button could, in this case, be called the Text Color button, although it can change the color of any foreground. The left side of the button shows the current text color. You use the down arrow to display a menu of optional colors.

6 Choose a dark blue color and click it.

The dark blue color, which appears in the sixth box to the right in the second row, would be a good choice (see Figure 2.5).

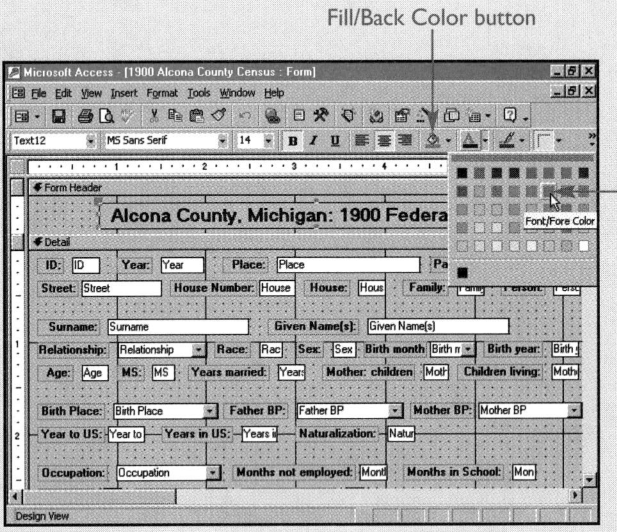

Figure 2.5
The Font/Fore Color drop-down palette offers a variety of colors for text.

> **Default Button Colors**
> Notice that the color on the Font/Fore Color button has changed to dark blue. After you choose a color for the foreground, background, or lines, it becomes the default choice for that button on the toolbar. The color of the button changes to indicate the current default, and you can apply that color to a selected object by clicking the button without using the drop-down menu.

7. **Click the gray background to the left of the title in the Form Header area. Click the down arrow on the Fill/Back Color button on the Formatting (Form/Report) toolbar.**
The Fill/Back Color drop-down palette is displayed.

8. **Choose a light blue background.**
A background color that goes well with dark blue text is the fifth box to the right in the fifth row. Notice that the background of the title is still gray.

9. **Click anywhere on the title to select it.**
The title should show a border with handles as it did when you selected it before.

10. **Click the down arrow on the Fill/Back Color button and click the Transparent option.**
When you want the background of a box to be the same as the background color of the area behind it, you can make the background of the box transparent.

11. **Click the down arrow on the Line/Border Color button.**
A drop-down palette appears. This menu is identical to the one found under the Fill/Back Color button. The most recently used colors are shown at the bottom of the palette (see Figure 2.6).

continues ▶

To Change the Color of Text, Backgrounds, and Borders Using Buttons (continued)

Figure 2.6
The Line/Border Color drop-down menu displays recently used colors.

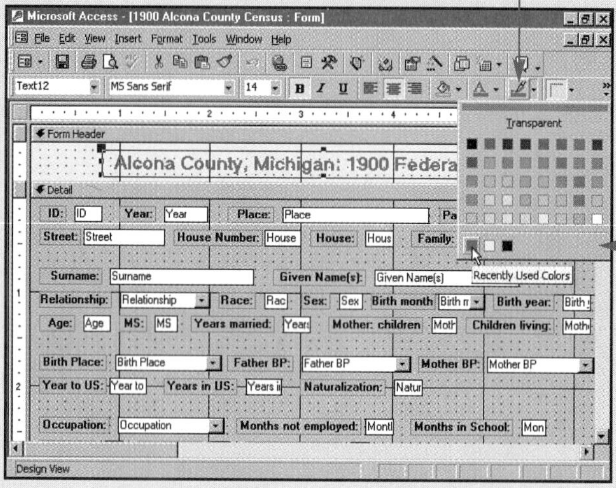

⑫ **Choose the same shade of blue you selected for the title text from the Recently Used Colors area.**
You can select the blue color from this area as well as from its original location on the menu.

⑬ **Click the View button on the Form Design toolbar.**
This switches from Design view to Form view. Notice the color combination in the Form Header area.

⑭ **Click the Save button to save your changes, and then close the form.**
Keep the database open for the next lesson.

Lesson 2: Using the Format Painter to Copy Formats Between Controls

You can easily copy the format from one control to another. The ***Format Painter*** button, on the Form Design toolbar, can be used in several ways to copy formats from one control to one or more other controls.

To Copy Formats Between Individual Controls

① **In the Federal Census database, click the Forms object button, if necessary, and open the 1900 Alcona County Census form in Design view.**

② **Click the label for the ID field (ID:) in the Detail section.**
Handles should appear around the label control box but not the field text control box (see Figure 2.7). Notice that the ID label is right aligned.

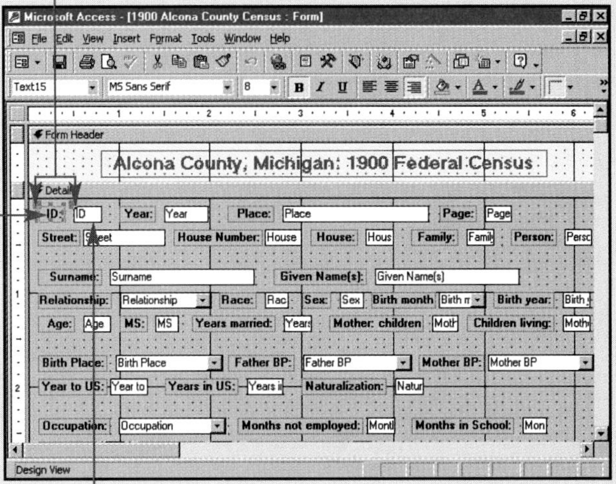
Handles appear around the label box
The ID label is right-aligned
No handles appear around the associated text box

Figure 2.7
The ID label box is selected.

3 Use the Font/Fore Color, Fill/Back Color, and Line/Border Color buttons to change the colors to those you used for the title in Lesson 1.

Change only the ID label box on the left, not the ID text control box on the right. Click the left side of each formatting button to apply the same colors you used in the previous lesson. If the default color for one of the buttons was changed, use the drop-down arrow on the right of the button and choose the color the way you did in Lesson 1.

4 With the ID label box still selected, click the Format Painter button on the Form Design toolbar.

The pointer changes shape, adding a paintbrush to the normal arrow (see Figure 2.8).

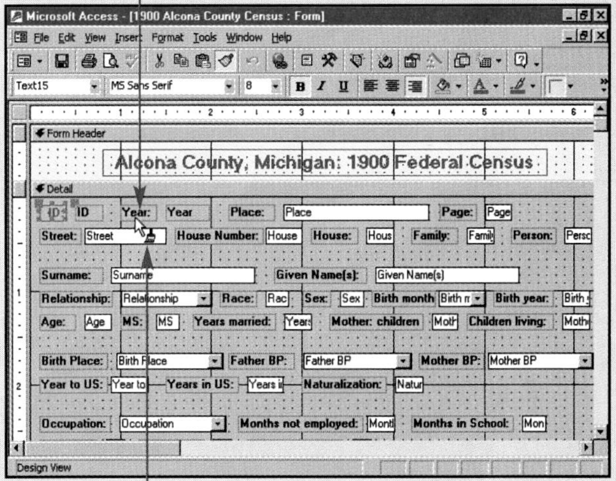
The Year label box
Mouse pointer for the Format Painter

Figure 2.8
The Format Painter pointer has a paintbrush added to the arrow.

continues ▶

To Copy Formats Between Individual Controls (continued)

5. **Click the label control box for the Year control box.**
   The Fore Color, Back Color, and Border Color now match the ID label. Notice that the pointer no longer has a paintbrush attached.

> **Unexpected Consequences of the Format Painter**
> The Format Painter also applies the settings for font style, point size, and alignment. Notice that the Year label is now right aligned. You need to keep an eye on alignment and number formatting to make sure the Format Painter doesn't make unexpected changes in your form!
>
> Also, if you use the Format Painter to copy the format of a label onto a text box, you will not see any immediate problem. However, when you use the form, the text box shows a gray background instead of white when you tab to it to enter data.

6. **With the ID label still selected, double-click the Format Painter button.**
   Double-clicking locks the button on for repeated use.
7. **Click the label control box for the Place field.**
   The Fore Color, Back Color, and Border Color now match the ID field label. Notice that the pointer still has a paintbrush attached. You can continue to paint as many label and field text controls as you want until you click the Format Painter button again to turn it off.
8. **Click the label control box for the Page field.**
   Notice that the paintbrush remains with the mouse pointer.
9. **Click the Format Painter button once to turn off the Format Painter.**
   Keep the form open for the next lesson.

Lesson 3: Formatting More Than One Control at a Time

Access provides you with a faster way to change the format of several controls simultaneously. To do this, you need to select a number of controls at the same time.

To Format Many Controls at One Time

1. **Move the pointer to the vertical ruler, immediately to the left of the ID field.**
   The pointer turns into an arrow pointing to the right.
2. **Click and hold down the left mouse button.**
   A thin line appears through the first row of controls.
3. **Drag the pointer down until it is to the left of the Age field.**
   A thin line should appear through the row of fields that begin with the Age field, and the ruler appears black between the two lines (see Figure 2.9).

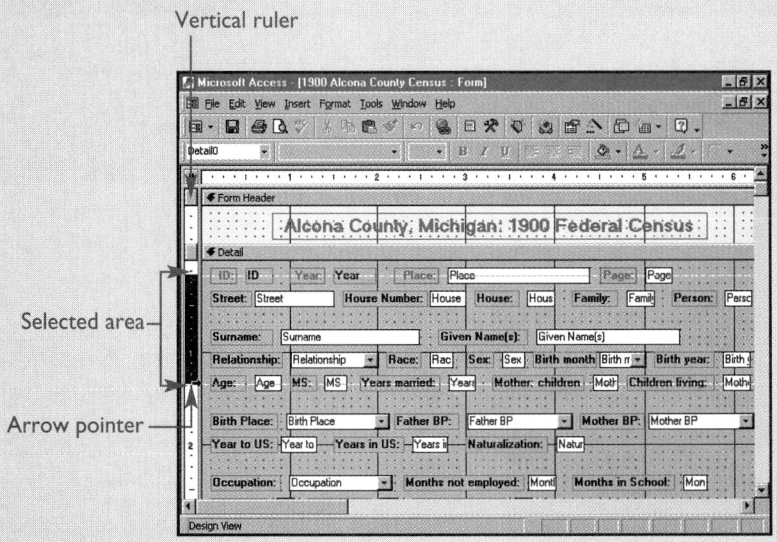

Figure 2.9
The vertical ruler turns black to show the selected area.

4 **Release the left mouse button.**
All the labels and controls to the right of the dark area of the ruler are selected (see Figure 2.10).

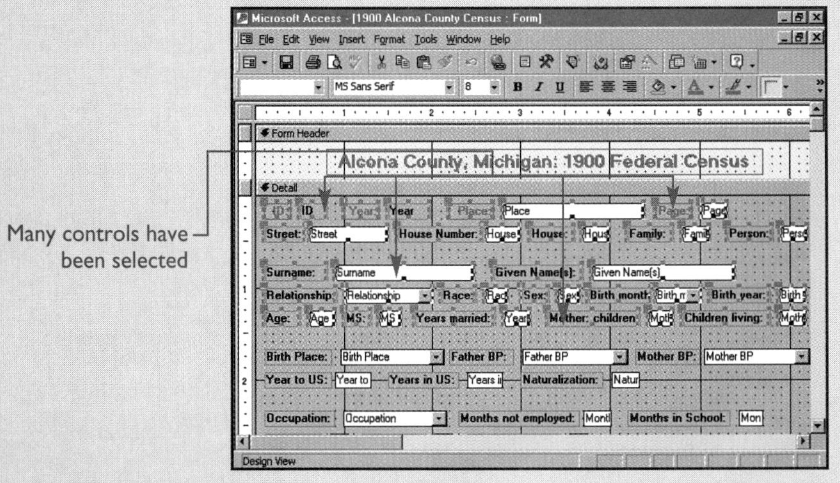

Figure 2.10
Text boxes and label boxes were selected at the same time.

5 **Use the Font/Fore Color, Fill/Back Color, and Line/Border Color buttons to change the colors to those you used in Lesson 1.**
The background, text, and border of the selected labels and controls should be changed. Notice that this method enables you to select the formats separately and does not change the text alignment.

6 **Repeat steps 1-5 to select the remaining controls in the Detail area of the form and change the colors.**

If you are using a screen with 640x480 resolution (which is the resolution that the figures were captured in), you may not be able to see all the remaining fields on the screen. Use the vertical scrollbar to scroll down so you can see all the fields that have not been changed.

continues ▶

To Format Many Controls at One Time (continued)

7 Click in a blank area of the Detail section.

The background, text, and border of all the labels and controls should now match the Form Header area.

8 Use the Fill/Back Color button to change the background of the unused portion of the Detail area to the same light blue you used for the Form Header area.

9 Click the View button.

Notice the color combination of the form. Also notice that the combo box buttons remain gray and black (or whatever colors were chosen as default colors), as do the perimeter portions of the screen, such as the status bar and the scrollbars (see Figure 2.11).

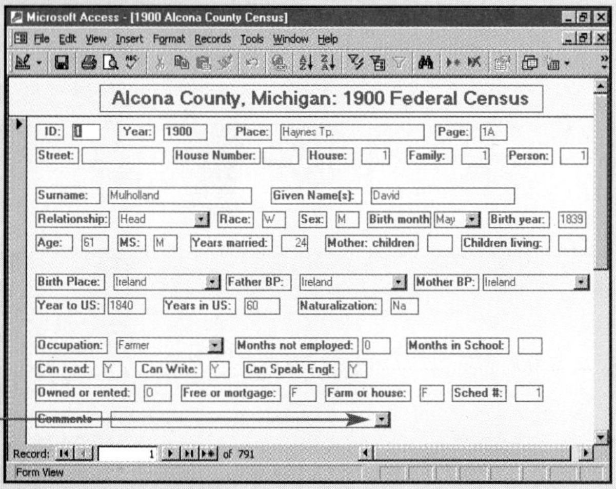

Figure 2.11
The colors of various elements of the form were changed.

10 Save your changes and close the form.

Other Shortcuts for Selecting Multiple Controls
The procedure used in Lesson 3 involves several steps to select all the components of the Detail area. If you know that all the objects on the form will be formatted the same way, you can use the Select All option from the Edit menu. If you are going to format most of the objects the same way, you can use the Select All option, and then hold Shift down and click the ones you don't want to format to deselect them. If you want to format only a few controls, you can hold down Shift and click to select all the controls that you want to format.

Lesson 4: Changing Colors Using Properties

In Lesson 2, you used the buttons on the Form Design toolbar to change the color of the background, text, and borders. Using the Properties box gives you many more colors and shades from which to choose. This is especially important if, for example, you are attempting to make your form colors match your company's colors. Several other formatting options are available in the Properties box.

In this lesson, you use the Properties box to change the color of the three required fields in this form. This warns users that these fields are special in some way.

To Change Colors and Align Text Using Properties

1. **Highlight the 1900 Alcona County Census form; click the Design button, and maximize the form, if necessary.**

2. **Right-click the Surname label control box.**
   The Surname field is one of the fields you want to identify as required by changing the color.

3. **Choose Properties from the shortcut menu and click the Format tab, if necessary.**

4. **Scroll down until you can click in the Fore Color text box.**
   The Fore Color is identified by a numeric code, and a Build button is displayed on the right side of the Fore Color text box (see Figure 2.12).

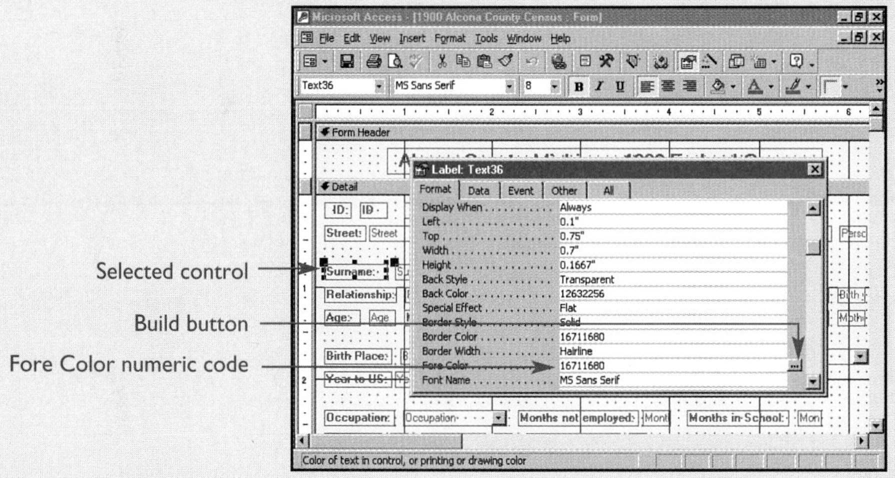

Figure 2.12
The Format tab in the Properties box offers a variety of formatting options.

5. **Click the Build button.**
   The Color dialog box is displayed.

6. **Click the Define Custom Colors button.**
   The Color dialog box expands to include a box showing a range of color options. The current color is indicated by an arrow on the right side and by crosshairs at the top edge of the multicolored box (see Figure 2.13). The look of your Color dialog box depends on your computer's display settings.

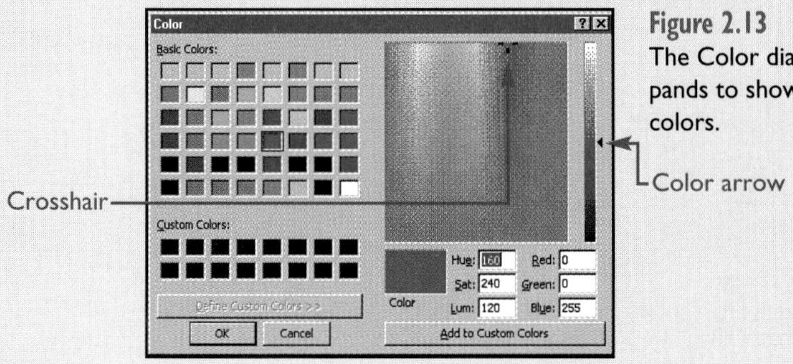

Figure 2.13
The Color dialog box expands to show custom colors.

continues ▶

To Change Colors and Align Text Using Properties (continued)

7 Click a bright red area of the multicolor box and click OK.

8 Close the Properties box.

You have now warned the user that the Surname field is special in some way. (You let them know exactly what is special about it in Lessons 5 and 6.) Now copy the format of the Surname label to the other two required fields.

9 With the Surname label control still selected, double-click the Format Painter.

10 Click the Given Name(s) and Relationship label controls to change the color of the text to match the color of the Surname label.

11 Click the Format Painter button again to turn it off.

12 Click the View button.

Notice that the three required fields stand out on the screen (see Figure 2.14).

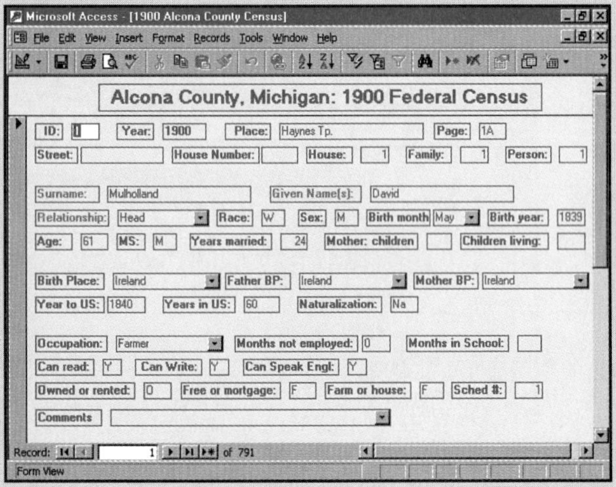

Figure 2.14
Colors were added to identify special fields.

13 Save your changes and close the form.

Lesson 5: Adding Status Bar Instructions in the Form View

In Lesson 4, you learned how to give the user a visual cue that there was something special about a field. If you want to make the form easy to use, you may also need to give the user help on what to put in the field and provide information on any special characteristics of the field. Access has several ways to help the user, including printed instructions, status bar messages, and custom ControlTips.

In this lesson, you add help to the status bar. In Lesson 6, you create custom ControlTips.

To Add Status Bar Instructions in the Form View

1. **Highlight the 1900 Alcona County Census form in the Forms window; click the Design button, and maximize the form, if necessary.**

2. **Right-click the Surname text control box.**
   Make sure you use the text control box, not the label control box you worked on in Lesson 4. A shortcut menu is displayed.

3. **Choose Properties from the shortcut menu and click the Other tab.**

4. **Click the Status Bar text box.**

> If you don't see the Status Bar text box, you probably right-clicked the Surname label control box instead of the Surname text control box in step 2. Leave the Properties box open and click the Surname text control box. The Properties box displays the properties of the currently selected object.

5. **Type the following text:**
   `Enter the surname. If unreadable, type a ?; if blank, type "not given".`

   This is the text that appears in the status bar when the cursor is in the Surname field (see Figure 2.15). The Properties box in Figure 2.15 is expanded to show the entire label in the Status Bar text box.

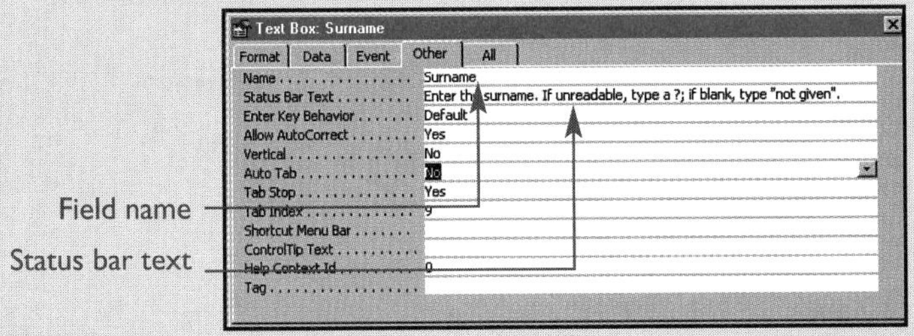

Figure 2.15
Whatever is typed into the Status Bar text box appears in the status bar.

> **Maximum Length of Status Bar Message**
> When creating a message for the status bar, you want to limit the length of the message so that the entire message is visible on the status bar when that field is selected. Try to keep your message under 75 characters.

6. **Click the text box of the Given Name(s) field. Enter the following text in its Status Bar text box:**
   `Enter the given name(s). If unreadable, type ?; if blank, type "not given".`

   This message is slightly altered from the text used for the Surname field.

> To see the text box of the Given Name(s) field, you may need to drag the Properties box out of the way. Click the blue title bar of the Properties box and drag it to another part of your screen so you can select the new control. When you click the Given Name(s) text box, the title on the Properties box changes to reflect the new field that is selected. Make sure the title bar says Text box: Given Name(s).

continues ▶

To Add Status Bar Instructions in the Form View (continued)

7 Click the Relationship text box and type the following text in the Status Bar text box:

```
Enter the relationship. If unreadable, type ?; if blank, type "not given".
```

8 Close the Properties box.

9 Click the View button and then click the Surname text box.

The message you typed appears in the status bar (see Figure 2.16).

If the status bar does not appear at the bottom of your screen, choose Tools, Options from the menu. Click the View tab in the Options dialog box, if necessary, and then click the Status Bar check box in the Show area.

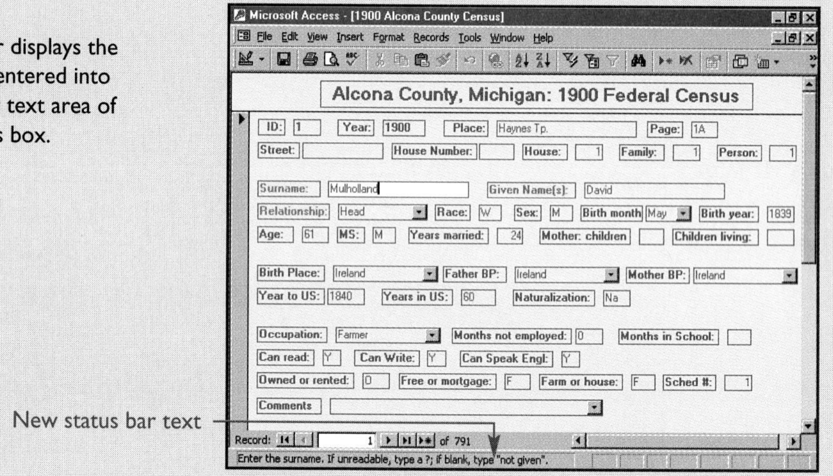

Figure 2.16
The status bar displays the message you entered into the Status Bar text area of the Properties box.

10 Save your changes and close the form.

Copying and Pasting Status Bar Text

It might seem that the Format Painter could be used to copy status bar text. The Format Painter, however, works on those functions that change the appearance of an object. It does not work on any of the customized features that require that text be entered. If you are entering identical (or similar) text to the status bar for several fields, type the text into a field, highlight it, and then use the Copy and Paste commands to place the text in the status bar text areas of subsequent fields. (You have to use the keyboard shortcuts or the right mouse shortcut menu to copy and paste because the menu and toolbar versions of copy and paste apply to the selected object, not the boxes in the Properties dialog box.)

Lesson 6: Adding Customized ControlTips to Controls

In Windows, when you move the pointer over a button on a toolbar and leave it there for a short time, a ScreenTip appears telling you what the button does. You can add the same feature to the controls on your forms, which can help make the form easier to use. In a form, these ScreenTips attached to controls are known as ***ControlTips***.

In this lesson, you add ControlTips to augment the status bar messages you created in Lesson 5. You also use a ControlTip to tell the user how to change a default value.

To Add Customized ControlTips to Controls

1. **Highlight the 1900 Alcona County Census form; click the Design button and maximize the form, if necessary.**

2. **Right-click the Surname text control box and choose Properties from the shortcut menu.**

3. **Click the Other tab, if necessary, and then click the ControlTip text box.**

> There should be 12 Other options. If there are only five, it means you selected the Surname label control box instead of the text control box.

4. **Type the following text; press Shift+Enter after each of the first three lines:**

```
Do not leave this blank.
Check the status bar on
the bottom of the screen
for further instructions.
```

This is the text that appears in the ControlTip when the pointer is moved over the Surname field. If you don't press Shift+Enter at the end of each line, the ControlTip displays as a single line and might disappear off the edge of the screen so that only the last line you entered for the ControlTip is displayed (see Figure 2.17).

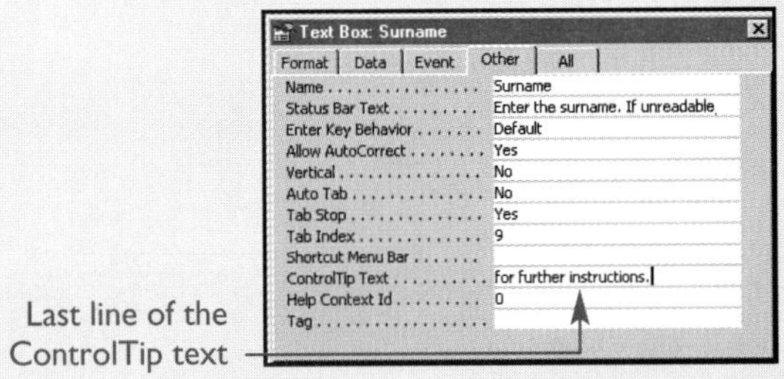

Figure 2.17
The ControlTip text box appears when the pointer is held over the field in Form view.

5. **Click the Given Name(s) text box. Locate the ControlTip text box in the Properties box and enter the same message.**

> **Copying and Pasting ControlTip Text**
> Instead of retyping the same text three times, you can copy the text from the Surname ControlTip text box and paste it into the ControlTip text boxes for the First Name(s) field. To copy the text, click another box; then click at the beginning of the ControlTip text box; hold the mouse button down, and drag to the right and down. This selects all four rows of text. Press Ctrl+C to copy the text. Move the Properties box until you can see the Given Names(s) text control box; click in the ControlTip text box, and press Ctrl+V to paste the text. Repeat the procedure for the Relationship text control box.

continues ▶

To Add Customized ControlTips to Controls (continued)

6 Repeat step 4 to place the identical text in the ControlTip text box of the Relationship text control box.

In each case, the ControlTip tells the user how to find more information. The same procedure can be used to give instructions for anticipated problems. In this database, for example, the Place field has a default value. As the user moves from township to township, this default value has to be changed.

Type ControlTip Text into More Than One Field at a Time

You can change the same property on several controls at the same time. For example, to add the ControlTip that you entered in this lesson, you could select the Surname text control box, hold down Shift, and click the other two controls; then open the Properties box. When you type the ControlTip text, it is entered into all three controls.

7 Repeat step 4 for the Place field, but enter the following text in the ControlTip text box. Remember to press Shift+Enter after each of the first four lines:

```
To change the Place default value, close this form and
click the Tables object button. Select the 1900 Alcona
County Census table and click the Design button. Select
the Place field; then type the new Default Value in the
Field Properties area.
```

A ControlTip message is limited to 255 characters. This message is close to the maximum size.

8 Close the Properties box.

9 Click the View button. Click the Surname field and leave the pointer over the Surname field.

Look at the ControlTip and the status bar. (The cursor is in the Surname field.) These types of messages can be very helpful, especially to a new user (see Figure 2.18).

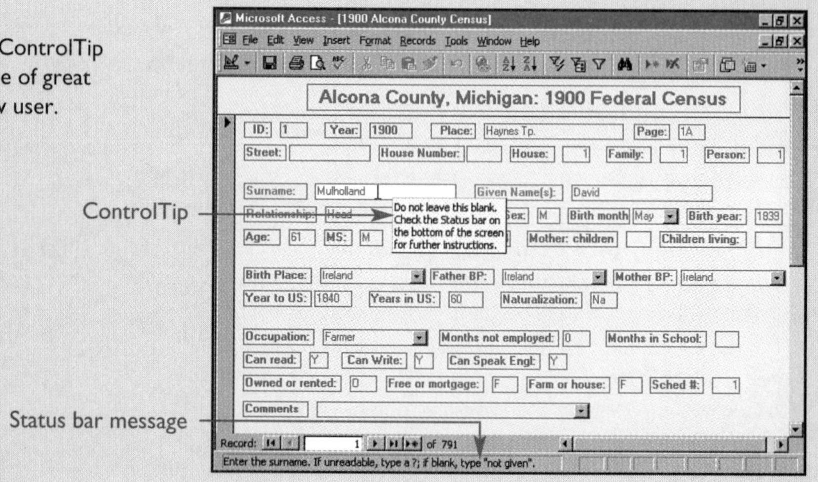

Figure 2.18
Status bar and ControlTip messages can be of great help to the new user.

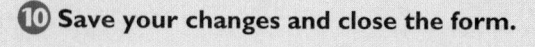

10 Save your changes and close the form.

ControlTip is Linked to Pointer
The ControlTip is linked to the pointer whereas the status bar is linked to the insertion point. If you have the insertion point in one box and point at another, the ControlTip and the status bar message will not refer to the same field.

Lesson 7: Creating a Custom Toolbar

The toolbars associated with the various components of Access are helpful to both the database designer and the end-user. Although end-users seldom use any of the buttons associated with the various design views, they often perform tasks using toolbars, such as sorting, filtering, and printing. More buttons are available than those shown in the default toolbars. You can add these buttons to toolbars and remove unused buttons.

In this lesson, you turn on an empty toolbar and add several buttons to it.

To Create a Custom Toolbar

1. **Highlight the 1900 Alcona County Census form; click the Open button, and maximize the form if necessary.**

2. **Right-click the Form View toolbar.**
   A shortcut menu is displayed.

3. **Choose Customize from the shortcut menu.**
   The Customize dialog box displays tabs for three sections: Toolbars, Commands, and Options (see Figure 2.19).

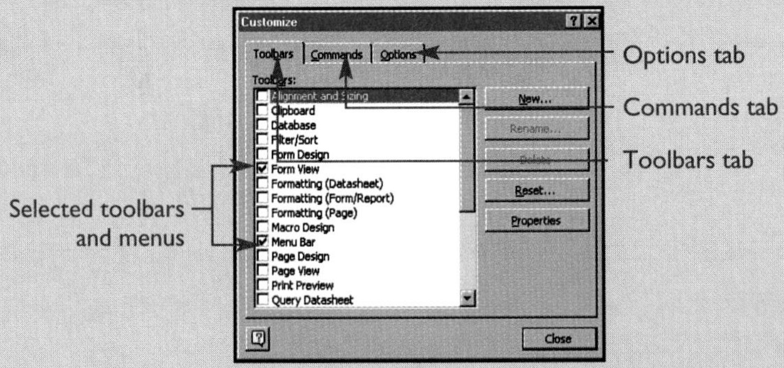

Figure 2.19
The Customize dialog box has three tabs. The Toolbars tab displays existing toolbars.

4. **Select the Toolbars tab, if necessary. Scroll down the list of toolbars and click the check box for the Utility 1 toolbar.**
   This toolbar is normally empty and can be used to create a customized toolbar. As soon as you click the Utility 1 toolbar check box, an extra toolbar is added (see Figure 2.20).

continues ▶

To Create a Custom Toolbar (continued)

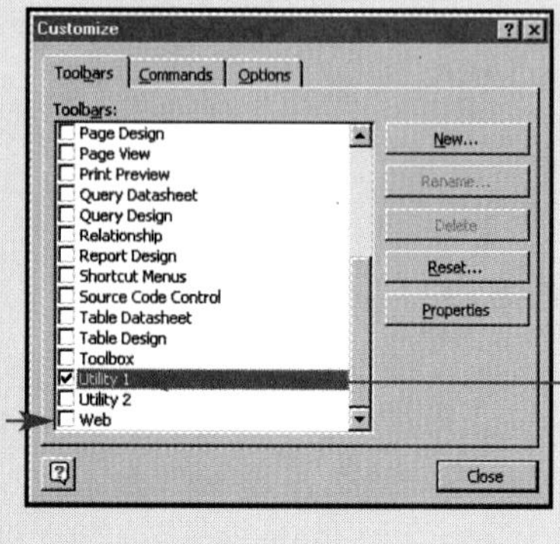

Figure 2.20
The Utility 1 toolbar is added as soon as you click its check box.

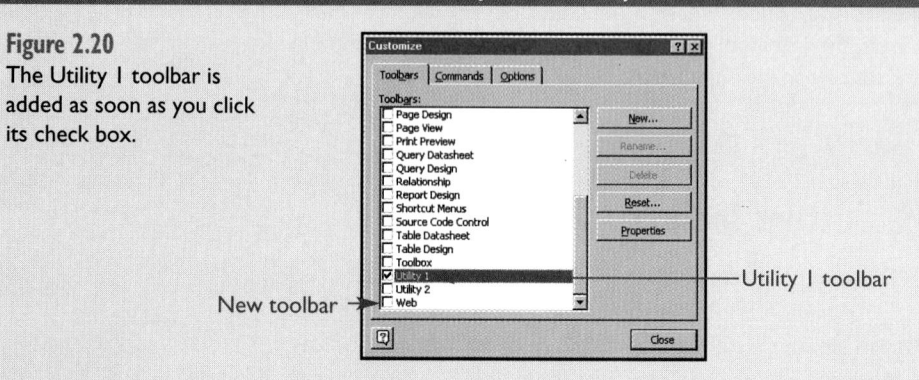

5 **Select the Commands tab in the Customize dialog box.**
Many buttons are available for you to add to the toolbar. They are grouped by the categories displayed on the left, with the individual buttons shown on the right.

6 **Click Records in the Categories section.**
A list of commands that are useful for dealing with records is displayed.

7 **Click the Filter Excluding Selection command and drag it up to the new Utility 1 toolbar (see Figure 2.21).**

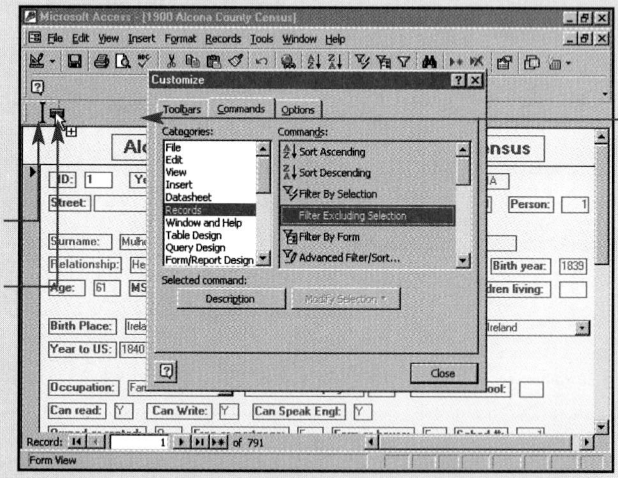

Figure 2.21
When you are adding a button to the toolbar, a small button appears to be attached to the pointer arrow.

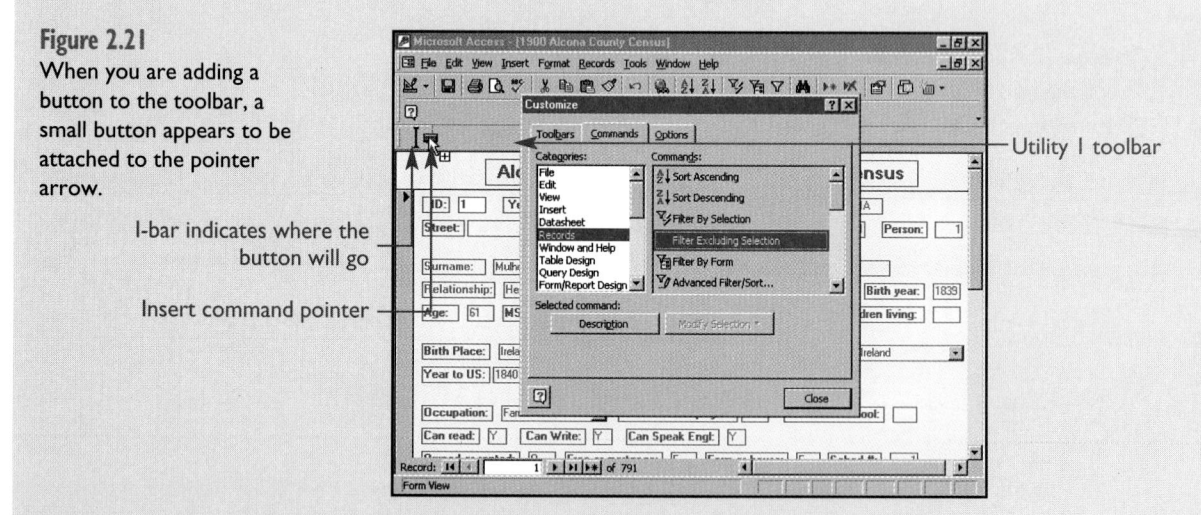

8 **Release the mouse button.**
The command is added to the toolbar. Because this command does not have a button icon, the text is included on the new button on the toolbar.

> **X** To add a new button, you need to drag the button to the beginning of the toolbar at the far-left end where a small box marks the current size of the toolbar. When the button is successfully placed, a large, bold I-bar (I) displays to show the insertion point.

9 **Scroll down the list of Records commands to select the command for First. Drag it onto the Utility 1 toolbar to the right of the Filter Excluding Selection button.**

10 Add the Previous, Next, and Last buttons to the right of the First button.

You may have to move the Customize dialog box out of the way so you can see your new toolbar, but do not close it. The Customize dialog box must be open for you to customize a toolbar. You now have five buttons on the Utility I toolbar. In the next step, you create a separation mark on the toolbar that is useful for visually grouping similar buttons. In this case, the first button is used to manage records, whereas the next four are navigation buttons that are larger and easier to use than the navigation buttons at the bottom of the window.

11 Click the First button (the one to the right of the Filter Excluding Selection button) and drag to the right about an eighth of an inch. Release the mouse button.

The button moves to the right, and a vertical separating bar is inserted (see Figure 2.22). The navigation buttons are now grouped together.

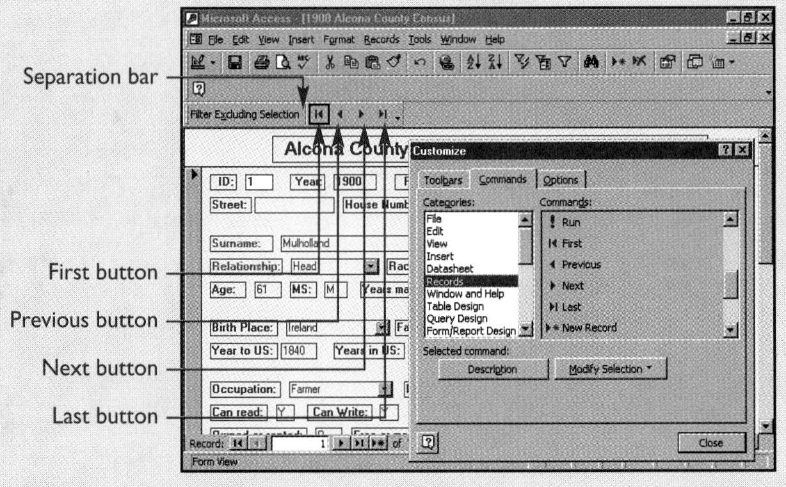

Figure 2.22
Dragging the button slightly to the right inserts a vertical bar on the toolbar that can be used to visually separate groups of buttons.

Removing Buttons from a Toolbar

You will use some buttons on the toolbars only rarely. You can easily remove these buttons using the Customize feature you used to add a toolbar and buttons. To remove buttons from a toolbar, right click any toolbar and select Customize from the shortcut menu. Click the button you want to remove and drag it below the toolbar. When you release the mouse button, the unwanted button disappears. (Note: You can always return the button to the toolbar; it is not removed permanently.)

12 Close the Customize dialog box. Try the new navigation buttons to make sure they work properly.

13 Right-click any toolbar and select Customize from the shortcut menu.

14 Click the Utility I check box to deselect it. Close the Customize dialog box.

15 Close the form and close the database.

If you have completed your session on the computer, exit Access and close Windows before you turn off the computer. Otherwise, continue with the exercises.

continues ▶

Resetting the Toolbars

The toolbars are part of the Access interface, not one particular database. When you change the toolbars, it affects anyone else who is using the application on that computer. Do not change the standard toolbars unless you have the permission of other users or it is your personal machine.

If you are working in a lab environment, you need to reset any toolbars you have modified to their original condition after you are finished with the exercises. To restore the Utility 1 toolbar, right-click any toolbar; click Customize, highlight the Utility 1 toolbar name, and click the Reset button. Click OK when prompted to reset the toolbar.

Checking Concepts and Terms

True/False

For each of the following, check *T* or *F* to indicate whether the statement is true or false.

__T __F **1.** Double-clicking the Format Painter button takes you to the Format Painter dialog box. [L2]

__T __F **2.** One reason you might use the Properties box to change a color is that this method gives you more color options than the toolbar button does. [L4]

__T __F **3.** If you customize a toolbar, the changes appear only when you use the database that was open when you customized the toolbar. [L7]

__T __F **4.** To apply the same format to the entire form, you can use the Select Entire Form command under the Format menu. [L3]

__T __F **5.** The number of characters you can put in a ControlTip is unlimited. [L6]

__T __F **6.** To change the color of the background for a control or a group of controls, you must first select the control(s). [L3]

__T __F **7.** A ControlTip is the Access name for a ScreenTip in a form. [L6]

__T __F **8.** A message that is entered on the Status Bar text box should be limited so that the entire message shows on the status bar when that field is selected. [L5]

__T __F **9.** You can use the Format Painter to copy a status bar message from one control to another. [L5]

__T __F **10.** To change the Properties box from one control to the next, you must close the first Properties box before you can open the next Properties box. [L4]

Multiple Choice

Circle the letter of the correct answer for each of the following questions.

1. Which button do you use to change the color of text in a form? [L1]

a. Fill/Back Color

b. Line/Border Color

c. Font/Fore Color

d. Special Effects

2. To remove a button from a toolbar, go to the Customize dialog box, and then______________. [L7]

a. drag the button below the toolbar and let go

b. select the button, and then press Del

c. select the button, and then choose Cut from the Edit menu

d. right-click the button and select Remove from the shortcut menu

3. A ControlTip is activated when you ________. [L6]
   a. place the insertion point in the appropriate control
   b. place the mouse pointer over the appropriate control for a short time
   c. click the field with the left mouse button
   d. click the field with the right mouse button
4. The Fore Color is found on the ________ tab of the Properties box. [L4]
   a. Data
   b. Event
   c. Format
   d. Other
5. To have a ControlTip break over several lines, press ________ to create breaks between the lines of text. [L6]
   a. Shift+F5
   b. Ctrl+Enter
   c. Shift+Enter
   d. Alt+Enter

Screen ID

Label each element of the Access screen shown in Figure 2.23 and Figure 2.24.

Figure 2.23

- **A.** Transparent Fill/Back Color
- **B.** Added button
- **C.** Visual cue
- **D.** Added navigation buttons
- **E.** Status bar message
- **F.** Blue Fill/Back Color
- **G.** Blue Font/Fore Color
- **H.** Toolbar button separator
- **I.** Modified toolbar
- **J.** ControlTip

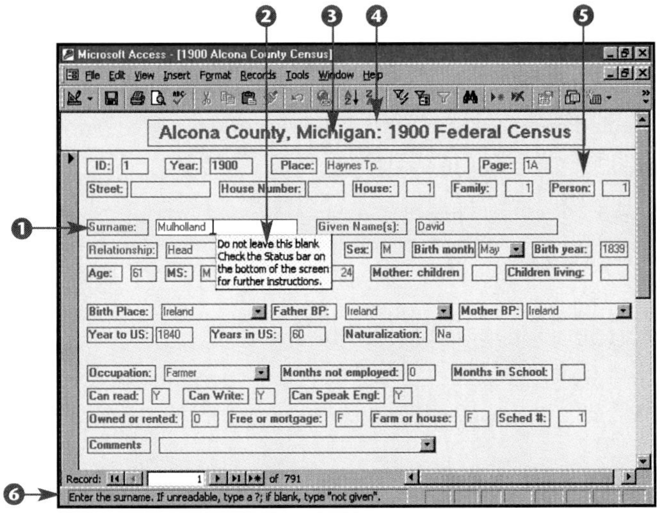

Figure 2.24

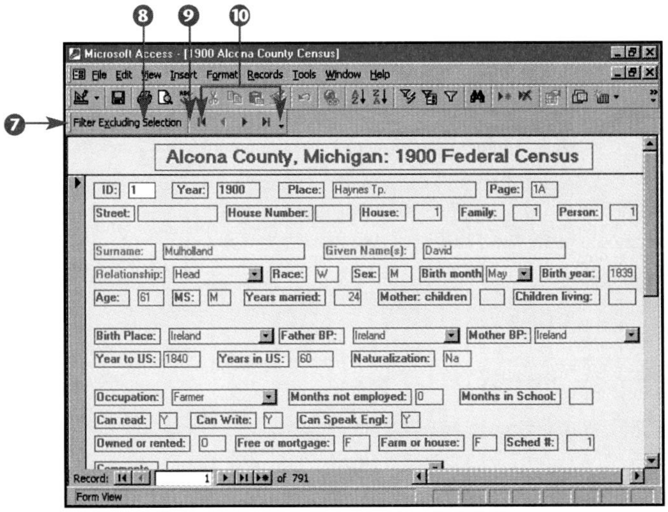

1. ________
2. ________
3. ________
4. ________
5. ________
6. ________
7. ________
8. ________
9. ________
10. ________

Discussion Questions

1. You can use several different colors to indicate different things on a form. Do you think you should limit the number of different colors you use on a single form? Would colorful forms be appealing to work with, or hard on the eyes? Can you think of any reason why you might want to be careful with certain color combinations?
2. In Lesson 4, you used the Properties box to change control properties. Take a look at the Properties box in form Design view again, but this time examine the various formatting options. What other types of visual cues might you use to alert the person using the form that a field is important?
3. You can put a lot of information into ControlTips, but some might argue that they are of limited value. Why?
4. ControlTips and status bar messages can be used to give some information. Can you think of a better way to get information to inexperienced database users?
5. You can easily remove buttons from toolbars. If you were having inexperienced users entering data, what buttons might you want to remove from the Form View toolbar? If you could turn off the menu, would that be useful?

Skill Drill

Skill Drill exercises reinforce project skills. Each skill reinforced is the same, or nearly the same, as a skill presented in the project. Each exercise includes a brief narrative introduction, followed by detailed instructions in a step-by-step format.

In these exercises, you work with a database that keeps track of a company's microcomputer purchases and the distributors you buy from.

1. Changing the Title Color and Background

In this exercise, you change the color of a form title and change the background to transparent to enable the background pattern to show through the title box. [L1]

To change the title color and background, complete the following steps:

1. Find the AC3-0202 database file on your CD-ROM; send it to drive A. Right-click the filename; choose Properties, and turn off Read-only status. Right-click the filename again; choose Rename, and call the file `Computer Inventory`. Open the file.
2. Click the Edit Hardware Information button on the Main Switchboard. Look at the way the title fill overlaps the background. Click the View button to switch to form Design view of the Vendor and Hardware form.
3. Select the title and click the drop-down arrow on the Font/Fore Color button. Select a dark blue color.
4. With the title still selected, select Transparent from the Fill/Back Color button.
5. Click the View button to see your changes.
6. Save your changes and leave the database open for use in the next exercise.

2. Changing Multiple Controls

The text in the label control boxes is black. In this exercise, you select and change the color for all the controls in the Detail section of the form. [L3]

To change the color of multiple controls, complete the following steps:

1. Click the View button to return to Design view.
2. Select the Vendors label and click the Font/Fore Color button, which should display the color you used for the title.
3. Choose Edit, Select All from the menu to select all the controls in the form.
4. Hold down Shift and click the title to deselect it.
5. Click the Font/Fore Color button to change the font color for all the form's controls.
6. With the controls still selected, select Transparent from the Fill/Back Color button. Click anywhere in the background to deselect all the controls.
7. Click the View button to see your changes. Notice that the check mark boxes are still black and the Close command button was not changed.
8. Save your changes and leave the database open for use in the next exercise.

3. Creating Visual Cues for Special Fields

Three of the fields in the Vendor and Hardware form are required—you cannot move to the next record unless you have entered a vendor name and inventory code number. (Both are primary key fields.) You also must enter one of a set number of responses in the RAM field. It would be a good idea to alert the users that these fields are special. [L2, 3]

To create visual cues, complete the following steps:

1. Click the View button to return to Design view.
2. Select the text control box for the Vendors field.
3. Click the Fill/Back Color button and select a pale yellow color.
4. Select the RAM text control box, and then hold down Shift and click the Inventory Code Number field.
5. Click the Fill/Back Color button to change the background to the same color as the Vendors text control box.
6. Click the View button to see your changes.
7. Save your changes and leave the database open for use in the next exercise.

4. Adding Status Bar Instructions to a Field

The RAM field is set up to accept only specific entries—4, 8, 16, 32, 64, 128. In this exercise, you add instructions to the status bar for this field. [L5]

To add a status bar message to the RAM field, complete the following steps:

1. Click the View button to return to Design view.
2. Right-click the text control box for the RAM field and select Properties from the shortcut menu.
3. Click the Other tab and locate the Status Bar text box.
4. Type the following message into the Status Bar text box:

   ```
   Enter either 4, 8, 16, 32, 64, or 128
   ```
5. Close the Properties box.
6. Click the View button to switch to Form view and test the status bar by selecting the RAM field.
7. Save your changes and leave the database open for use in the next exercise.

5. Adding a ControlTip to a Field

You have added a status bar message to the RAM field, now it would be a good idea to add a ControlTip with the same message. [L6]

To add a ControlTip to the RAM field, complete the following steps:

1. Click the View button to return to Design view.
2. Right-click the text control box for the RAM field and select Properties from the shortcut menu.
3. Click the Other tab and locate the ControlTip text box.
4. Type the following message into the ControlTip text box:

```
Enter:
4
8
16
32
64
128
```

Make sure you press Shift+Enter to start each new line.

5. Close the Properties box.
6. Click the View button to switch to Form view and test the ControlTip by moving the pointer over the RAM field.
7. Save your changes and leave the database open for use in the next exercise.

6. Adding Buttons to a Toolbar

When you are entering data using a form, you often need to go back and look at the table to see all the entries together. The form Datasheet view does the same thing, and you can add a button to a toolbar to make the Datasheet view one click away. In this exercise, you add a Datasheet View button and a Form View button so you can toggle back and forth between views. [L7]

To add the Datasheet View and Form View buttons to a toolbar, complete the following steps:

1. If the Utility 1 toolbar is not displayed on your screen, right-click any toolbar and select Customize from the shortcut menu.
2. Select the Toolbars tab, if necessary, and then click the Utility 1 check box to display it on the menu.
3. Click the Commands tab.
4. Highlight the View option in the Categories list box.
5. Scroll down the Commands list box until you can see the Datasheet View option.
6. Click and drag the Datasheet View button to the Utility 1 toolbar.
7. Click and drag the Form View button to the Utility 1 toolbar. (Note: Make sure you drag the button called Form View, and not the Forms button!)
8. Close the Customize dialog box.
9. Click the Datasheet View button. Now click the Form View button. Your form should look like Figure 2.25. (Note: If there were already buttons in your Utility 1 toolbar, your results will look different from the figure.)
10. Close the form and the database. If you are using a lab machine, restore the Utility 1 toolbar to its original condition, with no buttons, and turn it off.

Several improvements have been made to the Vendor and Hardware table.

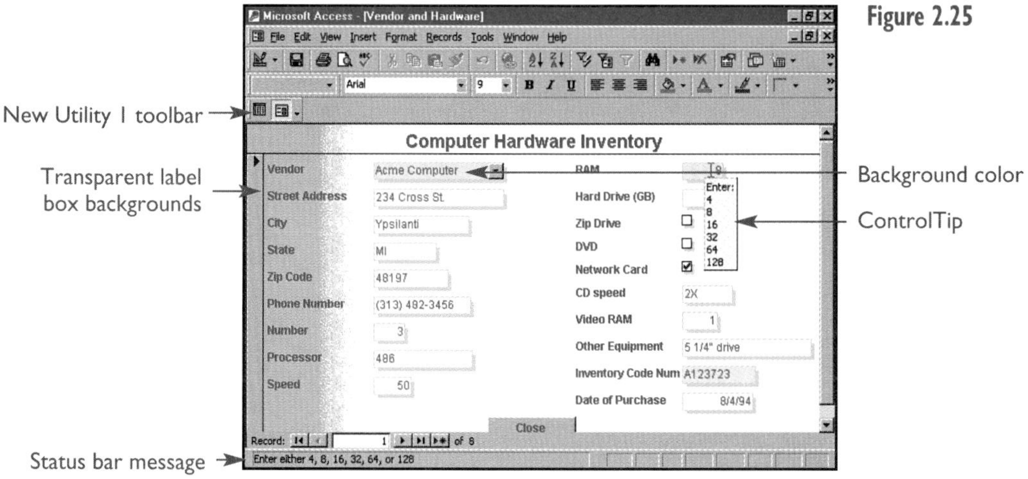

Figure 2.25

Challenge

Challenge exercises expand on or are somewhat related to skills presented in the lessons. Each exercise provides a brief narrative introduction followed by instructions that are not as detailed as those in the Skill Drill section.

The database used for the Challenge section is a modified version of the one used in the Skill Drill section.

1. Adding Instructions to a Form

One of the things you did in Project 2 was to add status bar instructions and ControlTips to an important field. You can also help the database user by adding instructions directly to the form.

1. Find the AC3-0203 database file on your CD-ROM; send it to drive A, and remove the Read-only status. Rename the file `Revised Computer Inventory` and open the file.
2. Close the Main Switchboard. Select the Vendor and Hardware form and open it in Design view.
3. Open the toolbox, if necessary, and add a label box to the right of the RAM field. The box should be about 3/4" wide and 1 1/2" tall.
4. Type the following text in the label box:

```
RAM:
   4
   8
  16
  32
  64
 128
 256
```

5. Select the label box and add a border using the Line/Border Width button. Color the border the same blue as the text.

6. Adjust the size and shape of the box. Switch to Form view to see your changes. Save your work and leave the form open for the next exercise.

2. Changing the Look of the Text Control Box

You can give text and label control boxes several special looks. The one most commonly used (because it is the default) is the Flat look.

Use the Office Assistant to find out how to apply special effects to text control boxes, and then add a shadowed effect to all of the text control boxes, but not the label control boxes.

Switch to Form view to see your changes. Save your work and leave the form open for the next exercise.

3. Hiding Controls on a Form

Some fields that you want to include on form printouts do not need to be displayed on the screen. You can hide fields that were filled in automatically from a linked table. Hiding these fields can also keep inexperienced users from trying to change information that shouldn't be changed.

In the Vendor and Hardware form, when you select a Vendor from the drop-down menu, the Street Address, City, State, ZIP Code, and Phone Number contain data from the Vendors table. Use the Office Assistant to figure out how to hide those fields on the form, but have them appear on a printout. (Note: If you can't find help on this topic, try looking through the text control box properties for one of the fields.) Save your work and leave the form open for the next exercise.

4. Setting Up a Toolbar for Form Design

In Lesson 7, you set up the Utility 1 toolbar to be used in Form view. You can use the other utility toolbar (Utility 2) to set up a toolbar with buttons that help you during the form design process. (Note: It doesn't matter what you use the utility toolbars for; you might use one of them for form buttons and the other for report buttons.)

1. Move to Design view, if necessary.
2. Choose Customize from the shortcut menu and turn on the Utility 2 toolbar. Turn on the Utility 1 toolbar also, if necessary.
3. From the Form/Report Design category add the Tab Order, Sorting and Grouping, Form Header/Footer, and Ruler buttons.
4. Also from the Form/Report Design category add the Align Left, Align Right, Align Top, and Align Bottom buttons.
5. Separate the alignment buttons from the first four buttons you added with a separator bar.
6. Close the Customize dialog box.
7. Grab the bar on the far left edge of the Utility 2 toolbar and drag it up and to the right of the Utility 1 toolbar. Both utility toolbars should now be on the same row.
8. Switch to Form view. Save your changes, but leave the form open for the next exercise.

5. Changing Toolbar Properties

After you have set up the toolbars the way you want them, you can use the toolbar properties (yes, even toolbars have properties!) to modify the way the toolbars work.

In either Form or Design view, activate the Customize dialog box. Click the Toolbars tab and select the Utility 2 toolbar. Be certain to click the name of the toolbar and not to remove the check mark from the Show check box. Click the Properties button. In the Toolbar Properties dialog box, deselect the Allow Moving check box. Do the same for the Utility 1 dialog box. Close the Customize dialog box and try to move either of the utility toolbars. Note: You can try some of the other options, if you want, but do not deselect the Allow Customizing option. Save your work and close the database.

After you complete these exercises, the Vendor and Hardware form should look like Figure 2.26.

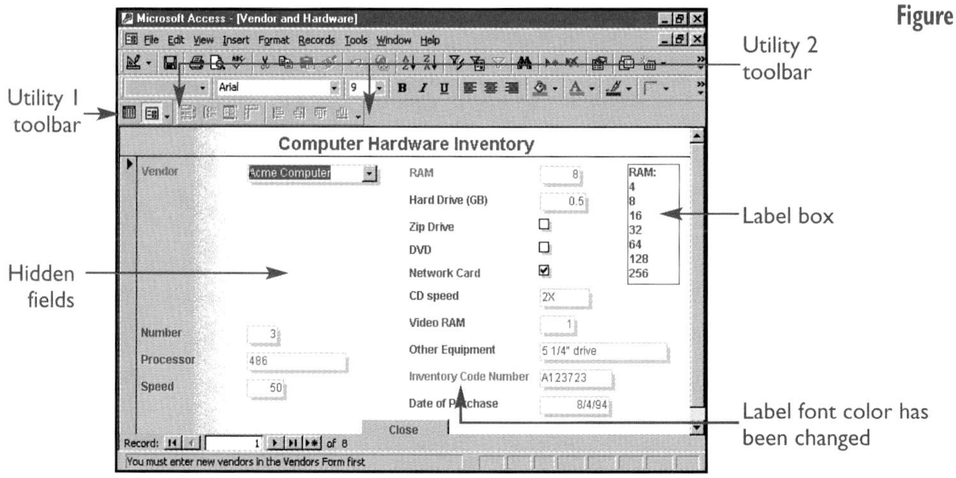

Figure 2.26

Discovery Zone

Discovery Zone exercises help you gain advanced knowledge of project topics and/or application of skills. These exercises focus on enhancing your problem-solving skills. Numbered steps are not provided, but you are given hints, reminders, screen shots, and/or references to help you reach your goal for each exercise.

In these exercises you use a modified version of the Federal census database you used in Lesson 1.

1. Creating a Custom Toolbar and Adding a Macro as a Button

At times you will want to create a brand new toolbar. In fact, some regular database users create a set of toolbars, making available exactly the buttons they want. When you create a custom toolbar, it is stored with the database, not with the Access program, as was the case with the built-in utility toolbars. If you are going to create a database that gets a lot of use, custom toolbars can make the database easier to use. You can even put macros on the new toolbar.

In this exercise, you use the AC3-0204 database, renamed `Creating a New Toolbar`.

Goal: Create a custom toolbar and add a macro to close the 1900 Alcona County Census form.

The toolbar should:

- be named `My Custom Toolbar`.
- contain one button—the macro called Close the 1900 Alcona County Census form.
- display both the macro icon and the name of the macro.
- have the button name changed to `Close the Form`.

Hint #1: After you create the toolbar, you can drag the macro to the toolbar.

Hint #2: The Customize dialog box has to be open before you can change the name of the new button.

Hint #3: If you are stuck, remember that shortcut menus are often the answer!

2. Editing a Button on a Toolbar

When you create buttons from macros, all of the buttons look exactly alike. You can change the button design to a pre-set shape, or you can create your own icons for these buttons. (You can also simply name the buttons and leave the icons off entirely.)

Goal: Create a button icon for the Close the Form button that looks like a red X.

The button should:

- look like a large red X.
- retain the Close the Form text.

Hint #1: Once again, think shortcut menu.

Your toolbar should look like Figure 2.27.

Figure 2.27

Project 3

Managing Changing Data

Objectives

In this project, you learn how to

- **Replace Data in a Table Using an Update Query**
- **Replace Portions of Fields Using an Update Query**
- **Update Tables Using a Calculated Expression**
- **Update a Table Based on Values in Another Table**
- **Update Linked Tables Automatically**

Key terms introduced in this project include

- Cascade delete
- Cascade update
- Null
- Update query

Why Would I Do This?

When you work with data in a database, you are usually doing one of two things: adding new records (and deleting or archiving old ones), or modifying data that is already in the table. In Project 2, you looked at ways to improve data entry by refining forms. In this project, you learn how to update existing data.

Update queries can be used to replace text fields or parts of text fields. This is useful in situations where textual information is changed—when a new area code is created or a part number is changed. You can also use Update queries to calculate changes in numeric fields. This feature is useful, for example, if you intend to raise prices by a certain percentage for an entire line of products.

In some cases, you may have a table that has new values for many individual records in another table. In this project, you learn how to use an Update query to update one table based on the contents of another.

Finally, when you have tables that are joined, you have the option of causing changes in one table to be automatically made in related tables. Changes in customer identification numbers in one table can be automatically updated in a table of customer purchases, or those purchases could be automatically deleted if the customer's name is deleted.

Visual Summary

When you have completed this lesson, you will have used Update queries to modify a table as shown in Figure 3.1:

Figure 3.1
Changes were made to the table using an Update query.

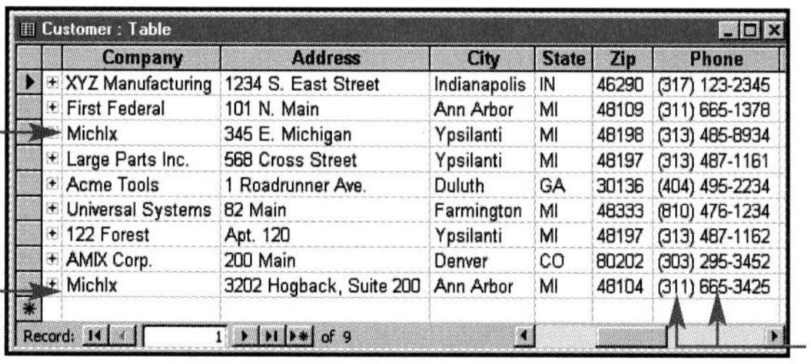

Customer : Table

Company	Address	City	State	Zip	Phone
XYZ Manufacturing	1234 S. East Street	Indianapolis	IN	46290	(317) 123-2345
First Federal	101 N. Main	Ann Arbor	MI	48109	(311) 665-1378
Michlx	345 E. Michigan	Ypsilanti	MI	48198	(313) 485-8934
Large Parts Inc.	568 Cross Street	Ypsilanti	MI	48197	(313) 487-1161
Acme Tools	1 Roadrunner Ave.	Duluth	GA	30136	(404) 495-2234
Universal Systems	82 Main	Farmington	MI	48333	(810) 476-1234
122 Forest	Apt. 120	Ypsilanti	MI	48197	(313) 487-1162
AMIX Corp.	200 Main	Denver	CO	80202	(303) 295-3452
Michlx	3202 Hogback, Suite 200	Ann Arbor	MI	48104	(311) 665-3425

Record: 1 of 9

Data is updated based on information in another field

Area codes were automatically updated based on the telephone exchange

Lesson 1: Replacing Data in a Table Using an Update Query

If you need to change the entire contents of a text field, such as a company's name that occurs in many records, you can use an ***Update query***, which enables you to set a condition which, when matched, cause changes to be made in the field. Using an Update query makes a permanent change to the affected database records. Therefore, it is best to run it first as a Select query, so you can verify how many records are going to be affected. If necessary, you can print the Select query to document the records that will be affected by the change. It is also a good idea to back up the affected table prior to making changes using an Update query, in case a mistake is made and you need to recover the original data.

In this example, a company that provides industrial cleaning supplies has a database that tracks its customers and their orders. We know that one of their customers, AMIX Corp., has spun off its Michigan offices into a new company named Michlx. All the company names for AMIX Corp. contacts in Michigan need to be changed.

To Replace Data in a Table Using an Update Query

1. **Make a copy of the AC3-0301 database file from the CD-ROM. Right-click the filename; select Properties from the shortcut menu, and remove the Read-only status. Use the shortcut menu to rename the file `Cleaning Supplies`, and then open the database.**
   The Database window should now be open to the Tables area (see Figure 3.2). If it is not, click the Tables object button.

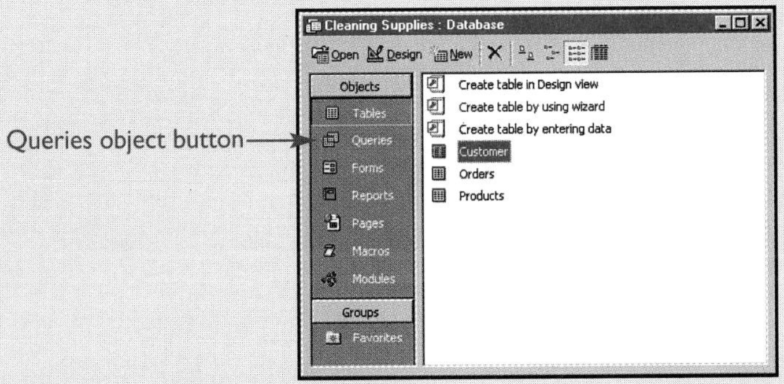

Figure 3.2
The Database window displays the Tables area of the Cleaning Supplies database.

2. **Click the Queries object button, and then click the New button on the Database toolbar.**
   The New Query dialog box displays.

3. **In the list box, select Design View, and then click OK.**
   The Show Table dialog box displays.

4. **Click the Customer table name and then click Add. Click the Close button to close the Show Table dialog box.**
   The Customer table is added to the Query Design window. The Query Design window contains the query design grid and one table (see Figure 3.3).

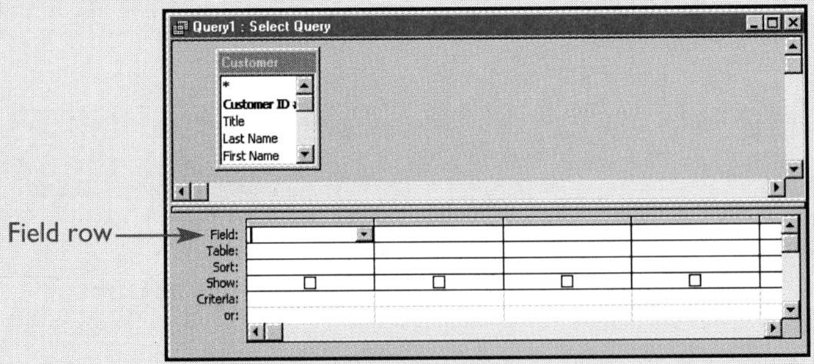

Figure 3.3
The Query Design window is shown with the Customer table added.

5. **Drag the Last Name, Company, and State fields (in that order) to the Field row of the query design grid.**
   The Last Name, Company, and State fields appear in the first three columns of the query design. You now want to set up the query to find all the companies named AMIX Corp. in Michigan.

6. **Enter the company name `AMIX Corp.` in the Criteria box in the Company column and press ↵Enter.**
   Remember to include the period following the abbreviation for corporation.

continues ▶

To Replace Data in a Table Using an Update Query (continued)

7 Enter `MI` in the Criteria box in the State column and press Enter.
The criteria for company and state should identify all the company's contacts in Michigan. Each of the entries is surrounded by quotation marks when you press Enter (see Figure 3.4).

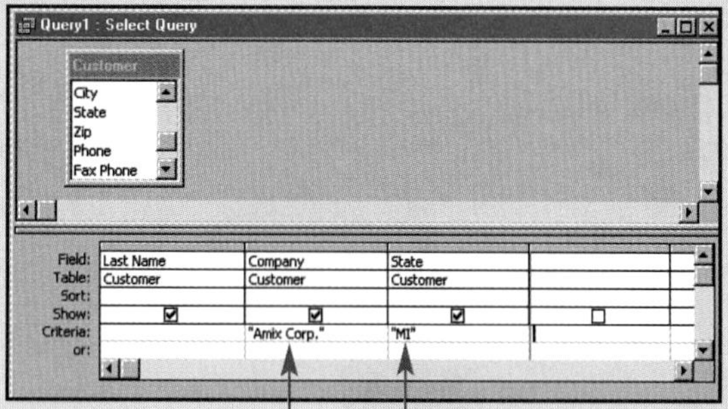

Figure 3.4
The criteria for finding the AMIX Corporation's Michigan contacts are entered

8 Click the View button to see if you have correctly identified the two Michigan contacts.
You only included three of the fields in this query for simplicity. The two Michigan contacts are shown (see Figure 3.5).

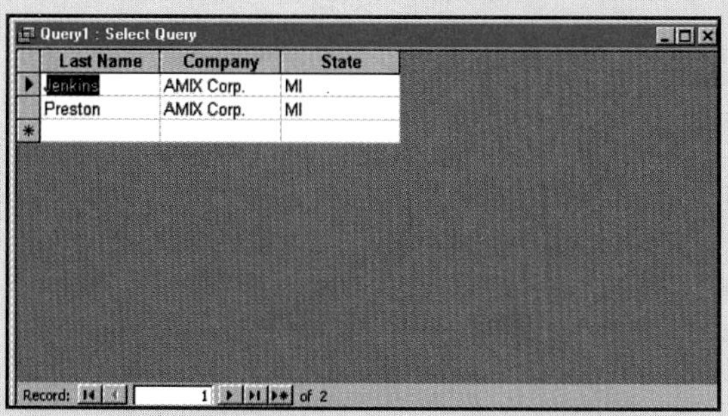

Figure 3.5
The two Michigan contacts are shown.

9 Click the View button again to return to the query design window.

10 Click the down arrow on the Query Type button.
A drop-down menu displays (see Figure 3.6).

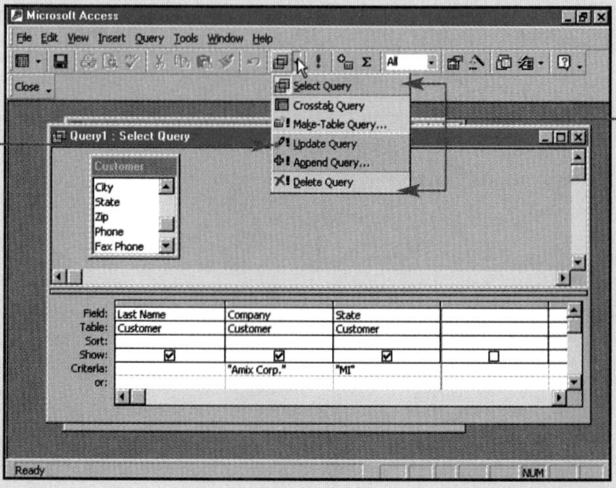

Figure 3.6
The drop-down menu of query types displays.

⑪ Select the Update Query option.
Notice that the Sort and Show rows were replaced by the Update To row in the query design window.

⑫ Type the new regional company name, `MichIx`, in the Update To box of the Company column and press ↵Enter.
The new company name is placed in the Update To box in the Company column (see Figure 3.7).

The Update To row

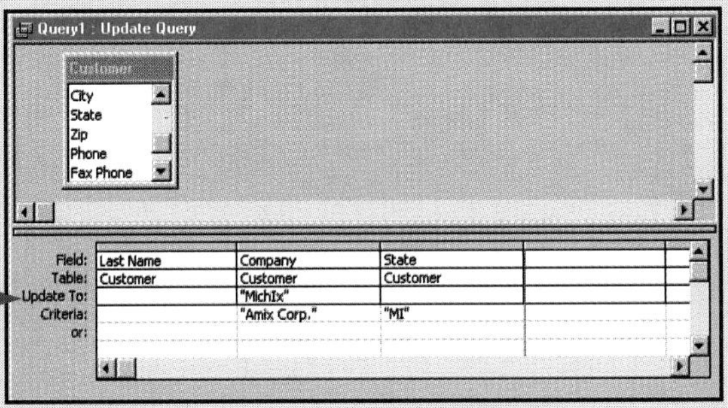

Figure 3.7
The new company name appears in the Update To box.

You are now ready to run the Update query to change the AMIX Corp. records in Michigan to MichIx.

⑬ Click the Run button on the toolbar.
A warning message displays, advising that you are about to make an irreversible change. The Undo button will not work following this step.

⑭ Click Yes to update the records.
The company names are changed. Make sure that you have made recent backups of your tables before you use this procedure on important tables. Notice that Access does not show you a dynaset of the updated records.

⑮ Close the query and save it with the name `Update Company Name`.

⑯ Click the Tables object button and open the Customer table.
Scroll through the records to confirm that the two customer contacts in Michigan have had their company name changed from AMIX Corp. to MichIx (see Figure 3.8).

These names were updated

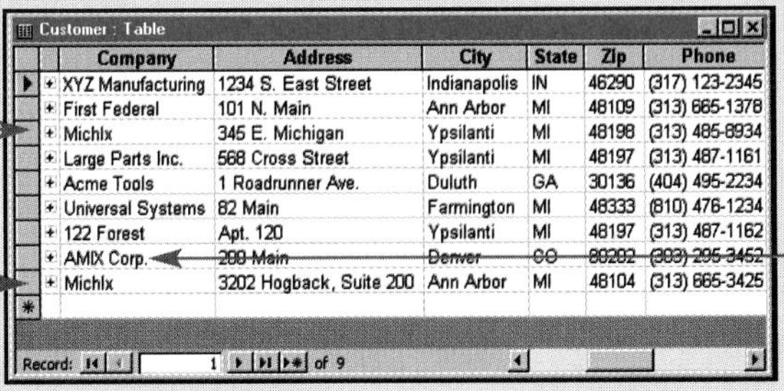

This name was not updated

Figure 3.8
The new company name appears in the appropriate records.

⑰ Close the table.
Leave the database open for use in the next lesson.

Fields Automatically Removed from Queries
If you were to go back to Design view to examine the query, you would find that the Last Name field was removed. The field was dropped automatically because it was not used in the query.

Lesson 2: Replacing Portions of Fields Using an Update Query

Some updates are based on a portion of a field. When the telephone company creates a new area code, it assigns some of the exchanges from the old area code to the new area code. To automatically update your database, you may need to determine whether part of the field matches a criterion and then change only part of the data in each field.

In this lesson, you learn how to use expressions for selecting the left, middle, and right portions of a string of text characters. You also learn how to use these expressions in an Update query.

To Update Tables Based on Selected Portions of Fields

1. **In the Cleaning Supplies database, click the Queries object button and click New.**
   The New Query dialog box displays.
2. **In the list box, select Design View, and then click OK.**
   The Show Table dialog box displays.
3. **Click the Customer table, and then click the Add button.**
   The Customer table is added to the query design.
4. **Click Close. Drag the Last Name, Company, City, and Phone fields to the query design grid.**
   The query design grid now has four fields (see Figure 3.9).

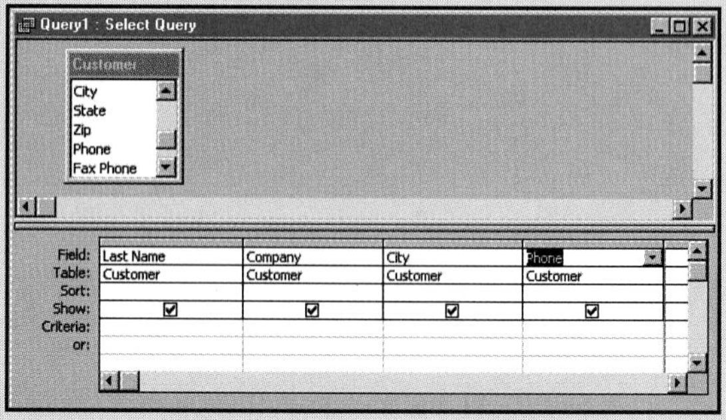

Figure 3.9
The query design grid displays four fields.

5. **Type the following expression in the Criteria box for the Phone field:**
   `Left([Phone],9)="(313) 665"`

   The Left expression extracts the characters at the left end of a string of text. In this example, you want to identify all phone numbers in the 313 area code that use the 665 exchange. You check for the first nine characters at the left end of the phone field. Notice that you count the parentheses and the space.

6 Click the View button to switch to the Datasheet view to confirm that the criteria found the two records that match.

The Datasheet view should show the two matching records (see Figure 3.10). If it does not show any records, you have made an error in entering the expression. Make sure you used the proper brackets and a space after the area code.

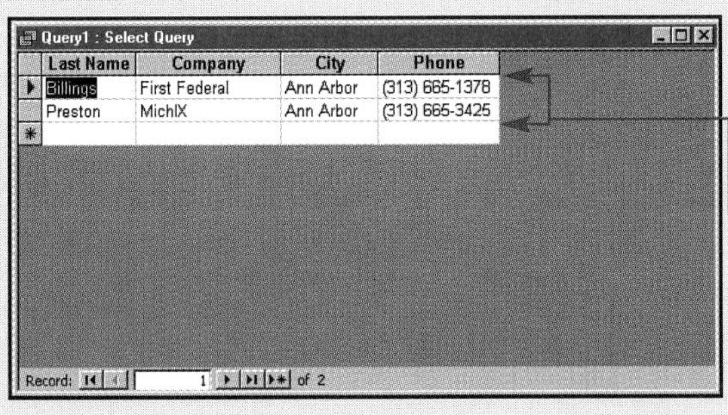

Figure 3.10
The query has found the records that match the phone number criteria.

7 Click the View button.

The program returns to Design view. Now, you change the query type and add another expression.

8 Click the down arrow on the Query Type button on the toolbar and select Update Query from the drop-down menu.

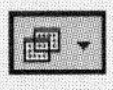

9 Enter the following expression in the Update To box of the Phone field:

```
"(311)"+Right([Phone],9)
```

The purpose of this expression is to create a new phone number that begins with the new area code and the old exchange and then attaches the nine characters from the right end of the phone number (see Figure 3.11). (Note: The Phone field column was widened, so that you can see the full expression.)

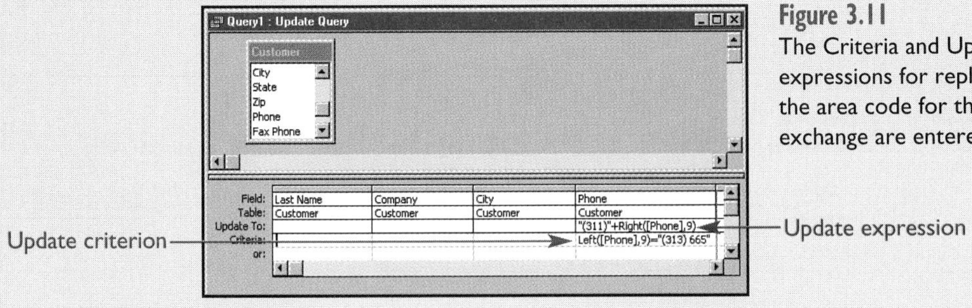

Figure 3.11
The Criteria and Update expressions for replacing the area code for the 665 exchange are entered.

Working with Input Masks
The Left and Right expressions use character counts based on the actual characters stored in the table. If the table was designed to use an input mask, the character count will be off. In the example in this lesson, the data was entered into the table with the parenthesis, spaces, and dashes, so they were counted. The phone numbers in the Fax Phone field were entered using an input mask and do not contain the extra characters.

continues ▶

To Update Tables Based on Selected Portions of Fields (continued)

The Mid Expression
A third expression is similar to Right and Left. The Mid expression selects characters from inside the string of characters. To select the exchange numbers 665 from a phone number in this lesson, you would use the expression Mid([Phone],7,3). It would start at the seventh character and select three characters.

10 Click the Run button on the toolbar.
A warning message displays, notifying you that you are about to make an irreversible change to two records. If it says that you are about to change more than two records, click No and look for a problem.

11 Click Yes to update the records.
The phone numbers change. Make sure you have made recent backups of your tables before you use this procedure on important tables.

12 Close the query and save it as `Update Area Code`.

13 Click the Tables object button and open the Customer table.
Scroll through the records to confirm that the two phone numbers that were formerly (313) 665, are now (311) 665 (see Figure 3.12).

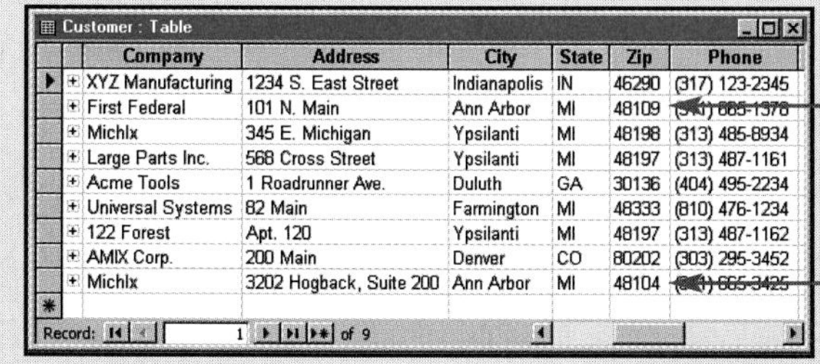

Customer : Table

Company	Address	City	State	Zip	Phone
XYZ Manufacturing	1234 S. East Street	Indianapolis	IN	46290	(317) 123-2345
First Federal	101 N. Main	Ann Arbor	MI	48109	[illegible] 665-1378
Michlx	345 E. Michigan	Ypsilanti	MI	48198	(313) 485-8934
Large Parts Inc.	568 Cross Street	Ypsilanti	MI	48197	(313) 487-1161
Acme Tools	1 Roadrunner Ave.	Duluth	GA	30136	(404) 495-2234
Universal Systems	82 Main	Farmington	MI	48333	(810) 476-1234
122 Forest	Apt. 120	Ypsilanti	MI	48197	(313) 487-1162
AMIX Corp.	200 Main	Denver	CO	80202	(303) 295-3452
Michlx	3202 Hogback, Suite 200	Ann Arbor	MI	48104	[illegible] 665-3425

Record: 1 of 9

These area codes were changed

Figure 3.12
The query changed the records that match the phone number criterion.

14 Close the table.
Leave the database open for use in the next lesson.

Lesson 3: Updating Tables Using a Calculated Expression

In the first two lessons, you revised data by using the Update query to replace all or part of the text in a field. The Update query can also be used to perform calculations on numeric fields through the use of algebra-like expressions.

In this lesson, you use a calculation to increase the price of goods by 10 percent as a late payment penalty. You also learn how to use more than one criterion to determine whether a bill is unpaid and overdue.

To Update Tables with a Calculated Expression

1 In the Cleaning Supplies database, open the Orders table and look at the Late Payment Factor field.
Notice that all the factors are 1.0.

2 Close the Orders table. Click the Queries object button and click New. Select Design view, and then click OK.
The Show Table dialog box displays.

3 Select the Orders table and click the Add button
The Orders table is added to the query design grid.

4 Click Close. Drag the Order #, Date of Purchase, Date of Payment, and Late Payment Factor fields to the query design grid, in that order.
The query design grid displays four fields (see Figure 3.13).

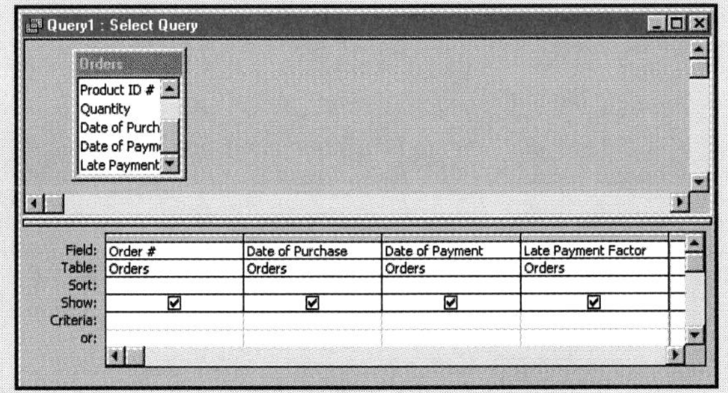

Figure 3.13
The query design shows the four selected fields.

5 Type the following expression in the Criteria box for the Date of Payment field:

```
Is Null
```

If a field has no entry, it is called a ***null*** value. This is not the same as a space or zero.

6 Click the View button to switch to Datasheet view.

In the Datasheet view, you can confirm that the query found the records without a date for the Date of Payment field. The Datasheet view should show the thirteen matching records (see Figure 3.14).

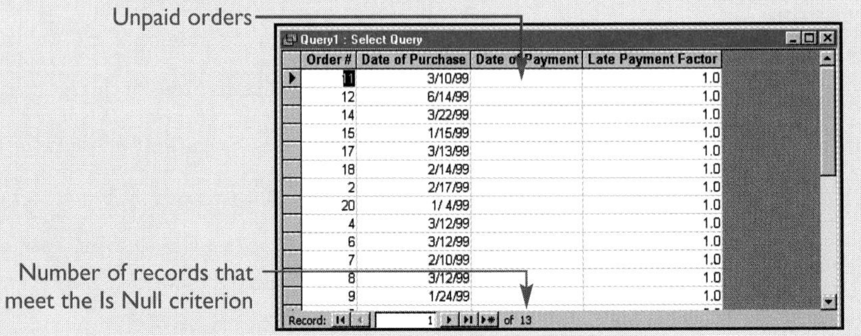

Figure 3.14
The query found the unpaid bills.

7 Click the View button to return to Design view.

continues ▶

To Start To Update Tables with a Calculated Expression (continued)

8 Type the following expression in the Criteria box for the Date of Purchase field:

`<2/1/99`

The computer treats dates as though they were sequential numbers that increase with time. The expression you just entered selects dates before February 1, 1999.

If two criteria are on the same line in the query design, they both must be met. In this case, the query finds records selected of purchases that have not been paid for and were made before 2/1/99.

9 Click the View button to switch to Datasheet view.

You can now confirm that the query found the records that have no date for the Date of Payment field and a purchase date before 2/1/99. The Datasheet view should show the three matching records with order numbers of 15, 20, and 9. (see Figure 3.15).

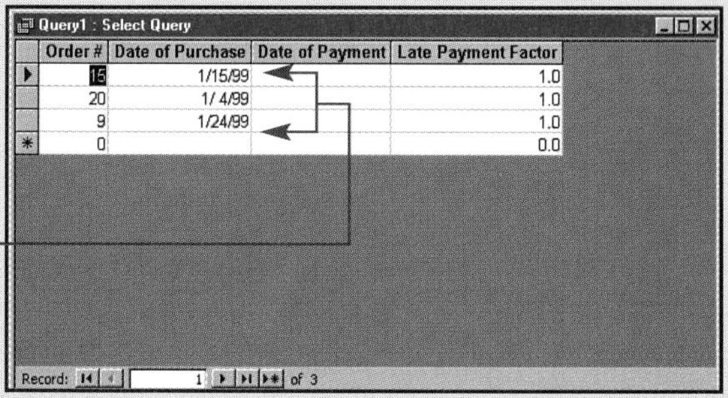

Figure 3.15
The bills are shown for purchases made before 2/1/99 that have not been paid.

These dates meet both conditions

10 Click the View button to return to Design view.

Identifying a Date
Notice that the program has added # symbols around the date. If you ever have problems with a complex criteria where the program has not correctly identified a date you entered, you may need to enclose the date with # symbols. If this step does not work, make certain that you have entered the date criterion in a Date/Time data type field.

11 Click the Query Type button on the toolbar and select Update Query from the drop-down menu.

12 Enter the following expression in the Update To box of the Late Payment Factor field:

`[Late Payment Factor]*1.1`

The purpose of this expression is to increase the price of the purchases that have not been paid on time by 10 percent (see Figure 3.16). The column width for the Late Payment Factor field has been widened to show the whole expression.

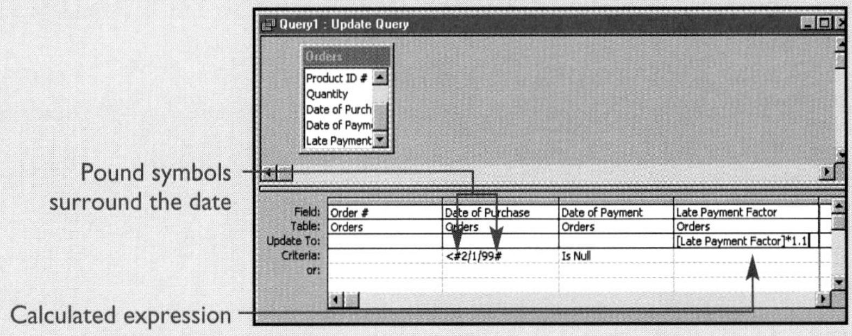

Figure 3.16
The Criteria and Update expressions for increasing the late payment factor are shown.

13. **Click the Run button on the toolbar.**
A warning message displays, notifying you that you are about to update three rows. Make sure you have made recent backups of your tables before you use this procedure on important tables.

14. **Click Yes to update the records.**
The Late Payment Factor values change.

15. **Close the query and save it as `Update for Late Payments`.**

> **Running a Calculated Update Query**
> Do not run the Update query more than once. It makes the calculation each time you run it. In this example, it increases the Late Payment Factor by 10 percent each time you run it.

16. **Click the Tables object button and open the Orders table. Check to make sure the Late Payment Factor has been changed to 1.1 for three records.**

17. **Close the table and close the database.**

Lesson 4: Updating a Table Based on Values in Another Table

In some cases, it is convenient to change several values in one table and then apply them to another table. In this lesson, you learn how to update the suggested sale price on a table that lists the stock on hand in a warehouse.

To Update a Table Based on Values in Another Table

1. **Make a copy of the AC3-0302 database file from the CD-ROM. Right-click the filename; select Properties from the shortcut menu, and remove the Read-only status. Use the shortcut menu to rename the file `Auto Parts`, and then open the database.**
The Database window should now be open to the Tables area (see Figure 3.17). If it is not, click the Tables object button.

continues ▶

To Update a Table Based on Values in Another Table (continued)

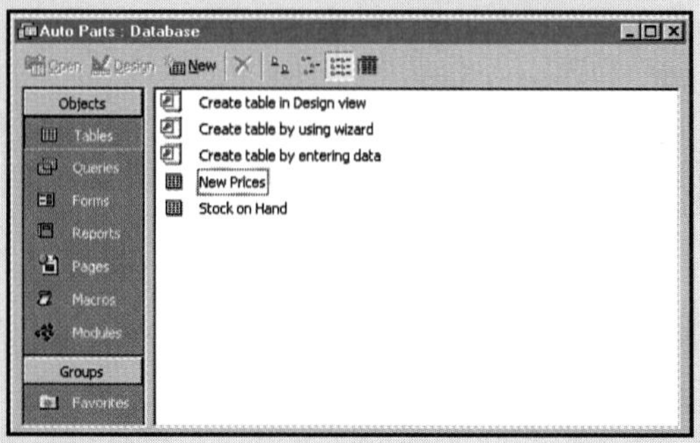

Figure 3.17
The tables in the Auto Parts database are displayed.

2 **Highlight the Stock on Hand table and click Open.**
Notice the field at the far right that indicates whether a particular lot of parts has been sold.

3 **Close the table. Click the Queries object button and click New.**
The New Query dialog box displays.

4 **Select Design View and click OK.**
The Query Design window appears with the Show Table dialog box open in front of it.

5 **Select the New Prices table and click the Add button.**

6 **Select the Stock on Hand table name and click the Add button.**

7 **Click the Close button to close the Show Table dialog box.**
The Query Design window displays the two tables joined by the Code field (see Figure 3.18).

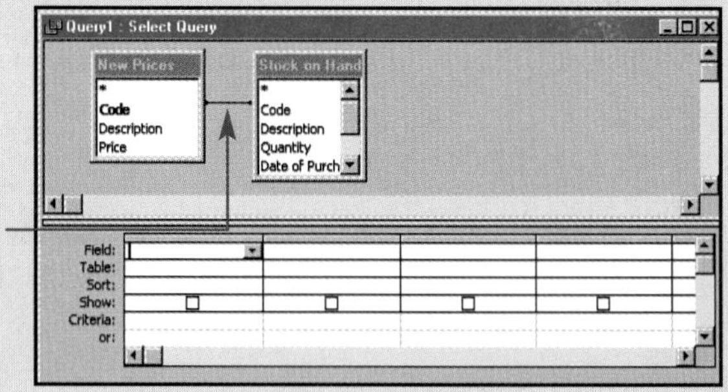

Figure 3.18
The Query Design window displays two tables joined by the Code field.

8 **Scroll down the list of fields in the Stock on Hand table. Drag the Suggested Price and Sold fields to the query design grid.**
The Query Design shows the Suggested Price and Sold fields.

9 **Click the Query Type button on the toolbar and click Update Query.**
A row is added to the query design for update expressions.

10 **Enter the following expression in the Update To box in the Suggested Price column:**

```
[New Prices].[Price]
```

The first part of the expression identifies the table, and the second part identifies the field in that table. Notice that the names are enclosed in square brackets and separated by a period.

This update replaces the values in the Stock on Hand table with those found in the New Prices table.

11 Type the following text in the Criteria box in the Sold column:

`No`

This condition restricts the price changes to those items not yet sold (see Figure 3.19).

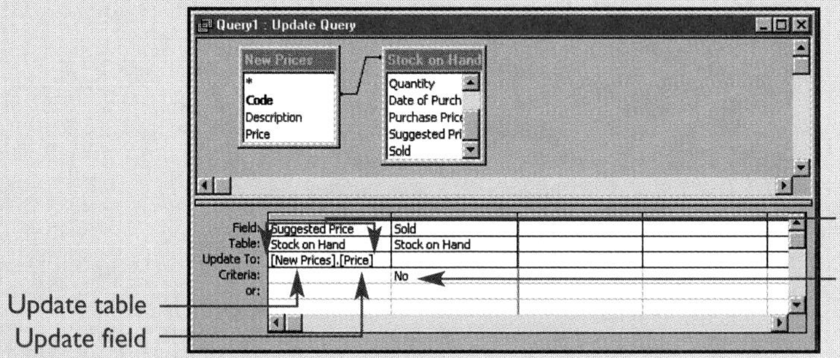

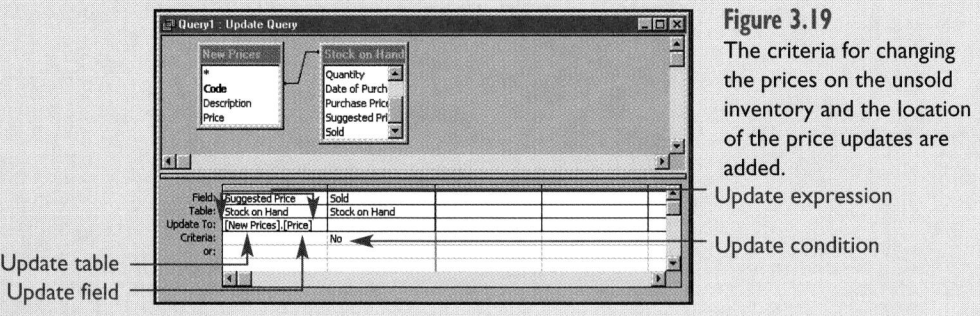

Figure 3.19
The criteria for changing the prices on the unsold inventory and the location of the price updates are added.

12 Close the query and name it `Update Prices`.

13 Click the Tables object button of the database. Open the Stock on Hand table.

Notice that the first lot of 45 axles has already been sold at $300.

14 Close the Stock on Hand table and open the New Prices table.

Notice that the new price for an axle is $285 for axles still in stock.

15 Close the New Prices table and click the Queries object button. Select the Update Prices query, if necessary.

16 Click Open.

This type of query is an Action query that acts like a program. When you open it, it performs its function. In this case, you see a dialog box that asks whether you want to run the query (see Figure 3.20).

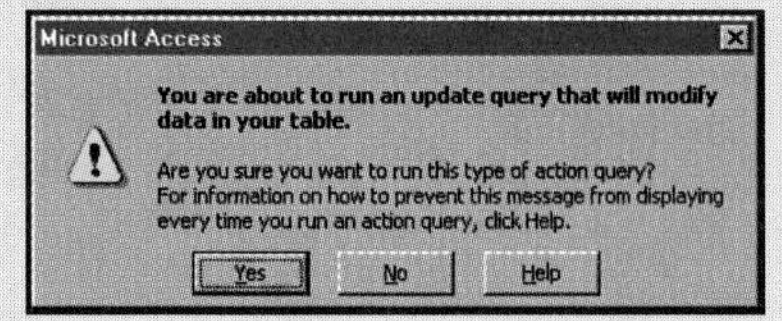

Figure 3.20
The dialog box cautions you that you are about to run an Action query.

17 Click Yes to continue.

Another message appears, telling you that you are about to make permanent changes to five rows of the table (see Figure 3.21). There were six rows in the table, but one of them did not meet the criteria you placed in the Sold column. This is an indication the query is working properly.

continues ▶

To Update a Table Based on Values in Another Table (continued)

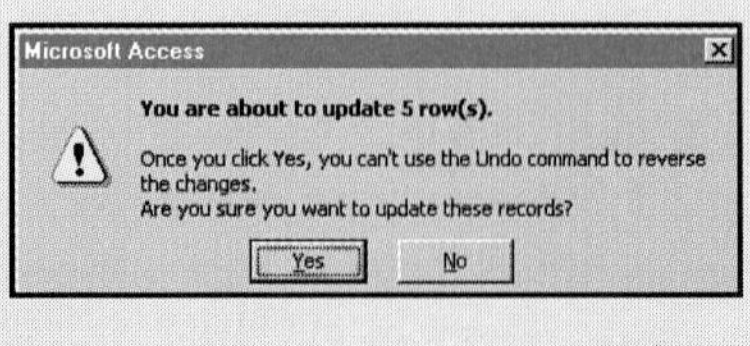
Microsoft Access
You are about to update 5 row(s).
Once you click Yes, you can't use the Undo command to reverse the changes.
Are you sure you want to update these records?
Yes
No

Figure 3.21
The dialog box informs you that you are about to make irreversible changes.

18 Click Yes to update the records.
The records are updated, but nothing appears to happen on the screen.

Back Up Your Work Before Running an Update Query
It is easy to make a mistake when you are designing an Update query, but very difficult to fix the results of a mistake. You can make a copy of the table before you attempt an update. To do this, click the Table object button; select the table you want to update, and use the Copy and Paste buttons from the menu bar to create a copy of the original table, but the program enables you to give the backup table a new name. This procedure should be performed before you try to update an important table.

19 Click the Tables object button and open the Stock on Hand table.
Notice that the suggested price for the stock has changed, except for the first record that was marked as already sold (see Figure 3.22).

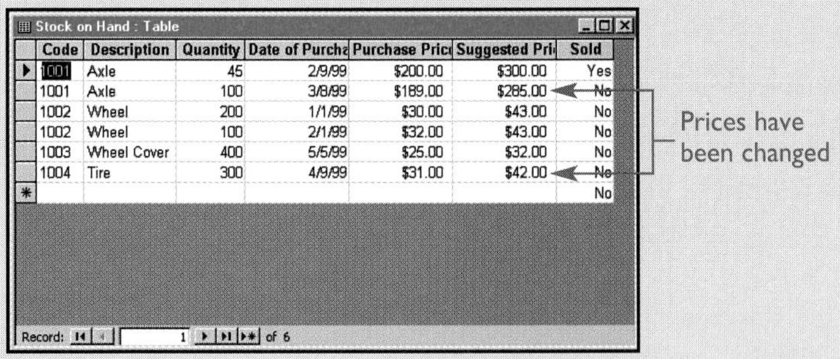
Stock on Hand : Table
Prices have been changed

Code	Description	Quantity	Date of Purcha	Purchase Pric	Suggested Pri	Sold
1001	Axle	45	2/9/99	$200.00	$300.00	Yes
1001	Axle	100	3/8/99	$189.00	$285.00	No
1002	Wheel	200	1/1/99	$30.00	$43.00	No
1002	Wheel	100	2/1/99	$32.00	$43.00	No
1003	Wheel Cover	400	5/5/99	$25.00	$32.00	No
1004	Tire	300	4/9/99	$31.00	$42.00	No
						No

Record: 1 of 6

Figure 3.22
The Stock on Hand table is shown after the prices were changed.

20 Close the table and the database.

Lesson 5: Updating Linked Tables Automatically

If two tables are linked, it is important to protect the linking fields from unexpected changes. If two companies merge and one of the companies has to change its parts codes to match those of the other system, it is important to update the related customer records.

In this lesson, you learn how to set the relationship between a primary key and a related field in another table, set referential integrity, and select automatic update options such as ***cascade update*** and ***cascade delete***. An automatic update is an alternative method of updating tables to the one you learned in Lesson 4. It is easier to use, but you also must always be careful when dealing with automatic updates.

To Update Linked Tables Automatically

1. **Make a copy of the AC3-0303 database file from the CD-ROM. Right-click the filename; select Properties from the shortcut menu, and remove the Read-only status. Use the shortcut menu to rename the file `Auto Parts 2`, and then open the database.**
   The Database window should now be open to the Tables area. If it is not, click the Tables object button. This is the same database you used in Lesson 4.

2. **Click the Relationships button on the toolbar.**
   An empty window titled Relationships displays.

3. **Click the Show Table button on the toolbar.**
   The Show Table dialog box displays the names of the two tables: New Prices and Stock on Hand.

4. **Click each table name and then click the Add button to add them to the Relationships window.**
   You may need to move the Show Table window to see the tables as they are added to the Relationships dialog box.

5. **Click the Close button to close the Show Table dialog box.**
   The Relationships window displays the two tables (see Figure 3.23). Notice that the Code field in the New Prices table displays in bold-faced type to indicate that it is the primary key field for that table.

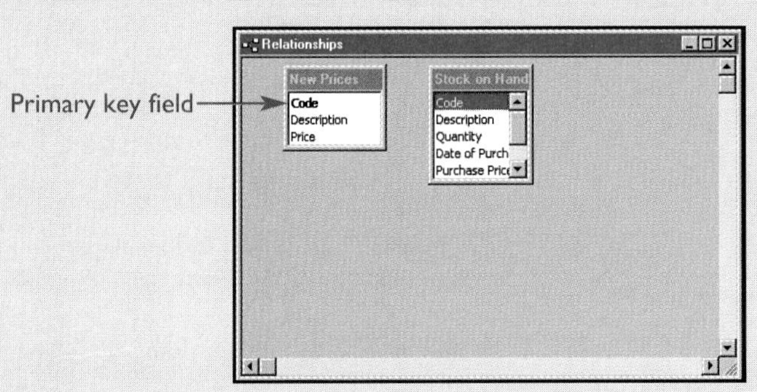

Figure 3.23
The Show Table window displays the two tables in the Auto Parts 2 database.

6. **Click and drag the Code field name from the New Prices table to the Code field in the Stock on Hand table.**
   The Edit Relationships dialog box displays to help you define the relationship (see Figure 3.24). A one-to-many relationship has been set automatically.

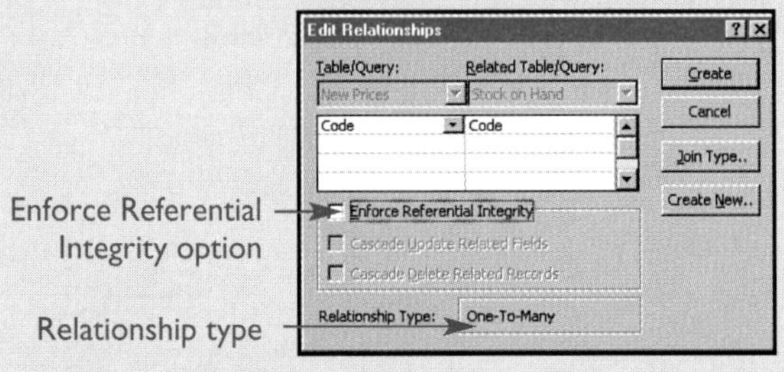

Figure 3.24
The Edit Relationships dialog box identifies the relationship as one-to-many.

7. **Click the Enforce Referential Integrity check box.**
   Two more options that were previously dimmed now become available.

continues ▶

To Update Linked Tables Automatically (continued)

8 Click both the Cascade Update Related Fields and the Cascade Delete Related Records check boxes.

This enables you to perform automatic updates and deletions of the records in the Stock on Hand table if changes are made to the code field in the New Prices table (see Figure 3.25).

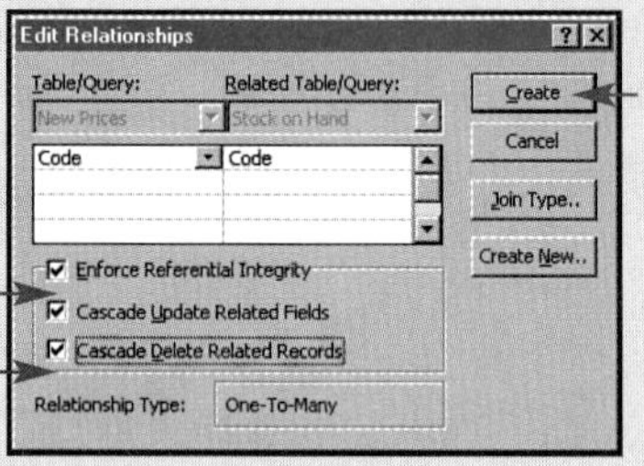

Create button

Cascade options

Figure 3.25
The Edit Relationships dialog box is set for automatic updating.

9 Click the Create button to create the relationship, and then close the Relationships window and save the changes to the layout.

10 Open the New Prices table.

11 Change the code for axles from 1001 to 1007 and close the table.

Because of the relationship you created, the records in the Stock on Hand table should now show that the new code for axles is 1007.

12 Open the Stock on Hand table.

The code for axles was automatically changed (see Figure 3.26). Notice that the axles are listed at the end of the table. This is because the Code field was indexed and the table was automatically sorted.

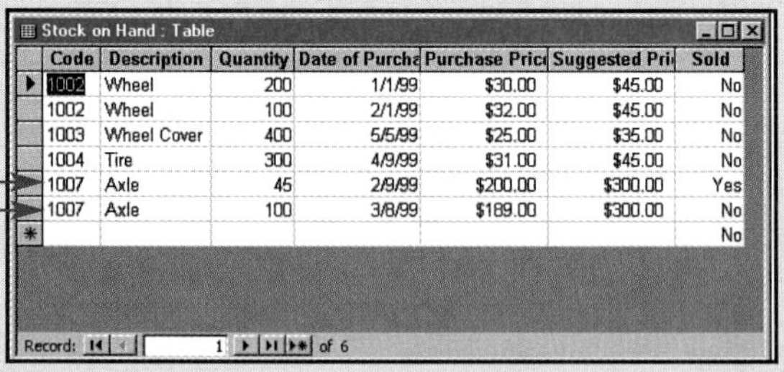

Figure 3.26
The code for axles was updated.

The data was automatically updated

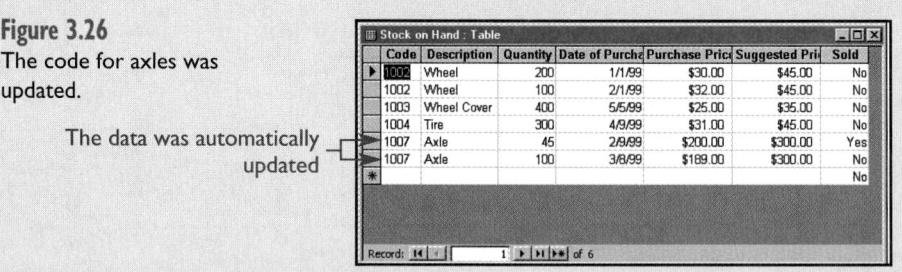

13 Close the Stock on Hand table and open the New Prices table. Click the record selector for the first row to select the record for Wheel.

The first row is selected (see Figure 3.27).

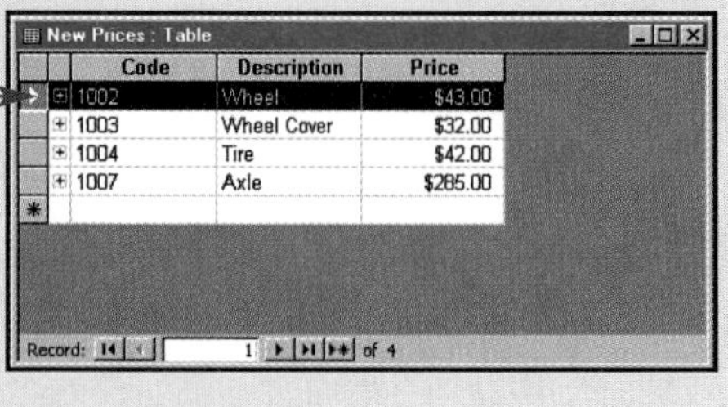

Figure 3.27
The first row of the New Prices table is selected.

Record selector

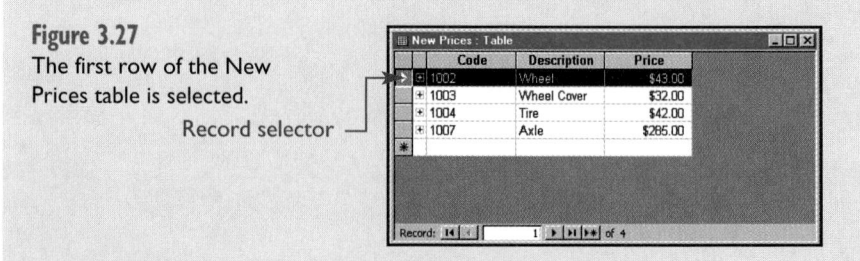

14 Press Del to delete this record.

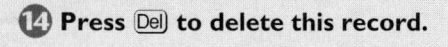

A cautionary message displays to inform you this record will be deleted, as well as an unspecified number of records in related tables (see Figure 3.28).

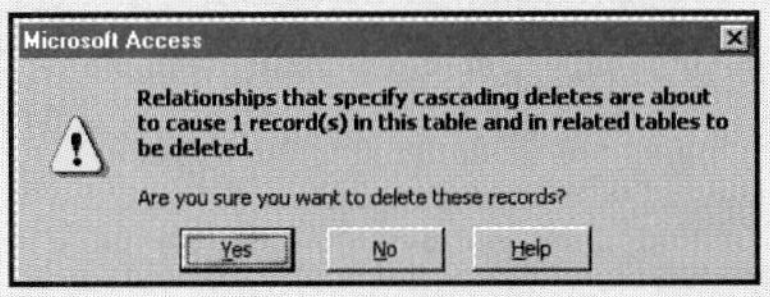

Figure 3.28
A warning message displays when the cascade delete feature is about to delete records in related tables.

15 **Click Yes to delete the records.**

16 **Close the New Prices table and open the Stock on Hand table.**
Notice that both records that had the code 1002 for Wheels were deleted from this table.

17 **Close the table and the database.**
Close Access unless you are going to proceed to the exercises.

Summary

In this project, you learned several methods that you can use to automatically update existing data in an Access table. You replaced whole fields and parts of fields using the Update query. You used the Update query to calculate a change in the values in a table, and to update a table based on values in another table. Finally, you learned to use the cascade update and cascade delete features to modify and delete records in a related table when changes are made to data in the primary or parent table.

You can learn more about Update queries by looking through the available Help on that topic using the Office Assistant.

Checking Concepts and Terms

True/False

For each of the following, check *T* or *F* to indicate whether the statement is true or false.

__T __F **1.** In an Update query you can use only two fields: the one you want to update and one other field for a single criterion. [L3]

__T __F **2.** If you make a mistake in the Update query design and update the wrong fields, you can use Edit and Undo from the menu to undo the mistake. [L1]

__T __F **3.** The expression, Left([Name],4) would identify the left four characters of a field called "Name". [L2]

__T __F **4.** One of the functions of an Update query is to create a new table for archiving records. [Why Would I Do This?]

__T __F **5.** If two tables are related using Cascade Delete Related Records as a condition of the join, deleting a record in the primary or parent table causes related records in the secondary or child table to be deleted. [L5]

__T __F **6.** When you run a calculation in an Update query, running it a second time has no effect. [L3]

__T __F **7.** If you run an Update query and decide you didn't want to make the change, click the Undo button immediately to undo the query. [L4]

__T __F **8.** When you are counting the number of characters you want to look at using a Left or Right expression, it is important to know whether an input mask is being used in that field. [L3]

__T __F **9.** It is a good idea to make a backup copy of a table before you use an Update query on it. [L4]

__T __F **10.** To use a cascading update, two tables must be joined. [L5]

Multiple Choice

Circle the letter of the correct answer for each of the following questions.

1. Which type of query would you use to calculate new values for an existing field? [L3]

a. Select

b. Append

c. Update

d. Crosstab

2. An Update query can be used to ________. [Why Would I Do This?]

a. replace data in a text field

b. make calculations in a numeric field

c. change data in a field based on data in another table

d. all of the above

3. To select the first five characters in the Name field, use the following expression: [L2]

a. Left[(Name), 5]

b. Left([Name],5)

c. Right([Name],5)

d. First([Name],5)

4. To update a field based on the Name field in the Customer table, which expression would you use?. [L4]

a. [Name].[Customer]

b. (Customer)+(Name)

c. [Customer].[Name]

d. Left[Customer]+Right[Name]

5. If two tables are joined with a one-to-many relationship, which option causes changes to the primary key field to be automatically made to any corresponding record in the joined table? [L5]

a. AutoUpdate

b. Cascade Update Related Fields

c. Table-to-Table

d. AutoUpdate Cascade

6. To change an ordinary Select query into an Update query, you start by clicking which button? [L1]

a. Query Type

b. Query View

c. Run

d. Preview

7. If you want to increase all the prices in the Price field by 10 percent, which expression could you use? [L3]

a. [Price] + 10%

b. [Price]*.1

c. [Price]*1.1

d. [Price]/.1

8. Null is the same as ________. [L3]

a. a blank field

b. the number 0

c. a space

d. all of the above

9. An expression used to identify the 3rd, 4th, and 5th letters in the Part# field would be [L2]

a. Right([Part#],3,3)

b. Left([Part#],3,3)

c. Middle([Part#],3,3)

d. Mid([Part#],3,3)

10. To update an existing field, type the new value in which box in the design grid?

a. Criteria

b. Update To

c. Field

d. Table

Screen ID

Label each element of the Access screen shown in Figures 3.29 and 3.30.

Figure 3.29

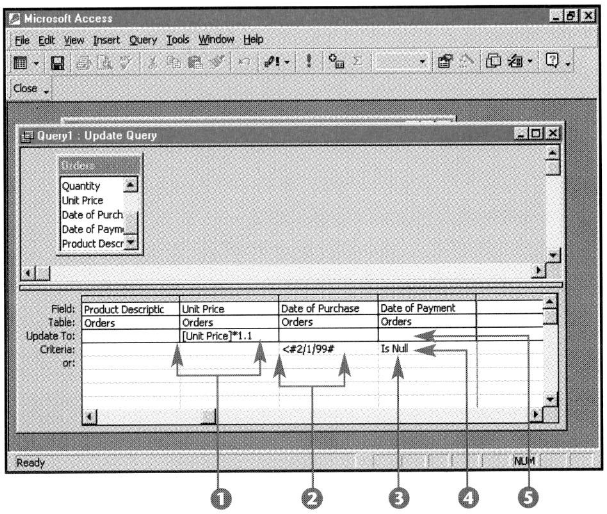

A. Empty field criterion

B. Field to update from

C. Query Type button

D. Calculation expression

E. Relationship line

F. Run button

G. Date criterion

H. Update expression row

I. Table to update from

J. Conditions are placed in this row

Figure 3.30

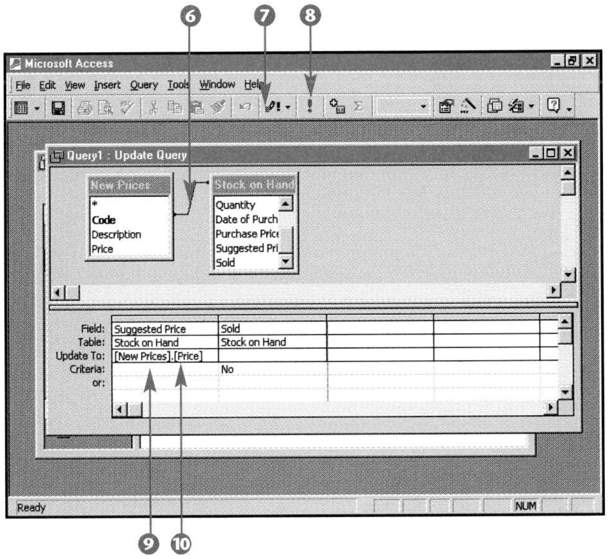

1. ____________ 5. ____________ 8. ____________

2. ____________ 6. ____________ 9. ____________

3. ____________ 7. ____________ 10. ____________

4. ____________

Discussion Questions

1. You can update a field using an Update query, but you can also use the Find and Replace feature. Under what conditions would you use the Find and Replace feature rather than the Update query?
2. Can you think of any possible problems with replacing just a portion of a field in a large database?
3. You are going to use a calculated expression to change the prices of your CDs for a big sale. Why might you want to back up your CD table before you run the calculation update?
4. Can you think of any reason you might want to use an Update query to take values from another table rather than simply using the cascade update feature to do the same thing?
5. Suppose you have a table of parts suppliers and a table of parts on hand. You decide to stop using one of your suppliers, so you remove the supplier from the parts suppliers tables. What problems would occur if you have the cascade delete option turned on?

Skill Drill

Skill Drill exercises reinforce project skills. Each skill reinforced is the same, or nearly the same, as a skill presented in the project. Each exercise includes a brief narrative introduction, followed by detailed instructions in a step-by-step format.

In these exercises, you work with a CD collection database. It consists of two tables—a table of CDs and a table of CD labels.

1. Updating a Table with a New Category

You have decided to change the category name Country to Country/Western. An Update query is one method you might use. While you are performing the following steps, think about other ways you might change the Category field.

To update a table with a new category:

1. Make a copy of the AC3-0304 database file from the CD-ROM. Right-click the filename; select Properties from the shortcut menu, and remove the Read-only status. Use the shortcut menu to rename the file `CD Collection`, and then open the database.
2. Click the Queries object button and click New.
3. Choose Design View; select CD Collection, and click the Add button.
4. Click the Close button to close the Show Table dialog box. Drag the Category field to the query design grid.
5. Use the Query Type button and select Update Query.
6. Type `Country` in the Criteria text box and `Country/Western` in the Update To text box.
7. Click the Run button on the toolbar to run the query. You should change 15 rows.
8. Close the query and save it as **`Country/Western`**.
9. Click the Tables object button and open the CD Collection table. Scroll down the Category field to make sure your changes were made. Close the table when you are done.
10. Leave the database open for the next exercise.

2. Updating a Table with a New Company Label

You find out that the full name of the RCA label is RCA Victor. In this exercise, you use a simple Update query to change the label name. This exercise is similar to the first one, but gives you an extra concern—a similar entry in another table.

To update a table with a new company label:

1. Click the Queries object button and click New.
2. Choose Design View; select CD Collection and click the Add button.
3. Click the Close button to close the Show Table dialog box. Drag the Label field to the query design grid.
4. Use the Query Type button and select Update Query.
5. Type `RCA` in the Criteria box and `RCA Victor` in the Update To box.
6. Click the Run button on the toolbar to run the query. This action should change 24 rows.
7. Close the query and save it as `RCA Victor`.
8. Click the Tables object button and open the CD Collection table. Scroll down through the Label field to make sure your changes were made. Close the table.
9. Open the Label table and change RCA to `RCA Victor`. (This was not changed automatically.) Now when you relate the two tables, you can establish referential integrity. Close the table.
10. Leave the database open for the next exercise.

3. Identifying Multiple Disk Sets by Analyzing the Serial Number

The serial numbers for certain CD labels identify multiple CD sets. In this exercise, you add a field and text to that field for records from a record company that begin with a specific prefix.

To identify multiple disk sets by analyzing the serial number:

1. Open the CD Collection table in Design view.
2. Add a new field called `Multiple Disks`; select the Yes/No data type; close the table and save your changes.
3. Click the Queries object button and click New.
4. Choose Design View; select CD Collection and click the Add button.
5. Click the Close button to close the Show Table dialog box. Drag the Label, Serial number, and Multiple Disk fields to the query design grid.
6. Use the Query Type button and select Update Query.
7. Type `Epic` in the Criteria box for the Label field.
8. Type `Left([Serial number],3)=E2K` in the Criteria box for the Serial number field.
9. Type `Yes` in the Multiple Disk Update To box.
10. Click the Run button on the toolbar to run the query. One row should change.
11. Close the query and save it as `Multiple Disk Update`.
12. Click the Tables object button and open the CD Collection table. Scroll down to see what happened. Notice that typing Yes in the Update To box of a Yes/No field places a check mark in the check box for that field. Close the table.
13. Leave the database open for the next exercise.

4. Using a Cascade Update

The table of Label names should be related to the CD Collection table. That way, any changes you make to the label name in the Label table can be automatically updated in all the related records in the CD Collection table.

To create a cascade update:

1. Click the Relationships button on the toolbar.
2. Click the Add button to add the CD Collection table.
3. Select the Label table and click the Add button. Click the Close button to close the Show Table dialog box.
4. Drag a link between the primary key in the Label table (the Label field) to the Label field in the CD Collection table.
5. In the Edit Relationships dialog box, select Enforce Referential Integrity and click the Cascade Update Related Fields check box.

6. Click the Create button to create the relationship, and then close the Relationships window. Choose Yes to save the relationship.
7. Open the CD Collection table and click anywhere in the label field. Click the Sort Ascending button to sort the labels. Scroll down to see the entries entitled MHS.
8. Close the CD Collection table and save your changes. Open the Label table.
9. Scroll down until you find the MHS record. Highlight MHS and type `Musical Heritage Society`. Close the Label table.
10. Open the CD Collection table. Scroll down to the previous location of the MHS entries. Notice that all of them were changed to Musical Heritage Society.
11. Close the table, but leave the database open for the next exercise.

5. Using a Cascade Delete

You own two CDs that were published under the Legacy label. They are both collections of Irish songs you got as a gift from a relative, but you never cared for either of them. Your boss is Irish, so you give her the CDs, and decide you want to remove not only the two CDs from the CD Collection table, but also the label reference from the Label table.

To create a cascade delete:

1. Click the Relationships button on the toolbar.
2. Double-click the relationships line between the two tables to activate the Relationships dialog box.
3. Click the Cascade Delete Related Records check box and click OK. Close the Relationships dialog box.
4. Open the CD Collection table and scroll down to see the Legacy entries. Close the CD Collection table.
5. Open the Label table. Scroll down to the Legacy record and click anywhere in the record.
6. Click the Delete Record button on the toolbar. Click Yes to agree to make this permanent change.
7. Close the Label table and open the CD Collection table. Scroll down and make sure the Legacy CDs were removed.
8. Close the CD Collection table and close the database.

Challenge

Challenge exercises expand on or are somewhat related to skills presented in the lessons. Each exercise provides a brief narrative introduction followed by instructions in a numbered step format that are not as detailed as those in the Skill Drill section.

You use three databases in the Challenge section. The first two exercises are based on the same database you used in the Skill Drill section. The second database is a company personnel file, and the third database uses U.S. motor vehicle statistics.

1. Using Multiple Criteria in an Update Query

In the third Skill Drill exercise, you created a new field and checked a check box if a serial number matched a criterion. You can use the same technique to match more than one value. In this exercise, you create an Update query that looks for Columbia CDs with serial numbers beginning with either C2K or C4K—both of which signify multiple-disk sets.

1. Copy the AC3-0305 database file from the CD-ROM; remove the Read-only status; rename the file `CD Collection 2`, and open the database. Sort using the Label field and look through the Columbia records in the CD Collection table.
2. Click the Query object button and create a new query in Design view, based on the CD Collection table.

3. Add the Label, Serial number, and Multiple Disks fields to the query design grid.
4. Change the query to an Update query and type **`Yes`** into the Update To box for the Multiple Disks field.
5. Type **`Columbia`** in the first Criteria box for the Label field. Type **`Left([Serial number],3)=C2K`** in the first Serial number Criteria box.
6. Type **`Columbia`** in the second Criteria box (the first 'or' box) for the Label field. Type **`Left([Serial number],3)=C4K`** in the second Serial number Criteria box. Without a criterion in the second Criteria row for Label, the query would find any record in the database with a serial number beginning with C4K.
7. Run the query. The warning message should tell you that you are about to update five rows. Click Yes.
8. Examine the CD Collection to make sure your updates worked. Save your query as **`Columbia Update`**. Leave the database open for the next exercise.

2. Adding Text to Fields Using an Update Query

In Lesson 3, you learned how to update a numeric field by using a mathematical expression (in that case, multiplying the value in a field by 1.1). You can also update a text field by adding text to it. While looking over your CD Collection table, you discovered that you forgot to use the proper prefix in about half of the Deutsche Grammophon serial numbers; they are all supposed to begin with the letter D, followed by a space. In this exercise, you create an Update query that identifies the mislabeled serial numbers and then you add the correct prefix.

1. Look through the CD Collection table to see the serial numbers for the Deutsche Grammophon CDs. Notice that all the incorrect entries begin with the number 4.
2. Create a new query in Design view, and base it on the CD Collection table.
3. Add the Label and Serial number fields to the query design grid.
4. Change the query to Update Query. Enter **`Deutsche Grammophon`** to the first Criteria box for the Label field. Be careful about the spelling!
5. Type **`Left([Serial number],1)=4`** in the first Criteria box for the Serial number field.
6. Type **`"D "+[Serial number]`** (including the quotation marks and the space after the letter D) in the Update To box for the Serial number field. This adds the letter D and a space to the beginning of the existing serial number.
7. Run the query to update the six incorrect serial numbers. Save your changes as **`DG Update`**.
8. Check the CD Collection table to make sure your query worked. When you are done, close the table and close the database.

[?] 3. Updating Salaries Based on Department

The Online Products Company has been through some rough times, but a new company name and focus have made them profitable again. It is time to calculate the raises, and the boss decides that everyone deserves a 5 percent raise. The Marketing department reminds the boss that they were the only group that made concessions in the previous two years, and convinces her that they deserve a 10 percent raise. The boss agrees. In this exercise, you create an Update query to calculate the new salaries.

Copy the AC3-0306 database file from the CD-ROM; remove the Read-only status; rename the file `Online Products`, and open the database. Use the available help to figure out how to give the Marketing people 10 percent raises, while giving the others a 5 percent raise. Call the query `Salary Update`.

Look up the IIf function and use it in the Update To row. Hint: You do not need to enter anything into the Criteria row. When you are done, close the table and close the database.

4. Creating a Calculated Field to Update a Table Field in Another Table

The database you work with in the next two exercises shows the number of privately and publicly owned cars and trucks in the 50 states and the District of Columbia. One table contains the raw data from the U.S. Department of Transportation; the second table contains projected increases of vehicles by location. (These numbers are not from the D.O.T.; they were estimated for these exercises only.) In this exercise, you use the Expression Builder to create a formula to update a new field.

1. Copy the AC3-0307 database file from the CD-ROM; remove the Read-only status; rename the file `Motor Vehicles by State`, and open the database. Look through both tables to get a feel for the data.
2. Create a relationship between the Location fields in both tables and enforce referential integrity.
3. Add a Number field to the Projected Increases table called `Cars in 10 Years`.
4. Create a new query in Design view. Add both the Projected Increases table and the Vehicles table.
5. Drag the Cars in 10 Years field to the query design grid from the Projected Increases table. Change the query type to an Update query.
6. Click in the Update To box and click the Build button on the toolbar. Open the Vehicles folder in the Tables folder. Double-click Cars Privately Owned to move it to the Build window.
7. Click the Plus button; then double-click the Cars Privately Owned field again.
8. Click the Times (*) symbol. Open the Projected Increases folder in the Tables folder and then double-click the 10 Year Projected Increase field. The last three steps added the current number of vehicles and the projected percentage increase time the same number.
9. Run the query and then save it as `Projected Number of Cars`.
10. Check the Projected Increases table to make sure your update was successful. (Alabama should have 1,833,647 cars and Alaska should have 249,124 cars.) Leave the database open for the next exercise.

5. Creating a Calculated Field Using More Than One Field

In the previous exercise, you calculated the projected number of privately owned cars in each of the states and the District of Columbia. In this exercise, you calculate the projected total number of privately owned vehicles in the United States.

Use the available help to calculate the total number of private cars and trucks by state. You will want to use the Expression Builder, as you did in the previous exercise. You will also need to create a new field, called `Vehicles in 10 Years`, in the Projected Increases table. Save the query as `Projected Numbers of Cars and Trucks`.

Check your results against the Projected Increases table shown in Figure 3.31. The Projected Increases table should look like this when you are done:

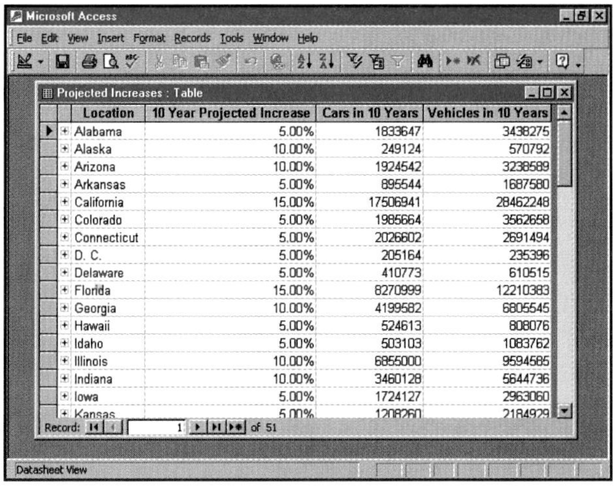

Figure 3.31

Discovery Zone

Discovery Zone exercises help you gain advanced knowledge of project topics and/or application of skills. These exercises focus on enhancing your problem-solving skills. Numbered steps are not provided, but you are given hints, reminders, screen shots, and/or references to help you reach your goal for each exercise.

In these exercises you use a PC Training database. This database contains two tables. The first contains information about each employee, including whether or not the employee has completed training in each of six Office applications. The other table is used for tracking software training and identifying the company's Microsoft Office experts.

1. Creating Update Queries to Update a Second Table

The Human Resources department tracks employee training, so that they can plan for upcoming workshops and seminars. They keep a list of employees, uniquely identified by their Social Security numbers. They track which type of computer each employee uses, and whether the employee has completed the company's rigorous training program for six Office applications. As employees complete the training for an application, the trainer enters an 1 into that column.

A second table needs to be updated every month. This table provides the information for a training chart that is sent to each supervisor in the company. It contains a list of employees and a column for each application. If the employee has completed the training, the word `completed` appears in that column. You are assigned the job of figuring out a way to update this table. You use the AC3-0308 file, renamed `Software Training`.

Goal: Create a way to update each of the six software application columns.

- You should create a relationship between the Social Security Number fields and enforce referential integrity.
- You may need more than one query to complete this assignment.
- Each query should be saved and named, so that it can be re-run each month.

Hint #1: After you have successfully tested one query, you can make copies and then modify each copy.

Hint #2: When you modify a copy of a query, make sure you modify all necessary fields. Rather than deleting and replacing fields, try using the drop-down menu in the Field box.

Keep the database open for the next exercise.

2. Updating a Field Based on Several Other Fields

The company sends employees to take Microsoft certification tests when they have completed the training on an application, and gives bonuses for each test passed. The company also has an internal certification program; when an employee completes training for all six applications, he or she is certified as a Company Office Expert and given a raise in pay to go along with the added responsibility of helping other users who have software problems. (To become a Company Office Expert, Macintosh users need to take Windows training for several of the programs.)

Goal: Create a query that puts a check in the Office Expert field check box when an employee has completed training in all six applications.

Remember that the employee must have completed training for all six applications. Call the new query `Office Expert Update`.

The Microsoft Software Level table should look like Figure 3.32.

Figure 3.32

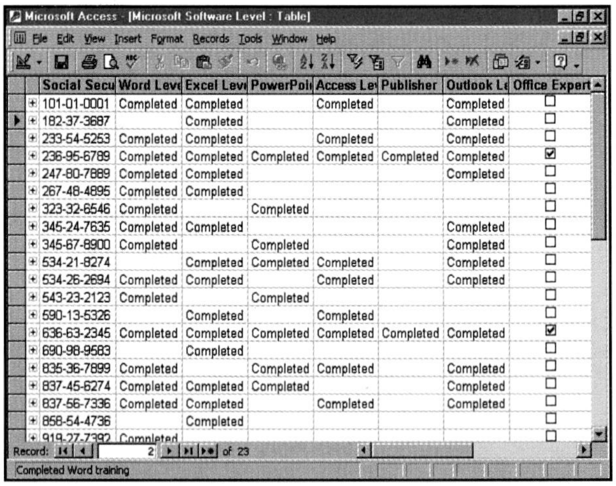

Project 4

Project 4

Using Access Tools

Objectives

In this project, you learn how to

- **Correct Spelling with the Spelling Checker**
- **Customize Data Entry Using AutoCorrect**
- **Analyze a Table**
- **Analyze Database Performance**
- **Update the Database Using Name AutoCorrect**
- **Use Office Links to Analyze Data with Excel**

Key terms introduced in this project include

- AutoCorrect
- Documenter
- Name AutoCorrect
- Office Links
- Performance Analyzer
- Spelling checker
- Table Analyzer

Why Would I Do This?

Access provides a full range of tools to help you edit data, analyze components of your database, and connect to other Microsoft Office applications. These tools help you, the database designer, to control and modify your database to best suit your needs. Access also includes a full set of security tools that you use in Project 7.

Access includes a ***Spelling checker***, which checks each word against a built-in dictionary, and an ***AutoCorrect*** tool, which corrects common mistakes and expands a few letters into short phrases. You may be familiar with these tools from Microsoft Word, Excel, or PowerPoint. Although the need for these tools is not as obvious in a database as it is in other applications, in certain situations, both can be very useful.

In addition to the ***Documenter***, which you used in Project 1, Access provides two other very powerful analysis tools, one for tables only and two for any database object. With the ***Table Analyzer***, an Access wizard helps you to determine whether there is redundant data in the database. If there is, it suggests ways of splitting up the table into smaller, more efficient, related tables. The ***Performance Analyzer*** is a wizard that makes recommendations about the structures of various database components.

Access 2000 has, for the first time, included a feature that automatically updates dependent parts of the database when an object or field is renamed. In the past, when you renamed a field in a table, you had to go through all the other database objects and update the new name. The ***Name AutoCorrect*** feature automatically updates new field names in other objects, such as forms and reports, and in calculated fields that contain the new field name. This feature automatically updates changes in object names, as well as fields.

Finally, Access offers ***Office Links*** to help you use the capabilities of other Microsoft applications to analyze and report your data. You can send data to Excel for further analysis or advanced graphing. You can also send information to Word if you need a quick, attractive report.

Visual Summary

When you have completed this lesson, you will have used Access tools and utilities to do such things as send data to be analyzed in Excel (see Figure 4.1).

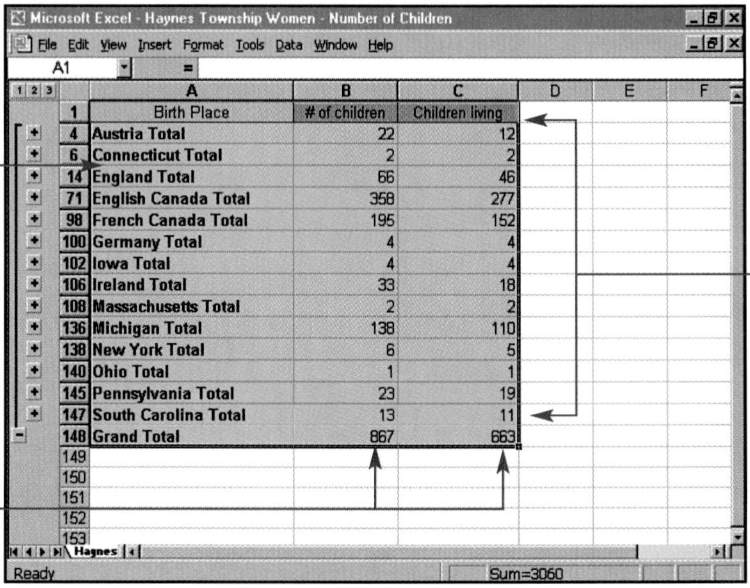

Figure 4.1
The results of an Access query were sent to Excel for analysis.

Lesson 1: Correcting Spelling with the Spelling Checker

The Spelling checker checks words in your database against a list of words in a Microsoft built-in dictionary. If the program can guess what you were trying to type, it presents you with a list of alternative words to choose from. In some cases, such as a last name field, a city field, or a numeric field, the Access Spelling checker would be of little or no use. At times, however, standard text is entered into a field. This would be true for fields such as memo fields in personnel databases or description fields in inventories.

In this lesson, you use a database of short story books and check the spelling of the book titles.

To Correct Spelling with the Spelling Checker

1 Make a copy of the AC3-0401 database file from the CD-ROM. Right-click the filename; select Properties from the shortcut menu, and remove the Read-only status. Use the shortcut menu to rename the file `Books of Stories`, and then open the database.

2 Click the Tables object button, if necessary. Open the Book Information table and maximize the window.

Of the fields in this table, only the Title field would benefit from a spell check. A check of the Author or Publisher fields would result in the majority of words being unrecognized.

3 Move the pointer to the column selector of the Title field and click the mouse button.

The Title column is now highlighted (see Figure 4.2). If anything in a table is selected, the Spelling checker checks only the highlighted word, phrase, or field.

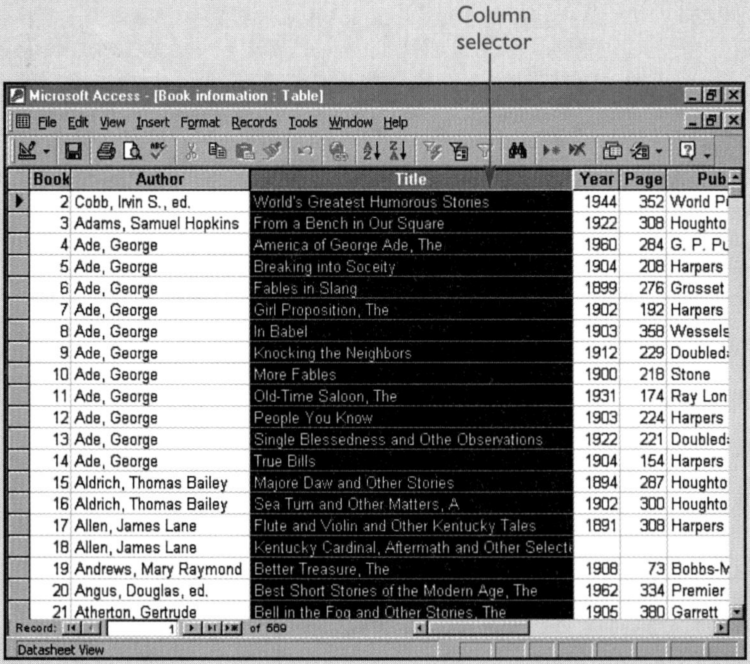

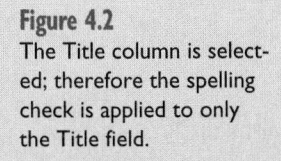

Figure 4.2
The Title column is selected; therefore the spelling check is applied to only the Title field.

4 Click the Spelling button on the toolbar.

continues ▶

To Correct Spelling with the Spelling Checker (continued)

The Spelling dialog box displays. The Spelling checker moves to the first word that does not match a word in its dictionary. It displays that word, in this case "Ade," and then offers alternatives (see Figure 4.3).

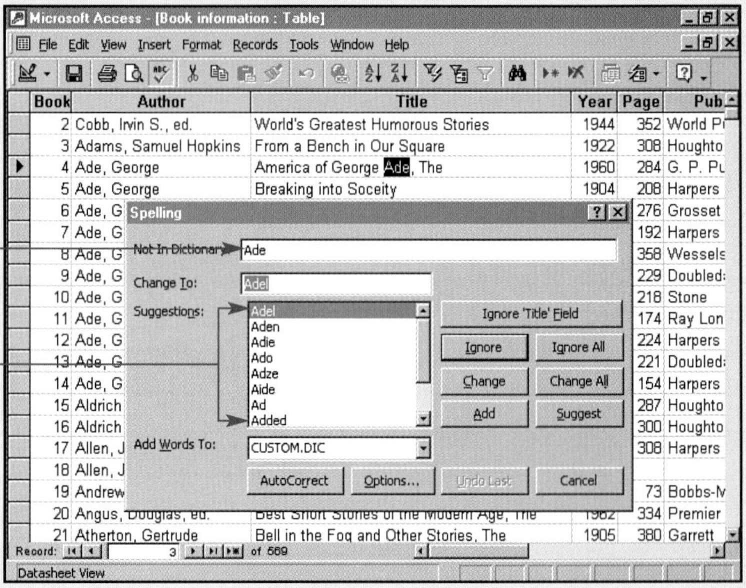

Figure 4.3
The Spelling dialog box finds the first unrecognized word.

Using the Spelling Checker

The program gives you several options when it finds an unrecognized word. You can type the replacement word directly into the Change To text box, or you can use one of several buttons on the right side of the Spelling dialog box. If the word is an unusual one, but spelled correctly, you can choose to ignore it, or ignore it for the entire document. You can select a new spelling from the list, and then change to that spelling. You can also change the spelling throughout the whole document. You can also add the word to your dictionary, but make sure it is spelled correctly! If you are using a computer in a lab setting, you should probably not add words to the dictionary.

5 Click Ignore All.

This causes the Spelling checker to ignore all instances of this word, which is an author's name. The Spelling checker then moves on to the next unrecognized word, "Soceity," which is misspelled.

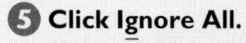

Sometimes the Spelling dialog box blocks your view of the word that is highlighted. If you want to see the unrecognized word in context, click the title bar of the Spelling dialog box and move it until you can see the highlighted word.

6 Select `Society`, if necessary, and then click the Change button.

The misspelled word is replaced with the correctly spelled word, and the program finds the next unrecognized word, `Othe`.

7 Select Other from the Suggestions list box, and then click the Change button.

The misspelled word is replaced and the program finds the word `Majore`, which is misspelled, but which doesn't have a correct entry in the Suggestions list box.

8 Type `Marjorie` in the Change To text box.

At this point, you can either change the current unrecognized word or add it to the dictionary (see Figure 4.4).

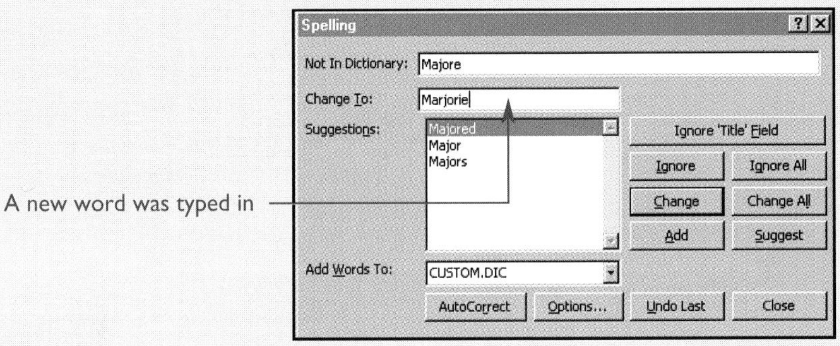

Figure 4.4
The correctly spelled word was entered into the Change To text box.

9 Click the Change button.

The word you typed replaces the misspelled word.

10 Click the Close button in the dialog box.

Close the Book Information table, but leave the database open for the next lesson.

Lesson 2: Customizing Data Entry Using AutoCorrect

Combo and list boxes offer an excellent way to create shortcuts for many data entry tasks. An alternative method for creating data entry shortcuts is to use the AutoCorrect feature in Access. The AutoCorrect feature is available in other Microsoft Office applications, such as Word, Excel, and PowerPoint. An advantage of using AutoCorrect rather than list or combo boxes is that the AutoCorrect feature works in every field in which you are entering data; AutoCorrect entries work in other Microsoft applications even if you create them in Access. AutoCorrect also works when you are adding a word or phrase that is only part of a field.

To Customize Data Entry Using AutoCorrect

1 In the Books of Stories database, click the Forms object button. Double-click the Book Information Data Input form and maximize the window.

2 Use the Next Record navigation button to move to record 8.

This record has a publisher (Doubleday, Page) that is not in the combo box for the Publisher field (see Figure 4.5). You can add this publisher as a new entry to the combo box, or you can use the AutoCorrect feature to see how it works.

continues ▶

To Customize Data Entry Using AutoCorrect (continued)

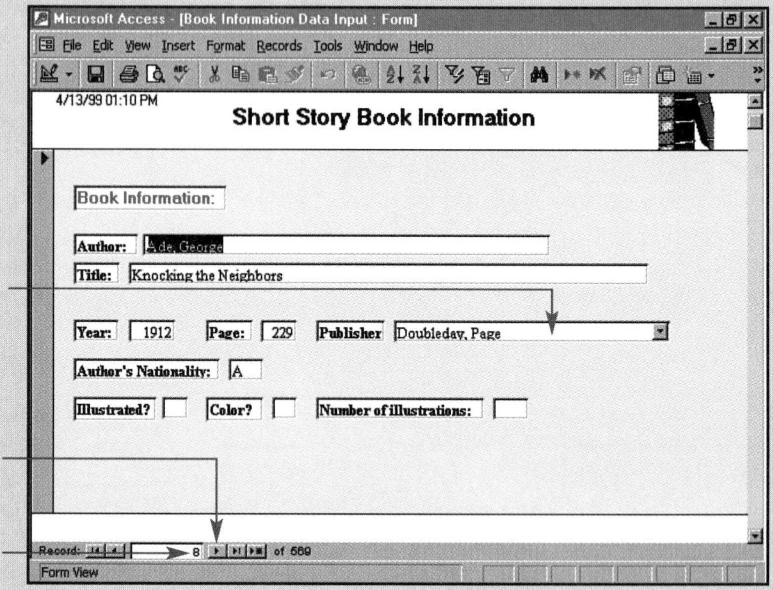

Figure 4.5
This record contains an entry in the Publisher field that is not in the combo box.

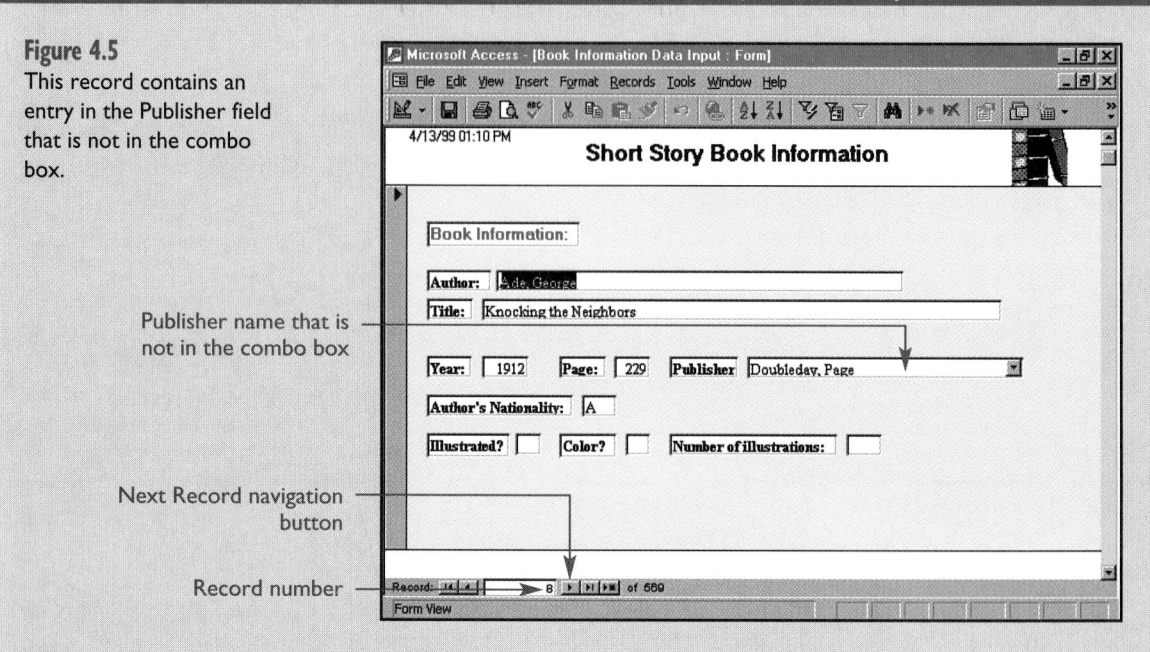

3 Choose Tools, AutoCorrect from the menu.

The AutoCorrect dialog box displays (see Figure 4.6). Notice the option to correct two capital letters at the beginning of a word. Access also offers options to capitalize the first letter of sentences, capitalize the days of the week, and adjust for accidental use of Caps Lock. The feature you want to use is Replace text as you type, so make sure that check box is selected.

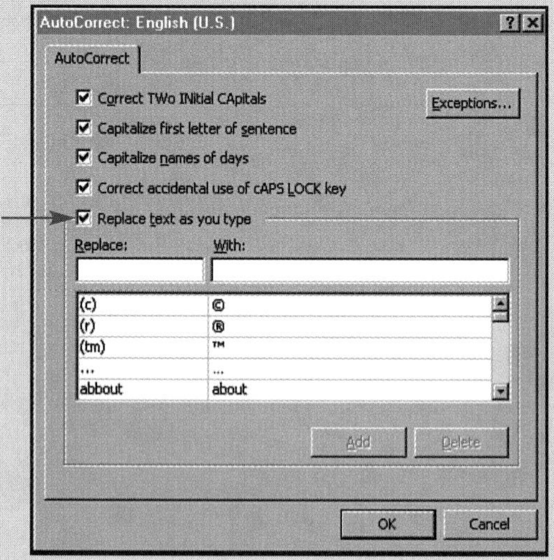

Figure 4.6
The AutoCorrect dialog box gives you five options.

If you take your database to a different computer and try your new AutoCorrect entry, it will not work. AutoCorrect entries are added to the Access program on the computer, not to your database file. This makes them very handy on machines that you use regularly, but of little use if you use several different computers.

4 Type `dp` in the Replace text box.
This is an abbreviation that is easy to remember.

5 Type `Doubleday, Page` in the With text box.
Make sure you type the text exactly as shown, including the capital letters and the comma (see Figure 4.7).

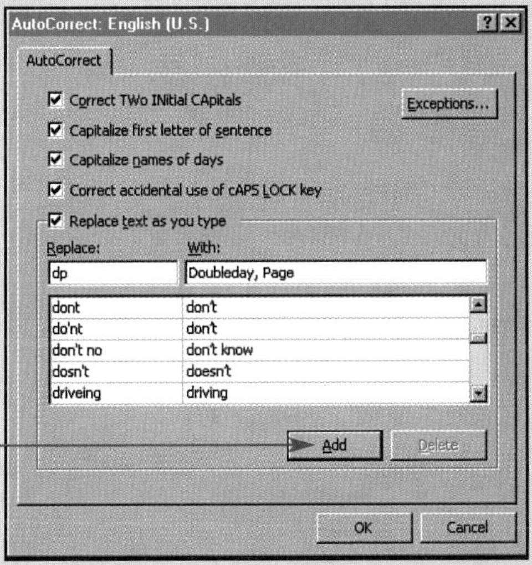

Figure 4.7
In the With text box, type exactly what you want to have appear in the field.

6 Click the Add button, and then click OK.
The shortcut is added to the AutoCorrect list.

7 Click the New Record button at the bottom of the screen.

8 Click in the Publisher field; type `dp`, and then press Enter.
Notice that the dp is replaced by Doubleday, Page exactly as you typed it into the AutoCorrect list (see Figure 4.8). This entry is now stored in a common location for all the Microsoft applications.

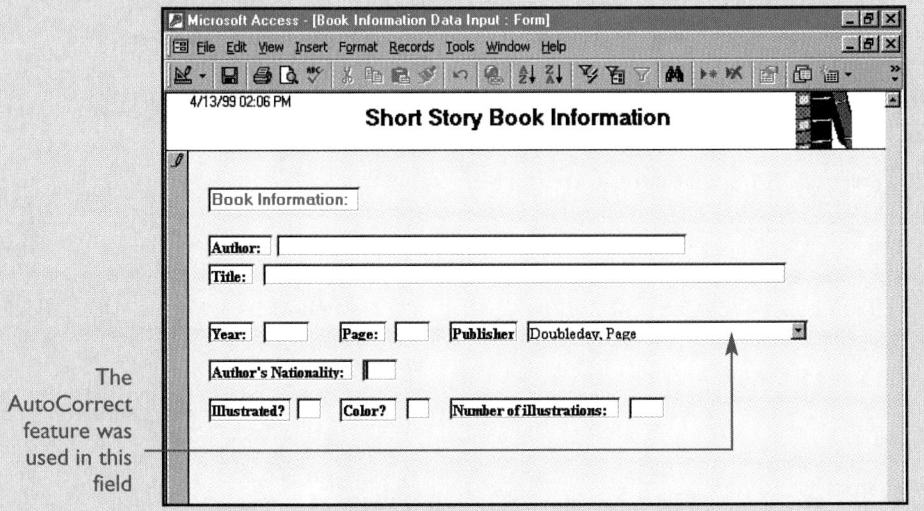

Figure 4.8
The AutoCorrect entry expands when you move to the next field.

continues ▶

To Customize Data Entry Using AutoCorrect (continued)

How To Activate an AutoCorrect Entry
In the previous example, you pressed ←Enter to activate the AutoCorrect entry. You can also activate it by pressing Spacebar, Tab, or a punctuation mark.

9 **Launch Microsoft Word.**

10 **Choose Tools, AutoCorrect from the menu and scroll down to see whether dp is there.**

Notice that it shows up in the Microsoft Word AutoCorrect list. It also appears in PowerPoint and Excel. This is because the AutoCorrect list is stored on the computer's hard drive as a shared file available to all Microsoft Office products. This can be a great timesaver for you.

The AutoCorrect Feature in Other Microsoft Applications
While you are in Word, take a look at the tabs at the top of the AutoCorrect dialog box. Several options are available for advanced features. Access has only the AutoCorrect tab, as do Excel and PowerPoint.

11 **Close the AutoCorrect dialog box in Word. Type dp and then press Spacebar**

The abbreviation expands into the publisher's name exactly as it did in your Access form.

Removing an AutoCorrect Entry
If you are using a computer in a lab, you need to remove the AutoCorrect entry you added. To do this, return to the AutoCorrect window; scroll down and select the entry you added and press Del.

12 **Close Word, but don't save your changes.**

13 **Close the Book Information Data Input form, and then close the Books of Stories database.**

Lesson 3: Analyzing a Table

Access provides three analysis tools to help you fine-tune your database: a Table Analyzer, a Performance Analyzer, and a Documenter. These tools help you in different ways. The Table Analyzer contains a wizard that looks at a table, determines which fields contain duplicated information, and then determines how you might want to break the large table into smaller, more efficient linked tables. If you are not interested in having the Access program determine which fields to break out of the original table, you can identify the fields yourself.

In this lesson, you analyze the table in a database of a television viewing log. This comes from a small study by a local cable company of the number of hours each person watches one of five major channels.

To Analyze a Table

1. **Make a copy of the AC3-0402 database file from the CD-ROM. Right-click the filename; select Properties from the shortcut menu, and remove the Read-only status. Use the shortcut menu to rename the file `TV Viewing Habits`, and then open the database.**
   It does not matter what area you are in. The analyzers work from anywhere in the database.

2. **Choose Tools, Analyze from the menu, and then select Table.**
   This wizard has two introductory screens that are optional. Compare your screen to Figure 4.9. (If your screen does not match the figure, click the Next button until you reach the correct screen.) This dialog box shows all the tables in the database. It also enables you to turn on the introductory screens that describe the process in detail. Turn those on if you are interested, and then click Back to view them.

> The Table Analyzer Wizard is not installed by default. If you are using a computer that has not had that option installed, follow the onscreen directions to install it using the Office CD-ROM, or ask your lab manager for further instructions.

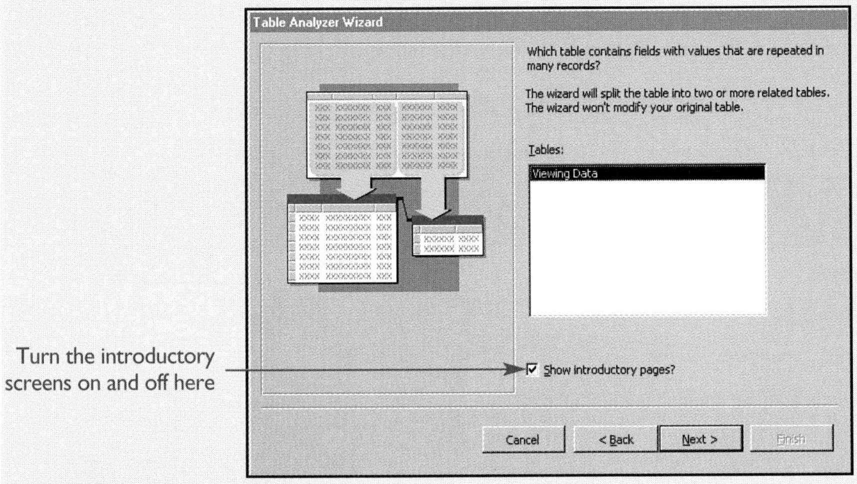

Figure 4.9
The first Table Analyzer Wizard dialog box enables you to choose a table to analyze.

3. **The Viewing Data table is already selected, so click Next.**
   The second Table Analyzer Wizard dialog box sets the program's level of control over the process.

4. **Select the Yes, let the wizard decide option, and then click Next.**
   Access decides which fields have sufficient duplication to warrant a separate table. It sets up the structure of the resulting tables and shows you the links it plans to create. If the potential tables are off the screen, click the title bars and drag the table lists until you can see them all. Notice that some of the changes make sense; others, such as separating the First Name and Last Name fields, make no sense at all (see Figure 4.10).

continues ▶

To Analyze a Table (continued)

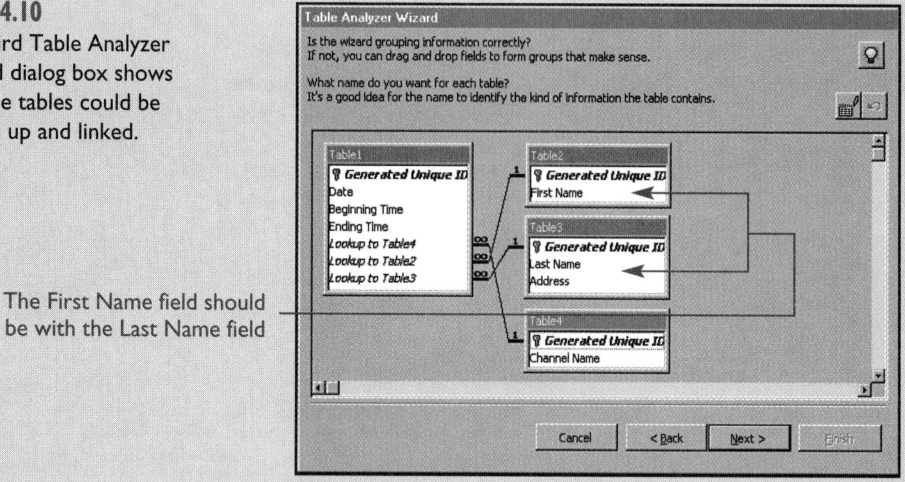

Figure 4.10
The third Table Analyzer Wizard dialog box shows how the tables could be broken up and linked.

Several fields were separated from the original table. Because the tables need to be linked, Access creates key fields called Generated Unique ID for each of the new tables. A lookup field is also included for each of the new tables.

5 Click the First Name field in Table2 and drag it to Table3.
Because the First Name field was the only original field in Table2, that table is removed, and the lookup field referring to it is removed (see Figure 4.11).

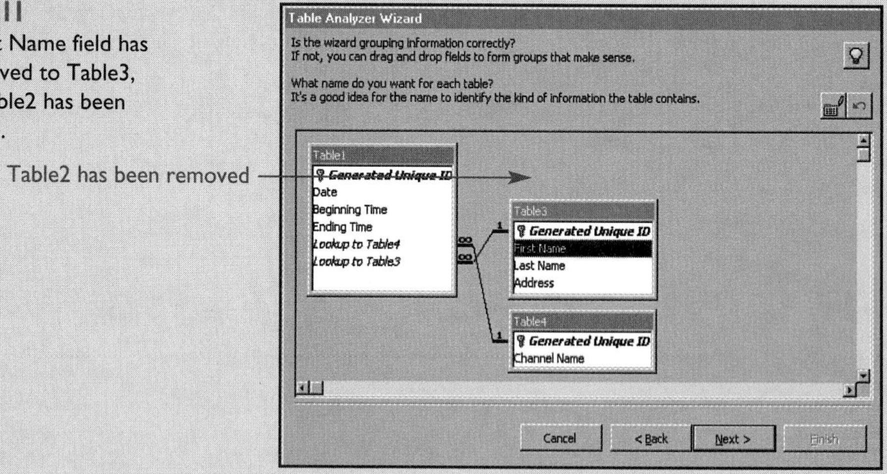

Figure 4.11
The First Name field has been moved to Table3, while Table2 has been removed.

It is now a good idea to rename the tables. Make sure you use descriptive names.

6 Double-click the title bar for Table1. Type `Dates and Times` in the Table Name box. Repeat this process until all three tables are renamed.
Your Table Name box should look like Figure 4.12.

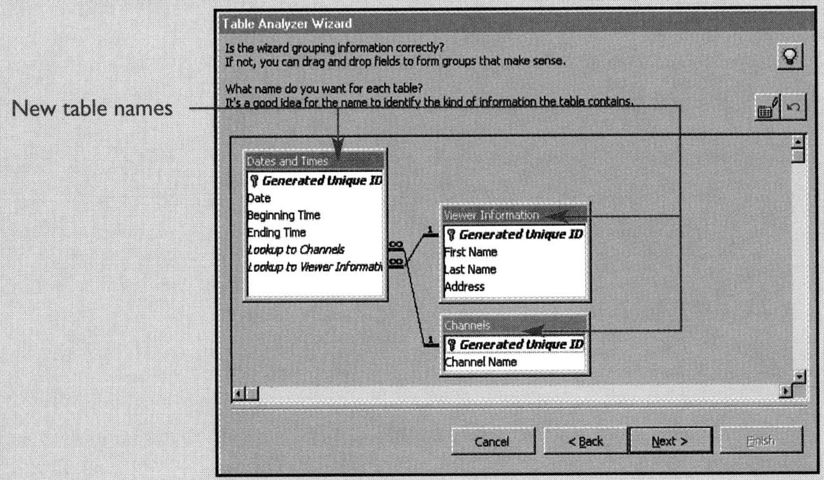

Figure 4.12
All three tables are renamed.

7 Click Next.
The next Table Analyzer Wizard dialog box displays and asks whether you are satisfied with the primary key field chosen by the program. If not, you are told how to assign another field as the primary key.

8 Click Next.
After a brief delay, the next Table Analyzer Wizard dialog box displays (see Figure 4.13). The purpose of this dialog box is to identify identical items, one or more of which might be misspelled or entered differently. If you want to change an entry, choose a correction from the drop-down list in the Correction column, or type a new entry. The data in this dialog box is often incorrectly identified as being a problem, although at times the wizard does catch errors. No changes should be made to this list.

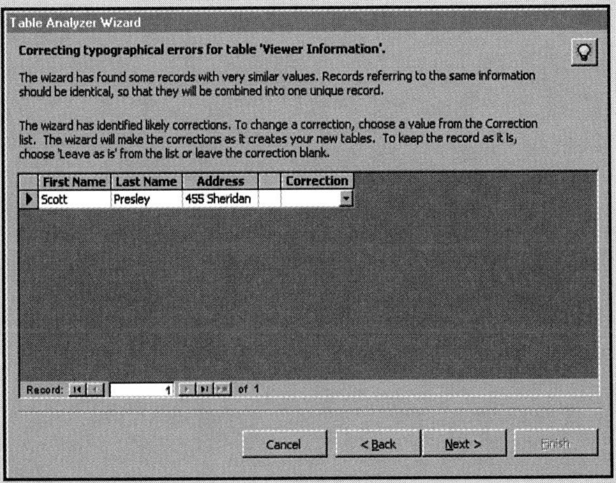

Figure 4.13
The next Table Analyzer Wizard dialog box looks for inconsistent duplicate entries.

9 Click Next.
A warning dialog box appears asking whether you are sure you want to continue (see Figure 4.14).

continues ▶

To Analyze a Table (continued)

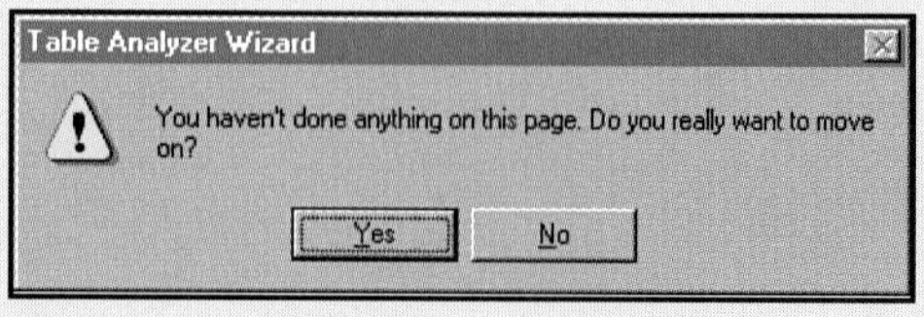

Figure 4.14
The program warns you that you have made no changes, even though changes were suggested.

10 Click Yes.
Possible errors are displayed for a second table.

11 Click Next; then click Yes to continue.
The next Table Analyzer Wizard dialog box displays and asks whether you want to create a query that looks like your original table.

Creating a Query To Look Like Your Original Table
It is usually a good idea to create this query because it enables you to work with the data as you originally set it up in the table. Additionally, Access makes the links to make sure all forms and reports can still find the necessary information.

---

12 Make sure the Yes, create the query option is selected, turn off the Help option, and then click Finish.
After a brief delay, the program shows the results of the query, which has the same information as the original table.

13 Close the query. Move to the Tables object button, if necessary, and open the Dates and Times table.
Notice that the Channels appear in a column called Lookup to Channels (see Figure 4.15). It is now a lookup field, taking its information from the Channels table. The same holds true for the Viewer Information table. In this case, the column widths were adjusted to enable you to see the results more clearly.

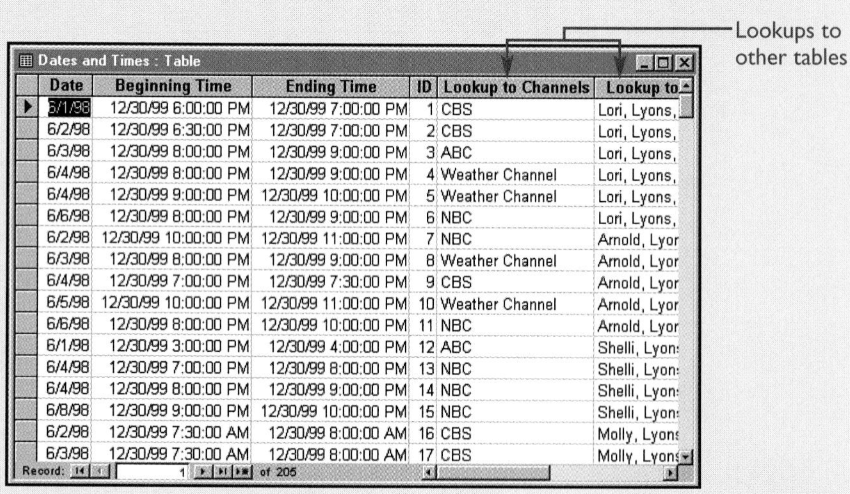

Date	Beginning Time	Ending Time	ID	Lookup to Channels	Lookup to
6/1/98	12/30/99 6:00:00 PM	12/30/99 7:00:00 PM	1	CBS	Lori, Lyons,
6/2/98	12/30/99 6:30:00 PM	12/30/99 7:00:00 PM	2	CBS	Lori, Lyons,
6/3/98	12/30/99 8:00:00 PM	12/30/99 9:00:00 PM	3	ABC	Lori, Lyons,
6/4/98	12/30/99 8:00:00 PM	12/30/99 9:00:00 PM	4	Weather Channel	Lori, Lyons,
6/4/98	12/30/99 9:00:00 PM	12/30/99 10:00:00 PM	5	Weather Channel	Lori, Lyons,
6/6/98	12/30/99 8:00:00 PM	12/30/99 9:00:00 PM	6	NBC	Lori, Lyons,
6/2/98	12/30/99 10:00:00 PM	12/30/99 11:00:00 PM	7	NBC	Arnold, Lyor
6/3/98	12/30/99 8:00:00 PM	12/30/99 9:00:00 PM	8	Weather Channel	Arnold, Lyor
6/4/98	12/30/99 7:00:00 PM	12/30/99 7:30:00 PM	9	CBS	Arnold, Lyor
6/5/98	12/30/99 10:00:00 PM	12/30/99 11:00:00 PM	10	Weather Channel	Arnold, Lyor
6/6/98	12/30/99 8:00:00 PM	12/30/99 10:00:00 PM	11	NBC	Arnold, Lyor
6/1/98	12/30/99 3:00:00 PM	12/30/99 4:00:00 PM	12	ABC	Shelli, Lyon
6/4/98	12/30/99 7:00:00 PM	12/30/99 8:00:00 PM	13	NBC	Shelli, Lyon
6/4/98	12/30/99 8:00:00 PM	12/30/99 9:00:00 PM	14	NBC	Shelli, Lyon
6/8/98	12/30/99 9:00:00 PM	12/30/99 10:00:00 PM	15	NBC	Shelli, Lyon
6/2/98	12/30/99 7:30:00 AM	12/30/99 8:00:00 AM	16	CBS	Molly, Lyons
6/3/98	12/30/99 7:30:00 AM	12/30/99 8:00:00 AM	17	CBS	Molly, Lyons

Figure 4.15
The Dates and Times table is now joined to two other tables.

14 Close the table and the database.
Leave Access open for the next lesson.

Lesson 4: Analyzing Database Performance

In Lesson 3, you learned how to use an analysis tool to analyze a table. Access also offers a tool to analyze the performance of a database. This analysis is not restricted to tables; it works on all database objects. It is always a good idea to back up your database before you run any of the analyzers.

In this lesson, you analyze all the database objects in a database and correct two of the problems found.

To Analyze Database Performance

1. **Make a copy of the AC3-0403 database file from the CD-ROM. Right-click the filename; select Properties from the shortcut menu, and remove the Read-only status. Use the shortcut menu to rename the file `Checking Performance`, and then open the database.**
   The Database window should now be open to the Tables area, although it does not matter what area you are in. The analyzers work from anywhere in the database.

2. **Choose Tools, Analyze from the menu, and then select Performance. Install the Performance Analyzer Wizard, if necessary.**
   The first Performance Analyzer Wizard dialog box displays (see Figure 4.16). This dialog box has several tabs that enable you to choose the database object type you want to work on.

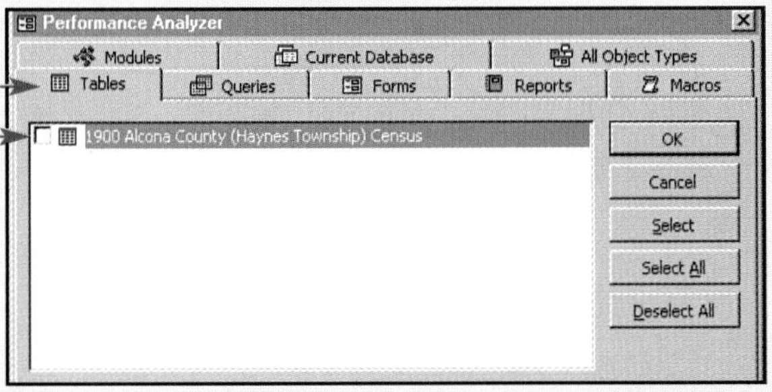

Figure 4.16
The first Performance Analyzer dialog box enables you to choose a table to analyze.

3. **Click the check box for the only table in the database and click OK.**
   The Performance Analyzer looks at the table and has no suggestions to improve it (see Figure 4.17).

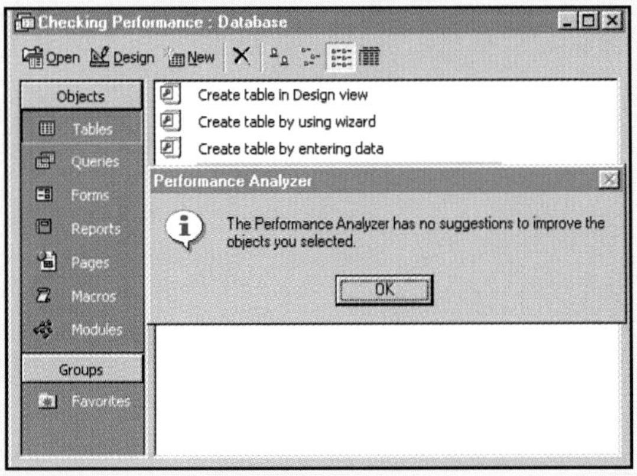

Figure 4.17
The Performance Analyzer found no problems with the table.

continues ▶

To Analyze Database Performance (continued)

4 Click OK, and then choose Tools, Analyze, Performance from the menu.

The first Performance Analyzer dialog box displays.

5 Choose the All Object Types tab, and then click Select All.

All the objects in the database are shown, and all of them are selected (see Figure 4.18).

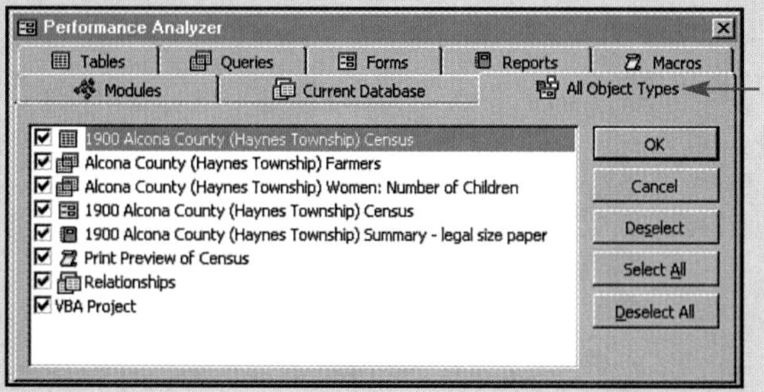

Figure 4.18
The Performance Analyzer dialog box now shows all the database objects.

6 Click OK.

The Performance Analyzer analyzes each object in the database. This procedure can take a long time in a complex database, particularly if you are using a slow machine or are operating on a network version of the software.

The recommendations, suggestions, and ideas are shown, along with the database object to which they refer. The Analysis Notes at the bottom of the dialog box further describe the Analysis Results for the first item on the list. (see Figure 4.19). When any other object listed in the Analysis Results is selected, the Analysis Notes change to describe the highlighted item. In this case, the only items you should act on are the two that are shown as recommendations.

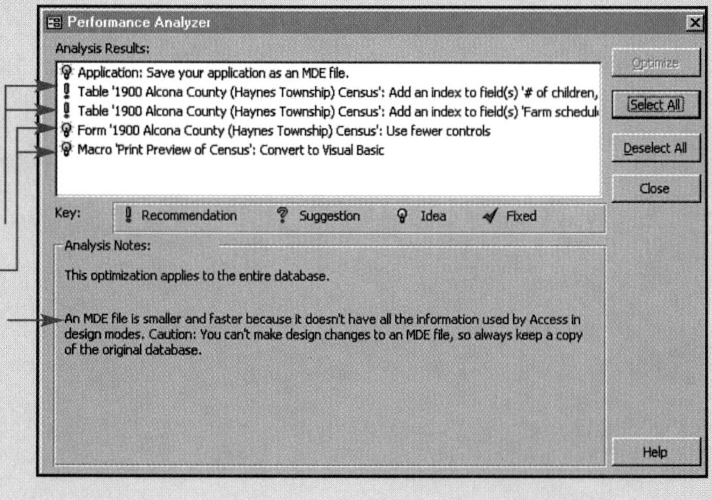

Figure 4.19
The Performance Analyzer gives recommendations, suggestions, and ideas about how to improve database performance.

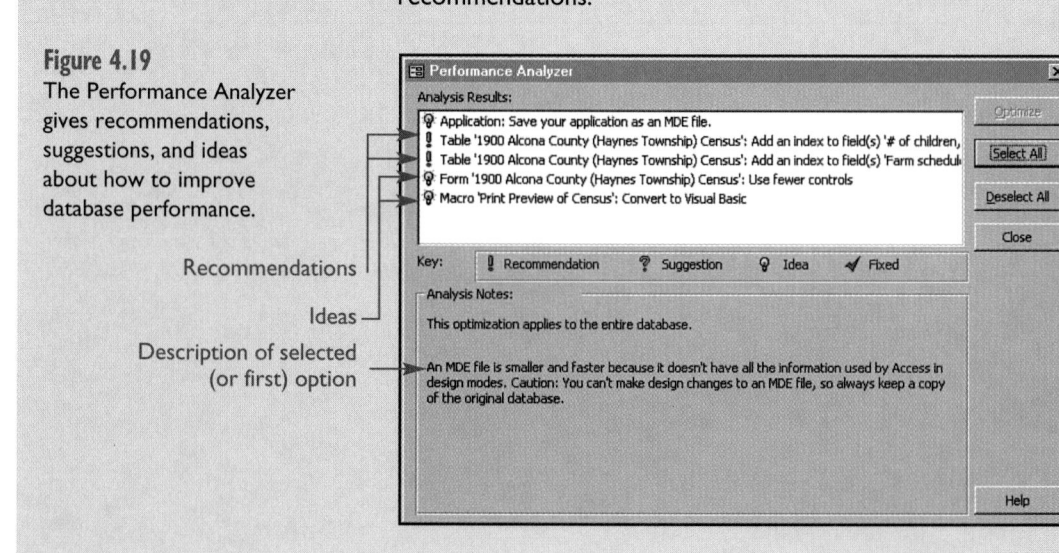

Accepting Performance Analyzer Recommendations
Some of the recommendations, suggestions, and ideas make great sense, whereas others make no sense at all. Be careful when you make changes based on the analyzers, particularly those you are not sure of. Back up your database before you run the Performance Analyzer.

7. **Select the second item in the list.**
This item recommends that an index be added to fields in the table to improve the operations of one of the queries. (Read the details in the Analysis Notes area.)

8. **Click the Optimize button in the dialog box.**
This tells the computer to accept the Performance Analyzer recommendation.

9. **Select the third item in the list.**
This item also recommends that an index be added to fields in the table to improve the operation of a second query.

10. **Click the Optimize button.**
Check marks indicate that optimization was performed on two of the items (see Figure 4.20).

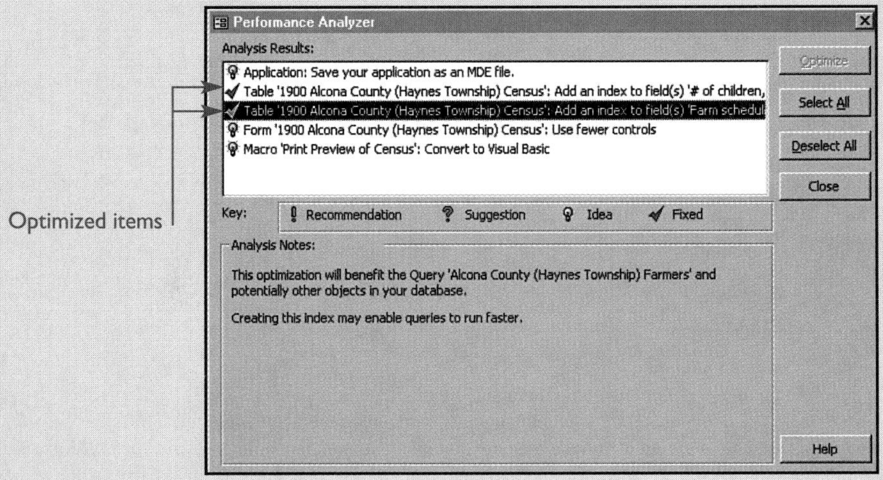

Figure 4.20
Two of the recommendations were performed.

11. **Click the Close button, and then close the database.**
Leave Access open for the next lesson.

Lesson 5: Updating the Database Using Name AutoCorrect

Databases tend to constantly evolve. Object names and field names are often changed, which has led to problems in the past. A change in a field name meant that the database designer had to change all references to that field in every query, form, report, or other object that depended on it. If the field was numeric, any formulas or expressions that used it also had to be changed. The same held true with object names. Access 2000 has now included a Name AutoCorrect feature that automatically updates the database every time a name change occurs.

In this lesson, you work with a database that contains statistics about publicly and privately owned cars and trucks in the United States.

To Update a Database Using the Name AutoCorrect Feature

1. **Make a copy of the AC3-0404 database file from the CD-ROM. Right-click the filename; select Properties from the shortcut menu, and remove the Read-only status. Use the shortcut menu to rename the file `Using Name AutoCorrect`, and then open the database.**

2. **Click the Queries object button, if necessary. Select the Total Cars and Trucks query, and click the Design button.**
The query opens in Design view (see Figure 4.21). Notice that the fourth field is an expression (as is the seventh field, which is off the screen). The fields in the second and third columns are added together to get a total of cars by state. It is difficult to read the expression in the narrow column.

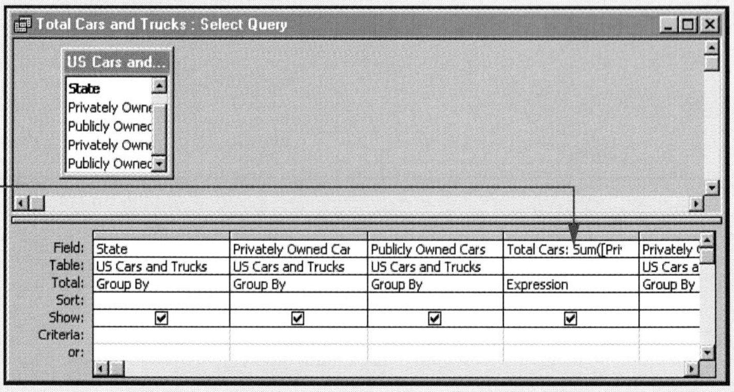

Figure 4.21
The query is open in Design view.

3. **Right-click the Field box of the fourth column and select Zoom from the shortcut menu.**
The expression is now easy to read (see Figure 4.22). Look at the field names in the expression; they match the field names in the second and third columns of the query design grid.

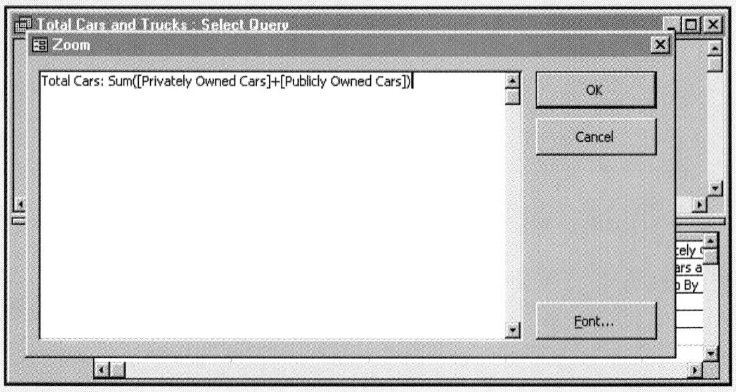

Figure 4.22
The Zoom button makes a long expression easy to read.

4. **Click OK, and then close the query.**

5. **Click the Tables object button. Click the Design button to open the US Cars and Trucks table in Design view.**

6 Change the name of the second field to Private Cars, the third field to Public Cars, the fourth field to Private Trucks, and the fifth field to Public Trucks.

Your table Design window should look like Figure 4.23.

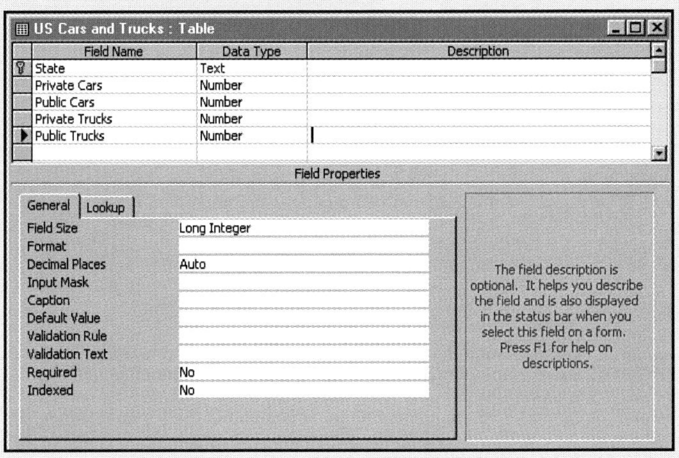

Figure 4.23
Four of the five field names were changed.

7 Close the table and save your changes. Click the Queries object button and open the Total Cars and Trucks query in Design view.

Notice that the field names were changed in the second and third columns.

8 Right-click the Field box of the fourth column and select Zoom from the shortcut menu.

The field names in the expression also changed (see Figure 4.24).

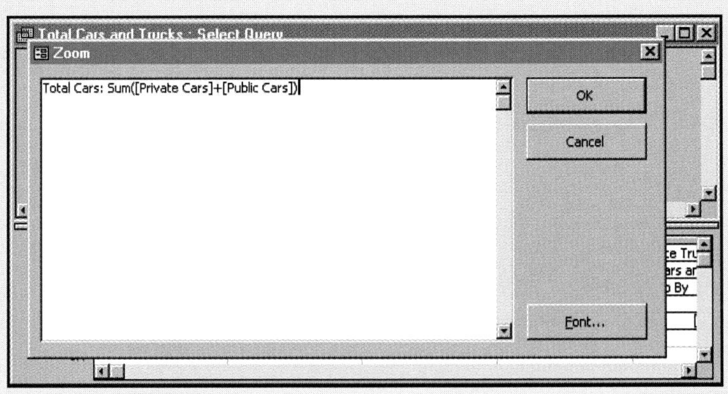

Figure 4.24
The field names in the expression were automatically changed to match the new field names in the table.

9 Close the Zoom box and the query; then click the Forms object button.

10 Open the Total Cars and Trucks form.

Notice that the numbers are correct, but the field labels did not change (see Figure 4.25). If you want to change the labels, you need to do that in Design view.

continues ▶

To Update a Database Using the Name AutoCorrect Feature (continued)

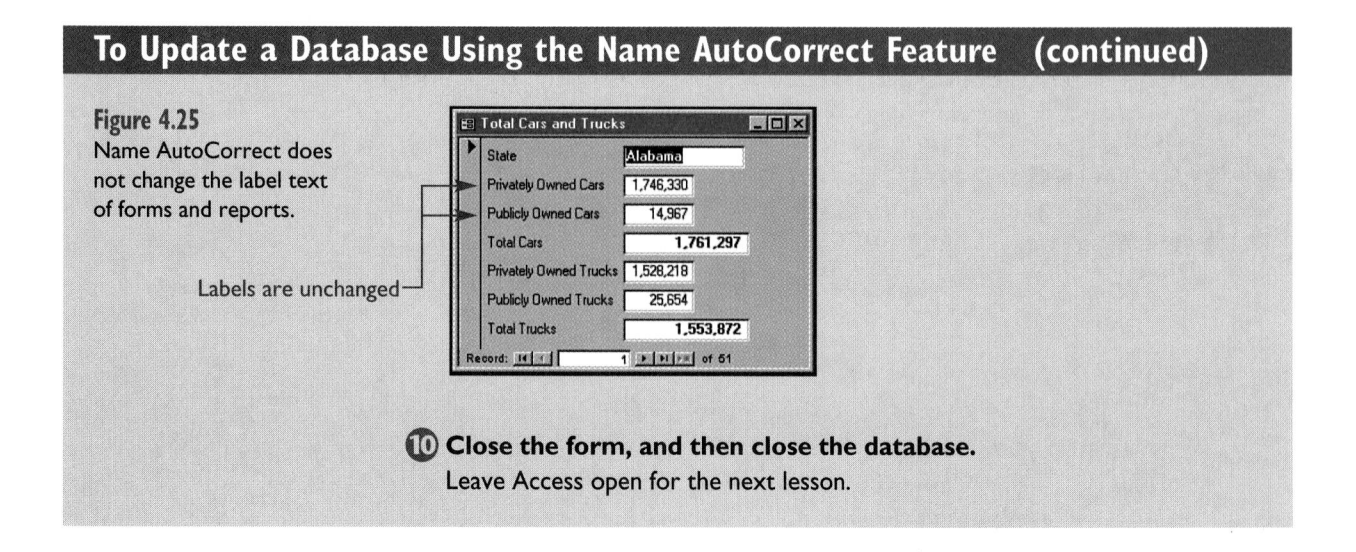

Figure 4.25
Name AutoCorrect does not change the label text of forms and reports.

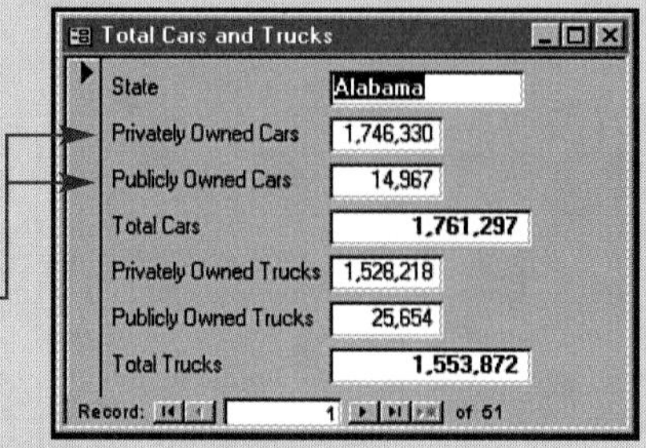

10 Close the form, and then close the database.
Leave Access open for the next lesson.

The Name AutoCorrect Feature and Older Versions of Access
If you are using a database created in Access 97, the previous procedure does not work automatically. After you convert the database to Access 2000, choose Tools, Options from the menu. Click the General tab and click the check boxes for the Track name AutoCorrect info and the Perform name AutoCorrect options in the Name AutoCorrect area.

If your database was created on an even earlier version of Access and then upgraded as new versions came out, you may have problems getting this feature to work. Try turning on the Name AutoCorrect feature, and then changing one of the field names in a table. If it does not work, you need to make these changes manually. If it is a simple database, you can export the data to Excel, create a new database, and import the data. You need to recreate the other database objects.

Lesson 6: Using Office Links to Analyze Data with Excel

In many cases, you want to perform calculations using the fields in your database. Although Access has many capabilities, such as calculated fields and summaries on reports, it is usually far easier to perform calculations in an Excel spreadsheet. You can send the contents of a table to Excel, but in many cases it is better to send a query that contains only the data you want to use. You can also send data to Excel from forms and reports.

In this lesson, you use a modified query from the census database you used in Lesson 4. The query is a summary of women who have had children, as reported in the 1900 census. It contains only three fields: the mother's birthplace, the number of children each woman had, and the number of children still living. This data is to be transferred to Excel for analysis. This lesson requires that you have Microsoft Excel available.

To Use Office Links to Analyze Data with Excel

1 Make a copy of the AC3-0405 database file from the CD-ROM. Right-click the filename; select Properties from the shortcut menu, and remove the Read-only status. Use the shortcut menu to rename the file `Analyze with Excel`, and then open the database.

2 Click the Queries object button. Select and Open the Haynes Township Women - Number of Children query.

Notice that the query contains only 3 of the 38 fields in the 1900 Alcona County (Haynes Township) Census table (see Figure 4.26).

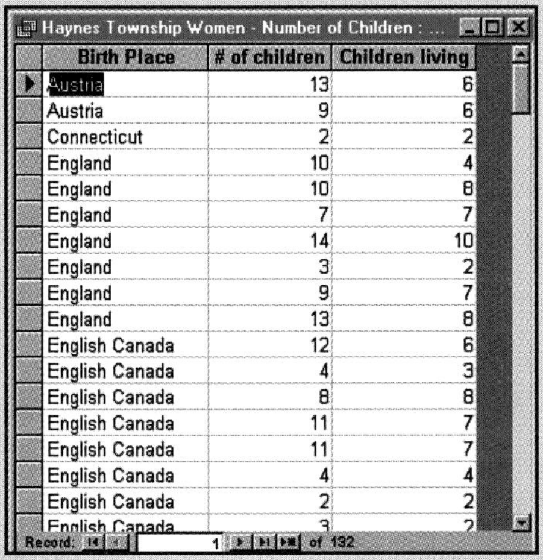

Figure 4.26
The query contains only three fields.

3 Choose Tools, Office Links from the menu, and then select Analyze It with MS Excel.

You can also click the OfficeLinks button on the Database toolbar and select Analyze It with MS Excel from the drop-down list. The program opens Excel and transfers the data from the query to the Excel program. This is now an Excel file and can be edited, modified, and saved in the same way you would work on any other Excel file (see Figure 4.27). Excel assigns it the same name as the database object from which it is derived.

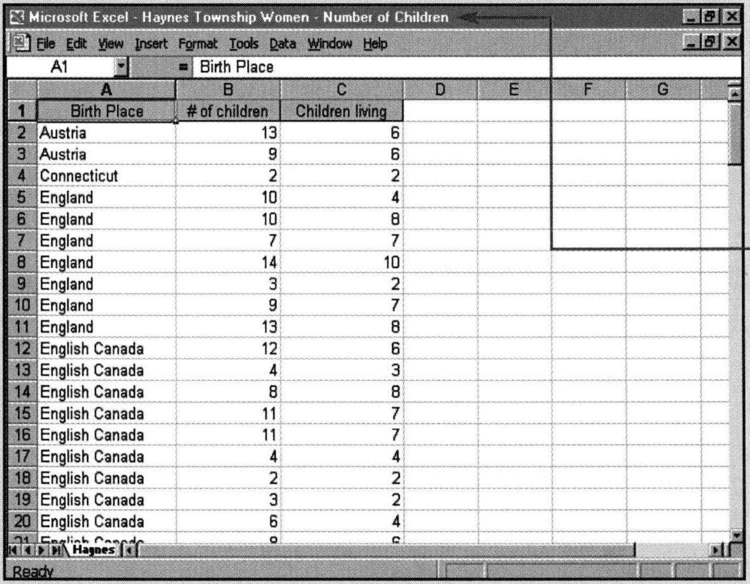

Figure 4.27
The Analyze It With MS Excel option creates a new Excel file and transfers data from Access.

continues ▶

To Use Office Links to Analyze Data with Excel (continued)

Interactivity Between Excel and Access
The Excel file created in this way is not linked to the original database source; updates that you make to the data in Access do not transfer to the new Excel file, and changes you make to the Excel spreadsheet are not reflected in the Access database.

7. **Click in cell A1, and then scroll to the bottom of the data; hold down Shift, and click in cell C133.**
All the data is selected.

8. **Choose Data, Subtotals from the menu to display the Subtotals dialog box. Click the check box for the # of children in the Add subtotal to scroll box.**
Excel calculates subtotals for # of Children and Children Living. Your Subtotal dialog box should look like Figure 4.28.

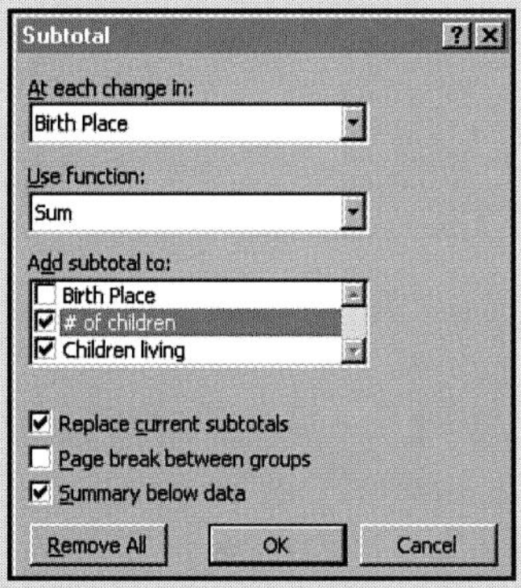

Figure 4.28
The Subtotals dialog box was set to group on Birth Place and add up the other two fields.

9. **Click OK, and then return to the top of the worksheet. Click the line on the right side of the column selector for the first column (the one labeled A), and widen the column by about 1/2".**

10. **Click the second level box at the top of the column at the very left side of the window.**
The worksheet displays only the group totals and grand total (see Figure 4.29). Notice how much easier it is to do sophisticated data analysis in Excel.

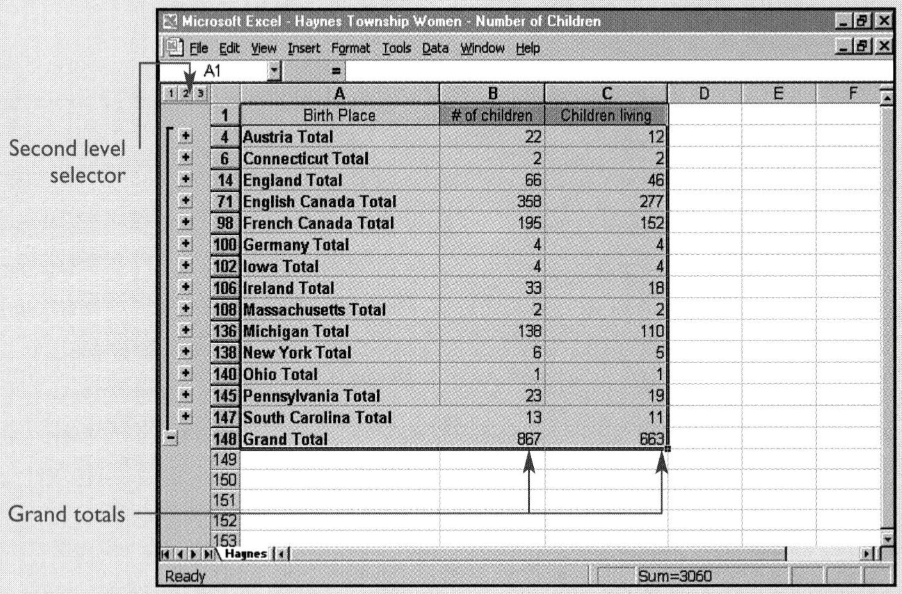

Figure 4.29
Excel displays group subtotals and grand total.

⑪ Close Excel and save your changes. If the program asks you to save it in the most recent format, click Yes.

⑫ Close the query and close the database.
Close Access unless you are going to proceed to the exercises.

Summary

In this project, you used some of the tools and utilities available to you in Access. These include a Spelling checker and an AutoCorrect feature, both of which are used in other Microsoft Office applications. You also used two of the analysis tools to analyze a table and optimize database performance. You used the Name AutoCorrect feature to update a changed field name in database objects and expressions. Finally, you used the Office Links tool to analyze data from a database query in Excel.

You can learn more about the Access analyzer tools by going to the help index and typing in `analyzer`.

Checking Concepts and Terms

True/False

For each of the following, check *T* or *F* to indicate whether the statement is true or false.

__T __F **1.** If you add a new word to your Custom dictionary in Access, it is not automatically included in the Custom dictionary in Microsoft Word. [L1]

__T __F **2.** An AutoCorrect shortcut added in Access is also available in Excel. [L2]

__T __F **3.** You can run the Analyze tools from anywhere in the database. [L3]

__T __F **4.** Choose Optimize to accept a Performance Analyzer recommendation. [L4]

__T __F **5.** You can add new words to the Microsoft dictionary. [L1]

__T __F **6.** An AutoCorrect entry is an alternative for a combo box or a list box. [L2]

__T __F **7.** The three analysis tools are the Table Analyzer, the Performance Analyzer, and the Office Links. [L3]

__T __F **8.** It is probably unnecessary to back up your database before using the Performance Analyzer. [L4]

__T __F **9.** The Name AutoCorrect feature works well with databases created in any version of Access. [L2]

__T __F **10.**. The Table Analyzer works only on tables and queries. [L3]

Multiple Choice

Circle the letter of the correct answer for each of the following questions.

1. Which tool enables you to enter shortcuts for longer words or phrases? [L2]

a. AutoCorrect
b. Documenter
c. Table Analyzer
d. Performance Analyzer

2. To activate an AutoCorrect entry, type the shortcut, followed by ______________. [L2]

a. a Spacebar only
b. a punctuation mark only
c. Tab only
d. all of the above

3. The Name AutoCorrect feature will not______________. [L5]

a. automatically update field names
b. automatically update object names
c. work automatically with Access 97 files
d. enable you to change a field name

4. It is usually a good idea to accept a Performance Analyzer recommendation to index a field if you ever plan to do which of the following on that field? [L4]

a. run a spelling check
b. do a performance analysis
c. sort
d. create a Crosstab query

5. When you send a query to Excel using Office Links, ______________. [L6]

a. the spreadsheet is not linked to the source database and won't be updated as you update information in the database
b. the file is automatically updated as you update the database
c. you can change information in the spreadsheet, and the changes are also made in the database
d. the query looks at the spreadsheet and imports the information to your database

6. The Spelling checker______________. [L1]

a. finds spelling and grammar mistakes
b. identifies misspelled words
c. identifies words that are not in its dictionary
d. updates words automatically

7. The Performance Analyzer offers ______________. [L4]

a. recommendations
b. suggestions
c. ideas
d. all of the above

8. Office Links are found in which menu option? [L6]

a. Tools
b. Insert
c. Records
d. Edit

9. The Table Analyzer ______________. [L3]

a. optimizes field names

b. makes sure tables interact properly with queries, forms, and records

c. provides a description of each field, data type, and relationship

d. determines whether a table should be broken into two or more smaller tables

10. The AutoCorrect feature is preferable to combo boxes or list boxes because ______________. [L2]

a. it can be used in any field, rather than in just one field

b. it can be used by other Microsoft applications

c. it can be used to enter only a part of a field

d. all of the above

Discussion Questions

1. In Lesson 1, you used the Spelling checker, which included options to change or ignore the unrecognized word, or add it to the dictionary. Under what situations would you ignore a word rather than add it to the dictionary? What possible problems can you foresee with a number of different people adding words to the same dictionary?

2. When would you use a combo box or list box in place of the AutoCorrect feature? What problems might you have adding abbreviations to the AutoCorrect tool?

3. In Lesson 4, you ran the Performance Analyzer. One of the ideas was to change the database file to an MDE file. What is an MDE file, and why might you want to use one? (You may need to use the Office Assistant if you can't remember how an MDE file is used.) What is the major drawback to using MDE files?

4. When using an Access 97 file, why would you want to turn the Name AutoCorrect feature on? What kinds of problems could you encounter by leaving it off?

5. You used Office Links in Lesson 6 to move some data from an Access query to an Excel worksheet. You then grouped the data and provided group totals and a grand total. How would you perform the same functions using Access?

Skill Drill

Skill Drill exercises reinforce project skills. Each skill reinforced is the same, or nearly the same, as a skill presented in the project. Each exercise includes a brief narrative introduction, followed by detailed instructions in a step-by-step format.

1. Using the Table Analyzer

The Table Analyzer can help you make your tables more efficient and easier to extract information from. In this exercise, you work with a table of Alaska geographical locations that was not set up using good design techniques.

To use the Table Analyzer

1. Make a copy of the AC3-0406 database file from the CD-ROM. Right-click the filename; select Properties from the shortcut menu, and remove the Read-only status. Use the shortcut menu to rename the file `Alaska Locations`, and then open the database.

2. Select Tools, Analyze, Table from the menu.

3. Skip the two introduction screens, if necessary, by clicking Next twice. Select the Geography table.

4. Let the wizard decide how to break up the table. Accept the three tables as they are shown.

5. Rename Table1 as `Location`.

6. Rename Table2 as `Borough`.

7. Rename Table3 as `Type`.

8. Click Next, and then click Next three times to accept the primary key fields and skip the typographical error screen. Click Yes when asked whether you really want to move to the next screen.

9. Choose to create a query to match the original table; deselect the Help check box, and then click Finish.
10. Close the query and close the database.

2. Checking the Spelling

The CD Collection database you used in Project 3 is ideal for the use of the Spelling checker. In this exercise, you check the spelling of the CD Title field.

To check your spelling:

1. Copy AC3-0407; remove the Read-only status, and rename the file `New CD Collection`.
2. Open the database, open the CD Collection table, and then select the CD Title column.
3. Click the Spelling button to begin the spelling check.
4. Change Gratest to Greatest.
5. Click Ignore for Antal, Dorati, and Kodaly.
6. Click Ignore All when you reach Bartok because this name appears several times in the field.
7. Ignore Bacchanales and Royale. Notice that the next unrecognized word is Oout, which is misspelled twice.
8. Click Change All to change both misspellings at the same time.
9. Click the Close button to close the Spelling dialog box.
10. Leave the table open for the next exercise.

3. Adding an AutoCorrect Entry

The AutoCorrect feature, when used by itself or in combination with combo and list boxes, makes data entry easy. In this exercise, you add an AutoCorrect entry to be used in the CD Title field.

To add an AutoCorrect entry:

1. Select Tools, AutoCorrect from the menu.
2. Type **gh** in the Replace text box.
3. Type **`Greatest Hits`** in the With text box.
4. Click the Add button to add this new entry.
5. Click OK to close the AutoCorrect dialog box.
6. Click the New Record button.
7. Type **`Kronos Quartet`** in the Artist/Group field.
8. Type **gh** in the CD Title field, press Spacebar, and then type **`of the Kronos Quartet`**.
9. Close the table, but leave the database open for the next exercise.

4. Analyzing Database Performance

The New CD Collection database contains tables, queries, forms, and reports. To see how they work together, and what might be done to improve operation, it is a good idea to run the Performance Analyzer. Remember, before you do this to an important database, make a backup copy!

To analyze database performance:

1. With the New CD Collection open, select Tools, Analyze, Performance from the menu.
2. Click the All Object Types tab from the Performance Analyzer dialog box.
3. Click the Select All button to select all the database objects.
4. Click OK to run the Performance Analyzer.
5. Select the second item in the list (the recommendation to add an index to the Label field).
6. Click the Optimize button.
7. Click the Close button to close the Performance Analyzer dialog box. Leave the database open for the next exercise.

5. Updating Field Names Using Name AutoCorrect

With five database objects, a change in one of the field names would have caused major problems in earlier versions of Access. In this exercise, you change the name of the Year Issued field, and then check to make sure the changes are reflected in the other database objects.

To use the Name AutoCorrect feature:

1. With the New CD Collection open, click the Tables object button, if necessary.
2. Select the CD Collection table and click the Design button.
3. Highlight the Year Issued field name and change it to `Year Recorded`.
4. Close the table and save your changes.
5. Click the Queries object button; select the Music from the 1990s query, and click the Design button.
6. Check to make sure the Year Issued field name changed to Year Recorded.
7. Click the View button and check to make sure the data appears in the Year Recorded field.
8. Use the same procedure to check the CD Collection Input Form and the CD Collection report.
9. When you are finished, close the database, but leave Access open for the next exercise.

6. Using Office Links to Analyze Data

Excel is an excellent program to use to analyze Access tables or queries that contain a lot of numerical fields. In this exercise, you use a database about Arizona tornadoes to look at casualties by county.

To use the Office Links feature:

1. Copy AC3-0408; remove the Read-only status, and rename the file `Updated Arizona Tornadoes`.
2. Open the database, and then click the Queries object button.
3. Highlight the Arizona Counties with Tornado Casualties query and click the Design button. Notice that this query displays only those counties in which a tornado-related injury or fatality has occurred in the 45 years of the study.
4. Click the View button to switch to Datasheet view.
5. Select Tools, Office Links, Analyze It with MS Excel.
6. Click in cell A1; hold down Shift, and click in cell C21.
7. Select Data, Subtotals from the menu.
8. Click the check box next to the Killed field, and then click OK.
9. Widen column A by about 1/2".
10. Click the second level button to view only the group totals and grand total.
11. Click the Print button to print the page.
12. Close Excel and save your changes in the latest Excel format.
13. Close the query and close the database.

Challenge

Challenge exercises expand on or are somewhat related to skills presented in the lessons. Each exercise provides a brief narrative introduction followed by instructions in a numbered step format that are not as detailed as those in the Skill Drill section.

The database used for the Challenge section is a modified version of the one you used in Project 1.

1. Publishing Access Data with MS Word

In Lesson 6, you sent data from a query to Excel for analysis. Another Office Link enables you to send information from an Access object to Microsoft Word. In this exercise, you send the information from the Employee Projects query to a Word document.

1. Copy AC3-0409; remove the Read-only status, and rename the file `Working with Access Tools`.
2. Open the database and open the Employee Projects query.
3. Select Tools, Office Links, Publish It with MS Word from the menu.
4. Click the Print button to print the table that was created.
5. Close the Word document and close Word. (Note: You won't be asked to save the Word document if you try to close it without having saved it.)
6. Close the Employee Projects query, but leave the database open for the next exercise.

2. Using the Documenter to Get Detailed Information About an Object

You used one of the analysis tools, the Documenter, in Lesson 1. In that lesson, you examined the properties of all the database objects, but turned off some of the details. In this exercise, you use the Documenter on one object, but with all the details turned on.

1. Choose Tools, Analyze, Documenter from the menu.
2. Select only the Employee Information table.
3. In the Options area, include all items for the table.
4. Include Names, Data Types, Sizes, and Properties for the fields.
5. Include Names, Fields, and Properties for the indexes.
6. Run the Documenter. (This takes a while.)
7. Find the page that displays the details about the relationships. Print only that page.
8. Close the Print Preview window, but leave the database open for the next exercise.

3. Changing the Default Field Settings

The common uses for Access databases depend on whether the database is designed for use at home, in an educational setting, or in the business world. The default field settings can be changed to accommodate the way you most often use a database.

In this exercise, you use the available help to figure out how to change several of the field defaults.

1. Change the default field size to 25, the default number type to Single, and the default field type to number. (Note: If you are doing these exercises in a lab setting, check with the lab manager before making these changes.)
2. Create a new table to make sure your changes took effect. Do not save the table.
3. Change the default field size back to 50, the default number type to long integer, and the default field type to text. Create a new table to make sure the default settings were properly restored. Do not save the table.

4. Changing the Way the Program Works

You can also change the way the pointer and arrow keys work while you are using Access. In this exercise, use Help to figure out how to do the following:

1. Single-click (rather than double-click) to open a database object.
2. Have the arrow keys move to the next character, rather than to the next field.
3. Make the insertion point go to the start of the field (rather than select the entire field) when you move to a new field.

Try out all these changes in the current database. When you are through, change the features back to the way they were and close the database.

Discovery Zone

Discovery Zone exercises help you gain advanced knowledge of project topics and/or application of skills. These exercises focus on enhancing your problem-solving skills. Numbered steps are not provided, but you are given hints, reminders, screen shots, and/or references to help you reach your goal for each exercise.

In these exercises, you use a database containing a table of business contacts. In the first exercise, you set up a mail merge with a Word document. In the second exercise, you change the look of the Access screen.

1. Creating a Mail Merge Document Based on an Access Table

You may have learned how to create a mail merge document in Word, but Access has a very effective way to create the same type of document. Because you probably have your mailing list in Access anyway, this is the preferred way to create mail merge documents in many situations.

Use the AC3-0410 file and save it as `Using Mail Merge`. Open up the Contacts table and select the Merge It with MS Word office link. You may be able to figure out how to create the document just by looking at the screen, especially if you already know how to use mail merge in Word. If not, use the Help menu.

Goal: Create a mail merge document based on an Access table.

(Note: Field names are displayed as <Field Name> in the following list).

The document should have:

- the current date in the first line, followed by a blank line.
- the customer's <First Name> and <Last Name> in the next line.
- the <Address> in the next line.
- the <City> followed by a comma and a space, followed by the <State>, followed by the <ZIP> in the next line.
- a blank line, followed by a line that reads `Dear` <<First Name>>`:`
- another blank line, followed by a paragraph that reads:

  `How are things in` <<City>>`? I'm just dropping you a line to let you know about our annual mid-winter sale!`

Figure 4.30

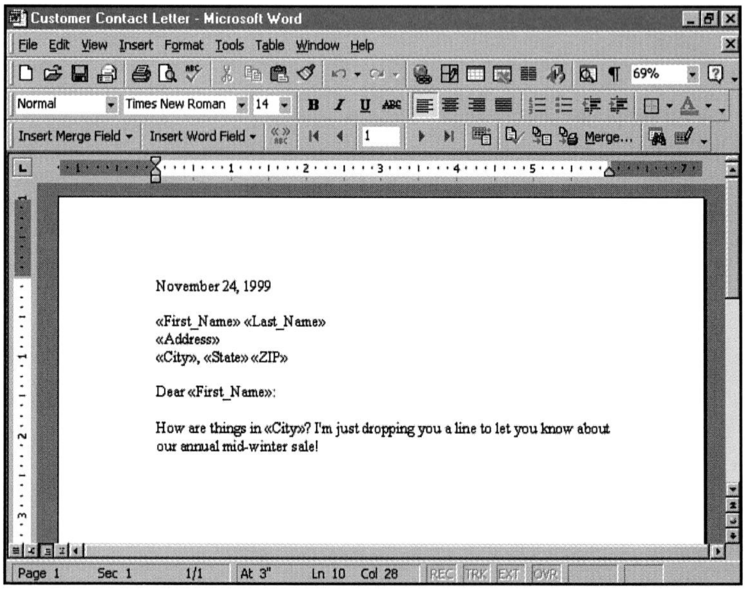

Your mail merge document should look like Figure 4.30.

Print the fifth record. Close Word and save the document as `Customer Contact Letter`. Close the Contacts table and leave the database open for the next exercise.

2. Changing the Look of the Access Screen

You may be able to make the Access window more visually appealing, although always remember that what is appealing to one person may be unsettling to another.

Goal: Change the look of the Access window.

Your new Access screen should:

- use a dark blue font instead of the default black font.
- have aqua gridlines instead of the default silver gridlines.
- use the Times New Roman font instead of the default Arial font.
- use a 12-point font instead of the default 10-point font.
- have a default column width of 1.5" instead of the default 1" column width.
- use a sunken cell effect instead of the default flat effect.

Test your new-look screen. If you like it, and you are using a one-person machine, you can leave it. Try other combinations. If you are on a multi-user machine, change the settings back to the defaults when you are through.

Project 5

Project 5

Analyzing and Reporting Data

Objectives

In this project, you learn how to

- **Use the Totals Tool in a Query**
- **Create Crosstab Queries and Reports**
- **Create Crosstab Queries with Conditions and Total Columns**
- **Analyze Data Using PivotTables**
- **Add a Subform to an Existing Form**
- **Insert Subreports into Reports Using the Subform/Subreport Wizard**
- **Create Reports Using the Chart Wizard**

Key terms introduced in this project include

- crosstab
- PivotTable
- subform
- subreport

Why Would I Do This?

The best database is of little use unless its data can be turned into information and communicated. You need to be able to summarize data in different ways depending on the type of information and the audience for whom it is intended.

If you need a quick analysis of one field in relation to another field, you can perform a quick calculation using a query and the Totals tool. If you need to analyze more than two fields, a crosstab query and its report are very useful.

A ***crosstab*** is a very powerful query used to produce a table that counts, averages, or sums data by the groupings that you specify. For example, if you sent out a survey with ten questions, you would enter each person's responses in a single record. If you got 1,000 responses, you would have 1,000 records, each with a numeric response (for example, a 1 to 5 rating scale) to the ten questions. Counting the number of times each response was given for each question would take a long time. A crosstab query can give you a table of responses in seconds. You can even set criteria and add calculations to the crosstab query.

PivotTables are forms that are similar to crosstab queries; they show the relationship between fields in a spreadsheet-like format. PivotTables have the advantage of being interactive. You can rearrange the fields in a PivotTable and even filter the data that you want to examine. PivotTables are set up in spreadsheet format and can be used to display subtotals and grand totals.

Subforms and subreports are also tools used to summarize and present data taken from joined tables. You may have created forms and subforms using a wizard, but you can also modify an existing form by adding a subform. You can also create reports that display related data from joined tables in a report/subreport format. These data presentation tools are very effective when tables are joined in a one-to-many relationship.

Sometimes data that can be presented in table form can be more effectively displayed as a chart. Access provides a charting tool that enables you to chart data from tables.

Visual Summary

When you have completed this lesson, you will have created a crosstab query, a PivotTable, a report with a subreport, and a chart (see Figures 5.1, 5.2, 5.3, and 5.4).

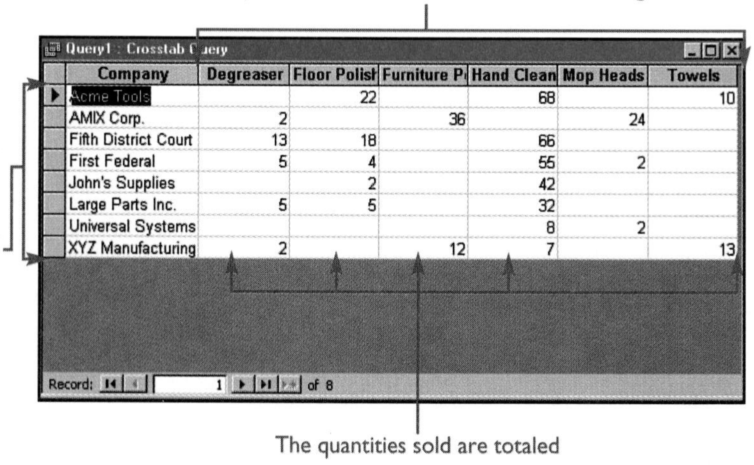
The product names are used as column headings
Query1 : Crosstab Query
Record: 1 of 8
The company names are used as row headings
The quantities sold are totaled

Company	Degreaser	Floor Polish	Furniture P	Hand Clean	Mop Heads	Towels
Acme Tools		22		68		10
AMIX Corp.	2		36		24	
Fifth District Court	13	18		66		
First Federal	5	4		55	2	
John's Supplies		2		42		
Large Parts Inc.	5	5		32		
Universal Systems				8	2	
XYZ Manufacturing	2		12	7		13

Figure 5.1
A crosstab query was set up to calculate the total sales of each product by the company that bought them.

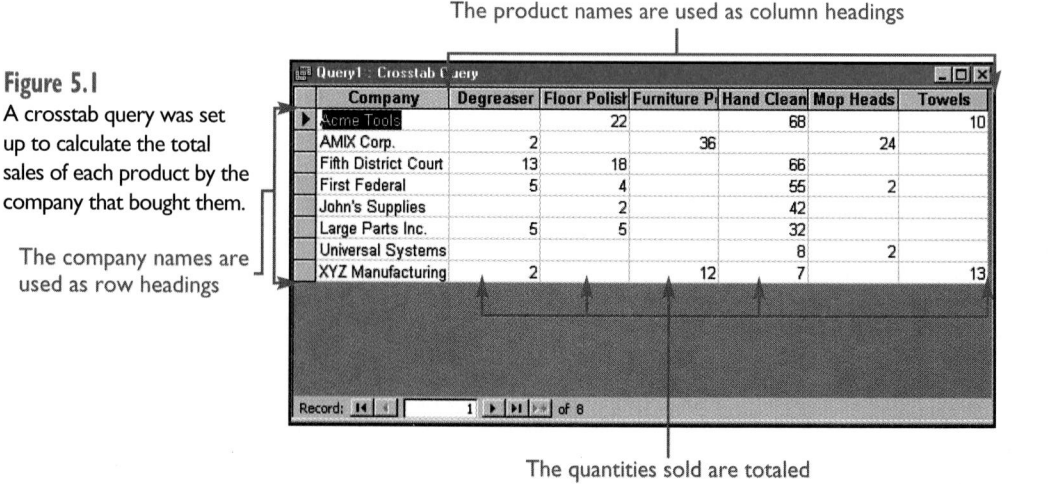

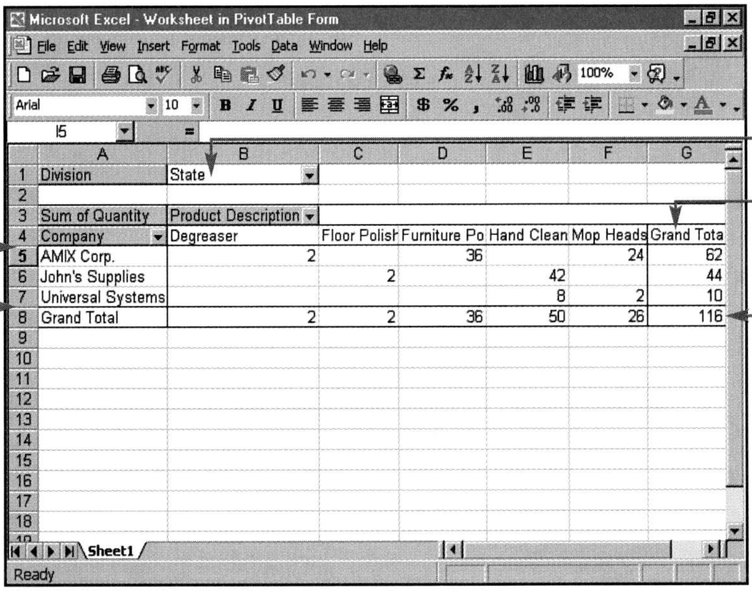

Companies in the selected Division

The division can be changed

Totals column

Totals row

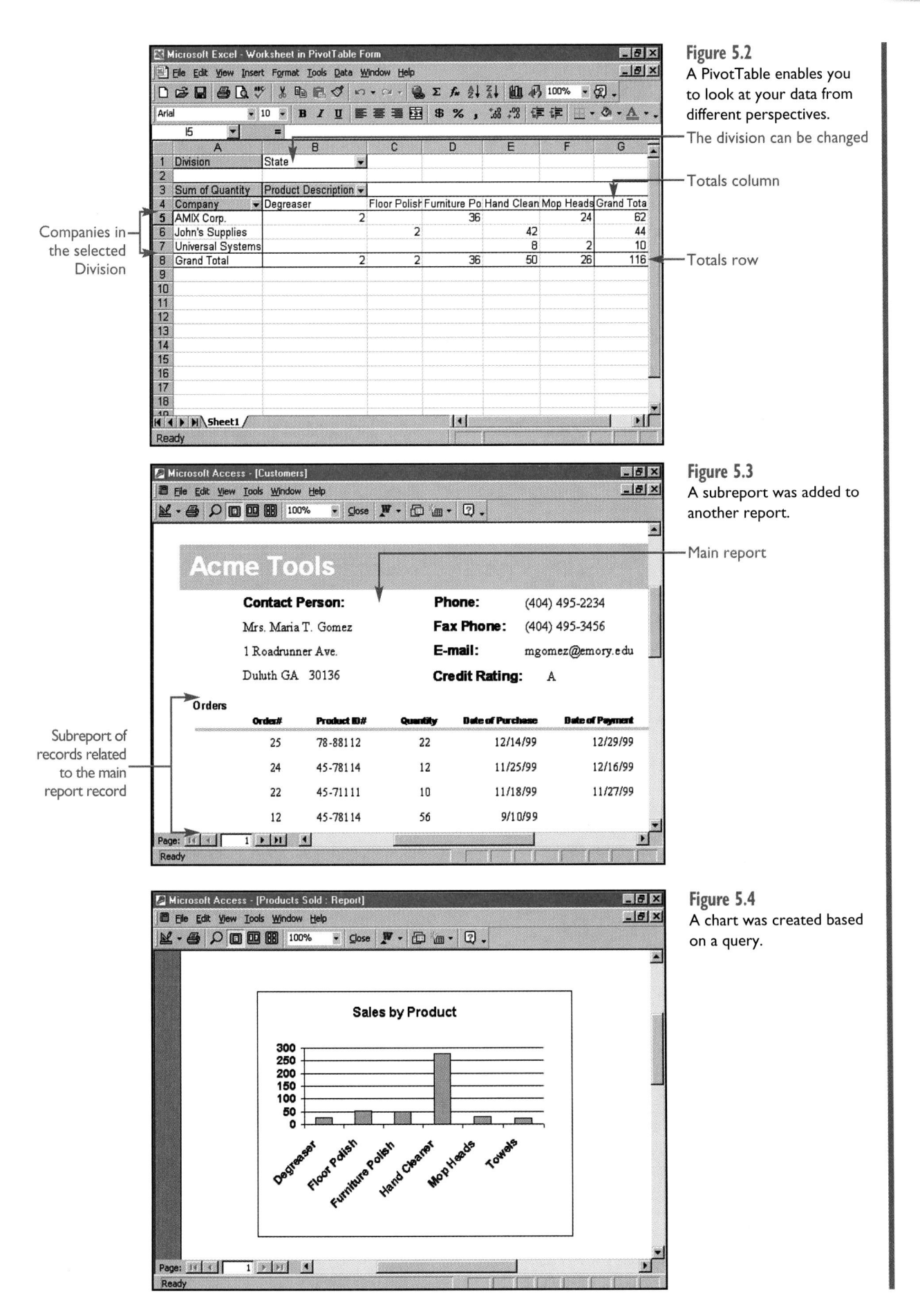

Figure 5.2
A PivotTable enables you to look at your data from different perspectives.

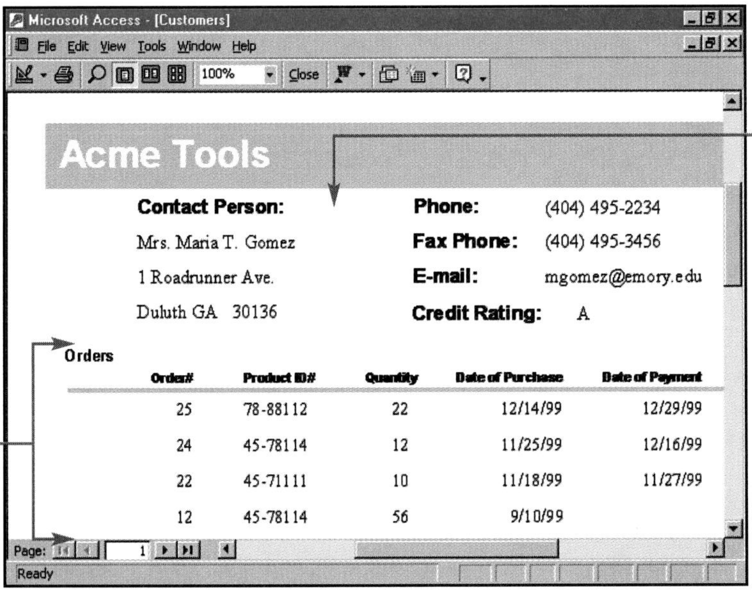

Main report

Subreport of records related to the main report record

Figure 5.3
A subreport was added to another report.

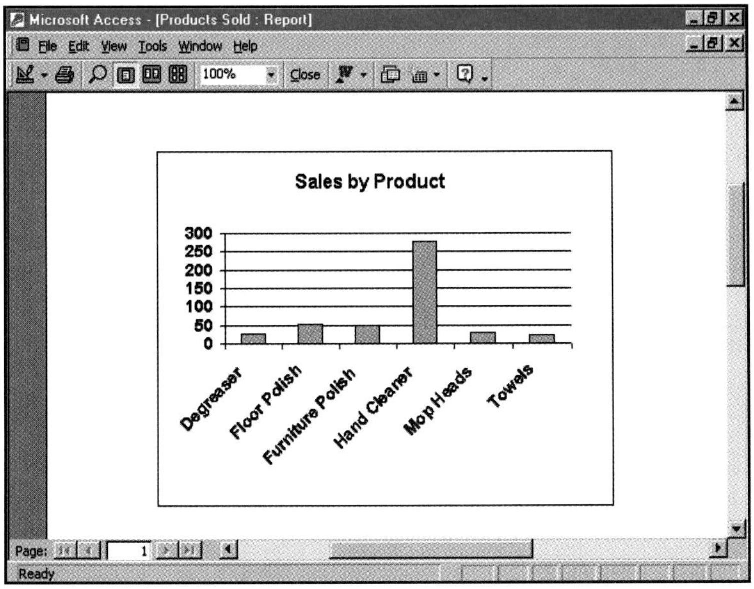

Figure 5.4
A chart was created based on a query.

Lesson 1: Using the Totals Tool in a Query

At times, you might want to use your database to retrieve simple summary information; that is, grouped data on one field and a calculation based on a second, related field. Access enables you to do this easily using a query and the Totals tool.

In this example, you create a query based on two tables that store the product name and the number of units sold for each product. The database you use for this project is a shortened database of information about the customers, products, and orders received by a small cleaning supply company during the second half of 1999.

To Use the Totals Tool in a Query

1. **Copy the AC3-0501 database file from the CD-ROM to drive A. Remove the Read-only status; rename the copy `Data Analysis`, and open the database.**
   The Database window should open in the Tables area.

2. **Click the Queries object button, if necessary, and then click the New button.**
   The New Query dialog box displays.

3. **Click Design View, and then click OK.**
   The Show Table dialog box displays four tables (see Figure 5.5).

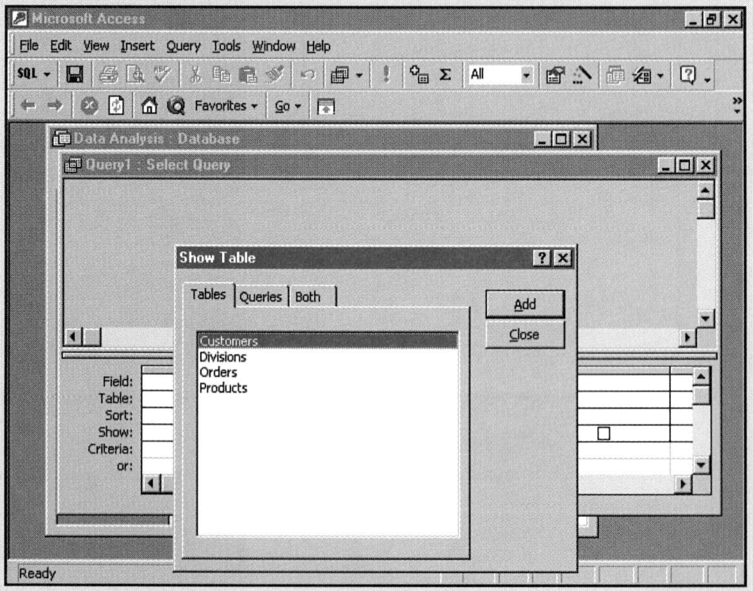

Figure 5.5
The Show Table dialog box displays the database tables.

4. **Select the Products table and click Add. Use the same procedure to add the Orders table, and then click the Close button in the Show Table dialog box.**
   The Products and Orders tables are added to the Query Design window. The Query Design window shows the Products and Orders tables and displays the one-to-many relationship between the Product ID# fields (see Figure 5.6).

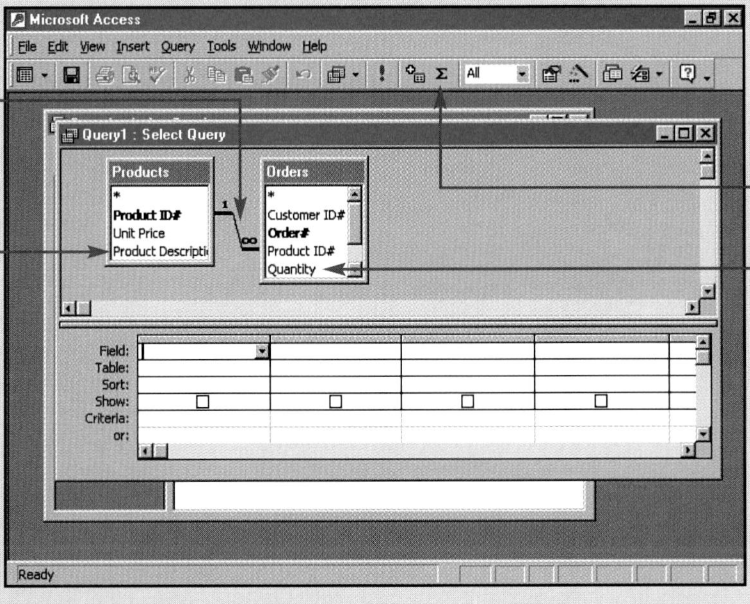

Figure 5.6
The Products and Orders tables were added to the Query Design window.

5 Double-click the Product Description field in the Products field list.
The Product Description field is added to the Field row.

6 Double-click the Quantity field in the Orders field list.
The Quantity field is added to the Field row.

7 Click the Totals button on the toolbar.
A new Total row is added to the query design grid (see Figure 5.7).

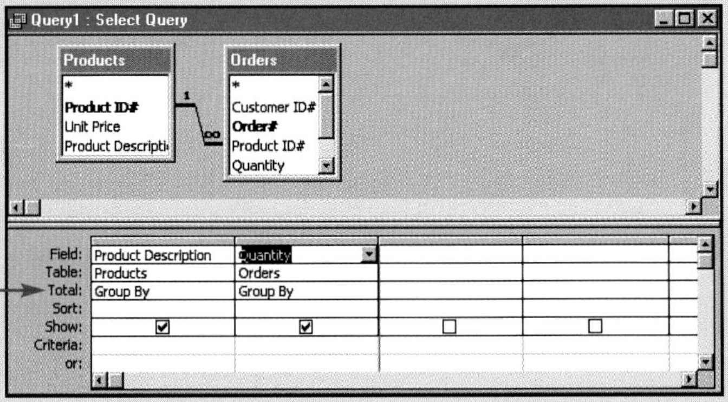

Figure 5.7
The query design grid now includes a Total row.

8 Click the Total box in the Quantity column in the query design grid. Click the down arrow and select Sum from the drop-down list.
The design grid shows you that when the query runs, you see the sums in the Quantity column displayed by product description (see Figure 5.8).

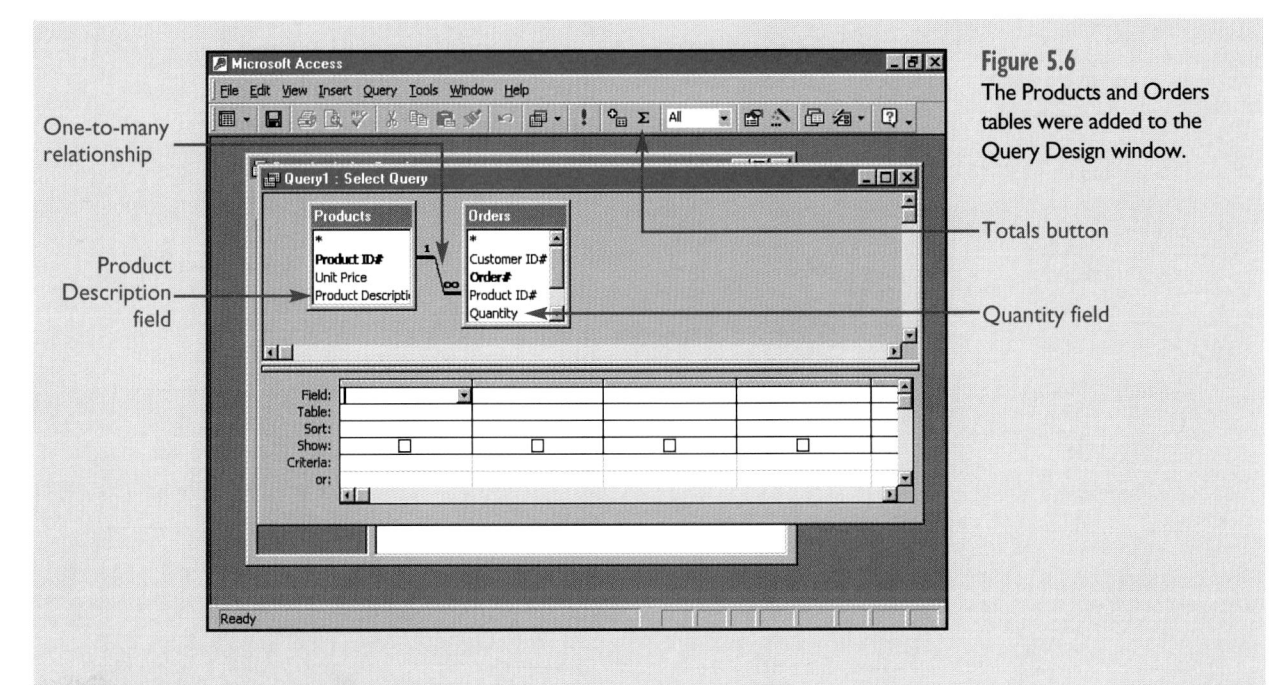

continues ▶

To Use the Totals Tool in a Query (continued)

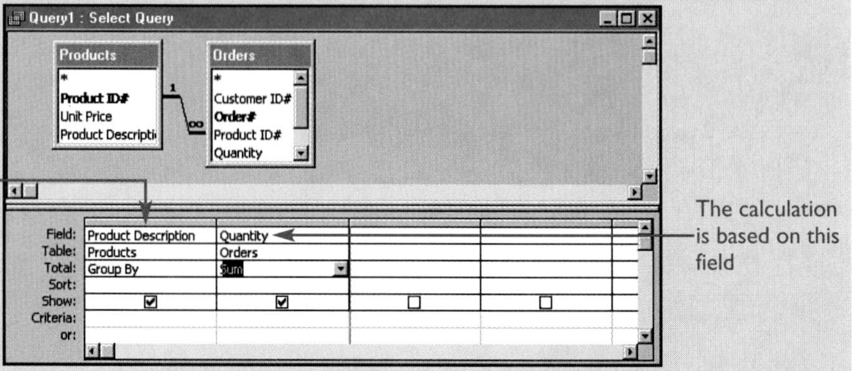

Figure 5.8
The resulting query displays the total number of orders by product description.

9. **Click the Run button to run the query.**
The query looks in the Products table to get the description of the product based on the Product ID# field, and then sums the total number of units ordered for each product (see Figure 5.9).

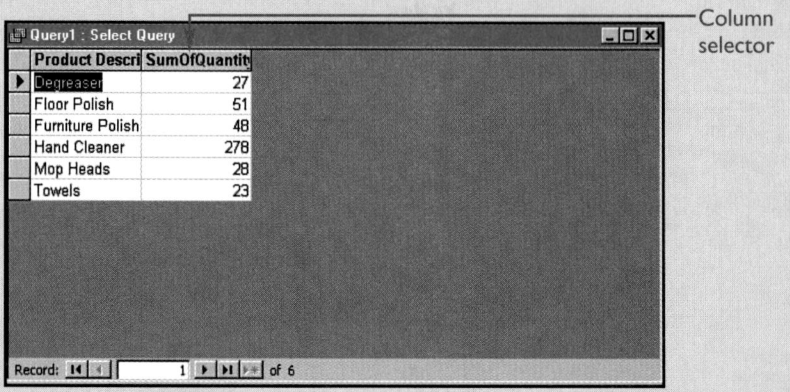

Figure 5.9
The query uses the Totals tool to calculate grouped data.

10. **Click the column selector for the SumOfQuantity column to select the column, and then click the Sort Descending button on the toolbar.**
The quantities are sorted from the highest to the lowest number of products ordered (see Figure 5.10).

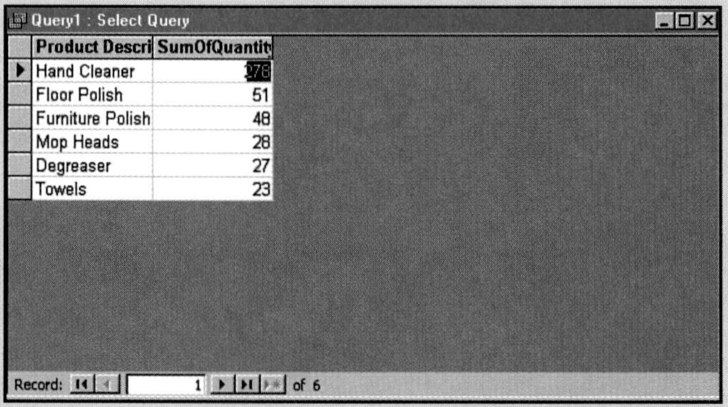

Figure 5.10
The quantities are sorted in descending order.

11. **Close the Query Design window and save the query as `Sales by Product`.**
Keep the database open for the next lesson.

Lesson 2: Creating Crosstab Queries and Reports

A Crosstab query produces a dynaset where the contents of one field provide the column headings and the contents of another field are used as row headings. The cells of the query are calculated based on the fields that match the values of both the row and column fields.

In this example, you create a Crosstab query based on three tables that show customer information and orders placed by those customers for various types of cleaning supplies. The Crosstab query calculates the quantity of each item sold to each customer.

To Create a Crosstab Query Based on Multiple Tables

1. **Click the Queries object button, and then click the New button.**
   The New Query dialog box displays.

2. **Click Design View, and then click OK.**

Using the Crosstab Query Wizard
You can also use the Crosstab Query Wizard to create a Crosstab query as you do in the Challenge exercises. In addition, the Design View option enables you to create Crosstab queries, but gives you more control over the process and lets you see how the process works—important knowledge when you need to create or modify more complex Crosstab queries.

3. **Select the Customers table and click Add. Use the same procedure to add the Orders and the Products tables; then click the Close button in the Show Table dialog box.**
   The Customers, Orders, and Products tables are added to the Query Design window. Notice that all three tables are related.

4. **Click the Query Type button and select the Crosstab Query option.**
   Notice that the query design grid has two new rows named Total and Crosstab (see Figure 5.11). The Show row is no longer shown because all the fields used in a crosstab query must be displayed.

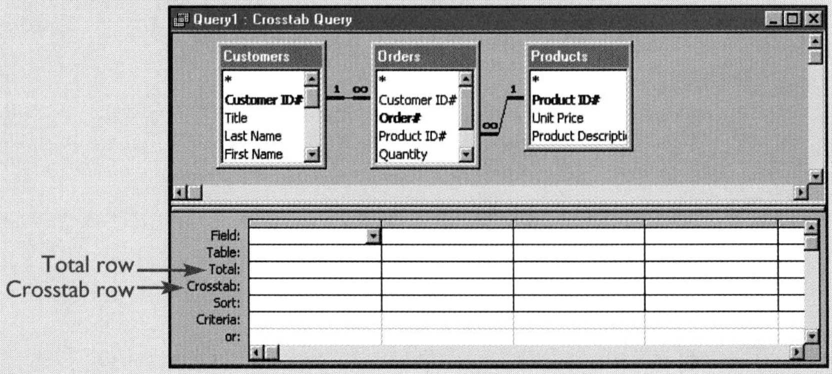

Figure 5.11
The Crosstab Query table includes Crosstab and Total rows in the query design grid.

5. **Scroll down the list of fields in the Customers table to the Company field. Double-click the field name to add this field to the first column of the query table.**

continues ▶

To Create a Crosstab Query Based on Multiple Tables (continued)

The first column shows the Company field and fills in the next two boxes with the table name and the default setting of Group By in the Total box.

The company names display as row headings on the left side of the Crosstab dynaset that is produced.

6. **Click the Crosstab box in the Company column, and then click the down arrow at the right side of the box to reveal a menu of choices.**
A menu of options for the Crosstab box is displayed (see Figure 5.12).

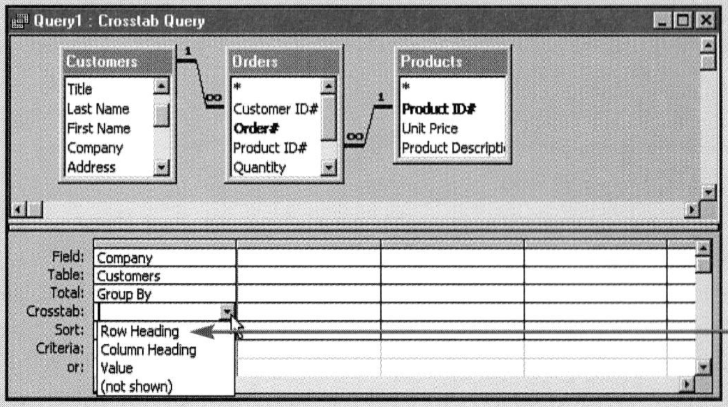

Figure 5.12
The Crosstab drop-down list gives you several options.

7. **Click the Row Heading option.**

8. **Scroll down the list of fields in the Products table. Double-click the Product Description field.**
The Product Description field displays in the second column in the query design grid. The names of each type of product are used as the column headings in the resulting Crosstab dynaset.

9. **Click the Crosstab box in the Product Description column and click the down arrow in that box. Select Column Heading from the list of options.**

10. **Double-click the Quantity field from the Orders table to place it in the third column.**
You want to know the quantity of each type of product sold to each customer and to display it in the cells of the resulting Crosstab dynaset.

11. **Click the Crosstab box in the Quantity column and click the down arrow in that box. Select Value from the list of options.**
This selection specifies that the program calculate a numeric result to be placed in the table. The last step in creating the Crosstab query is to change the Total box from Group By to a mathematical operation.

Minimum Requirements for a Crosstab Query
When you create a Crosstab query, you must identify at least one field as a column heading, one field as a value, and at least one field as a row heading. The order of these three fields is irrelevant.

You can have more than one row heading, which creates subheads in the rows, but the main row head field needs to be to the left of the subhead field.

⑫ **Click the Total box in the Quantity column, and then click the down arrow. Select Sum from the drop-down list.**

Your query design grid should look like Figure 5.13.

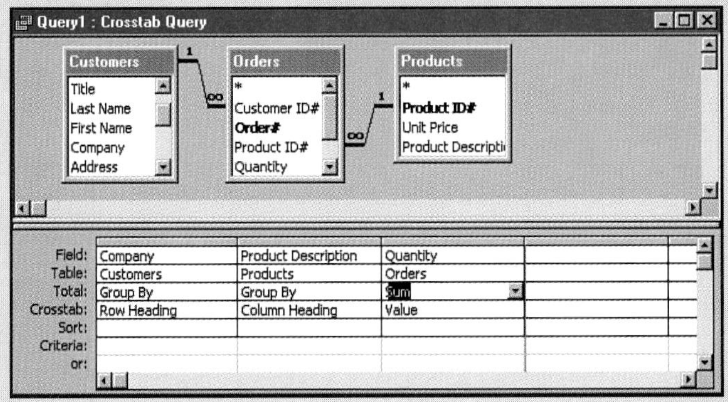

Figure 5.13
The Crosstab query setup is complete, with a row heading, a column heading, and a value field selected.

⑬ **Click the Run button on the toolbar.**

The Crosstab query displays in Datasheet view (see Figure 5.14). (Note: The column widths were decreased in this figure to fit all the fields on the screen.)

The crosstab query added all the sales of each product by company. The Customers table includes nine companies, but only eight are listed here because one of the customers did not place an order.

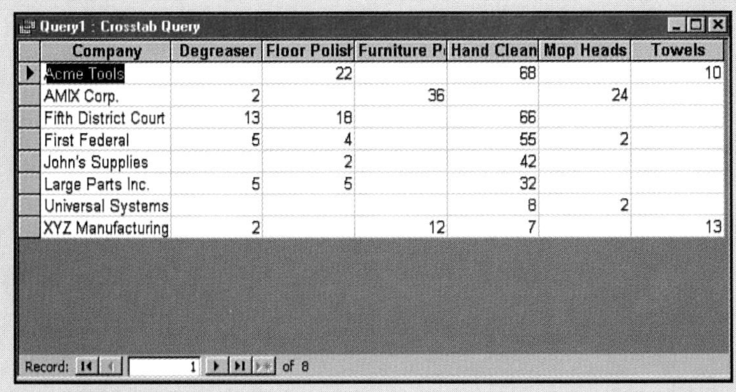

Company	Degreaser	Floor Polisl	Furniture P	Hand Clean	Mop Heads	Towels
Acme Tools		22		68		10
AMIX Corp.	2		36		24	
Fifth District Court	13	18		66		
First Federal	5	4		55	2	
John's Supplies		2		42		
Large Parts Inc.	5	5		32		
Universal Systems				8	2	
XYZ Manufacturing	2		12	7		13

Figure 5.14
The Crosstab query Datasheet view displays total unit sales by company and product.

⑭ **Close the query and save it with the name `Products Sold Listed by Customer`.**

Lesson 3: Creating Crosstab Queries with Conditions and Total Columns

It is possible to use criteria to limit the Crosstab query calculations. You can also include additional columns of summary data. Because the last quarter of the year is always slow, you offered an incentive for ordering more products; any purchasing agent who ordered more than $500 worth of cleaning supplies between October 1 and December 31 would receive a free gift. To find out who met your criteria, you need to create a Crosstab query that calculates the total dollar amount of orders by company for the fourth quarter of 1999.

In this lesson, you limit the orders in the Crosstab query to those sold between two given dates. You also add a column to the table to calculate the total amount of the orders for each customer.

To Use Criteria Based on Another Field in a Crosstab Query

1. **Select the Products Sold Listed by Customer query and click the Copy button.**
   You can use this query as the basis for your new query.

2. **Click the Paste button and type `Sales Incentive` in the Paste As dialog box. Open the Sales Incentive query in Design view.**

3. **In Design view of the crosstab query in the Data Analysis database, double-click the Date of Purchase field from the Orders table.**
   It is placed in the fourth column of the query design grid.

4. **Click the Total box in Date of Purchase column, and then click the down arrow to reveal the menu choices. Scroll down and click Expression.**
   The Total box in the fourth column now contains the word Expression.

5. **Enter the following expression in the Criteria box for the Date of Purchase column:**

   `Between 10/1/99 and 12/31/99`

   If you press ↵Enter or click another cell, the program adds # signs on either side of the dates (see Figure 5.15). (The fourth column in the figure was widened to show the expression. It is not necessary for you to do so.)

Figure 5.15
A Criteria expression is added to the Date of Purchase field.

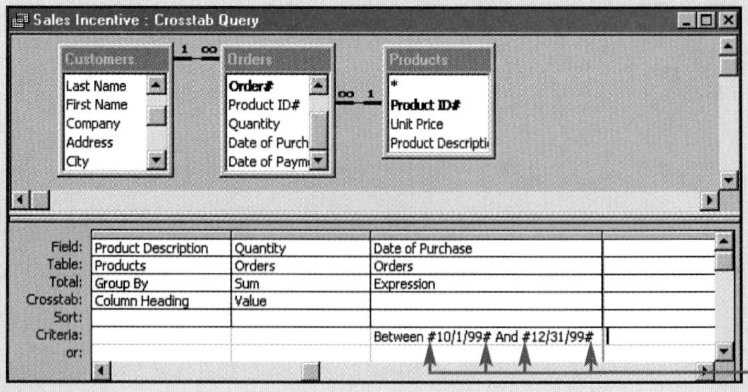

The Between Expression
The Between expression is inclusive; that is, purchases made on the beginning and ending dates are included in the query table.

6. **Click the Run button to view the Crosstab Query datasheet.**
   The table includes only those purchases made between October and December 1999 (see Figure 5.16). Refer to Figure 5.14 in Lesson 2 to see the differences between the numbers. Notice that there are only seven companies listed; one of the companies that placed orders in the third quarter did not place any orders in the fourth quarter.

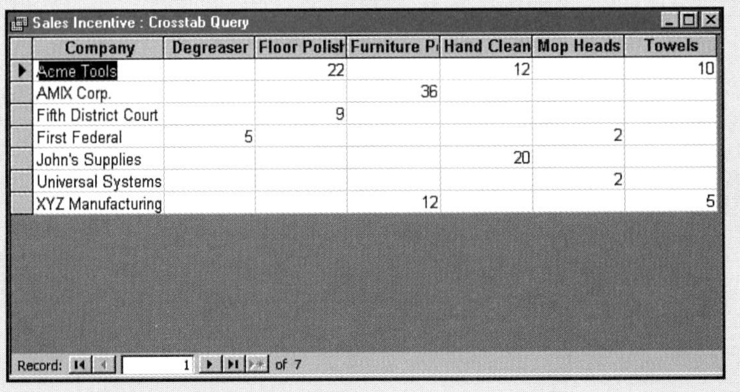

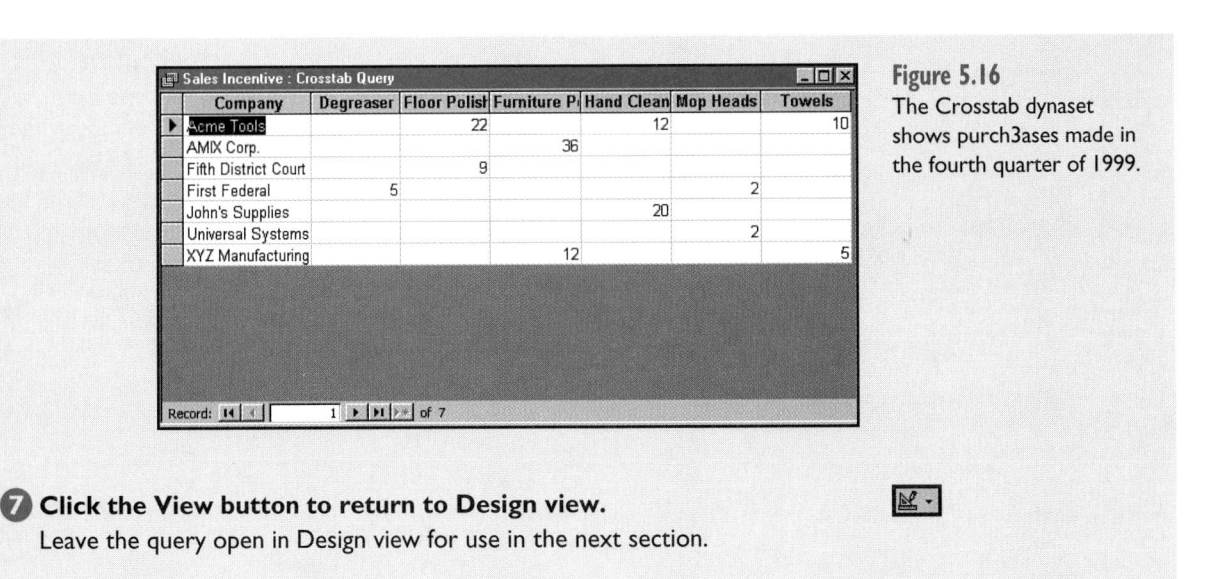

Figure 5.16
The Crosstab dynaset shows purch3ases made in the fourth quarter of 1999.

7 Click the View button to return to Design view.
Leave the query open in Design view for use in the next section.

Now you know the number of units of each product sold to each company during the fourth quarter of 1999. To find out which purchasing agents should be receiving gifts, you need to get a total dollar volume of sales to each company for the same period.

To Include a Column of Totals in a Crosstab Query

1 Enter the following expression in the fifth Field box:

`Amount: [Quantity]*[Unit Price]`

The words to the left of the colon are the label for the new column. The expression to the right of the colon multiplies the contents of the Quantity and Unit Price fields for each type of purchase by each customer. Each field in the expression must be enclosed by its own set of brackets. The mathematical symbol (in this case *) is outside of square brackets.

2 Click the Crosstab box in the new column. Click the down arrow, and then click Row Heading.
Even though you are seeking to produce a column of totals, the program considers the totals to be row headings. Notice that the Total box has the default entry Group By (see Figure 5.17).

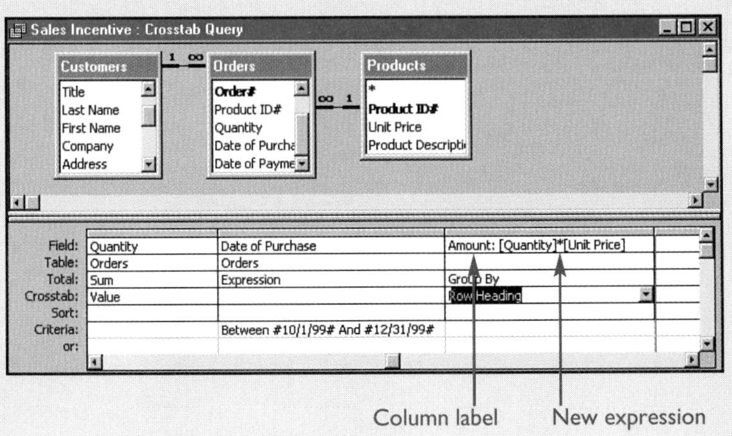

Figure 5.17
The Row Heading option has been selected in the Crosstab row.

continues ▶

To Include a Column of Totals in a Crosstab Query (continued)

3 Click the Run button to run the Crosstab query.

The Crosstab query displays the cost for each purchase by customer with a separate row for each purchase (see Figure 5.18). This is useful in some situations, but is not what you want here.

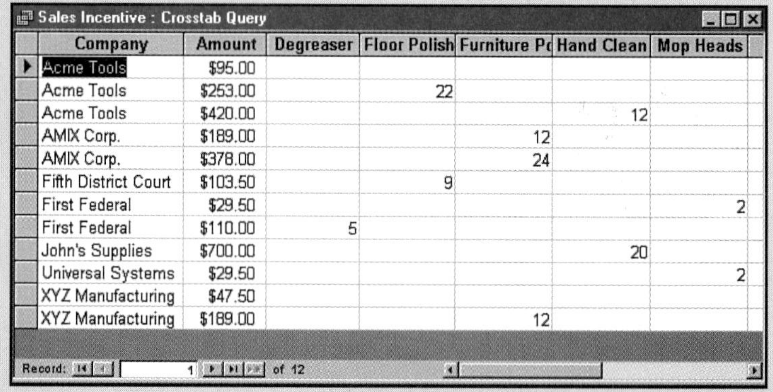

Company	Amount	Degreaser	Floor Polish	Furniture P(	Hand Clean	Mop Heads
Acme Tools	$95.00					
Acme Tools	$253.00		22			
Acme Tools	$420.00				12	
AMIX Corp.	$189.00			12		
AMIX Corp.	$378.00			24		
Fifth District Court	$103.50		9			
First Federal	$29.50					2
First Federal	$110.00	5				
John's Supplies	$700.00				20	
Universal Systems	$29.50					2
XYZ Manufacturing	$47.50					
XYZ Manufacturing	$189.00			12		

Figure 5.18
The Crosstab query shows the cost for each purchase by customer with a separate row for each purchase.

4 Click the View button to return to Design view.

5 Click the Total box in the Amount column that was added in step 1, and then click the down arrow and select Sum.

This creates a sum to show the total cost of all purchases for each customer.

6 Click the Run button to view the Crosstab Query datasheet.

The Orders expression column now shows a total for each customer for each product. These totals are considered row headers (see Figure 5.19).

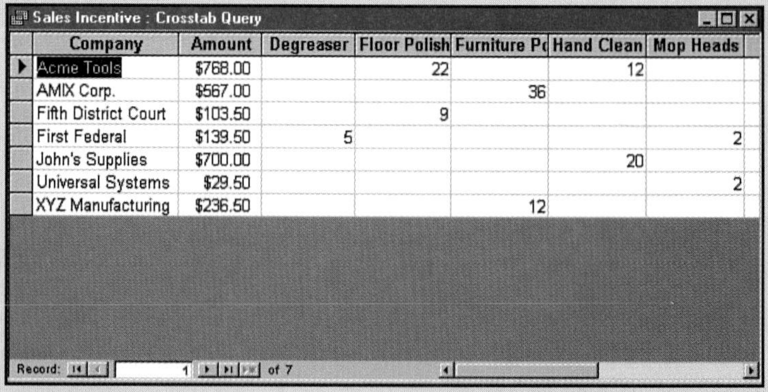

Company	Amount	Degreaser	Floor Polish	Furniture P(	Hand Clean	Mop Heads
Acme Tools	$768.00		22		12	
AMIX Corp.	$567.00			36		
Fifth District Court	$103.50		9			
First Federal	$139.50	5				2
John's Supplies	$700.00				20	
Universal Systems	$29.50					2
XYZ Manufacturing	$236.50			12		

Figure 5.19
The Crosstab query displays the total dollar value of orders for each customer during the fourth quarter.

7 Close the query and save your changes.

Leave the database open for use in the next lesson.

Creating Crosstab Queries

Crosstab queries can be confusing if you jump into the design of one without a clear objective in mind. Decide ahead of time which field should be used as a row header or column header. Determine which field should be used to calculate the value in each cell and what mathematical expression to use.

The Crosstab Query Wizard creates simple Crosstab queries for you. You must have at least one choice for row, column, and value fields. You have an option of adding a totals column. If you want to use a calculated expression, you can use the wizard to create most of the query and then modify the design.

Lesson 4: Analyzing Data Using PivotTables

A PivotTable is an interactive table used to perform calculations, and is often the best way to analyze large amounts of complex data. PivotTables are usually associated with Excel worksheets, but can be created in Access and edited using Excel tools. In Access, a PivotTable displays as a form enabling you to print data on a separate page for each change in a selected category. Although a PivotTable performs in a similar manner to a crosstab query, it offers greater flexibility to analyze data in different ways. Rather than having to create a new query, you can use a PivotTable and rearrange row headings, column headings, and page fields until you achieve the desired results.

In this example, you create a PivotTable based on a query in the Data Analysis table.

To Create a PivotTable

1. **Click the Forms object button and click the New button.**
2. **Select PivotTable Wizard and choose the Sales by Product, Customer, and Division query from the drop-down list in the New Form dialog box. Click OK.**

   The first PivotTable Wizard screen displays a sample PivotTable on the left and a good description of PivotTables on the right (see Figure 5.20). Take a few moments to look at the example figures and read the description.

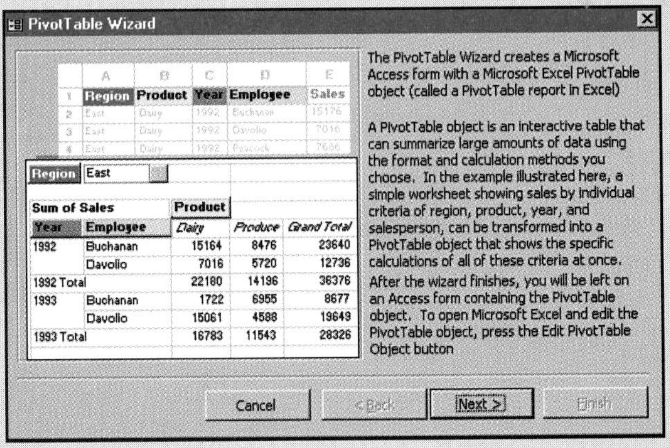

Figure 5.20
The first PivotTable Wizard dialog box contains information about the use and structure of PivotTables.

continues ▶

To Create a PivotTable (continued)

3 Click Next, and then click the Select All button.

All the fields in the query move from the Available Fields box to the Fields Chosen for Pivoting box (see Figure 5.21).

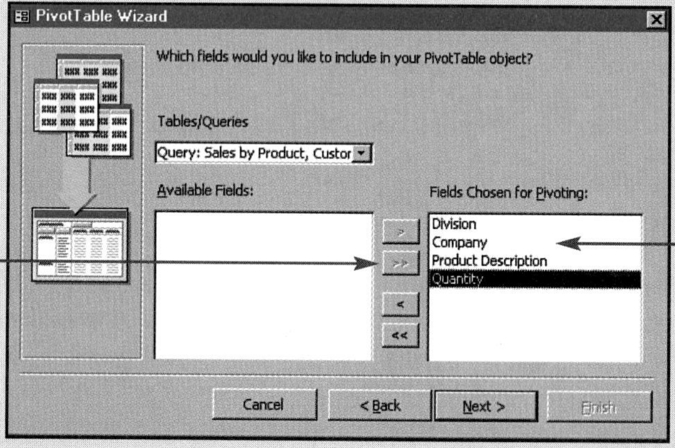

Figure 5.21
All the query fields are selected.

4 Click the Next button.

After a few moments, a third PivotTable Wizard dialog box displays. This dialog box enables you to make changes in the layout and operation of the PivotTable (see Figure 5.22). If it is the first time the PivotTable Wizard is used, the program asks whether you want help with this feature.

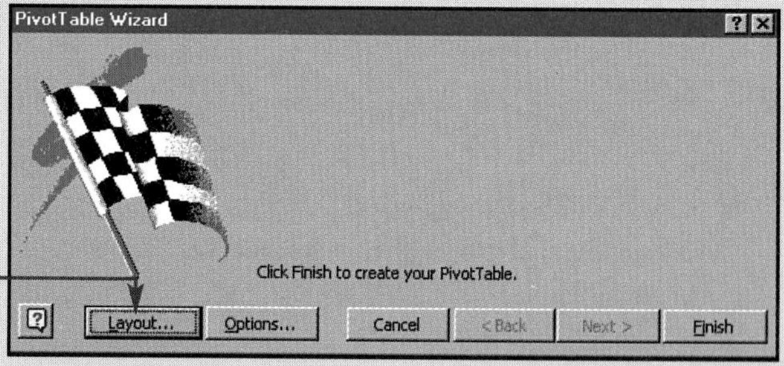

Figure 5.22
The third PivotTable Wizard dialog box enables you to change the layout and options of the PivotTable.

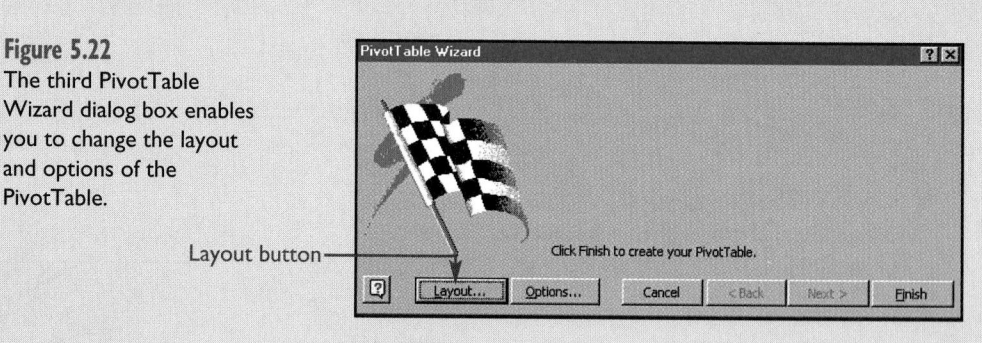

You must have Excel installed on your machine for this procedure to work. If you get an error message telling you that the program can't find Excel, install Excel on your current machine, move to another machine, or skip the rest of this lesson.

5 Click the Layout button.

A layout screen displays. In this screen, you drag the fields that you selected from the list on the right edge of the dialog box to their desired locations on the form.

6 Drag the Division field to the PAGE box, the Company field to the ROW box, the Product Description field to the COLUMN box, and the Quantity field to the DATA box.

Your screen setup should look like Figure 5.23.

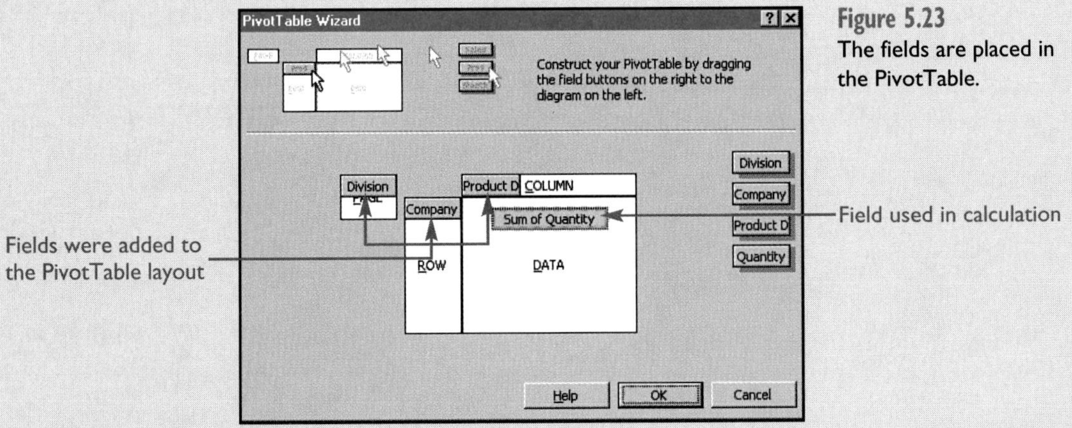

Figure 5.23
The fields are placed in the PivotTable.

Using the PivotTable Effectively
Several options are available to you for displaying data in a PivotTable. You can always move back to this layout form and move the fields between the four parts of the PivotTable. You can also use subgroups. For example, in the PivotTable you are currently creating, if each Company field had several locations, the field containing the location data could be added to the ROW box and the data would then display with location totals, company totals, and a grand total.

7 Click OK to close the Layout dialog box, and then click Finish to close the last PivotTable Wizard dialog box.
The PivotTable displays in Access (see Figure 5.24).

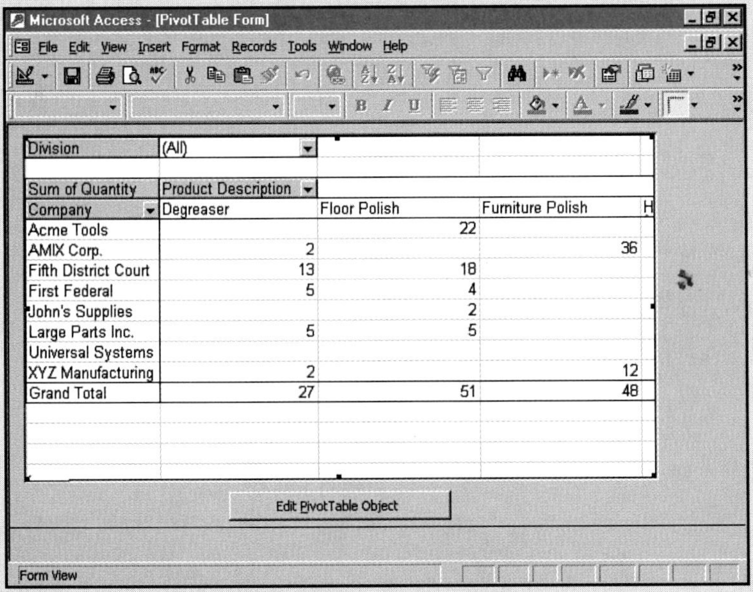

Division	(All)		
Sum of Quantity	Product Description		
Company	Degreaser	Floor Polish	Furniture Polish
Acme Tools		22	
AMIX Corp.	2		36
Fifth District Court	13	18	
First Federal	5	4	
John's Supplies		2	
Large Parts Inc.	5	5	
Universal Systems			
XYZ Manufacturing	2		12
Grand Total	27	51	48

Figure 5.24
The PivotTable form displays in Access.

8 Click the Save button and save the form as `PivotTable`.

continues ▶

To Create a PivotTable (continued)

9 Maximize the PivotTable Form window. Click the Edit PivotTable Object button at the bottom of the PivotTable.

The PivotTable opens in Excel. This enables you to change the way you look at your data. It also enables you to modify the page layout.

10 Maximize the window, if necessary. Click anywhere inside the PivotTable, and then select Data, Refresh Data from the menu.

This refreshes the underlying Access data for the Excel PivotTable. If the pointer is in a cell outside the PivotTable boundaries, the Refresh Data option is unavailable in the menu.

11 Click the drop-down arrow for the Division page; select State, and click OK.

12 Maximize the window, if necessary, and then click the column selector for column B and drag to the right until you have selected all the columns containing data, including the Grand Total column.

13 Double-click one of the column separator lines to resize the column widths. Adjust the columns individually, if necessary, to see all the fields on screen at the same time.

Your screen should look like Figure 5.25.

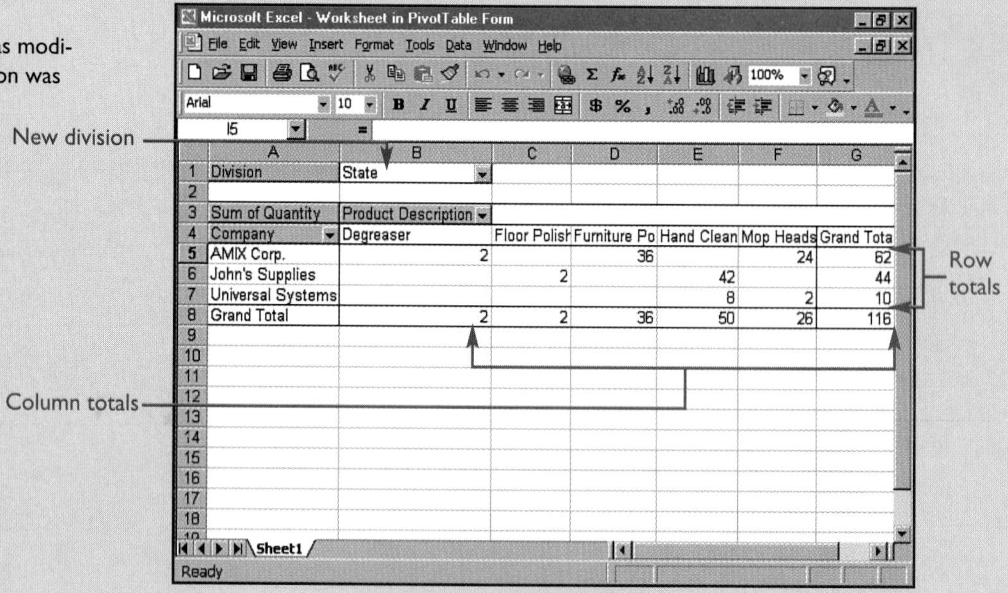

Figure 5.25
The PivotTable was modified, and the division was changed.

14 Click the drop-down arrow for the Division page; select International, and click OK.

The two companies in the International division are listed.

15 Close Excel, and then close the PivotTable form.

Leave the database open for the next lesson.

Lesson 5: Adding a Subform to an Existing Form

It is often useful to be able to review the data in joined tables simultaneously. Using the form/subform approach, you can create an individualized statement that shows all the orders placed by one customer on a single form. The ***subform*** is a form placed within another (main) form, showing data from another table related to the selected record from the main form. This provides a reporting tool that could be used to communicate with customers, or it could be used by sales representatives to track sales by customer.

If you used the *Access 2000 Essentials Intermediate* book, you learned how to create a form/subform using the Form Wizard. In this lesson, you take an existing form, open it in Design view, and add another existing form to it. You also modify the new form so that you can print a copy of it as a report of a customer's orders. You place a form based on a customer orders table (the subform) within another form based on a table of general customer information.

To Add a Subform to an Existing Form

1. **In the Data Analysis database, click the Forms object button; click the Company Information form, and then click the Design button.**
The Company Information form opens in Design view.

   The first step in adding a subform to an existing form is to open the form that is based on the table that has the primary key field on the "one" side of the one-to-many relationship. This is the main part of the form. In this case, the Company Information table contains the primary key field, Customer ID#.

   The Primary Key Field in the Main Form
   The main form needs to contain the primary key field that links to the subform, but it is not necessary to display the primary key field in the form.

2. **Maximize the Design window, if necessary. Click the Toolbox button on the toolbar if the toolbox is not already displayed on the screen.**

3. **Click the Subform/Subreport button on the toolbox. Draw a rectangle that fits in the lower portion of the open form.**
When you draw the rectangle, it appears as a thin line. This marks the boundary of the subform (see Figure 5.26).

continues ▶

To Add a Subform to an Existing Form (continued)

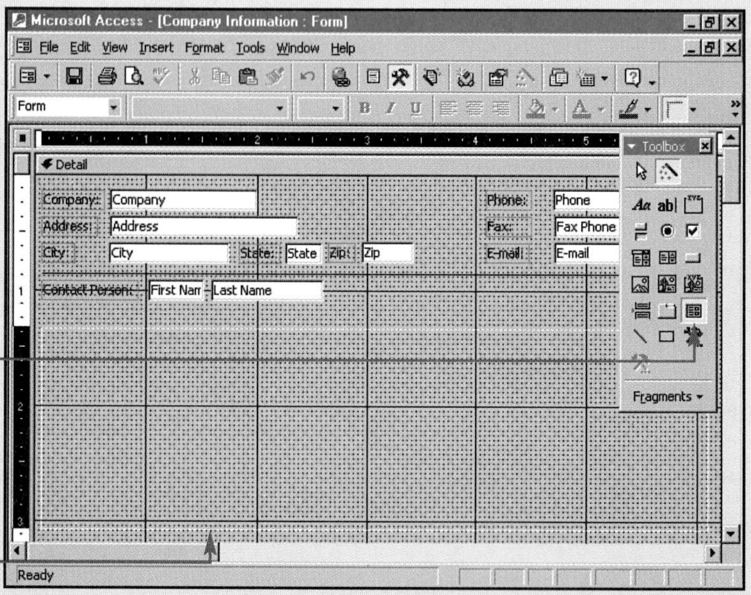

Figure 5.26
The Company Information form displays the designated area for the subform.

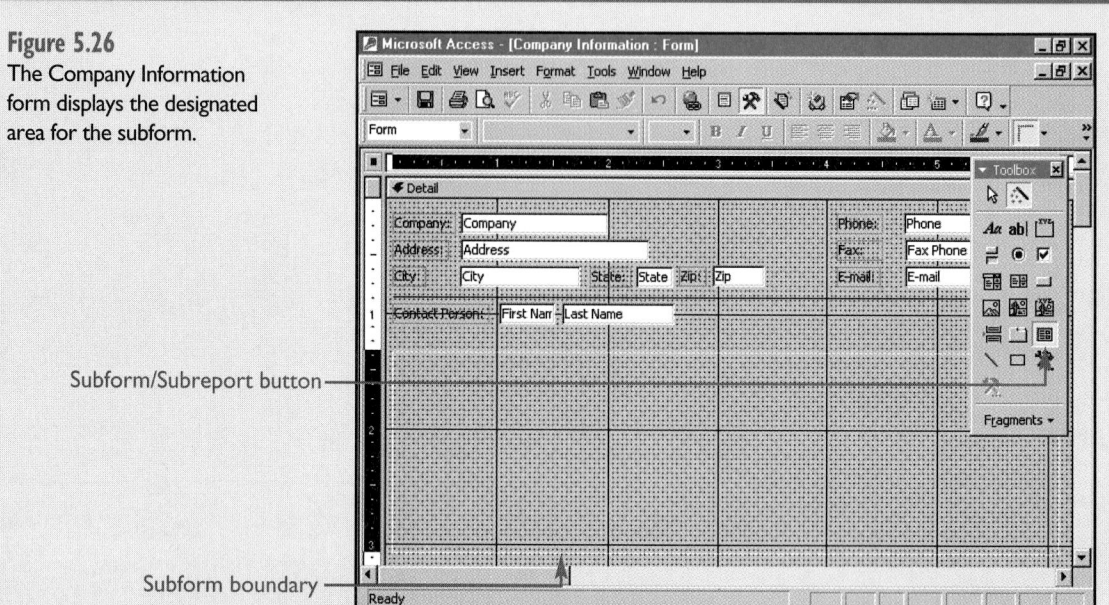

❹ **Release the mouse button.**
When you release the mouse button, the Subform/Subreport Wizard is activated. After a short delay, the first SubForm Wizard dialog box displays and asks whether you want to draw the data from a table or query, or to use an existing form.

❺ **Select the Use an existing form option, and then select the Orders form, if necessary.**
The SubForm Wizard dialog box should look like Figure 5.27.

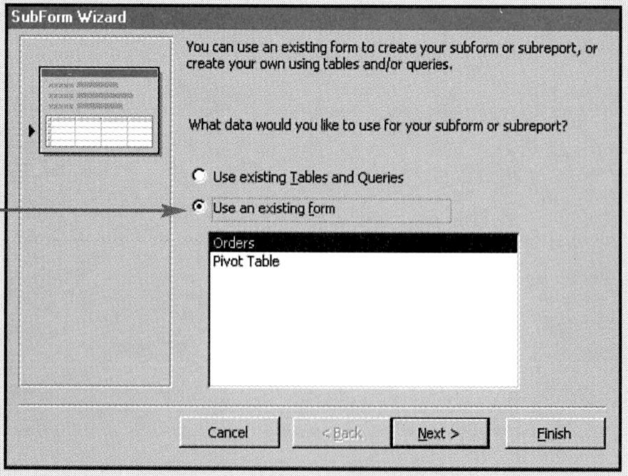

Figure 5.27
The first SubForm Wizard dialog box asks for a data source.

❻ **Click Next.**
The second SubForm Wizard dialog box displays (see Figure 5.28). It identifies the field that links the two tables and gives you the option of linking the two forms using that field, leaving the two forms unlinked, or defining your own link.

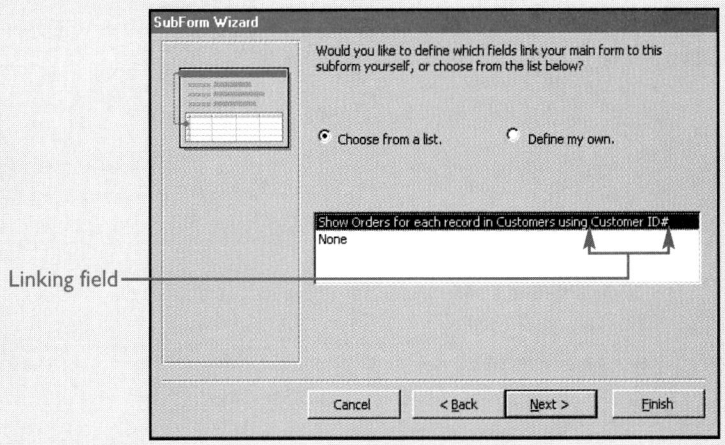

Figure 5.28
The second SubForm Wizard dialog box enables you to identify the field you want to link between the main form and the subform.

7. **Accept the default settings to use the Customer ID# field as the link. Click Next.**
   The final SubForm Wizard asks for a name for the subform.

8. **Click the Finish button to accept the default name, Orders.**
   The wizard finishes the design and returns you to the design of the Company Information form.

9. **Click the View button to switch to Form view.**
   The Company Information form displays with the subform Orders embedded in it. The subform used in this example is a tabular form (see Figure 5.29).

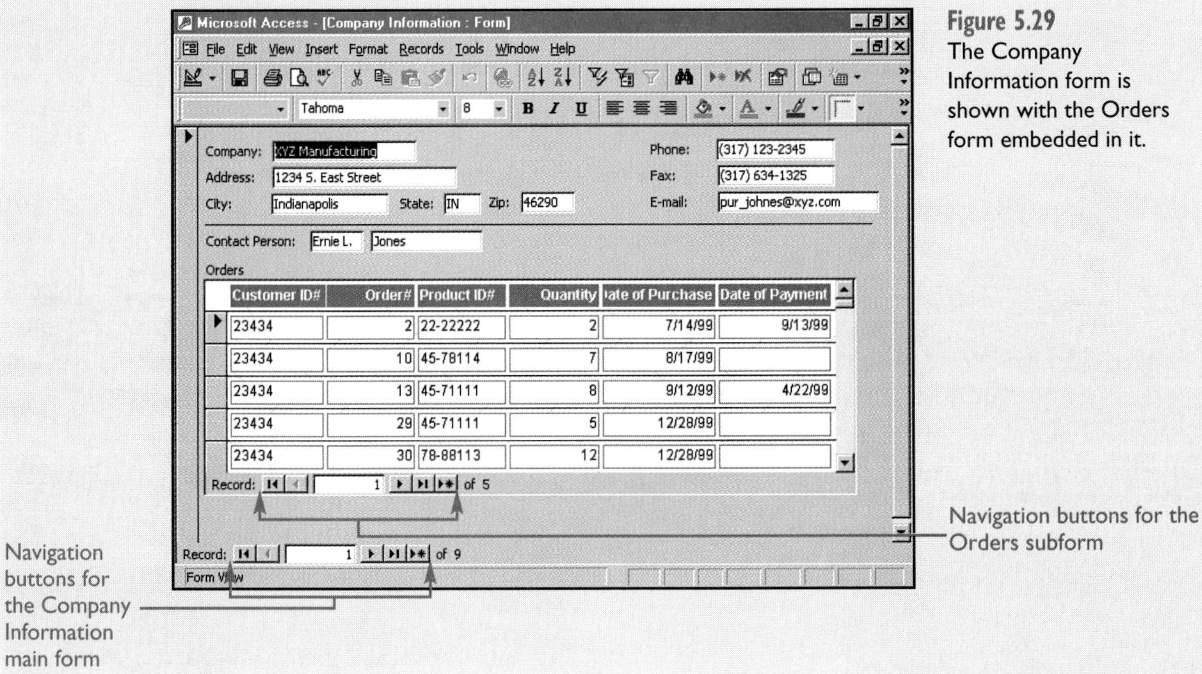

Figure 5.29
The Company Information form is shown with the Orders form embedded in it.

continues ▶

To Add a Subform to an Existing Form (continued)

Formatting the Subform
If you don't like the way the subform looks, you can move back to Design view and adjust the size of the subform by clicking anywhere in the subform and using the sizing handles. You can also resize column widths and change character formatting, as you can with the main form.

10. **Click the Next Record navigation button for the Company Information form.**
Notice that the Orders form shows only the records that match the customer in the Company Information form.

11. **Continue to click the Next Record button for the Company Information form until you get to the seventh record.**
Notice that the Orders subform remains empty because there are no related records for that company.

12. **Close the form and save the changes.**

Creating a Separate Subform
When you use the Form Wizard to create a form with a subform, the subform is saved separately. When you use the previous procedure to add a subform, it is embedded in the main form and no separate form is created.

Lesson 6: Inserting Subreports into Reports Using the Subform/Subreport Wizard

It is also possible to combine two reports that are based on joined tables. In this lesson, you learn how to combine a report that shows the customer information from the Customers table with the individual orders by that customer shown in a tabular format report.

First, you preview the two reports that are to be joined. These reports are already provided. The Customers report is based on the Customers table and was created with a columnar AutoReport and then modified by rearranging the fields. The Orders report is based on the Orders table and was created with a tabular AutoReport.

To Preview the Two Reports

1. **In the Data Analysis database, click the Reports object button. Double-click the Customers report.**
The preview of the Customers report displays. This will be the main report.

2. **Maximize the Report window, if necessary. Scroll around to view the report, and use the navigation buttons to examine more than one page.**
Information about each company displays (see Figure 5.30).

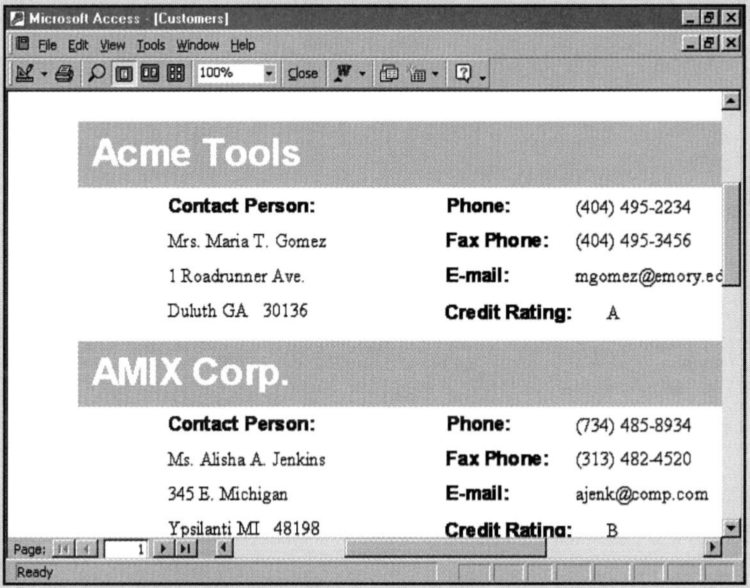

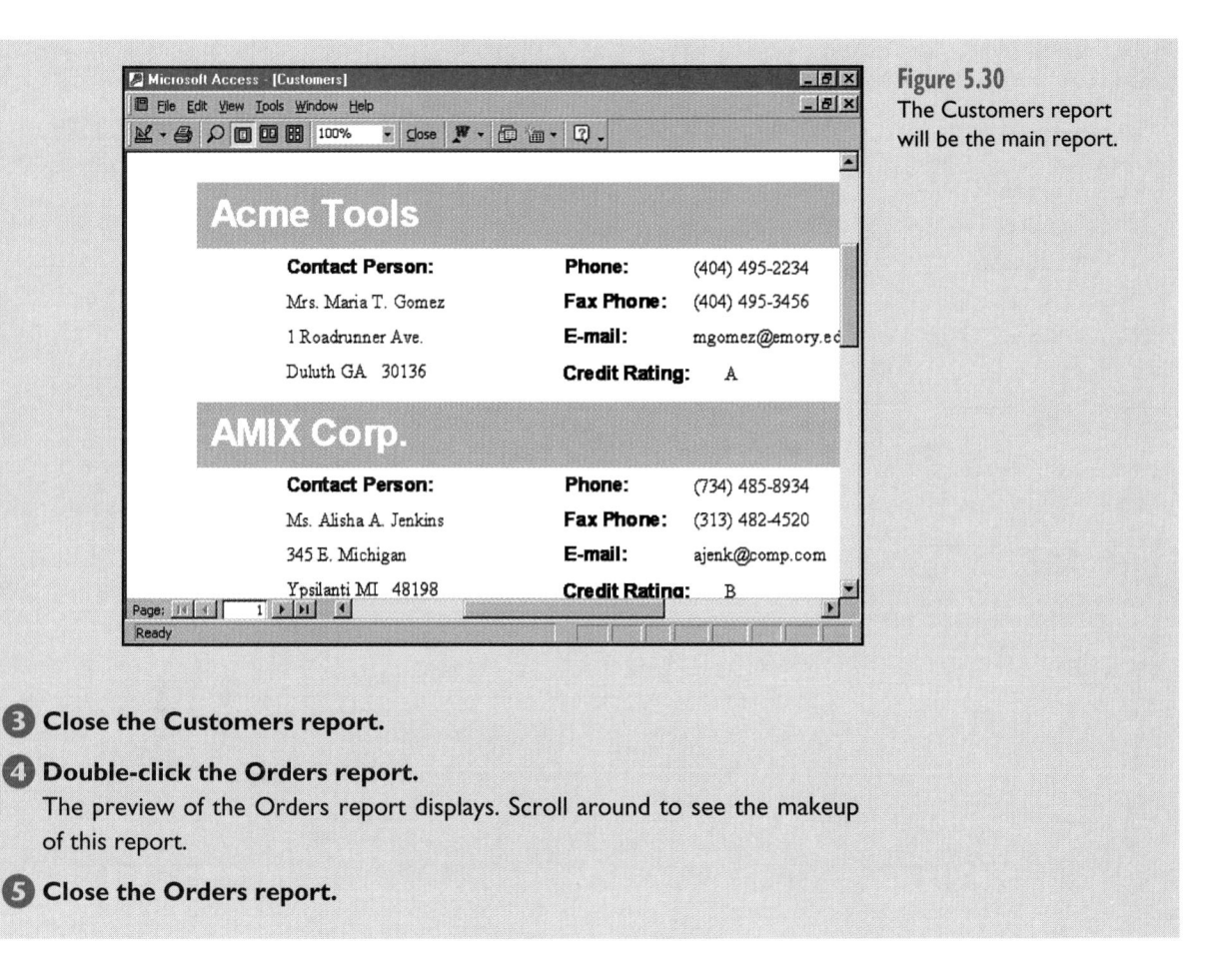

Figure 5.30
The Customers report will be the main report.

3. **Close the Customers report.**
4. **Double-click the Orders report.**
   The preview of the Orders report displays. Scroll around to see the makeup of this report.
5. **Close the Orders report.**

In the next section, you learn how to make the Orders report a subreport of the Customers report. A ***subreport*** is a report placed within another (main) report, showing data from another table related to the selected record from the main report.

To Combine the Reports

1. **Click the Customers report to select it, and then click Design. Click the Toolbox button to open the toolbox, if necessary.**
   The Customers report opens in Design view (see Figure 5.31).

continues ▶

To Combine the Reports (continued)

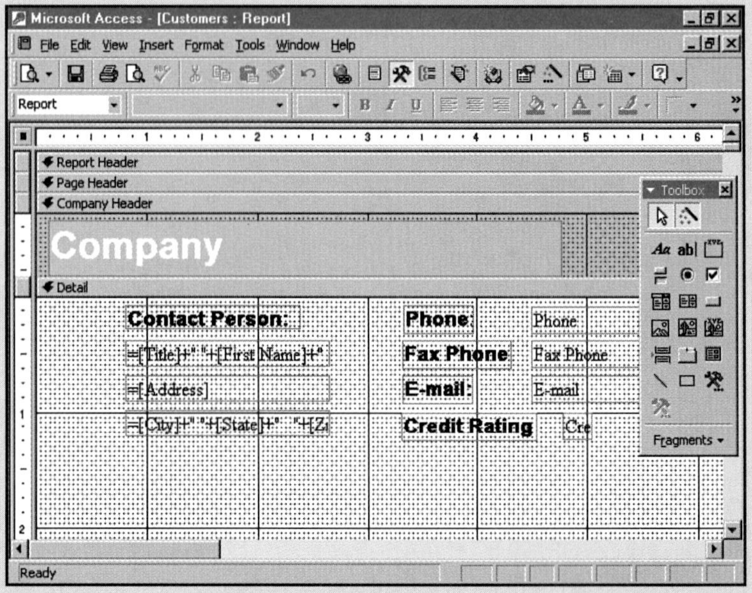

Figure 5.31
The Design view of the Customers report shows the report layout.

2 **Maximize the report Design window, if necessary, and scroll down to show the bottom part of the report design.**

The bottom portion of the Detail area is empty. This is where the subreport will be added.

3 **Click the Subform/Subreport button in the toolbox and draw a rectangle in the Detail area of the report design.**

The rectangle indicates the location of the subform (see Figure 5.32).

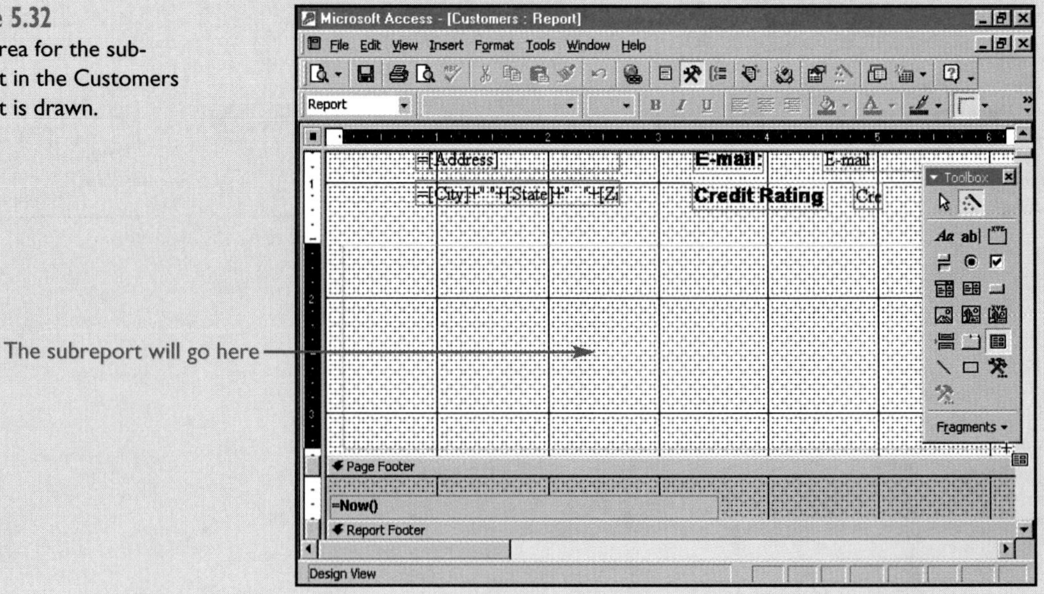

Figure 5.32
The area for the subreport in the Customers report is drawn.

When you release the mouse button, the first Subform/Subreport Wizard dialog box displays.

4 Select the Use an existing report or form option and make sure the Orders report is selected.

The Subform/Subreport Wizard dialog box enables you to select an existing report, to create a new report from a table or query, or use an existing form. Make sure you choose the Orders report, not the Orders form.

5 Click Next.

The second dialog box displays. If the reports you selected are based on tables that are joined in a one-to-many relationship, you see a choice that links the reports in the same way.

6 Select the Choose from a list option, if necessary. Select the first link, entitled Show Orders for each record in Customers using Customer ID#. Click Next.

Both of these options should be the defaults. The final dialog box asks for a name for the subreport.

7 Accept the default name `Orders` and click Finish.

The wizard places the subreport in the report design. The title of the subreport may overlap the bottom row of fields in the Customer table. Notice that the size of the subreport does not match the rectangle you drew (see Figure 5.33).

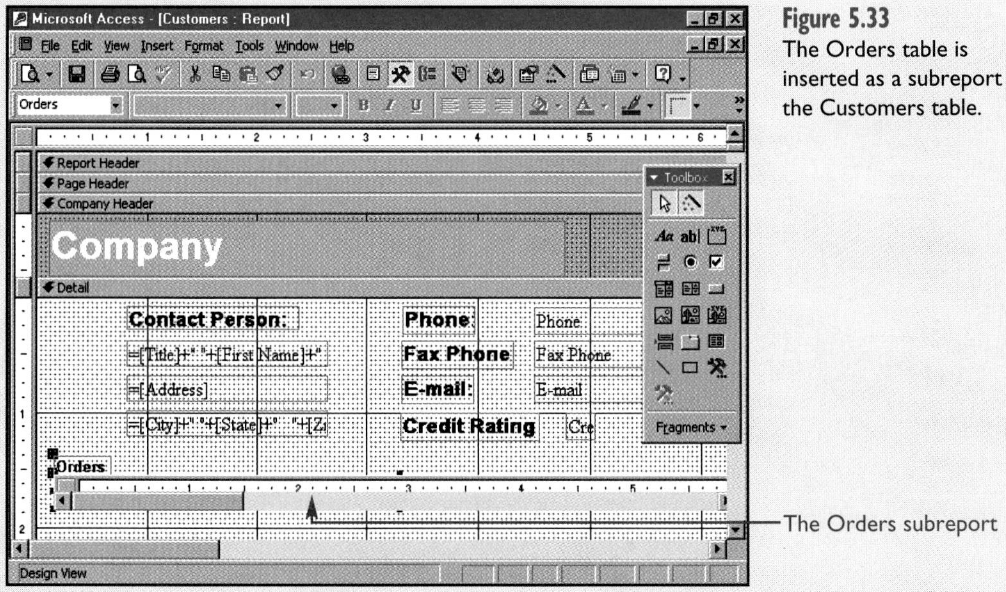

Figure 5.33
The Orders table is inserted as a subreport in the Customers table.

If the Orders subreport overlaps the bottom fields in the Customers report, you can move it down. Click the subreport. Move to the top of the subreport until the pointer changes to a hand, and then click and drag the subreport to the desired location.

continues ▶

To Combine the Reports (continued)

8 Click the Print Preview button on the toolbar to preview the report. Maximize the window, if necessary.

Notice that the list of orders is restricted to those that match the customer information above. Also, an extra "Orders" title is automatically included in the program (see Figure 5.34).

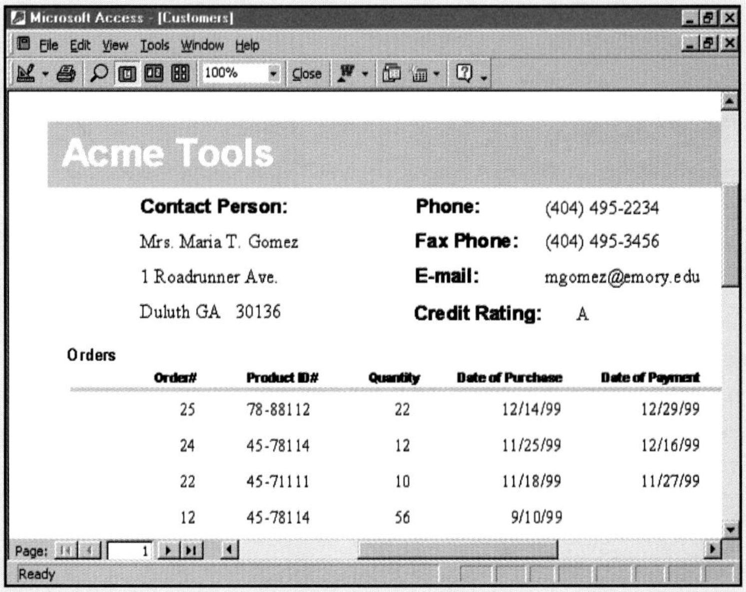

Figure 5.34
A preview of the final report shows the orders for one customer.

9 Use the navigation buttons to scroll through the report. Click anywhere on the report to see a full-page view.

Notice that the report shows only one company per page.

10 Close the report and save the changes.

Leave the database open for use in the next lesson.

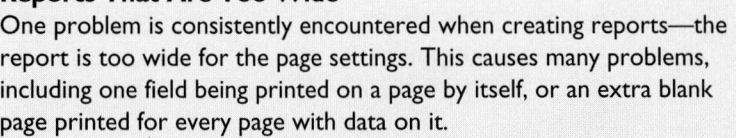

Reports That Are Too Wide

One problem is consistently encountered when creating reports—the report is too wide for the page settings. This causes many problems, including one field being printed on a page by itself, or an extra blank page printed for every page with data on it.

When you get a message telling you that your report does not fit, check the margins by choosing File, Page Setup from the menu (you may be able to fix the problem by decreasing the left and right margins). Figure out the maximum width of your report, and then use the ruler to move all the fields and lines so that the report width is slightly less than the allowed page width. Finally, grab the right edge of the report area and drag it to the left until it is narrower than the maximum page width.

Lesson 7: Creating Reports Using the Chart Wizard

Some types of information are best presented using charts instead of numbers. Access has a built-in Chart Wizard that uses an application called Microsoft Graph 2000 to help you create a chart. You can create most of the common chart types, including column charts, pie charts, and bar charts. Charts created in Access are somewhat difficult to edit, however, and the chart module has only limited charting capabilities. If you have Excel, you may find it easier to export or copy your data to a worksheet and create your charts there.

In this lesson, you create a chart to show how many of each product have been ordered.

To Create a Report Using the Chart Wizard

1. **In the Data Analysis database, click the Report object button, if necessary, and then click New.**
   The New Report dialog box displays.

2. **Select the Chart Wizard. Select the Sales by Product query from the drop-down list, and then click OK.**
   The first Chart Wizard dialog box displays, asking which fields contain the data you want to chart. This is the query you created in Lesson 1.

   If Microsoft Graph 2000 is not installed on your machine, you need to get the original installation disks to install this feature, or install it from your network.

3. **Select both the Product Description and SumOfQuantity fields, and then click Next.**
   The second Chart Wizard dialog box displays, asking what type of chart you want to use (see Figure 5.35). When you click a chart type, a description of that type appears in a box on the right side of the dialog box.

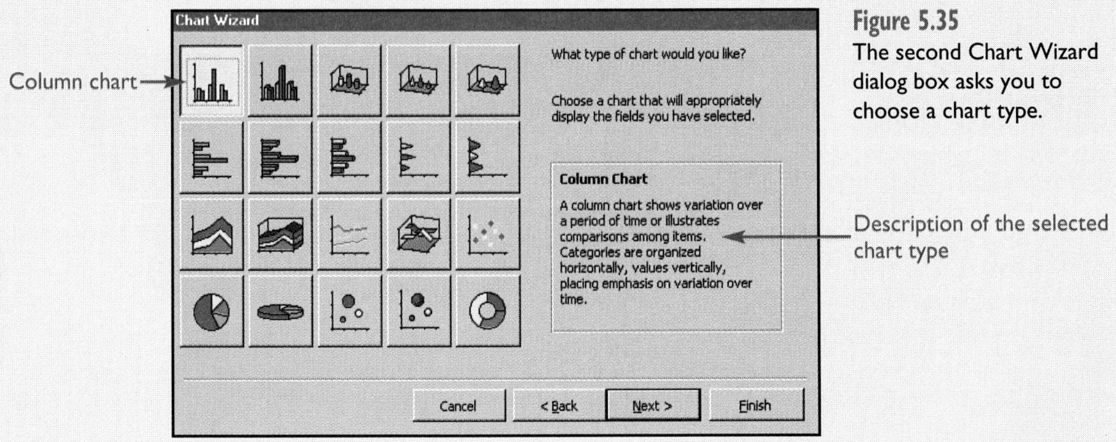

Figure 5.35
The second Chart Wizard dialog box asks you to choose a chart type.

continues ▶

To Create a Report Using the Chart Wizard (continued)

4 Select the Column Chart, the first example in the first row, and then click Next.

The third Chart Wizard dialog box displays, showing the Product Description field along the bottom (x) axis and the quantity along the vertical (y) axis (see Figure 5.36). No changes are made in this dialog box.

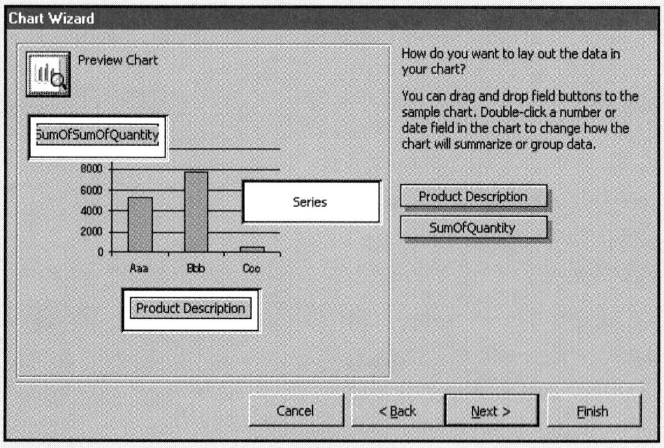

Figure 5.36
The third Chart Wizard dialog box shows the chart layout.

5 Click Next.

The fourth Chart Wizard dialog box displays.

6 Accept `Sales by Product` as the chart title. Select No, don't display a legend, and then click Finish.

Because there is only one data set in this chart, a legend is unnecessary. If you had two or more data sets, a legend would be necessary.

The final report is shown in Preview mode. The chart has major problems, particularly the data labels on the x-axis (see Figure 5.37). The Chart wizard automatically chose to display every other label on the x-axis.

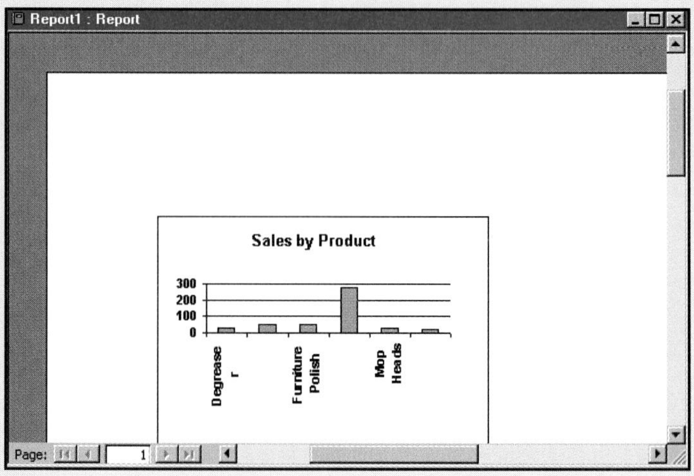

Figure 5.37
The x-axis labels display only every other label on the initial chart produced by the wizard.

7 Click the Close button on the toolbar.

You are now in the report Design view.

8 Double-click the chart to launch Microsoft Graph 2000.

A chart and a sample datasheet display (see Figure 5.38). Notice that the graph and numbers are not those you requested. Instead, they are the default values from Microsoft Graph 2000.

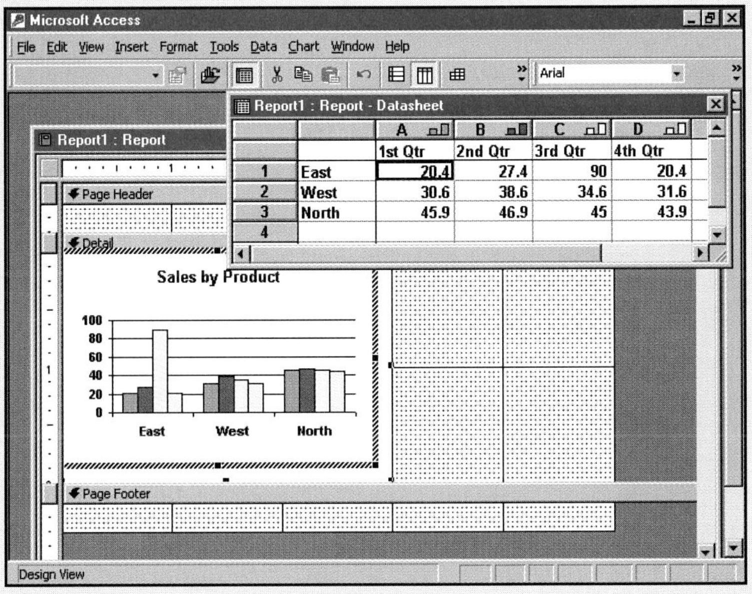

Figure 5.38
The chart and datasheet displayed bear no relationship to the chart you created.

9 Close the Datasheet window and maximize the report Design window, if necessary.

Notice that there are two handles in the lower-right corner of the Design window. You need to increase the size of both objects.

10 Move the pointer to the lower-right corner of the chart window and drag the handle for the Display area down and to the right about an inch.

11 Move the pointer to the lower-right corner of the chart window and drag the handle for the Chart area down and to the right so that it fits in the Display area.

Your report Design window should look like Figure 5.39.

continues ▶

To Create a Report Using the Chart Wizard (continued)

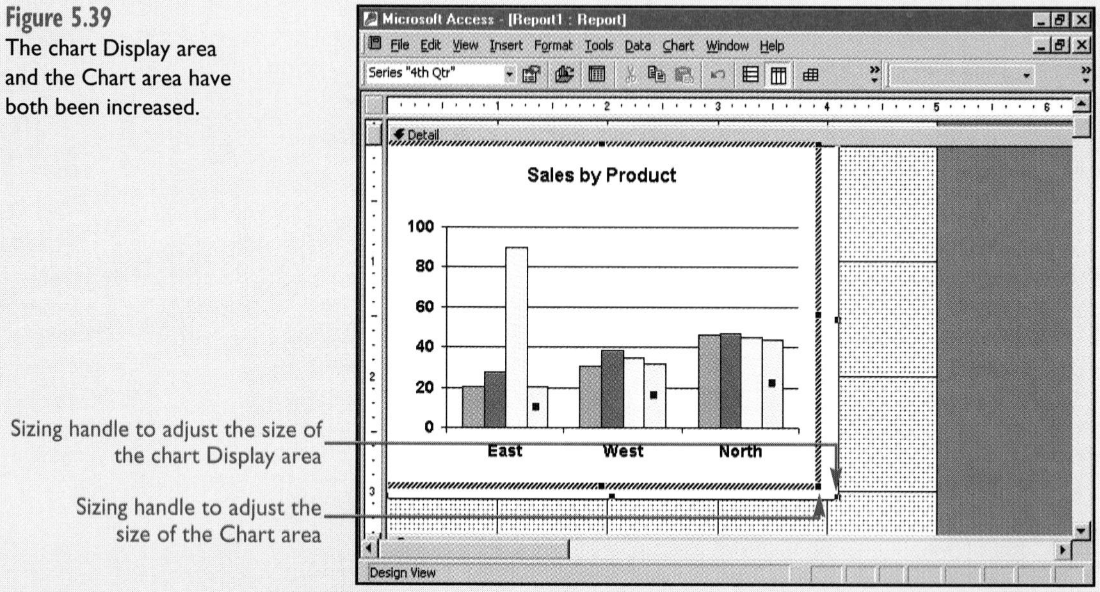

Figure 5.39
The chart Display area and the Chart area have both been increased.

You might not be able to accomplish these steps the first time you try. Each time the heavy line around the chart disappears, double-click the chart and try again. Working on Access charts can be very frustrating.

12. **Choose File, Close from the menu. Save the chart as `Products Sold`.**

13. **Select the Products Sold report and click the Preview button. Maximize the window and scroll down until you can see the whole chart.**

    Your chart should appear with all six data labels (see Figure 5.40). If you have cut off any of the chart, or have too much room on the right edge, adjust the size again. Your chart may appear slightly different.

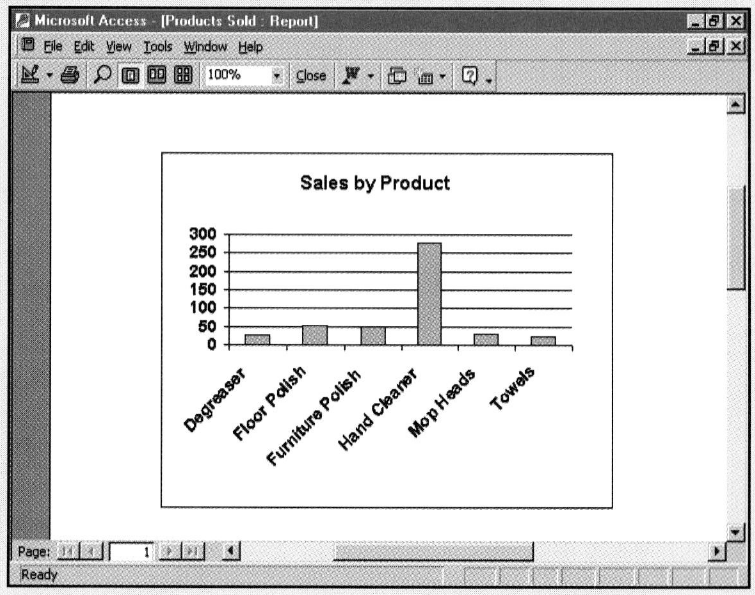

Figure 5.40
The chart displays all the product labels after it was resized and reformatted.

14 Close the Preview window, and then close the Data Analysis database.
If you have completed your session on the computer, exit Access and shut down Windows before you turn off the computer. Otherwise, continue with the following exercises.

Summary

In this project, you worked with several data analysis and reporting tools using queries, forms, and reports. You added totals to a query, and summarized data using a Crosstab query. You also added totals and criteria to a Crosstab query. The final data analysis tool you used was a PivotTable, which is a form that enables you to interact with the data. You also embedded a subform in a main form and a subreport in an existing report. Finally, you created (with some difficulty) a chart.

Crosstab queries and PivotTables are very powerful data analysis tools. You can learn more about their advanced features by looking up each topic in the Help index and examining the many help topics available for each.

Checking Concepts and Terms

True/False

For each of the following, check *T* or *F* to indicate whether the statement is true or false.

__T __F **1.** The Totals query feature needs to be based on a minimum of three fields. [L1]

__T __F **2.** The design for a Crosstab query must have at least one row header, one column header, and one value. [L3]

__T __F **3.** In a Crosstab query design, the field that is chosen to provide the values in the cells must have its Totals box changed to Group By. [L2]

__T __F **4.** If the records in a subform are going to be linked to the records in the main form, the tables on which they are based must be joined in a one-to-many relationship. [L5]

__T __F **5.** If you want to display data in chart form, you must export the table to Excel and use the Excel charting option. [L7]

__T __F **6.** To add a restriction on a Crosstab query using another field, add the field to the Field box, and write the limitation in the Crosstab box. [L3]

__T __F **7.** The Between expression is inclusive; that is, purchases made on the beginning and ending dates are included in the table. [L3]

__T __F **8.** To create a main form/subform, you use the SubForm Wizard found in the New Form dialog box. [L5]

__T __F **9.** When you edit a chart in Access, the data displayed in the Microsoft Graph program is the data that is being charted. [L7]

__T __F **10.** A Crosstab query produces a dynaset where the contents of one field provide the column headings and the contents of another field are used as row headings. [L2]

Multiple Choice

Circle the letter of the correct answer for each of the following questions.

1. If a field name is used in an expression, it must be enclosed by _____. [L3]
   a. []
   b. ()
   c. {}
   d. <>

2. To add an additional set of values such as totals to a Crosstab query, a new column needs to be set up with the Totals box set to _____. [L3]
   a. Column Header
   b. Row Header
   c. Value
   d. Expression

3. If a form and its subform are based on tables that are joined in a one-to-many relationship, _______. [L5]
   a. the records shown in the subform are limited to those that match the record shown in the main form
   b. they use the same navigation buttons
   c. they cannot both show a record with the same primary key field value
   d. you cannot change the contents of a field in the subform

4. To add a subreport to a report, you can _____. [L6]
   a. choose from a list of existing reports
   b. create a report based on a table
   c. create a report based on a query
   d. all of the above

5. Charts can be created in Access as a type of _____. [L7]
   a. Report
   b. Macro
   c. Query
   d. Table

6. The types of charts you can create in Access include _____. [L7]
   a. bar charts
   b. column charts
   c. pie charts
   d. all of the above

7. The SubForm/Subreport Wizard found in the toolbox can be used to _____. [L5,L6]
   a. add a subreport only from an existing report
   b. add a subform from an existing report
   c. create both reports with subreports and forms with subforms
   d. create the main part of the form

8. In a Crosstab query, the data that appears in the intersection of the columns and rows is known as the _____. [L3]
   a. value field
   b. quantity field
   c. amount field
   d. count field

9. A PivotTable _____. [L4]
   a. is interactive
   b. is actually run in Excel
   c. is more flexible than a Crosstab query
   d. all of the above

10. In a query, to create a new label for a column that will be used for a calculated field, type the label name followed by a _____. [L3]
    a. semi-colon
    b. colon
    c. period
    d. comma

Screen ID

Label each element of the Access screen shown in Figure 5.41 and Figure 5.42.

Figure 5.41

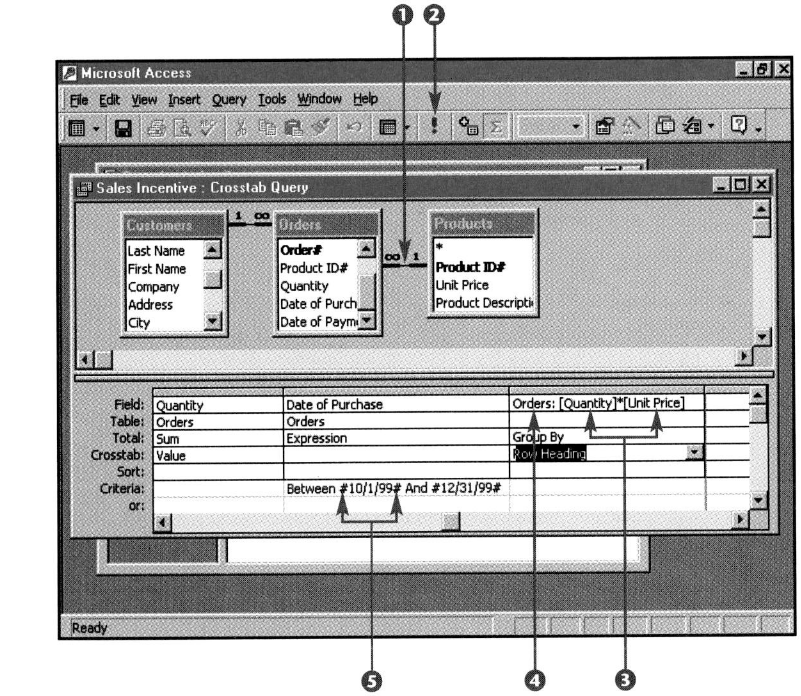

A. Run button
B. Column label
C. Subform/Subreport button
D. Subreport label
E. Date indicators
F. Subreport
G. Relationship
H. Toolbox button
I. Main report name
J. Fields

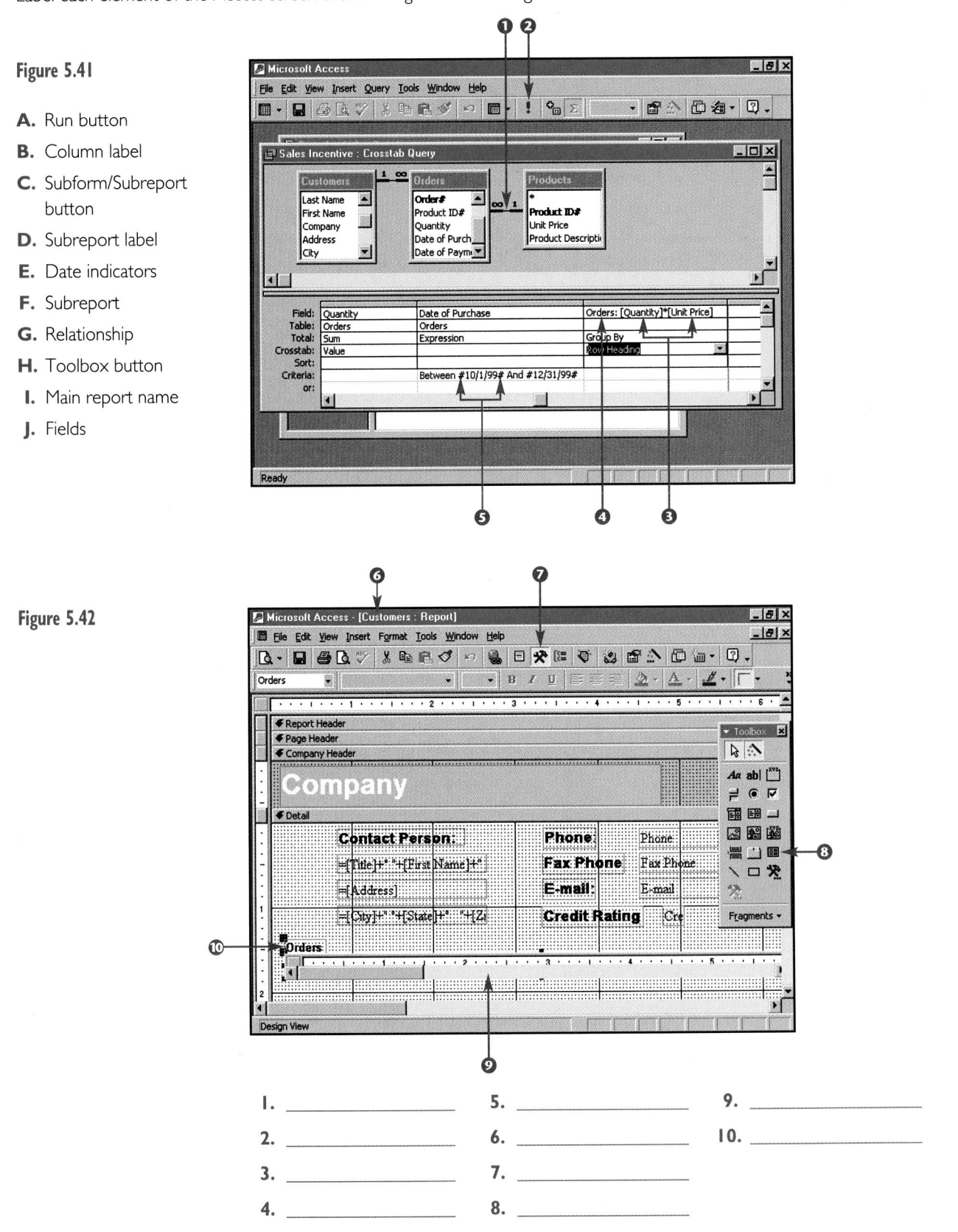

Figure 5.42

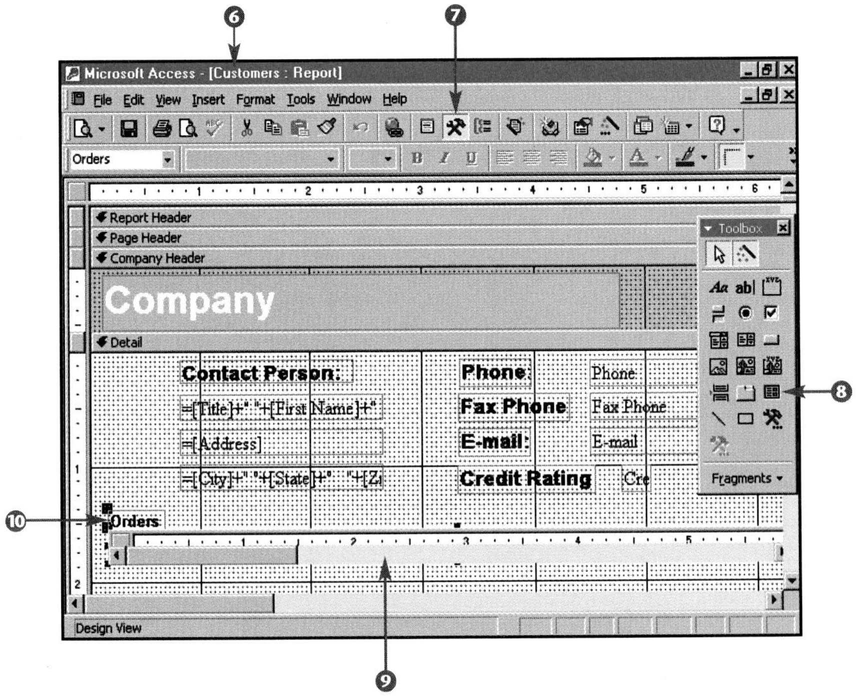

1. ____________________
2. ____________________
3. ____________________
4. ____________________
5. ____________________
6. ____________________
7. ____________________
8. ____________________
9. ____________________
10. ____________________

Discussion Questions

1. In Lesson 1, you used the Totals feature of the Data Analysis database to add up the number of units sold for each product in a table. The Totals feature includes, in addition to the Sum function, functions for such things as averages, minimums, maximums, and standard deviations. Can you think of a use for each of these functions? Would any of them be appropriate for the Sales by Product query you created in Lesson 1?
2. Take a look at the Customers table. Assume that there are hundreds of customers listed. Can you think of a way you might use a crosstab query using only the data from this table?
3. The PivotTable you created in Lesson 4 enables you to group data by division and then subgroup the data by company. PivotTables enable you to create subgroups for the subgroups (grouping on a third level). Have you ever worked on a database that could benefit from three levels of grouping? If not, can you imagine a situation where three levels might be useful?
4. In Lesson 6, you added the Orders report as a subreport to the Customers report. The Orders report was based on the Orders table and showed the Product ID# rather than the more descriptive product name. What steps could you have taken when you first designed the database to display the product name rather than the Product ID#?
5. Now that you have created a chart in Access, what do you think of the charting feature? If you need a chart in the future, will you use Access or another program? How would you get the data to another program (such as Excel) in a proper format for charting? Why do you think Microsoft included the charting feature in this program, knowing how difficult it is to use?

Skill Drill

Skill Drill exercises reinforce project skills. Each skill reinforced is the same, or nearly the same, as a skill presented in the project. Each exercise includes a brief narrative introduction, followed by detailed instructions in a step-by-step format.

In the first five exercises, you use a transcription of the 1880 Alcona County, Michigan federal census. Some of the entries have been standardized for such things as spelling and occupation names. You will notice that this database has a field (Place) with repetitive data. When this database was designed, it was felt that all the fields should be in one table because of the nature of the data.

1. Using the Totals Feature in a Query

In 1880, Alcona County was still sparsely settled (population 3,107), with the main occupation being lumbering. Because of the rough conditions and types of jobs available, nearly two-thirds of the residents were males. You might also suspect that the average age would be quite young, and the Totals query feature is just the way to find out whether that is true.

To use the Totals feature in a query, complete the following steps:

1. Copy the AC3-0502 database file from the CD-ROM to drive A. Right-click the filename; select Properties from the shortcut menu, and remove the Read-only status. Use the shortcut menu to rename the file `1880 Alcona Census`, and then open the database.
2. Click the Queries object button and click New.
3. Select Design View and click OK.
4. Click Add to add the 1880 Alcona County Census table, and then click the Close button in the Show Table dialog box.
5. Drag the Place field to the first column in the design grid, and then drag the Age field to the second column.

6. Click the Totals button.
7. Change the Total box for the Age field from Group By to Avg (which displays the average value of the numbers).
8. Click the Run button to view the query in Datasheet view. Notice the average ages for each place in the county. Print the query.
9. Close the query and save it as `Average Age`. Leave the database open for the next exercise.

2. Creating a Crosstab Query

A glance through the data shows you that there were a number of different occupations in the county in 1880. A Crosstab query enables you to find out how many people are listed in each job category and display them by gender. (Note: At School was an occupation, as was At Home for girls who were out of school but not yet married.)

To create a Crosstab query, complete the following steps:

1. Click the Queries object button, if necessary, and then click New.
2. Select Design View from the New Query dialog box, and then click OK.
3. Click Add to add the 1880 Alcona County Census table, and then click the Close button in the Show Table dialog box.
4. Drag the Occupation field to the first column in the design grid, and then drag the Sex and ID fields to the second and third columns.
5. Click the Query Type button on the toolbar and select the Crosstab Query option.
6. Click in the Crosstab box for the Occupation field and select Row Heading from the drop-down list. Use the same procedure to select Column Heading for the Sex field and Value for the ID field.
7. Click the Total box for the ID field and select Count from the drop-down list. It does not matter which field you choose to be counted, as long as there are entries in it for every record. The primary key field is often used for this type of situation.
8. Click the Run button. Notice that the first column shows that 393 females and 367 males have no occupation listed. (These are usually small children, but not always.)
9. Scroll down the list to see the different occupations for men and women in this county in 1880. When you are through, close the query and name it `Occupations`. Leave the database open for the next exercise.

3. Creating a Crosstab Query with Conditions

Schooling was not mandatory at this time and place, so some children attended regularly, some for only a few years (until they were capable of doing adult work), and some not at all. You can use a Crosstab query to find out how many children between the ages of 5 and 18 attended school the year the census was taken.

To create a query that uses conditions, complete the following steps:

1. Open a new query in Design view and add the 1880 Alcona County Census table.
2. Drag the Age, Attended School, ID, and Age fields to the query design grid. The second Age field will be used for the criterion.
3. Click the Query Type button on the toolbar and select the Crosstab Query option.
4. In the Crosstab row, select Row Heading for the Age field, Column Heading for the Attended School field, and Value for the ID field.
5. In the Total box, select Count for the ID field and Expression for the second Age field.
6. Type `Between 5 and 18` in the Criteria box for the second Age field.
7. Click the Run button to see the results of your query. The first column shows the ages. The second column shows how many children of each age did not attend school, and the third column shows how many children did attend school (that is, how many had an X in the Attended School field). Notice that more than half of the children between the ages of 6 and 13 attended school, but very few of the older children attended school (see Figure 5.43). Think how difficult it would have been to extract this data by hand!

8. Print the query.

9. Close the query and name it `Attended School`. Leave the database open for the next exercise.

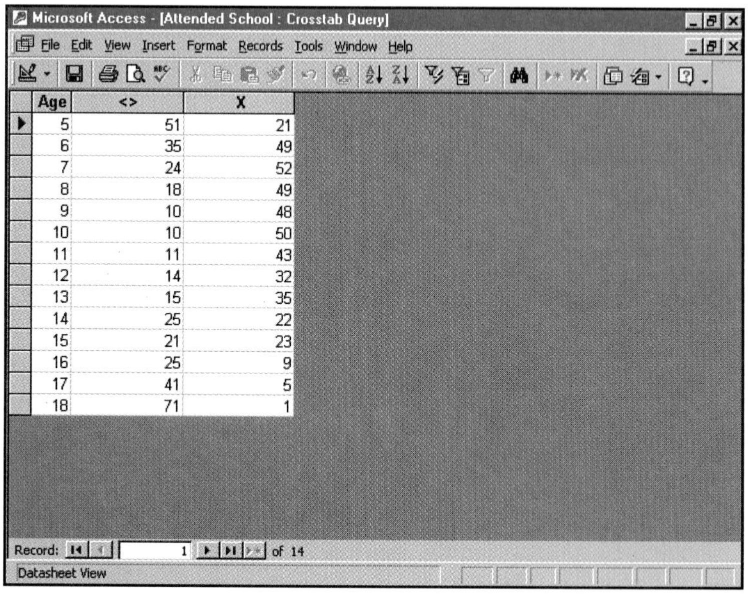

Figure 5.43
The Crosstab query shows how many children of each age attended school.

4. Creating a PivotTable Form

As you saw in the previous exercise, a Crosstab query is a powerful data analysis tool. If you want to be able to interact with the data, however, a PivotTable works better. For example, you might want to look at the place of birth of the men and women in the county by their location in the county. Remember that you need to do this on a machine that has Excel installed.

To create a PivotTable form, complete the following steps:

1. Click the Forms object button and click the New button.
2. Select the PivotTable Wizard; choose the 1880 Alcona County Census from the drop-down list, and click OK.
3. Click Next to move to the second PivotTable Wizard dialog box and select the Place, Sex, and Birth Place fields. Click Next.
4. Click the Layout button in the third PivotTable Wizard dialog box. Drag the Place field to the PAGE box, the Birth Place field to the ROW box, the Sex field to the COLUMN box, and the Birth Place field to the DATA box.
5. Click OK, and then click Finish. Click the Edit PivotTable Object button in the Form window. (You may have to scroll down to get to this button.)
6. Close the PivotTable toolbar, if necessary; then choose Data, Refresh Data from the menu.
7. Look at the data in the PivotTable; then select Harrisville Vlg. from the Place drop-down list and click OK. Notice that the numbers change, and the empty Birth Place rows (such as At Sea) are eliminated.
8. Try a few other locations; then select (All) from the Place drop-down list. Your PivotTable should look like Figure 5.44.

9. Print the PivotTable.

10. Close the Excel window, and then close the Access form and call it `Birth Places`. Leave the database open for the next exercise.

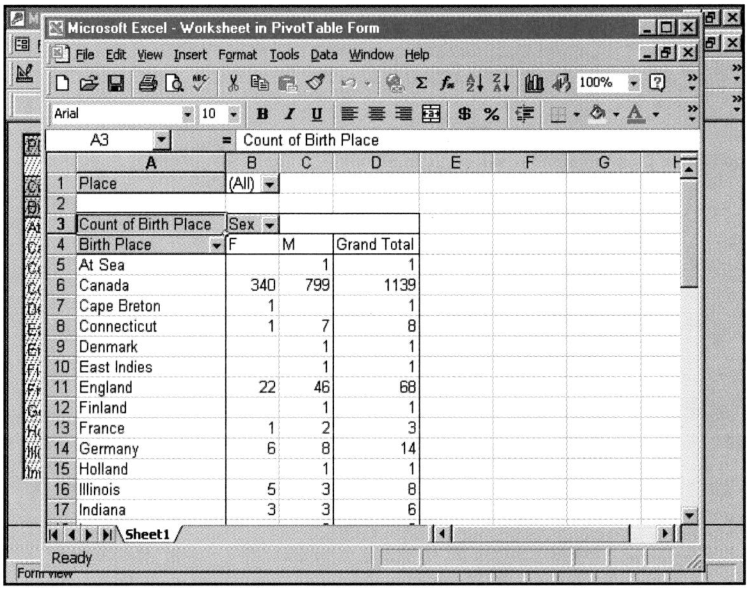

Figure 5.44
A PivotTable shows the birthplace of the residents of Alcona County, Michigan in 1880.

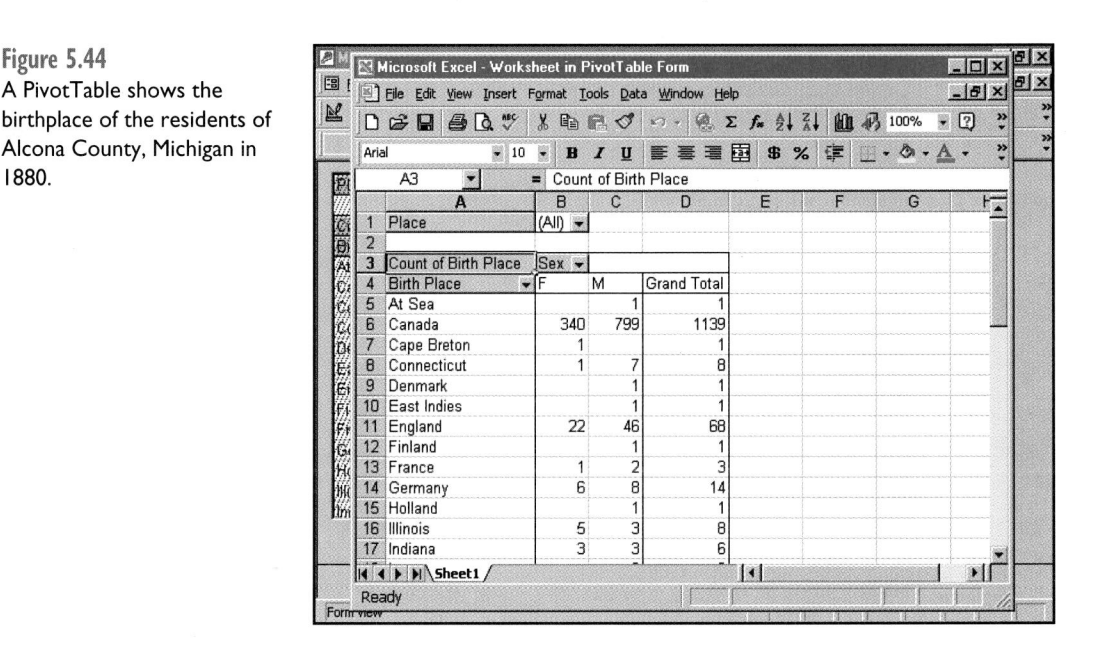

5. Creating a Chart

In the first exercise, you used the Totals function in a query to show the average age by location in the county. This is the type of data that is ideal for a chart.

To create a chart that displays the average age of the population by location, complete the following steps:

1. Click the Reports object button and click the New button.
2. Select the Chart Wizard; choose the 1880 Alcona County Census from the drop-down list, and click OK.
3. Add the Place and Age fields to the Fields for Chart box and click Next.
4. Select the Column chart type and click Next.
5. Double-click the SumOfAge button near the upper-left corner of the Chart Wizard dialog box. Choose Avg from the list, and click OK.
6. Click Next. Choose not to display a legend, and then click Finish.
7. Click the View button to switch to Design view. Maximize the window.
8. Click to select the Chart area and drag down and to the right until the Chart area is about 5" wide and about 3" high. Use the rulers to help you, and adjust the size as necessary.
9. Double-click the chart. Grab the handle in the lower-right corner and drag down and to the right until the chart fills the Chart area. You may have to move (or close) the datasheet to do this.
10. Select File, Print Preview from the menu. Your chart should look like Figure 5.45. If you need to change it, click the View button and repeat the previous procedure. Click the Print button to print the chart.

11. When you are through, close the report and save it as `Average Age Chart`. Close the database.

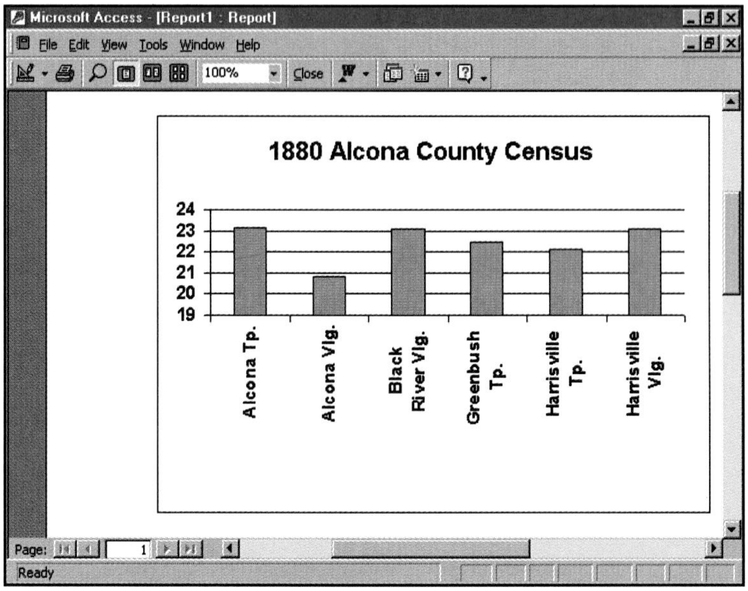

Figure 5.45
An Access chart shows the average age of residents by location.

6. Adding a Subreport to an Existing Report

In this exercise, you create a report with a subreport using two existing reports. The database you use is the short story database you used earlier in this book. You open a report on the information about each book and then add a subreport showing each story in the book, along with the author and year published information.

To add a subreport to an existing report, complete the following steps:

1. Copy the AC3-0503 database file from the CD-ROM to drive A. Right-click the filename; select Properties from the shortcut menu, and remove the Read-only status. Use the shortcut menu to rename the file `Short Story Collections`, and then open the database.
2. Click the Reports object button and click to select the Book Information report.
3. Click the Design button and maximize the screen.
4. Grab the Page Footer bar and drag it down an inch or so to make room in the Detail area.
5. Click the Subform/Subreport button in the toolbox and draw a box for the subreport about 1/2" under the beginning of the Year of Publication label. Drag the box to the right to about the 6 1/4" mark and make it about 1/2" deep.
6. Choose to use the existing Short Stories report as the subreport. Click Next.
7. Choose to link to each record in Book Information using the Book Title field.
8. Change the subreport label to read `Short stories in this book:`.
9. Click the View button on the toolbar to see your report/subreport. It should look like Figure 5.46. If you need to, return to Design view and modify the report design.

10. Print the first page of the report, and then close the database.

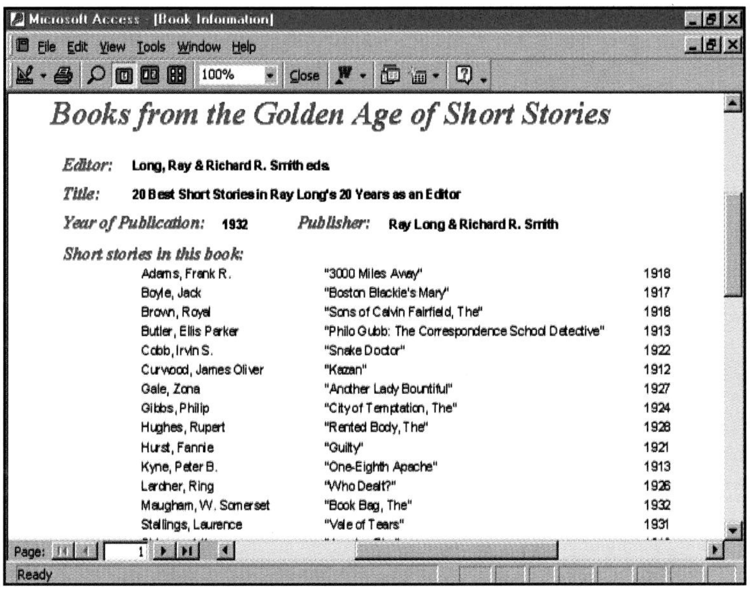

Figure 5.46
The short stories included in each book are listed below the book information.

Challenge

Challenge exercises expand on or are somewhat related to skills presented in the lessons. Each exercise provides a brief narrative introduction followed by instructions in a numbered step format that are not as detailed as those in the Skill Drill section.

You use two databases in the Challenge section. The first is the consulting database you created in Project 1. The second is a five-year database of U.S. tornadoes.

1. Adding Conditions to the Totals Feature in a Query

In this exercise, you create a query based on another query. You then show the costs of each project for a one-week period using the criteria based on a field that is not displayed.

1. Copy the AC3-0504 database file to drive A; remove the Read-only status. Rename the file `Consulting Projects`, and then open the database.
2. Create a new query in Design view. Add the Cost to Client query, and then add the Project Name, Cost, and Date fields to the design grid.
3. Add the Total row. Group on the Project Name field and create a Sum on the Cost field.
4. In the Total row of the Date column, select the Where option; this turns off the Show check box. Type `Between 4/3/00 and 4/7/00` in the Criteria box.
5. Run the query. The totals are for one week only.
6. Print the query.
7. Close the query and save it as `One Week Costs`. Leave the database open for the next exercise.

2. Creating a Crosstab Query Using the Crosstab Query Wizard

The Crosstab Query Wizard enables you to quickly create crosstabs, although if you want to place any conditions, you need to move to Design view after the wizard is completed. You want to find information about pay scales by gender. In this exercise, you use the Count feature to count the number of males and females in the company at each pay scale.

1. Create a new query using the Crosstab Query Wizard.
2. Select the Private table. Select the Pay Rate field as the Row Heading.
3. Select the Sex field as the Column Header.
4. Accept the Count function for the Employee ID field. Deselect the row sums.
5. Call the query `Pay Scale by Sex`.
6. Look at the results of the crosstab query. Does there seem to be a problem with pay by gender?
7. Print the query. Close the query and close the database.

3. Creating a Crosstab Query with Two Levels of Row Headers

You can group data in a Crosstab query using the row header and column header. Sometimes, you need to create a subgroup on a main group. You can do this in a Crosstab query by adding a second row header, but you can't subgroup on the column header. In this exercise, you use a database of five years of U.S. tornado data. You display the F-scales (intensity levels) of the tornadoes grouped on the county and subgrouped on the year.

1. Copy the AC3-0505 database file to drive A; remove the Read-only status. Rename the file `Five Year Tornado Data`, and then open the database.
2. Create a crosstab query using the Crosstab Query Wizard. Use the List of 1991-95 US Tornadoes query.
3. Add the County Name field, and then add the Year field as Row Headings.
4. Add the FScale field as the Column Heading. Accept the Count function for the State Name field as the calculation. Deselect the row sums.
5. Call the query `F-Scales by County and Year`.
6. Switch to Design view and add the State Name field again. Select Where in the Total column of the new field, and then type `Texas` into the Criteria row. This limits the crosstab query to Texas tornadoes.
7. Print the first page of the query.
8. Close the query and rename it `F-Scales by County and Year in Texas`. Leave the database open for the next exercise.

4. Creating a Query That Displays More Than One Function

You can create a query that displays more than one function. In this exercise, you work with the `Five Year Tornado Data database`. Use the Totals function to display the state-by-state statistics for the number of people killed and injured, and the average F-Scale of the tornadoes. Use the available Help to do this, if necessary. You also need to use Help to make the average F-Scale appear with two decimal places, and then sort the query by the average of the F-Scale in descending order (see Figure 5.47). Name the query `Summary Statistics by State`. Print the query.

Figure 5.47

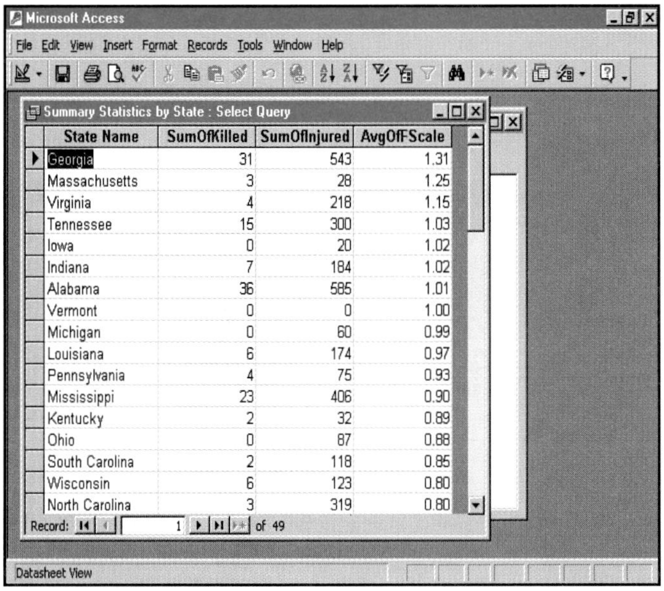

Discovery Zone

Discovery Zone exercises help you gain advanced knowledge of project topics and/or application of skills. These exercises focus on enhancing your problem-solving skills. Numbered steps are not provided, but you are given hints, reminders, screen shots, and/or references to help you reach your goal for each exercise.

In these exercises, you use a modified version of the tornado database you used in the Challenge exercises.

1. Creating a PivotTable with a Third Subgroup

PivotTables, like Crosstab queries, can be grouped and subgrouped on rows, which in turn are subgroups of the PivotTable page. Use the available help, if necessary, to figure out how to change the F-Scale data function and format.

Copy the AC3-0505 database file to drive A; remove the Read-only status. Rename the file `Five Year Tornado Data2`, and then open the database.

Goal: Create a PivotTable that has a third level of grouping.

The PivotTable should

- Use a table or query with the necessary information
- Use the State field as the page
- Use the County field as the main row header
- Use the Year field as the secondary row header
- Use the F-Scale field as the column header
- Use an average of the F-Scale as the data
- Show the average F-Scale to two decimal places

Hint: When in doubt, double-click!

Name the PivotTable `Third Level PivotTable`.

Your PivotTable should look like Figure 5.48.

Figure 5.48

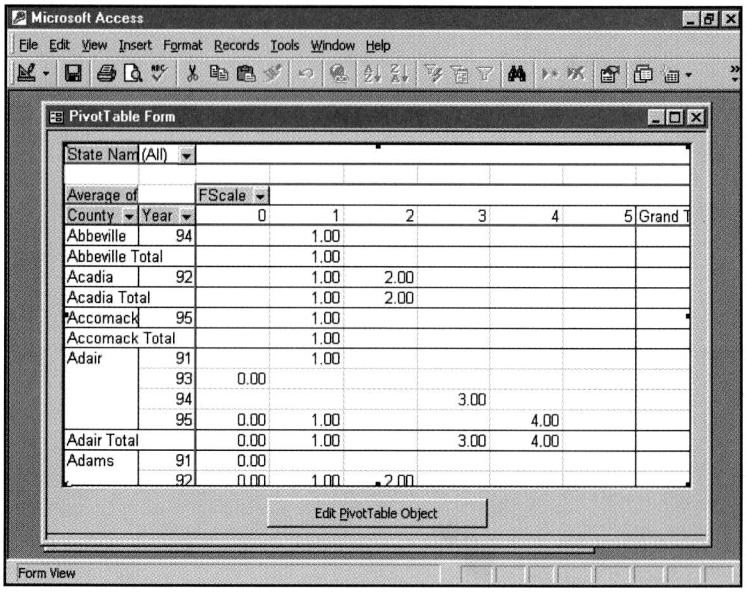

2. Using Access Data to Create an Excel Chart

As you may well have noticed, Access does not do charts very well—in fact, the Chart feature is probably the weakest link in the Access program. If you need to create a chart from Access data, by far the best alternative is to send the data to Excel and create the chart there. Creating a chart in Excel simply requires that you find the Chart Wizard button and follow instructions. In this exercise, you create a query to count the number of tornadoes at each F-Scale level and send the data to Excel for charting. (Note: You must have Excel available to complete this exercise.)

Goal: Create a chart in Excel based on a query created in Access.

For this exercise you should

- Create an Access query that has two columns; one with the different F-Scale levels and one with the total number of tornadoes at each level.
- Send the data to Excel.
- Change the F-Scale column numbers to text.
- Use the Excel Chart Wizard to create a chart. (You may need to use the Excel Help.)
- Use `Number of Tornadoes by F-Scale` as the chart title. The x-axis label should read `F-Scale`.
- Add Data labels to the columns.

  Print the chart. Name the query `F-Scale Chart` and the Excel spreadsheet `F-Scale`.

Hint #1: An easy way to change a number to text in Excel is to put an apostrophe (') before the number.

Hint #2: If you want to change something on an Excel chart, double-click it.

Your finished chart should look like Figure 5.49.

Figure 5.49

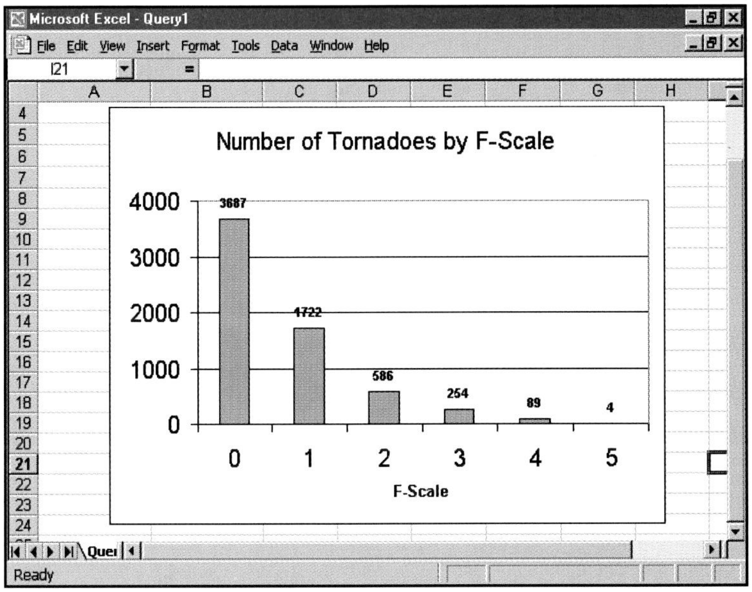

Project 6

Project 6

Filtering Data in a Linked Table Using Parameters and Form Filters

Objectives

In this project, you learn how to:

- **Link to a Large Table in Another Database**
- **Select Records Using Filter by Selection**
- **Select Records Using Filter by Form**
- **Use Parameters as Matching Criteria in a Query**
- **Use Parameters with Comparison Operators in a Query**
- **Use Parameters with Wildcards as Criteria in a Query**

Key terms introduced in this project include

- comparison operators
- dynaset
- excluding operators
- Filter by Form
- Filter by Selection
- Null
- parameter
- wildcard

Why Would I Do This?

Sometimes you will want to use information that is contained in another database. You may be able to import the table to your database and use it, or you may prefer to link to the table and use it without importing the data. Linking to a table is useful when the database is particularly large or is restricted in some manner that would prevent you from importing it.

Once you have linked to the data you want to use, you can extract and examine it for a variety of purposes. You seldom need to look at all of the records at any one time. You already know how to use criteria in a query to restrict the data that is displayed. You can also use quick methods that use both queries and forms to view the desired subset of data, which is also called a ***dynaset***.

In this project, you learn how to link to a large database table and create a query that enables you to control the output each time the query is run. A ***parameter*** query asks you for input whenever the query is used and uses your input as the criteria for the query. In this way, you can use the same query structure repeatedly and vary the criteria without having to open up the design of the query and make changes. If you base a report on a query that uses a parameter, you can control the output of the report by entering a value in the parameter value box that displays when the report is run.

You also learn how to use two of the most powerful data-searching features of Access—***Filter by Selection*** and ***Filter by Form***. The Filter by Selection feature enables you to scroll through a form and select the desired entry in a field. When you click on the Filter by Selection button, all records that match the entry in the field are displayed. The Filter by Form feature gives you a blank copy of the form and enables you to type desired field entries in one or more fields at a time.

Visual Summary

When you have completed this project, you will have created a parameter query to limit records displayed and used a form to filter data.

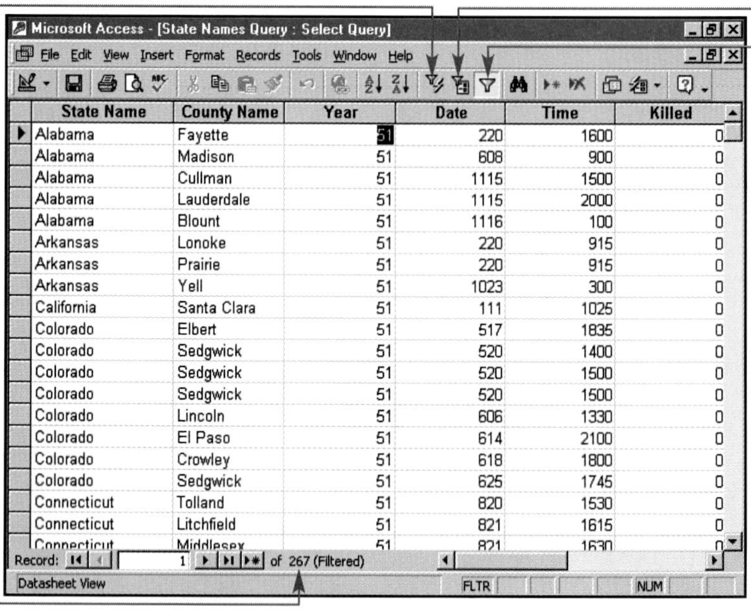

Figure 6.1
Filters may be applied to limit the records displayed.

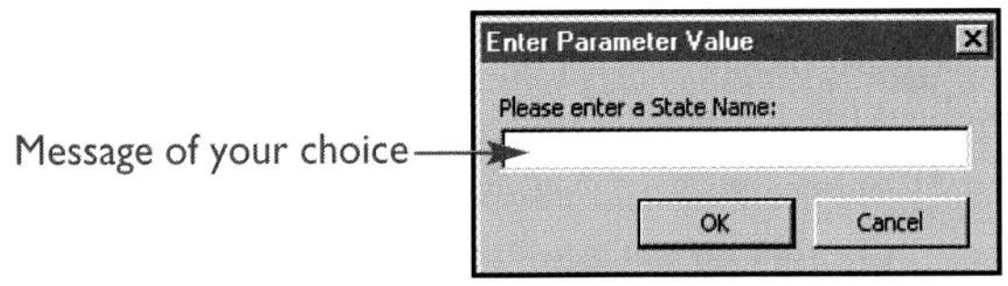

Figure 6.2
Parameter queries enable the user to enter the criteria each time the query is run.

Lesson 1: Linking to a Large Table in Another Database

In this lesson, you open a database that contains two tables; one lists the states in the United States, whereas the second lists the names of the counties in those states. You then link to a large table of tornado data in another database that resides on the CD-ROM included with this book. The tornado database contains over 38,000 records of all of the reported tornadoes that occurred in the United States from 1950 to 1995. This database was originally extracted from a government database over the Internet. It does not list the states or counties by name; rather, it assigns a number to these fields. Later in this project you will use this information in combination with the other two tables to extract useful information about the number and effects of tornadoes in the United States. To use the three tables together, you create a relationship using the Relationships window.

To Link to a Table in Another Database

1. **Launch Access. Choose Open an existing file or click the Open button if the program is already open.**

2. **Locate the student data file, AC3-0601, in the Student/Project06 folder on the CD-Rom disk and copy it to a folder on your hard drive. Remove the Read-only property; then rename the copy `Tornado Analysis`.**

3. **Open the Tornado Analysis database.**
   The database window displays the Tables area (see Figure 6.3).

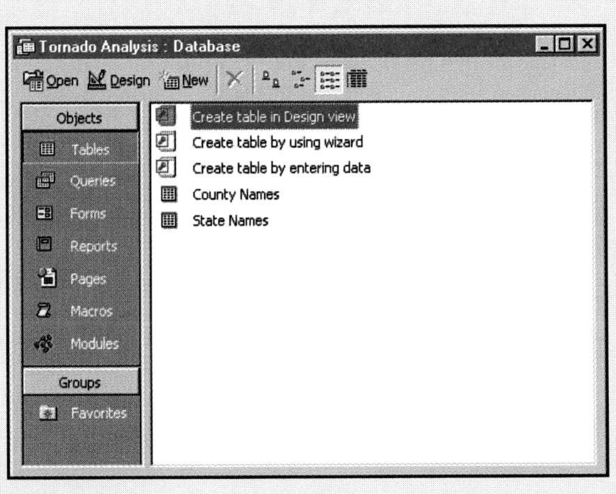

Figure 6.3
The database window displays the Tables area of the Tornado Analysis database.

4. **Choose File, Get External Data, Link Tables from the menu.**
   The Link dialog box opens. This works just like the Open or Save As dialog boxes.

continues ▶

To Link to a Table in Another Database (continued)

5 In the Look in drop-down list box, select the Student/Project06 folder on the CD-ROM drive; then select the 45 Year Tornado Records database.

Figure 6.4 shows the Link dialog box with the 45 Year Tornado Records database selected.

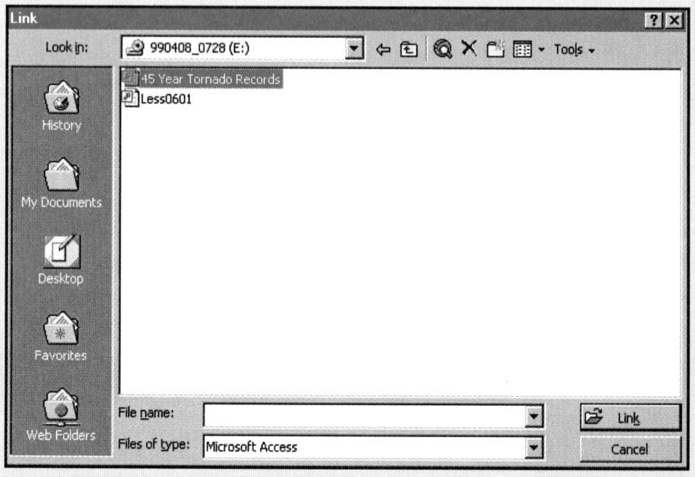

Figure 6.4
Use the Link dialog box to link to data in another database.

6 Click the Link button and choose the Tornadoes table from the Link Tables dialog box. Click OK.

Figure 6.5 shows the Tornadoes table listed in the table area with an arrow next to it to indicate that this is a linked table.

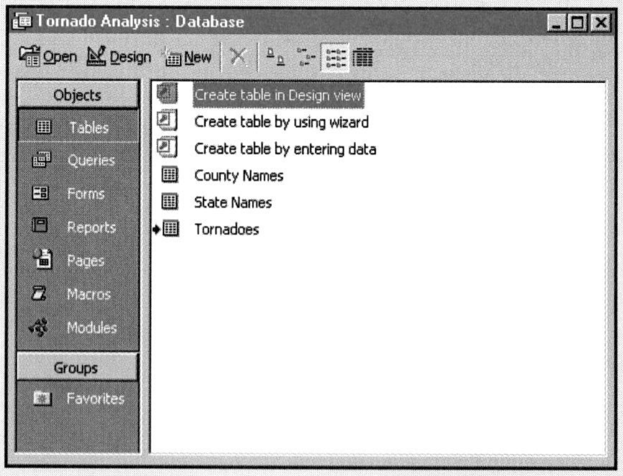

Figure 6.5
The tornadoes table is shown as a linked table.

7 Open each table and examine its contents.

The County Names table lists the name of every county and an identifying number for each. The same is true of the State Names table. The Tornadoes table contains data about when and where the Tornado occurred. It also includes several categories of statistical data, such as a damage rating, FScale rating, the number of injuries, and the number of people killed.

Before you can use these tables to extract meaningful data, they must first be related.

You use the State field and the CountyID field to create one-to-many relationships with the Tornadoes table. Both of these fields are the primary key in the one side of the relationship. The Tornado table does not have a designated primary key.

To Create a One-to-Many Relationship

1. **Make sure all of the tables are closed. Click the Relationship button. If necessary, click the Show Table button to display the Show Table dialog box.**

   The Relationships window opens and the Show Table dialog box is displayed as shown in Figure 6.6.

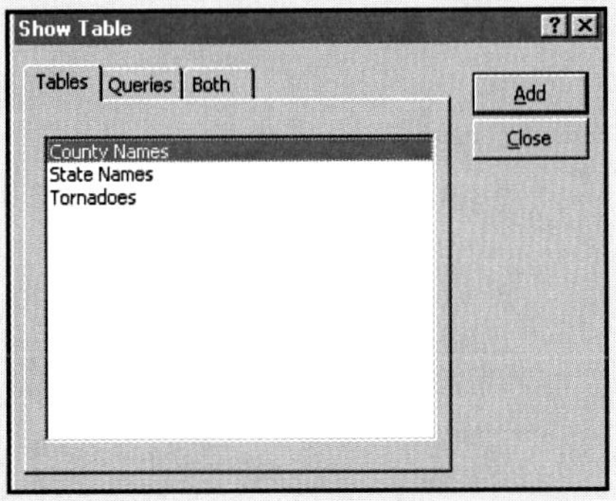

Figure 6.6
The Show Table dialog box is used to select tables and queries you want to include in the Relationships window.

2. **Double-click on each of the three table names to add them to the Relationships window; then close the Show Table dialog box.**

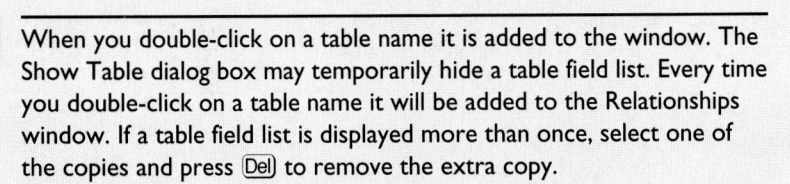

> When you double-click on a table name it is added to the window. The Show Table dialog box may temporarily hide a table field list. Every time you double-click on a table name it will be added to the Relationships window. If a table field list is displayed more than once, select one of the copies and press Del to remove the extra copy.

3. **Click and drag the lower edge of the Tornadoes field list box until you can see all of the fields. Drag the right edge of the box to display the names as shown in Figure 6.7**

4. **Click and drag the Tornadoes field list box to the center of the window and drag the State Names field list box to the right as shown in Figure 6.7.**

   This step is not necessary, but it makes it easier to see the relationships when the join lines are added.

continues ▶

To Create a One-to-Many Relationship (continued)

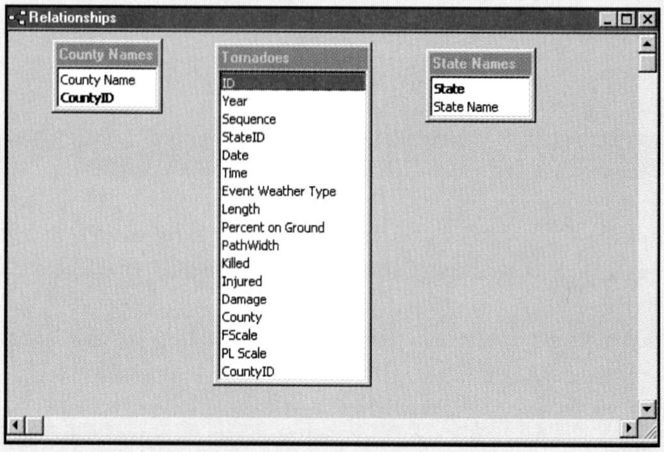

Figure 6.7
The Tornado field list is expanded and placed in the center of the window between the other two tables.

5 Click CountyID from the County Names table and drag it to the CountyID field in the Tornadoes table.

The Edit Relationships dialog box opens as shown in Figure 6.8. Notice that the Enforce Referential Integrity option is dimmed. You cannot choose this option when using a Linked table in a relationship.

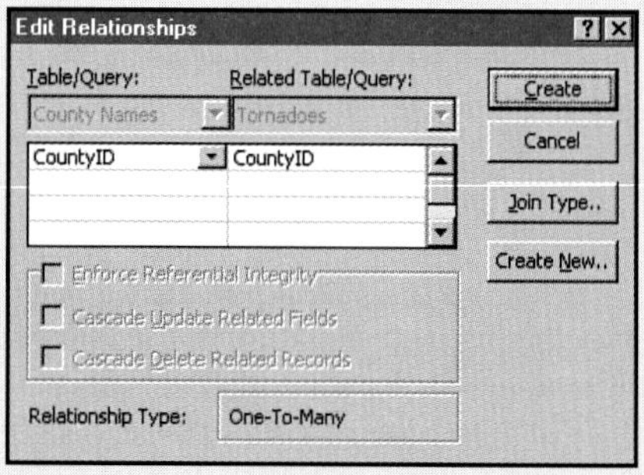

Figure 6.8
The relationship is created using the Edit Relationships dialog box.

6 Click Create. Click State from the State Names table and drag it to the StateID field in the Tornadoes table. Click Create in the Edit Relationships dialog box.

The Relationships window now shows a join line between County Names and the Tornadoes field list. There is also a join line between State Names and the Tornadoes field list (see Figure 6.9).

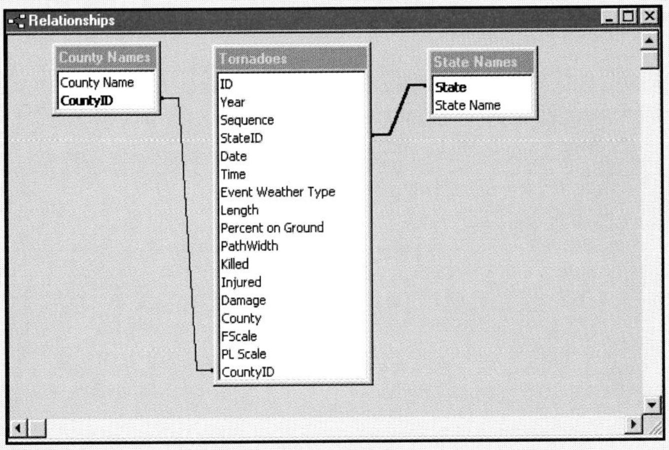

Figure 6.9
The relationships between the tables are defined.

7. **Click the Close button to close the Relationships window. Choose Yes when prompted to save the changes to the layout of the window.**

8. **Click the Queries Object button. Double-click the Create query by using wizard shortcut.**
   The Simple Query Wizard dialog box opens.

9. **Choose the State Names table and select the State Name field. Choose the County Names table and select the County Name field. Choose the Tornadoes table and select the Year, Date, Time, Killed, and Injured fields.**
   The Simple Query Wizard dialog box now displays the list of fields (see Figure 6.10).

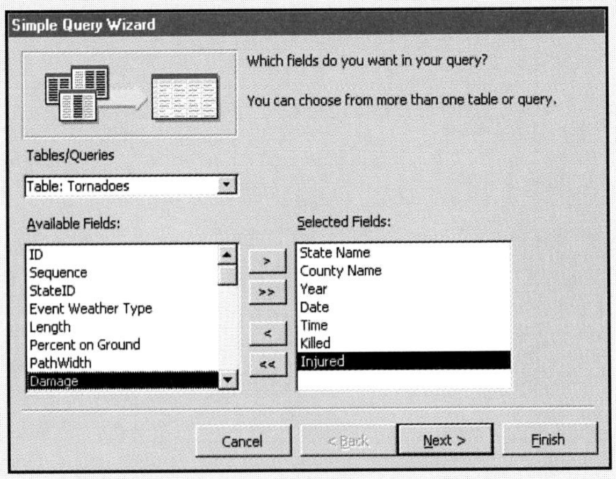

Figure 6.10
Use the Simple Query Wizard to create a query.

Why Fewer Records Display in the Query

The State Names query only displays 37,957 records out of the 38,486 records in the Tornadoes table. This discrepancy is due to the fact that all of the state and county identification numbers do not have matching records in the State Name and County Name tables. Some counties have merged with others or changed their names since 1950 when these records begin.

continues ▶

To Create a One-to-Many Relationship (continued)

10 Click Finish. The query is automatically named after the first field, `State Names Query`.

The Query now displays the list of tornadoes. Leave this query open for use in the next lesson.

Lesson 2: Selecting Records Using Filter by Selection

A quick method that can be used to examine data in a table is to select an entry in one of the fields and click the Filter by Selection button. A matching filter is immediately applied to the table and only those records that have the same value in that field are shown.

In this lesson, you learn how to use the Filter by Selection feature to display the records for one year. Open the Tornado Analysis database and run the State Names Query if you closed it after the previous lesson.

To Filter Records Using a Selected Value

1 If necessary, maximize the query window. Click 51 in the year field.

In this table, the tornadoes are displayed by State. You would like to see all the tornadoes that occurred in 1951 for all states.

2 Click the Filter by Selection button.

A filter is applied that limits the display to tornadoes that occurred in 1951 as shown in Figure 6.11. Notice that there were 267 such tornadoes.

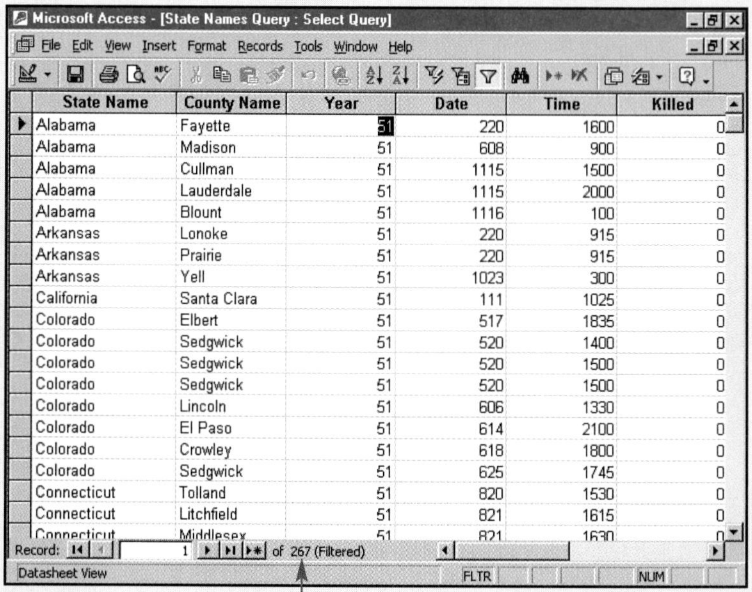

Number of records

Figure 6.11
Use the Filter by Selection window to select the data you want to view.

3 Click the Remove Filter button. Leave the query open for use in the next lesson.

The filter is removed and all 37,957 records are displayed again.

Lesson 3: Selecting Records Using Filter by Form

Another quick method that can be used to examine data displayed in tables, queries, and forms is to use a form filter. A form filter provides more options than using Filter by Selection. Although it is not as flexible as a query, and is not generally saved, the form filter technique can give you a quick and easy way of limiting data.

In the following steps, you apply additional criteria in more than one field of the State Names Query to filter the records shown. The following example is used to identify the tornadoes that occurred in Texas in 1953.

To Use Filter Criteria in More Than One Field

1. **In the State Names Query, click the Filter by Form button. Click in the State Name field, type Texas, and press Enter.**
   Notice that quotation marks are automatically added to the name. This is typical of criteria for a text field.

2. **Enter 53 in the Year field.**
   This field is a number data type and quotation marks are not used. These two criteria will be used to filter the records to display those that match (see Figure 6.12).

The program adds quotation marks to criteria in text fields

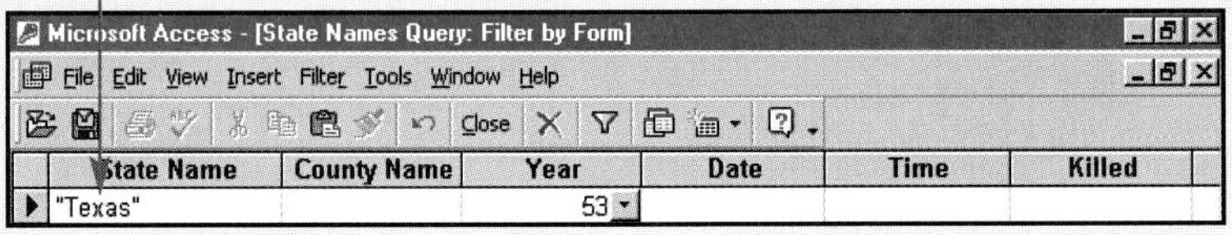

Figure 6.12
The form may be used to enter multiple filtering criteria.

3. **Click the Apply Filter button.**
   A list of the thirty-three tornadoes that occurred in Texas that year are displayed.

4. **Click the Remove Filter button.**
   All the records are displayed. Leave the query open for use in the next section.

You can fill in several fields in the form filter. Records will have to match all of the entries to be displayed. In some cases, you may want to see all the records that meet two different sets of criteria.

Next, you filter the records to see the tornadoes that occurred in 1953 in Texas and Oklahoma.

To Filter Using Two Sets of Criteria

1. **Click the Filter by Form button to reveal the design of the filter.**
   Notice that the previous set of conditions was not deleted. They still specify the Texas tornadoes from 1953.

continues ▶

To Filter Using Two Sets of Criteria (continued)

2 Click the Or tab at the bottom of the window.

A second form displays in which you can enter a new set of criteria.

3 Enter `Oklahoma` in the State field and `53` in the Year field.

A second set of conditions may be used. A third window is also added—note the second Or tab (see Figure 6.13).

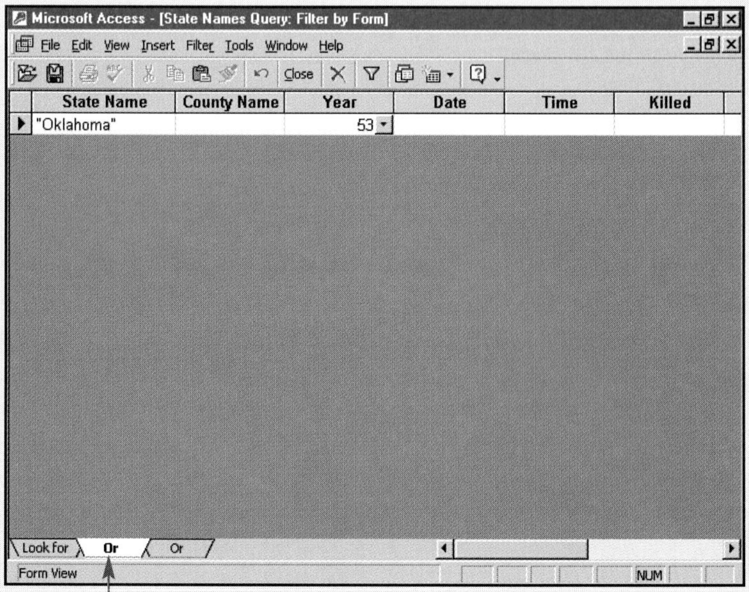

Additional sets of criteria may be added

Figure 6.13
A second set of criteria may be added.

4 Click the Apply Filter button.

The eighty-nine tornadoes that meet one set of criteria or the other set are displayed.

5 Click the Filter by Form button. Click the Clear Grid button.

The Clear Grid button removes all the criteria from the Filter by Form grid.

6 Click the Apply Filter button.

The empty criteria are applied. This is the method used to erase the criteria. Notice the Apply Filter button is dim, indicating that no filter criteria exist.

Storing Filter Conditions

If you create a filter, it is stored with the database object if you save the changes. When the table, query, or form is open, you can tell if a filter condition exists by looking at the Apply Filter button. If it is dim, no filter condition exists. If it is active, a filter condition exists that may be removed by clicking the button. The name of the Remove Filter button may be misleading. It does not erase the filter conditions; it only removes the application of the filter.

7 Close the query and save the changes. Leave the database open for use in the next lesson.

Lesson 4: Using Parameters as Matching Criteria in a Query

Form filters have several uses but there are many more things that you can do to filter data using queries. One of the most useful features in a query is the use of parameters.

In this lesson, you learn how to enter a prompting message in the criteria box instead of a value. When the query is run, a dialog box that displays your message will open and allow the user to enter a value. This method allows the user to enter a different value each time the query is run.

To Use a Parameter as a Matching Criteria

1. **Right-click on the State Names Query in the database window and choose Copy from the shortcut menu.**

2. **Right-click on an empty part of the queries window and select Paste from the shortcut menu. Enter `Times` as the new query name and click OK.**

3. **Repeat the previous step to create another copy of the State Names query but name it `County`.**

4. **Select the State Names query and click the Design button.**
   The State Names query opens in Design view.

5. **Enter the following in the criteria box under State Names, `[Please enter a State Name:]`**
   Be sure to use square brackets, not parentheses (see Figure 6.14).

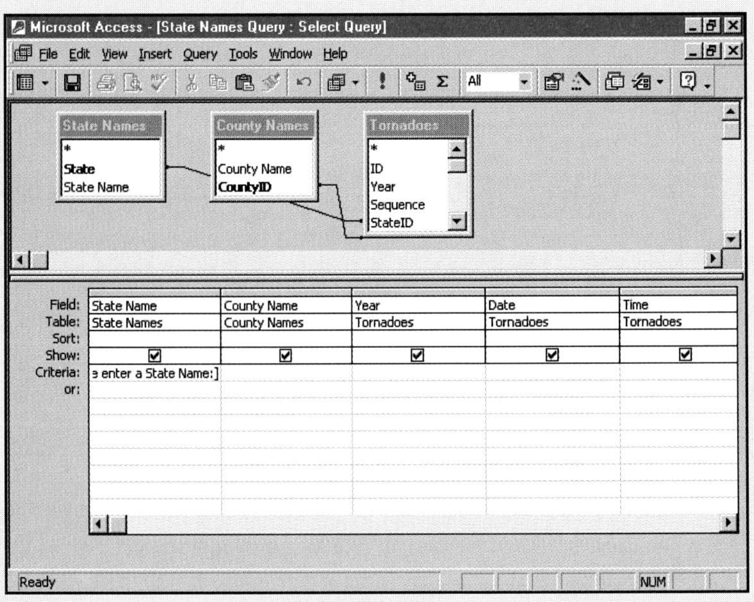

Figure 6.14
Messages enclosed in square brackets may be used instead of entering a single criterion.

Contents of a Parameter
If you enclose a phrase inside square brackets in a query design, the program prompts you to enter a value to be used in place of the phrase, unless the word or phrase in the brackets is a field name. If a field name is placed within the brackets, the current value of the field is used.

continues ▶

To Use a Parameter as a Matching Criteria (continued)

6. **Click the Run button.**
   A dialog box displays that contains the message you placed between the square brackets (see Figure 6.15).

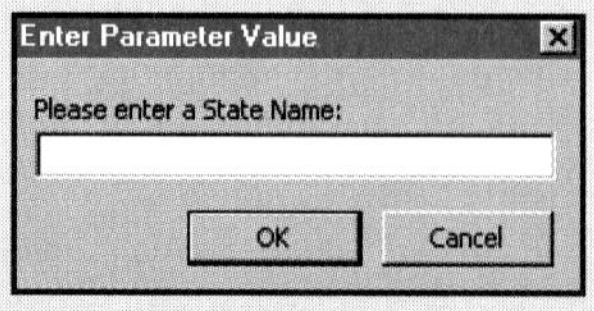

Figure 6.15
A parameter query enables the user to enter the criteria.

7. **Type `Ohio` and click OK.**
   The 731 tornadoes that occured in Ohio are displayed.

8. **Click the View button to switch to Design view. Click the Run button again. Enter `Indiana` and click OK.**
   The 1,035 records for Indiana are displayed.

9. **Close the query, and save the changes. Leave the database open for use in the next lesson.**

Lesson 5: Using Parameters with Comparison Operators in a Query

Parameters may be used in place of field names in criteria that determine ranges. The user can specify a range of dates, upper, or lower limits each time the query is run.

In this lesson, you learn to use parameters in a criterion that selects a range of times. You also learn to use the Zoom property when working with long criteria. Continue using the Tornado Analysis database.

To Use a Parameter in a Comparison Criteria

1. **Select the Times query and click the Design button.**

2. **Right-click on the criteria box in the Time field. Select Zoom from the shortcut menu.**
   The Zoom dialog box opens. It may be used to enter and edit long criteria that would not be easily viewed in the criteria box.

3. **Enter the following expression:**
   Between [Enter the starting time:] and [Enter the ending time:]
   The user will be able to enter starting and ending times when the query is run (see Figure 6.16).

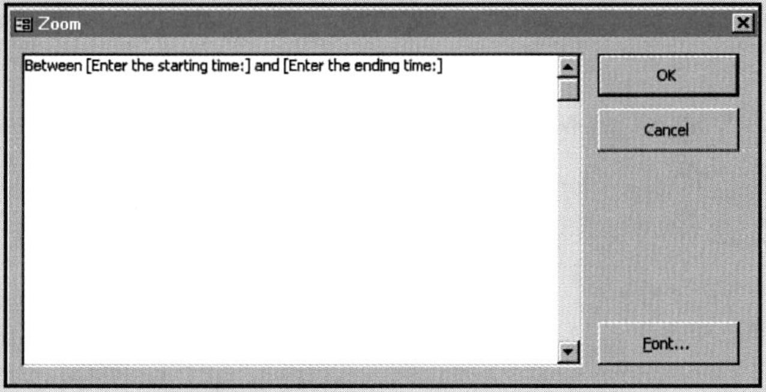

Figure 6.16
Long criteria may be entered using the Zoom dialog box.

4. **Click OK; then click the Run button.**
   The Enter Parameter Value dialog box appears.

5. **Type `0000` and click OK.**
   The data is stored using a twenty-four hour time format, starting at midnight. All times are given in local time. The second window opens with the second message.

6. **Type `0100` and click OK.**
   The 713 tornadoes that occurred between midnight and one o'clock a.m. are displayed. Scroll down the records. Notice that 0 and 100 are included. The Between operator includes values entered to define the range.

7. **Close the query and save the changes. Leave the database open.**

Comparison Operators
You may use a variety of ***comparison operators*** in filters or parameter queries, such as: (Equal, =; Greater Than, >; Less Than, <; Less Than or Equal,<=; Greater Than or Equal, >=; and Not Equal <>.) Operators like <> are called ***excluding operators*** because they are used to exclude the records that meet the criteria rather than include them.

Working with Empty Fields
At times you may want to exclude records that have empty fields. For example, if you do a calculation in a query where you divide one field by the other, it is important that you do not try to divide by an empty field because it will result in an error message. An empty field is a ***Null*** value. You may use a criterion of Is Not Null to make sure that no records with an empty field are included. You may use the Is Null operator to select empty fields.

Lesson 6: Using Parameters with Wildcards as Criteria in a Query

An asterisk may be used in place of text to complete an entry in a text field if the Like operator is used. The Like operator allows a match between a partial entry and the value in a field.

In this lesson, you use ***wildcards*** to locate counties when you only know part of the correct name.

To Use the Like Operator with a Wildcard

1. **In the Tornado Analysis database, select the County query and click the Design button.**
2. **Right-click on the criteria box in the County Name field and select Zoom from the shortcut menu.**
3. **Type the following operator and message:**
   `Like [Enter county name, may be completed with *:]`
   The Like operator enables the use of asterisks. Remember to use square brackets.
4. **Click OK; then click the Run button.**
   The Enter Parameter Value dialog box appears.
5. **Type `Tus*` and click OK.**
   All the county names that begin with Tus are displayed.
6. **Scroll down the list of county names to display the two other counties whose names start with Tus.**
   It is important to inspect the results to see if any unintended matches are included in the records.
7. **Close the query, and save the change. Leave the database open.**

Summary

You do not have to import a large table into your database to analyze it. It is possible to link to a large table and incorporate it into the relationships, queries, and other database objects.

The Filter by Selection option is used for simple matching criteria based on the currently selected field. The Filter by Form option has more capabilities and can be used to filter on several fields, in more than one combination.

Specific criteria may be replaced by prompting phrases enclosed between square brackets. A query that uses this feature to input a criterion is known as a parameter query. It allows the user to specify a different criterion value each time the query is run.

Checking Concepts and Terms

True/False

For each of the following, check *T* or *F* to indicate whether the statement is true or false.

__T __F **1.** If you enclose a phrase inside square brackets in a query design, the program prompts you to enter a value to be used in place of the phrase, unless the word or phrase in the brackets is a field name. [L4]

__T __F **2.** In the query design, a parameter is enclosed in parentheses. [L4]

__T __F **3.** Using parameters enables user input to restrict the output of a report. [L4]

__T __F **4.** If the Apply Filter button is gray (or dim), no filter conditions exist to be applied. [L3]

__T __F **5.** If you click the Remove Filter button, the filter is erased and you have to create it again if you need it in the future. [L3]

__T __F **6.** A wildcard may be used to replace numbers, not text. [L6]

__T __F **7.** In the design of a query, if the words inside square brackets match a field name, the program will use the current contents of that field. [L4]

__T __F **8.** To use the Zoom window for writing a long expression, right-click the field box or criteria box in the design grid and choose Zoom from the shortcut menu. [L5]

__T __F **9.** If you close a table and reopen it, the most recently created filter is no longer available for use. [L3]

__T __F **10.** If a field has no entry it is a Null value. [L5]

Multiple Choice

Circle the letter of the correct answer for each of the following questions.

1. Which of the following are used to enclose a parameter? [L3]

a. ( )

b. { }

c. < >

d. [ ]

2. Which of the following expressions correctly uses a parameter to prompt the user for input? (Assume that Company and Product are field names.) [L3]

a. (Enter the Company Name)

b. [Enter the Product Name]

c. [Company]

d. [Product]

3. Filter buttons used in Access are ______________. [L2]

a. Apply Filter, Create Filter, Remove Filter

b. Filter by Selection, Filter by Form, Filter by Design

c. Apply/Remove Filter, Filter by Selection, Filter by Form

d. Create Filter, Delete Filter

4. If you had a database of books that had been loaned out from a library and wanted to show all the books by a certain popular author that had been loaned out during a particular month, you would ______________. [L2]

a. place the cursor in the author field and use filter by selection

b. place the cursor in the date field and use filter by selection

c. scroll through the records using the navigation buttons and place a bookmark in each record that met the criteria

d. use the Filter by Form button and put the author's name in the author field and a logical criteria such as, Between 1/1/97 and 1/31/97, in the date field

5. Operators you can use with a Filter include ______________. [L5]

a. comparison operators

b. minimizing operators

c. pivotal operators

d. all of the above

6. When you click the Remove Filter button, the filter is ______________. [L3]

a. deleted

b. permanently removed and would have to be recreated to be used again

c. no longer active but still available to be reapplied until another filter is created

d. removed but saved as a permanent filter that can be reapplied at anytime by right-clicking on the Apply Filter button

7. To remove a filter permanently, ______________. [L3]

a. create a new empty filter and apply it to the form or query; then save the changes
b. click the delete button on the keyboard
c. right-click on the filter and click delete from the shortcut menu
d. click the Remove Filter button

8. If you link to a table rather than import it, you cannot ______________. [L1]

a. use it to create a query
b. use it in a relationship
c. change the data in the table
d. use its data in a report

9. An advantage of using a parameter query is ______________ [L3]

a. users can control the output of the query by entering a value in the Parameter Value dialog box
b. you can use the same query structure repeatedly without having to open the design of the query and make changes
c. a form or report can be based on a parameter query
d. all of the above

10. In a query, if the text entered inside square brackets is not a field name, the program ______________. [L3]

a. gives you an error message and tells you it cannot locate the field
b. uses the text as the heading for a column
c. assumes you want to enter a value from a parameter value dialog box
d. ignores the text that has been entered

Screen ID

Label each element of the Access screen shown in Figures 6.17 and 6.18.

Figure 6.17

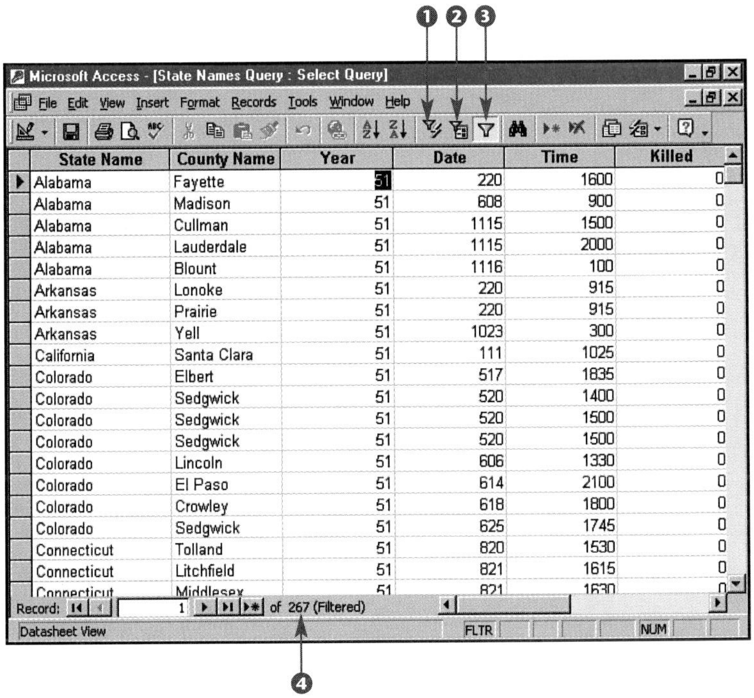

A. Number of records that meet the criteria

B. Mark used to enclose text criteria

C. Clear Grid

D. Filter by Selection

E. Closes the Filter by Form grid

F. Filter by Form

G. Apply Filter

H. Remove Filter

I. Criteria in a number field

J. Tab indicating second set of criteria

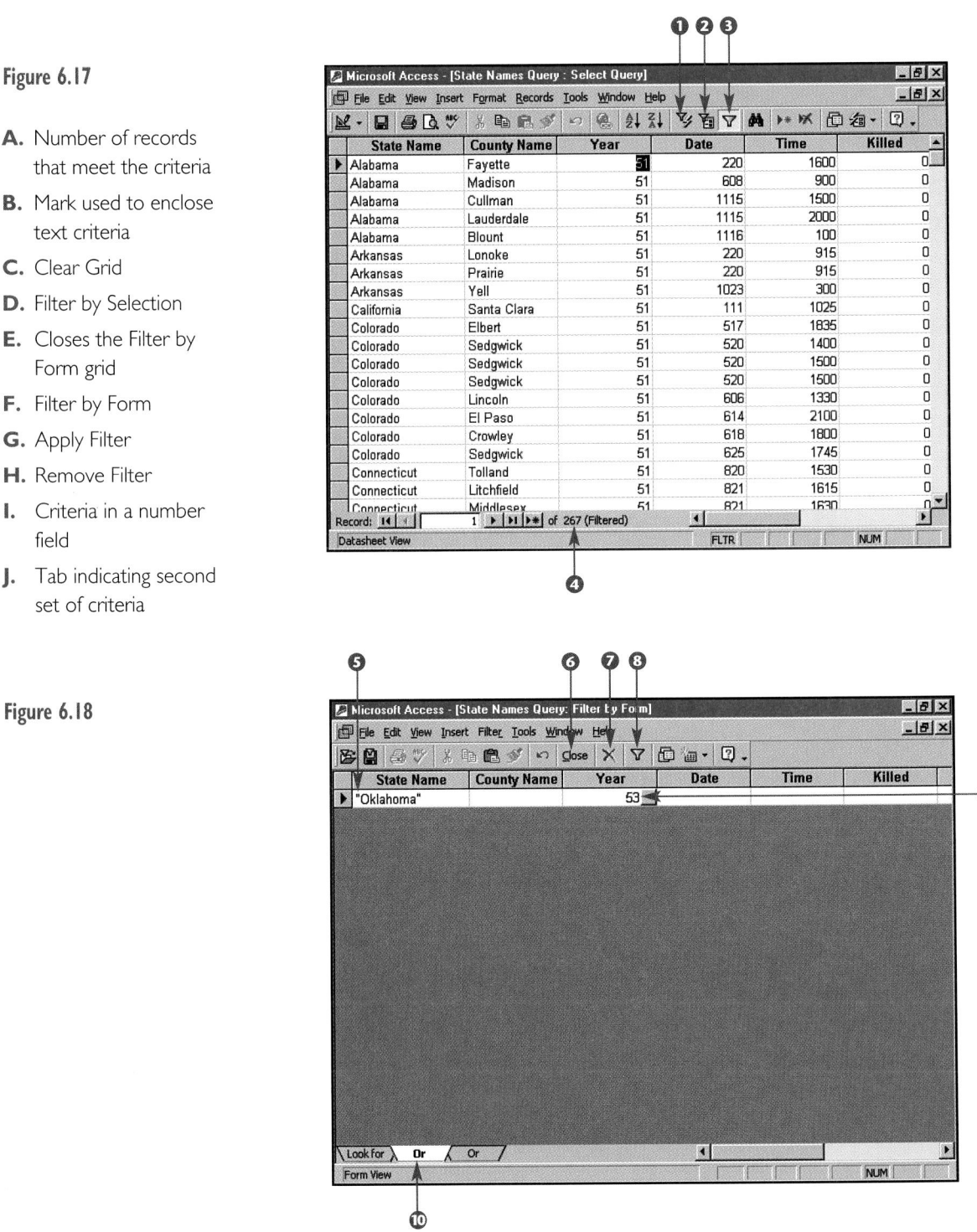

Figure 6.18

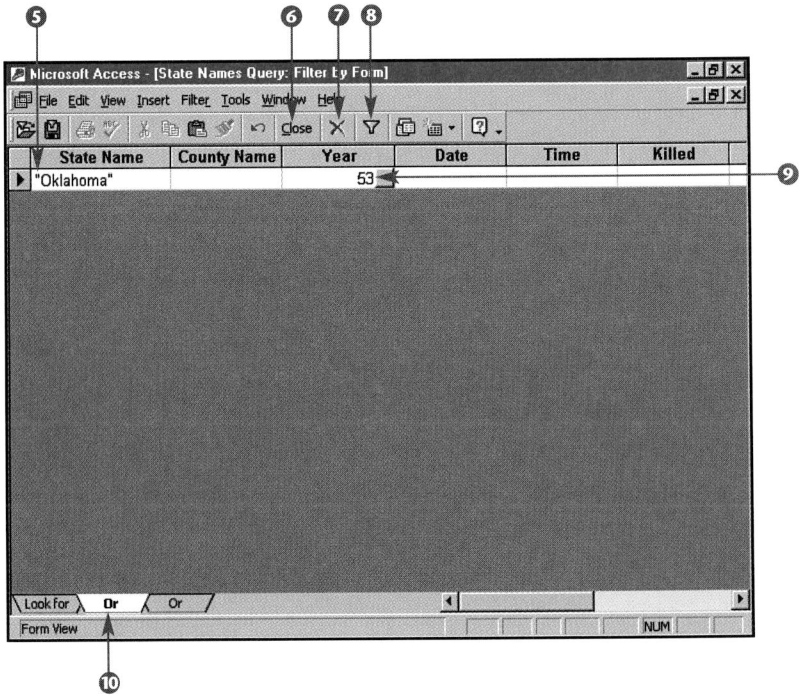

1. ____________
2. ____________
3. ____________
4. ____________
5. ____________
6. ____________
7. ____________
8. ____________
9. ____________
10. ____________

Discussion Questions

1. Describe situations in which it is best to link to a table rather than import it. State your reasons.
2. What kinds of fields would be appropriate for use with the Filter by Selection feature?
3. When is it most appropriate to use the Filter by Form feature instead of creating a query?
4. Under what circumstances would you use the wild-card feature with the parameter? When would it be a bad idea?

Skill Drill

Skill Drill exercises reinforce project skills. Each skill reinforced is the same, or nearly the same, as a skill presented in the project. Each exercise includes a brief narrative introduction, followed by detailed instructions in a step-by-step format.

All of the Skill Drill exercises use the same database. Before you begin, copy file AC3-0602 from the Student/Project06 folder on the CD-ROM disk to your floppy disk, remove the Read-only property, and rename it `Library`.

1. Using Filter by Selection to Find All the Books Published in 1992

Practice what you have learned on a different database. Open the Library database. Use the Filter by Selection feature to display only books published in 1992.

To Use the Filter by Selection feature

1. Open the Library database and open the Books table.
2. In the Publication Dates field, click on one of the 1992 dates.
3. Click the Filter by Selection button.

   The four books published in 1992 are displayed.
4. Click the Print button to print the table.
5. Click the Remove Filter button and close the table. Do not save the changes. Leave the database open.

2. Creating a Filter Based on a Form Using the Between Operator

In this exercise, you open a form that shows the books that have been borrowed from a library and create a filter for those that were borrowed in 1997.

To Create a Filter Using a Form

1. In the Library database, open the form Books on Loan.
2. Click the Filter by Form button.
3. Enter the following condition in the Borrow Date box:

   `Between 1/1/97 and 12/31/97`
4. Click the Apply Filter button.
5. Click the Print button to print the three books.
6. Click on the Remove Filter button to disable the filter.
7. Close the form but leave the database open.

3. Using a Parameter with the Like Operator for Partial Matches

Create a query that uses the Like operator with a parameter that enables you to enter the first few letters of a selection and produce matches.

To Use a Parameter with the Like Operator in a Query:

1. Open the Library database, if necessary, and open the query Mysteries in the Design mode.
2. In the Type of Book column, replace the "Mystery" criteria with the following:

   `[Enter the type of book:]`

3. Click the Run button to look at the Datasheet view. When the Enter Parameter Value dialog box appears, type any one of the following and click OK.

   Mystery, Fiction, Classic, Non-Fiction, Science Fiction, or Humor

4. Return to the Design view. Add the conditional word `Like` to the criteria. The new criteria should be:

   `Like [Enter the type of book:]`

5. Run the query again. Enter an asterisk to see all of the titles.

6. Click the View button to return to Design view. Click the Run button. Enter **`Mys*`** and click OK.

   Asterisks can be used to replace parts of fields you are trying to match when you use the Like operator; for example, Mys* would find any book type starting with "Mys".

7. Close the query, and save the changes. Leave the database open for use in the next exercise.

4. Use the Between Operator with Two Parameters

In the following exercise you use the Between operator with two parameters to determine which books were borrowed between any two dates.

To use the Between operator with two parameters

1. Open the Library database, if necessary.
2. Click the Queries tab and select the Borrowed Books query. Open it in Design view.
3. Enter the following criterion in the criteria box of the Borrower Date field:

   `Between [From:] and [To:]`

4. Click the Run button. Enter **`5/1/00`** in the From: box, and click OK. Enter **`8/31/00`** in the To: box to see which books were borrowed during the summer.
5. Print the list. There should be only one book.
6. Close the Query, and save the changes.

Challenge

Challenge exercises expand on or are somewhat related to skills presented in the lessons. Each exercise provides a brief narrative introduction, followed by instructions in a numbered step format that are not as detailed as those in the Skill Drill section.

Use the Tornado Analysis database that you created for all of the following Challenge exercises.

1. Use a Parameter to Provide User Input in a Calculation

In this exercise, you enable the user to enter a conversion factor to display the measurement in miles, meters, or kilometers.

To create a parameter query that allows the user to input a value used in a calculation

1. Open the Tornado Analysis database and click the Queries button.
2. Double-click the Create query by using the wizard shortcut button.
3. Choose the State Names table and select the State Name field. Choose the County Names table and select the County Name field. Choose the Tornadoes table and select the Year, Date, and Length from the Tornadoes table. Click Next.
4. Click Next to accept the Detail setting. Enter **`Path Length`** as the title. Click Finish to create the query.
5. Open the Path Length query in Design view. Scroll to display the empty field to the right of the Length field. Right-click in the Field box and choose Zoom from the shortcut menu.
6. Enter the following calculation:

   `Length (other units):[Length]*[Enter length conversion factor:]`

7. Click OK; then click the Run button.
8. Enter `.0001894` to convert the path length to miles. Click OK. Scroll the display to view the new, calculated field.
9. Close the query and save the changes.

2. Use the Like Operator with Two Asterisks to Match Any Part of the Field

When you use the Like operator with a parameter, you can finish the entry using a single asterisk. This method may require some user training and does not work if you are looking for part of a name that is not at the beginning of the name.

To use the Like operator with two asterisks

1. Right-click on the County query and select Copy from the shortcut menu. Right-click on the empty white area, and select Paste from the shortcut menu.
2. Enter `Find Partial County Names`, and click OK.
3. Open the Find Partial County Names query in the Design view.
4. Right-click the existing criteria in the County Name field and select Zoom from the shortcut menu.
5. Replace the existing criterion with the following:
   ```
   Like"*"+[Enter partial county name:]+"*"
   ```
6. Click OK; then click the Run button.
7. Enter `town` in the dialog box and click OK. Tornadoes in Towner County and Georgetown County are displayed.
8. Print the list of fifteen tornadoes in these two counties.
9. Close the query and save the changes.

3. Use the Not Null Operator to Remove Irrelevant Records

When working with large tables, it is valuable to be able to remove records that have no entry in a particular field. The path length was not recorded in many cases and there is no reason to display records in the Path Length query that do not have an entry. Some of the records have a path length of zero so it is necessary to distinguish between an empty field and one that contains a zero.

To use the Is Not Null operator to limit the display of records

1. Open the Path Length query (created in the first challenge exercise). Enter a conversion factor of .3048 to convert the length measurement to meters.
2. Observe that many records have a zero for the Length, whereas many others have no entry at all. The empty fields are said to have a Null value. Notice that all 37,957 records display.
3. Click the View button to switch to Design view. Enter the following criterion for the Length field:
   ```
   Is Not Null
   ```
4. Click the Run button. Enter .0003048 to convert the lengths to kilometers. Notice that the number of records displayed is reduced to 25,303. The records with empty fields are not displayed.
5. Close the query and save the change.

4. Using the Shortcut Menu to Filter by Exclusion

In this exercise, you create a filter using the shortcut menu to view everything except the records that match the selection.

To create an exclusion filter

1. Copy the State Names Query and rename the copy `Tornado Information`. Open the Design view and remove the parameter from the State Name field. Switch to Datasheet view of the query.
2. Right-click on Alabama in one of the records. Choose Filter Excluding Selection. None of the Alabama records are displayed.
3. Click the Filter by Form button. Notice that the not equal operator, <>, was automatically applied to the selected field value.
4. Close the Filter by Form view. Click the Remove Filter button. Close the query and save the changes.

5. Use the Shortcut Menu to Create a Compound Filter

You can combine filter conditions with the operator, and. In this example, you exclude all the Tornadoes from Texas and Florida.

To Create a Compound Exclusion Filter

1. Open the Tornado Information query.
2. Right-click on one of the state names. Click in the Filter For box.
3. Enter the following criterion:
   `Not "Texas" and Not "Florida"`
4. Drag the scroll box down the list to confirm that no tornadoes from Texas or Florida are listed.
5. Click the Filter by Form, clear the grid, and apply the empty filter.
6. Close the query and save the changes. Leave the database open to use in the following exercises.

Discovery Zone

Discovery Zone exercises require advanced knowledge of project topics and application of skills. These exercises focus on enhancing your problem-solving skills. Numbered steps are not provided, but you are given hints, reminders, screen shots, and references to help you reach your goal for each exercise.

In these exercises, you will be using the Tornado Analysis database you created in the project.

1. Using the Concatenation Operator

Sometimes it is useful to combine two fields together. This type of operation is called concatenation. It is possible to use this operator with parameters to create a calculated field that combines two other fields. The symbol used for concatenation is the ampersand, &.

Goal: Use the concatenation operator in a calculated field to combine the Date and Year fields.

To produce a calculated field that uses two parameters, Date and Year, and concatenates them into a single field:

- Open the Tornado Analysis database, if necessary, and open the Tornado Information query in Design view.

- Create a calculated field that contains the Date and Year field names within square brackets, separated by an ampersand.
- Run the query. The new column should display the date information (day and month in this case) and year in one field. An example of date information for May 13, 1992, would be 51392.
- Close the query and save the changes.

2. Use a Parameter to Find Matches Between Fields

If you use a parameter in one field that contains the name of another field, the query will display the records that contain the same value in both fields.

Goal: Create a query that displays the tornadoes that occurred in counties that have the same names as their states.

The solution should do the following:

- Make a copy of the State Names Query and name it `State and County Names that are the Same`.
- Open the query in Design view and remove the criterion in the State Name field.
- In the criteria box under the County Name field, enter a parameter that contains the State Name field.
- Run the query. What are the six counties that bear the name of the state in which they exist? Use Word to write a list of those names and include your own name. Close the query and save the changes.

3. To Filter a Database to Answer Specific Questions

Use the skills that you have learned about filters and queries to answer the following questions about the tornadoes that occurred in the United States and its territories during the period from 1950 to 1995.

Ultimately, you will need to decide what combination of filters and queries to use to determine answers to questions regarding a table of data.

Goal: Create queries and use appropriate filters to answer a set of questions.

Create a new query named `Questions` that contains the State Name and County Name fields and whichever fields you deem appropriate from the Tornadoes table to answer the following questions:

- How many tornadoes have killed more than 20 people?
- How many tornadoes have occurred in the county where you live? How many of them killed someone?
- How many tornadoes occurred in Texas in 1955?
- How many tornadoes occurred in Michigan in 1953?
- How many tornadoes occurred in Oklahoma in 1993?
- How many tornadoes occurred in Florida in 1990?

Open a Word document and enter these questions and the answers that you found. Add your name to the document and print a copy.

Close the Questions query and save the changes. Close the database.

Project 7

Sharing a Database with Others

Objectives

In this project, you learn how to:

- **Assign a Password to Your Database**
- **Change or Remove a Database Password**
- **Encrypt a Database**
- **Create a Switchboard**
- **Set Startup Parameters**
- **Set Access Defaults**

Key terms introduced in this project include

- Add mode
- Edit mode
- encryption
- password
- Read-only mode
- share-level security
- Startup parameters
- switchboard
- user-level security

Why Would I Do This?

Many features of Access are designed to enable users to share data and to gain access to data used by others. Problems can arise from sharing data with others, however. Someone may make changes to the tables, forms, reports, or queries you have created, or he or she may enter data into the tables in a non-standard format. In some cases, your database may contain sensitive information that is not for general distribution or proprietary information that is valuable to the company. In this lesson, you learn some techniques that will provide some protection from accidental changes. You also learn some useful safeguards to protect your database from intentional damage or theft.

Many people who need to use databases do not have the need or the time to learn how to use Access. You can customize a database to guide these users through the functions they need to use. You can do this by setting startup and default parameters that will lead these users to custom menus that open forms with customized toolbars.

Visual Summary

When you have completed this project, you will have designed a database with related tables:

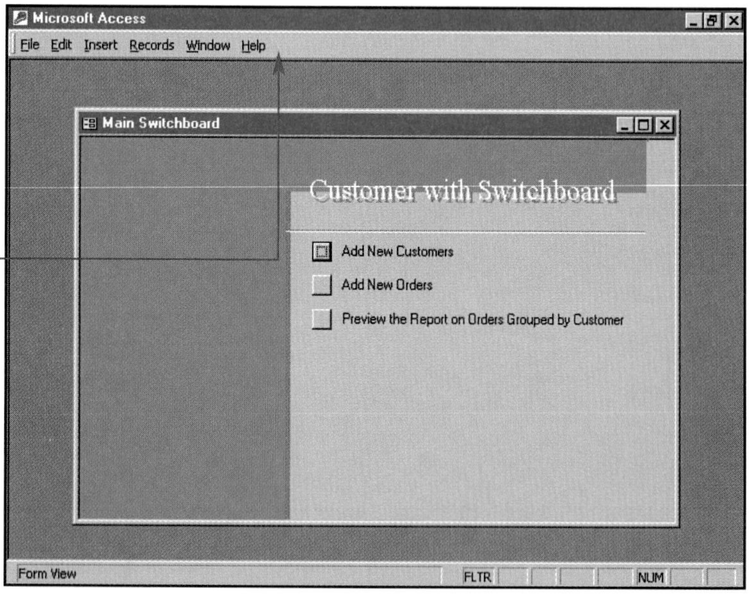

Figure 7.1
You can create a user-friendly form called a Switchboard for use by those who are less familiar with Access.

Lesson 1: Assigning a Password to Your Database

Adding security to your database is like putting a new lock on a door. It provides a measure of protection from some intruders, but it also has several drawbacks, such as:

- It slows you down every time you want to pass through the door.
- Other people who need to pass through the door must disturb you to ask you for the key.
- If you give a duplicate key to someone, you do not always know what he or she has done with it.
- There are people who have master keys to that type of lock.
- There are people who understand how the lock works and know how to pick it.
- If you lose the only key, it can be very inconvenient.

In spite of these disadvantages, most of us still use locks on our doors. Similarly, you may also want to add a measure of security to your database.

In this lesson, you learn how to require a ***password*** to open a database. Passwords are a mix of letters, numbers, and symbols used to identify an authorized user. Using a password to protect a database is called ***share-level security***.

To Assign a Password to Your Database

1. **Launch Access. Choose Open an existing file. In the Open dialog box, locate AC3-0701 on your CD-ROM. Right-click the file, and select Send To, 3 1/2 Floppy (A) from the shortcut menu. Change the Look in box to 3 1/2 Floppy (A:).**

2. **Right-click AC3-0701, select Properties, and remove the Read-only property. Right-click AC3-0701 again, and select Rename. Change the name of the file to `Prices` and press Enter.**

3. **Click the Prices database to select it, if necessary. Click the drop-down arrow on the Open button.**
   Several options are available. Opening the database in Exclusive mode prevents any other users from accessing the database while you are making this change. It is required for the following procedure, even if you are not using Access in a network environment (see Figure 7.2).

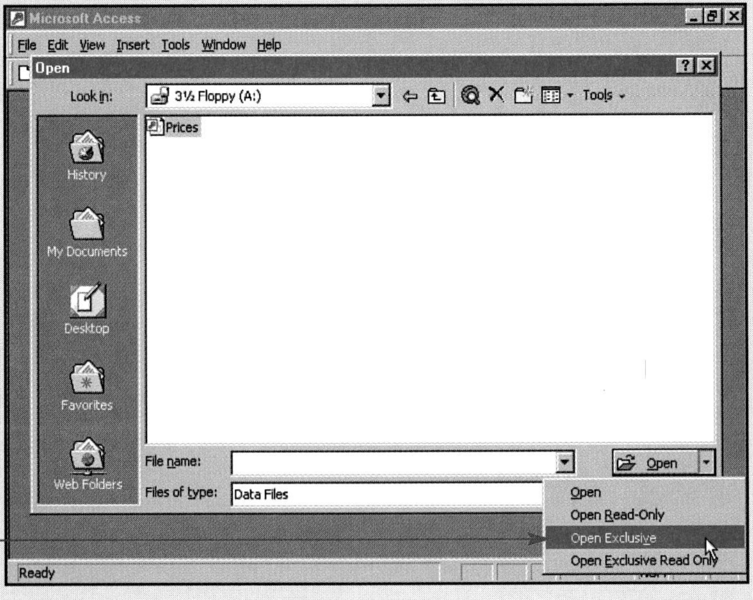

Figure 7.2
Use the Open Exclusive option to open the Prices database for exclusive use.

4. **Click Open Exclusive.**
   The Prices database opens.

5. **Choose Tools, Security from the menu; then select Set Database Password.**
   The Set Database Password dialog box appears (see Figure 7.3).

continues ▶

To Assign a Password to Your Database (continued)

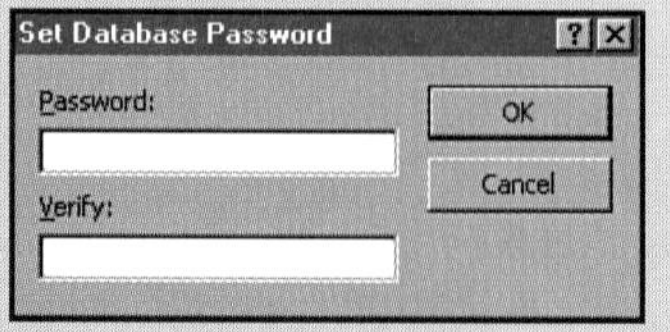

Figure 7.3
The Set Database Password dialog box enables you to set a new password.

6. **Type the following password in the Password text box:**

   ABCabc!

   The asterisks that appear represent the letters you type. If you are not sure what you typed, press Backspace and try again carefully.

7. **Press Tab, and type the same password in the Verify box. Click OK.**
   Be sure to use the same case (uppercase or lowercase) that you typed in the Password text box. The Set Database Password dialog box closes and the database window reappears.

8. **Close the database; then open it again.**
   You do not have to select the Exclusive option this time. The Password Required dialog box appears (see Figure 7.4).

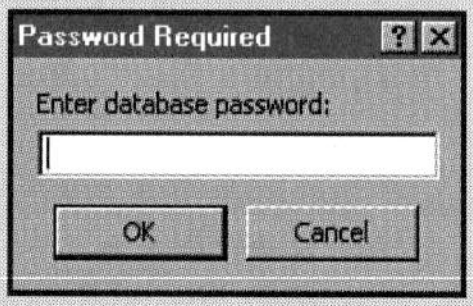

Figure 7.4
The Password Required dialog box is shown before the password has been entered.

9. **Carefully type the password and click OK.**
   The database opens if you correctly matched the password. If you did not match the password exactly, including the proper upper and lowercase characters, you see a warning box, and you return to the Password Required dialog box to try again.

10. **Close the database. Leave Access open.**

Guidelines for Choosing Passwords
Passwords in Access can be simple and short or complex and up to 14 characters in length. To get the best security out of your password, do not use a date or a word that would be listed in a dictionary. Do not use passwords others might be able to guess, such as a family member's name, your social security number, or a commonly used phone number. Make the password at least six characters long and include a character that is not a letter. If you do want to use an easily recalled word or date, insert an extra symbol. In the example in this lesson, the password included an exclamation mark for this purpose.

Lesson 2: Changing or Removing a Database Password

Once you have added a password to your database, you may need to change or remove it.

In this lesson, you learn how to change or remove the database password.

To Change or Remove a Database Password

1. **Choose File, Open. Select the Prices database on Drive A; then click the drop-down arrow next to the Open button, and choose Open Exclusive.**
   The Password Required dialog box appears.
2. **Enter the password you created in Lesson 1; then choose OK.**
3. **Choose Tools, Security from the menu bar; then choose Unset Database Password.**
   The Unset Database Password dialog box appears.
4. **Type the original password you created in Lesson 1 and click OK.**
   The database may now be opened without a password.
5. **Close the database. Leave Access open.**

When to Use the Open Exclusive Option
It is not necessary to use the Open Exclusive option if you are not changing the password.

Lesson 3: Encrypting a Database

Even though the database program is protected by a password, it is possible to view the data by opening the database with a word processing program. When you do this, most of the screen of the word processing program fills with unrecognizable characters, but some of the data in the tables is still readable.

In this section, you copy a database to your floppy disk and confirm that it is password protected.

To Confirm That a Database Is Password Protected

1. **Click the Open button. In the Open dialog box, locate AC3-0702 on your CD-ROM. Right-click the file, and select Send To, 3 1/2 Floppy (A) from the shortcut menu. Change the Look in box to 3 1/2 Floppy (A:).**
2. **Right-click AC3-0702, select Properties, and remove the Read-only property. Right-click AC3-0702 again, and select Rename. Change the name of the file to `Performance Evaluation`, and press Enter.**
3. **Select the Performance Evaluation file and click the Open button.**
   The Password dialog window opens.
4. **Enter a password of your choice. Click OK.**
   An error message displays when the program detects the incorrect password.
5. **Click OK. Click the Cancel button. Leave Access open.**
   You were not successful in opening the password-protected database.

It is still possible to read some of the text in a database by using a word processing program.

In this section, you use the Word program to view the database code and search for embedded text.

To View Embedded Text in a Database Using a Word Processing Program

1 Launch Word. Click the Open button. In the Files of type drop-down list, select All Files and locate the Performance Evaluation file on your floppy disk. Select the file, and click the Open button.

2 Click the Plain Text option button, and click OK.

The computer codes that Access uses to manage the database do not translate into meaningful text. The contents of the text fields, however, may be read. The problem is to find useful information in hundreds of pages of symbols (see Figure 7.5). The symbols that are displayed may vary from one computer to another. The code is shown in Normal view.

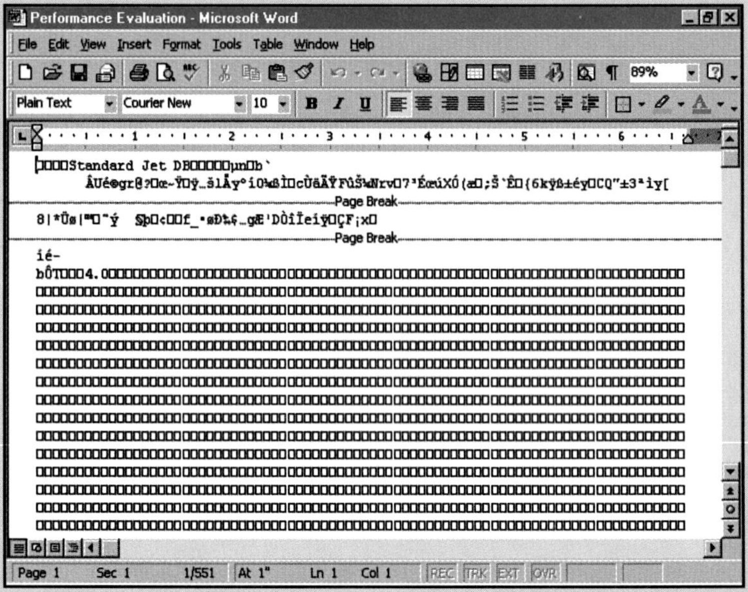

Figure 7.5
Most of the code in the database file is meaningless when viewed in Word.

3 Choose Edit, Find from the menu.

Because the topic of this database is performance evaluations, you can search for words that are likely to be used.

4 Type `expectations` in the Find what box. Click the Find Next button. Click Cancel to close the Find and Replace dialog box.

Social Security numbers and performance evaluations are easily recognizable (see Figure 7.6). Clearly, password protection is useful but not sufficient by itself to keep someone from reading the contents of text fields.

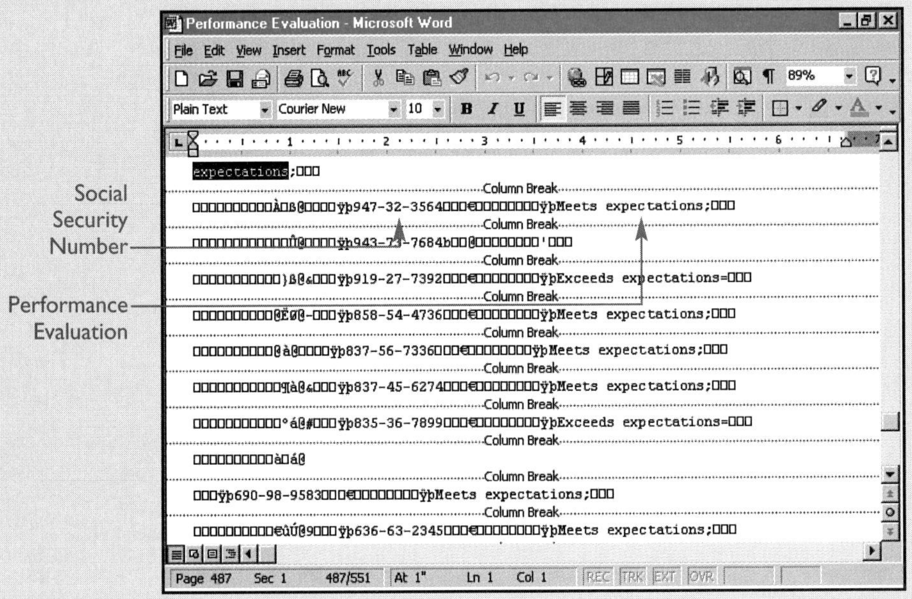

Figure 7.6
Important data may not be protected by using a password.

5 **Close the document. Leave Word open.**

Access has an ***encryption*** feature that encodes the contents of the fields so they are not easily read.

In the next section, you encrypt the database.

To Encrypt a Database

1 **Switch to Access. Choose Tools, Security, Encrypt/Decrypt Database.**
The Encrypt/Decrypt Database dialog box opens.

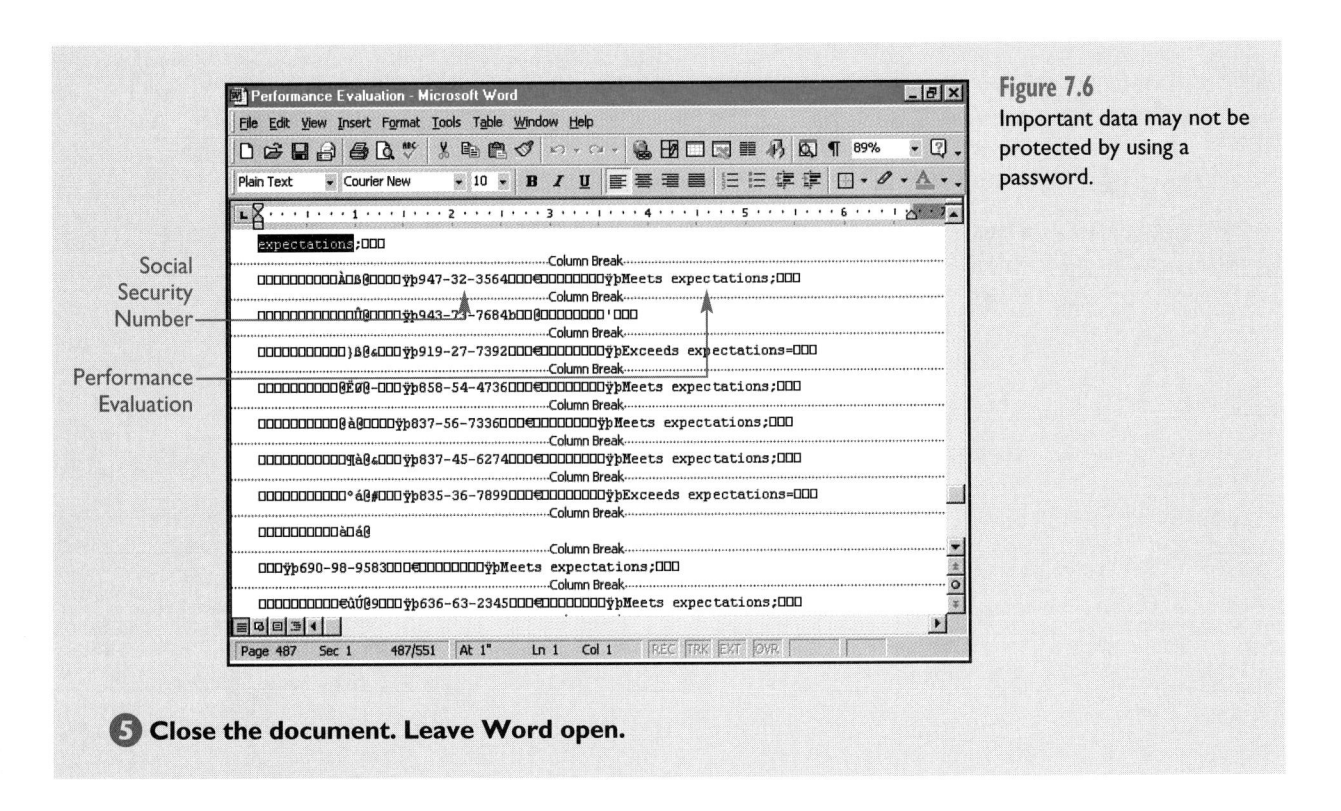

2 **Change the Look in box to display the files on the floppy disk in drive A. Select Performance Evaluation, and click OK.**
The Password Required dialog window opens. Because this database is password protected, you cannot make changes to it without the password. The password is provided in the next step.

3 **Type `jmp`, and click OK.**
The Encrypt Database As window opens.

4 **Enter `Encrypted Evaluations` in the File name text box, and click Save.**
The database is encrypted and saved under the new name.

5 **Switch back to Word. Follow the procedure described previously to open the Encrypted Evaluations database in Word and search for expectations.**
This time the search is unsuccessful. The text has been encoded and is no longer readable by this method.

6 **Close the file and close Word. Leave Access open.**

continues ▶

To Encrypt a Database (continued)

User-Level Security

The share-level security measures mentioned in these lessons are useful in providing a first line of defense. Access provides a more sophisticated level of security called ***user-level security*** that is particularly useful in a network environment. Do not attempt to make changes to user-level security on a network without the permission and cooperation of the network administrator. You could end up reinstalling Access or locking yourself and others out of a database. To learn more about user-level security, see the Discovery Zone exercises at the end of this project.

Lesson 4: Creating a Switchboard

As a database designer, you are often preparing databases for others to use, many of whom have little experience with databases. It is important that they are able to do their jobs quickly and efficiently. It is also important that they do not make changes to the design.

Access provides a feature called a ***switchboard*** that is a special purpose form. This form contains buttons that may be used by inexperienced people to open forms for inputting data, editing, or reviewing, as well as printing existing reports.

In this lesson, you learn how to create a switchboard using the Switchboard Manager. The sample database you will use already includes tables, forms, and reports that can be used in a switchboard.

To Create a Switchboard

1. **Launch Access, if necessary. Click the Open button. In the Open dialog box, locate AC3-0703 on your CD-ROM. Right-click the file, and select Send To, 3 1/2 Floppy (A) from the shortcut menu. Change the Look in box to 3 1/2 Floppy (A:).**
2. **Right-click AC3-0703, select Properties, and remove the Read-only property. Right-click AC3-0703 again, and select Rename. Change the name of the file to `Customer with Switchboard`, and press Enter.**
3. **Select the Customer with Switchboard file, and click the Open button.**
4. **Choose Tools, Database Utilities, Switchboard Manager from the menu bar.**

   Because there is no switchboard to manage yet, a dialog box appears that asks if you would like to create one (see Figure 7.7).

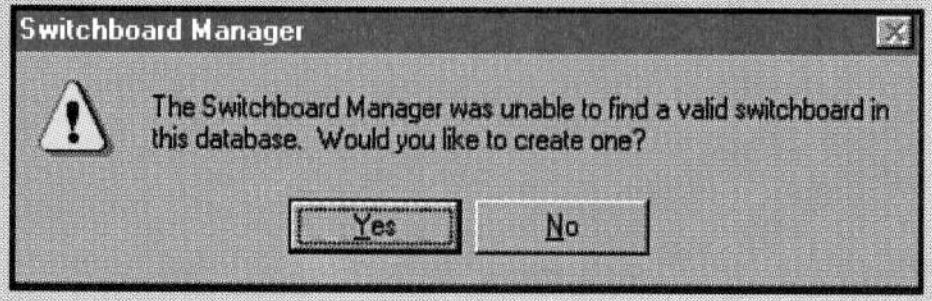

Figure 7.7
This dialog box appears if a switchboard does not already exist.

5 Choose Yes.

After a brief delay, another Switchboard Manager dialog box appears that displays the default switchboard (see Figure 7.8).

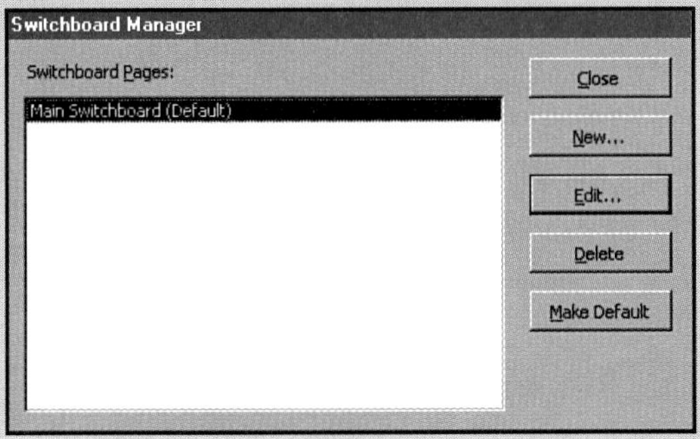

Figure 7.8
The Switchboard Manager dialog box displays the default switchboard option.

6 Click Edit.

This enables you to add action buttons to the switchboard. The Edit Switchboard Page dialog box appears (see Figure 7.9).

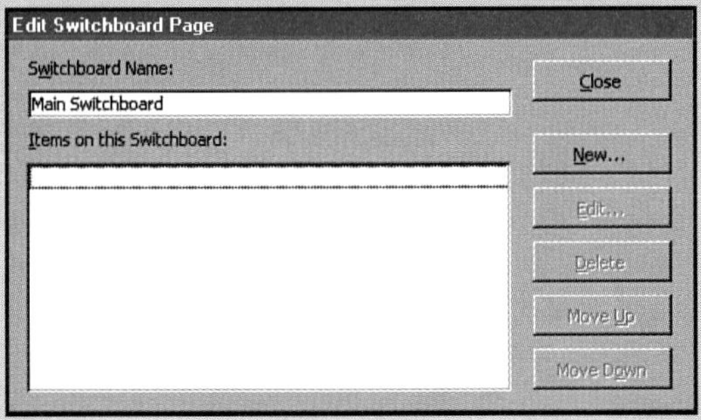

Figure 7.9
Use the Edit Switchboard Page dialog box to add action buttons to the switchboard.

7 Click New.

This action opens the Edit Switchboard Item dialog box (see Figure 7.10). This box contains a Text box that can be used to create a label for the action button. The Command drop-down list can be used to select commands to do things like open forms or preview reports.

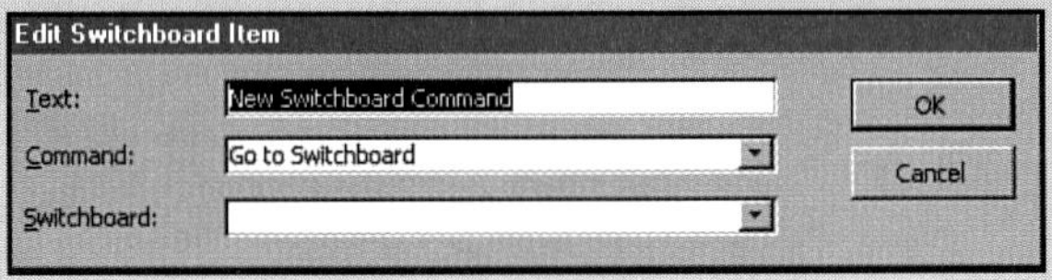

Figure 7.10
The Edit Switchboard Item dialog box is used to specify actions.

continues ▶

To Create a Switchboard (continued)

Use the Switchboard to Open the Same Form in Three Different Ways

The same form may be used three different ways and each of them can have its own button on the switchboard. If you open a form in ***Read-only mode***, it can only be used to view the records. The ***Add mode*** displays the form without showing any existing records and is useful for entering new data. The ***Edit mode*** is the one you have been using and allows the user to make changes, view existing records, and add new records.

8. **Change the text in the Text box to the following:**
`Add New Customers`

9. **In the Command drop-down list, select the Open Form in Add Mode option.**
The Add mode enables the user to enter new records but not to view existing records. Notice that the title of the third drop-down list box changes depending on your choice in the Command drop-down list box (see Figure 7.11).

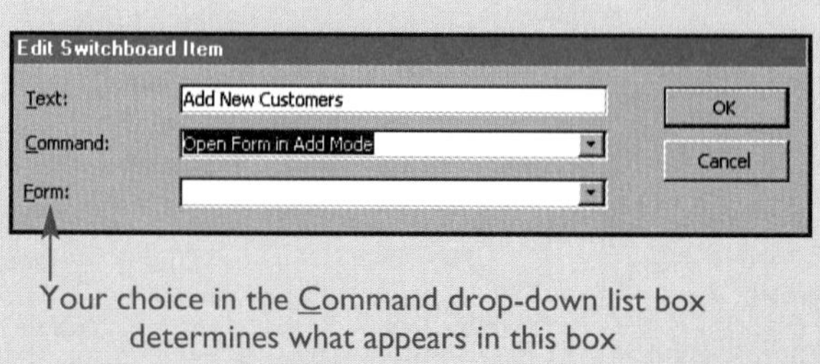

Figure 7.11
The Edit Switchboard Item dialog box changes the third choice in response to the contents of the Command drop-down list box.

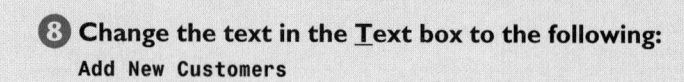

10. **In the Form box, select the Customer Information form. Click OK.**
The Edit Switchboard Page dialog box reappears, showing the Add New Customers item on its list of switchboard items (see Figure 7.12). Leave this dialog box open for use in the next section.

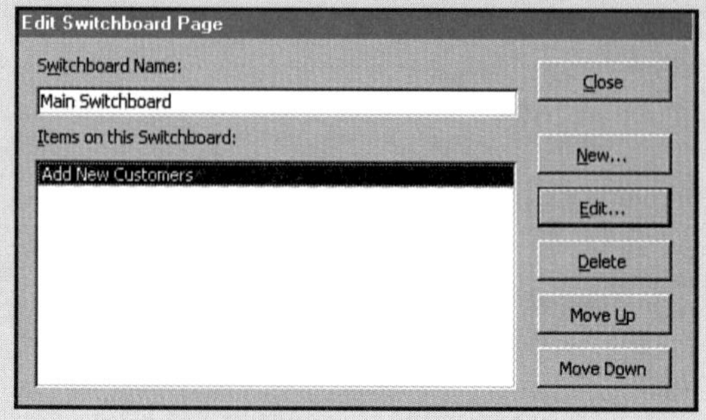

Figure 7.12
The Edit Switchboard Page dialog box displays the items that have been added to the switchboard.

This process may be repeated to produce several other switchboard items.

In the next section, you create switchboard items that allow the user to open the Customer Orders form in Add mode and to preview the Orders Grouped by Customer report.

To Create Additional Switchboard Items

1. **Click New to add another new item named `Add New Orders`. Choose the Open Form in Add Mode, and select Customer Orders in the Form box.**
The next switchboard item is defined as shown in Figure 7.13.

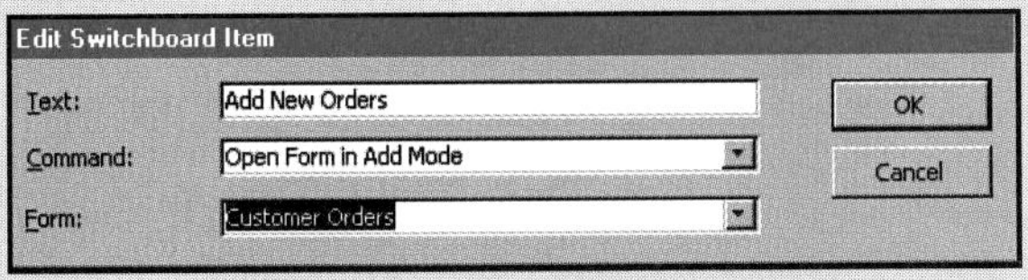

Figure 7.13
The Edit Switchboard Item dialog box is defined to add the next item.

2. **Click OK. Repeat the process again to add another new item named `Preview the Report on Orders Grouped by Customer`. This time, select the Open Report command, and pick the Orders Grouped by Customer report.**
The last item is defined to open a report (see Figure 7.14).

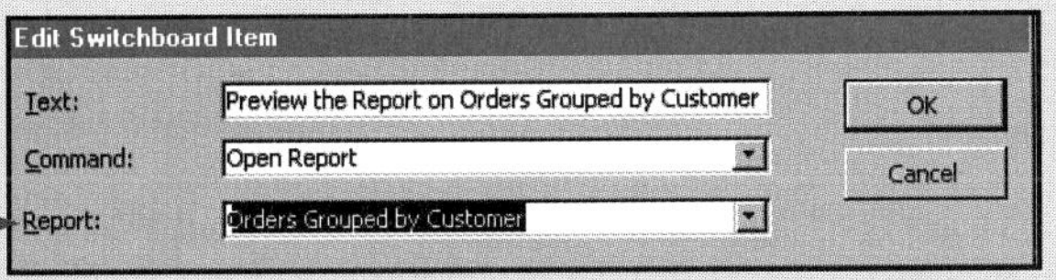

The box changes to Report to match the command

Figure 7.14
The Edit Switchboard Item dialog box is prepared to open a report.

3. **Click OK.**
The Edit Switchboard Page dialog box displays the three action items (see Figure 7.15).

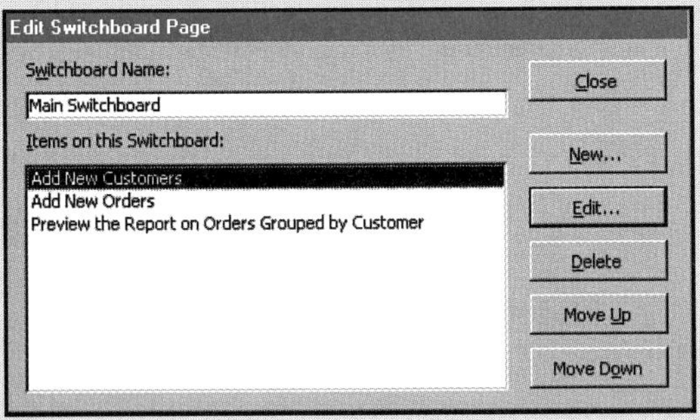

Figure 7.15
The Edit Switchboard Page dialog box displays the three action items.

4. **Click Close.**
The Switchboard Manager dialog box appears, displaying the single switchboard that has been created to this point.

5. **Click Close.**
The Switchboard Manager dialog box closes, and the database window is displayed. The database now has an extra table named Switchboard Items and a new form named Switchboard.

6. **Click the Forms object button to display the available forms. Click Switchboard to select it; then click Open.**
The new switchboard appears (see Figure 7.16).

continues ▶

To Create Additional Switchboard Items (continued)

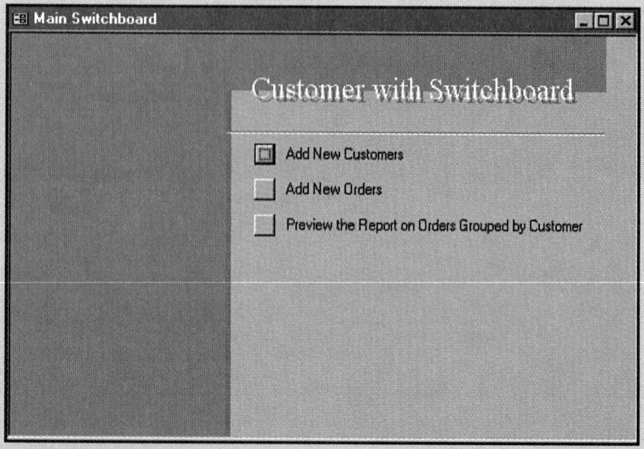

Figure 7.16
The new switchboard form opens.

7. **Test the switchboard by clicking on one of the buttons.**
It should automatically open the appropriate form or report.

8. **Close the form or report, and close the switchboard form.**
Leave the database open for the next lesson.

Switchboards May Be Linked or Launched on Startup
If you have more options than will fit on one switchboard or you would like to have multiple levels of switchboards, one of the commands available in the Command box is Go to Switchboard. You can use this to string together several switchboards and to branch from one to another.

The switchboard may be opened automatically by using the Startup settings whenever the database is opened. Startup settings are covered in the next lesson.

Lesson 5: Setting Startup Parameters

It is possible to control the way the database appears when it is opened. You can decide which toolbars are available to the user and you can open a switchboard form automatically. These options are called ***Startup Parameters***.

In this lesson, you learn how to open the switchboard automatically whenever the database is opened. You can also disable several features that are very useful while the database is being designed but that are not necessary while someone else is using it.

To Set Startup Parameters

1. **Open the Customer with Switchboard database, if necessary, and choose Tools, Startup from the menu.**
The Startup dialog box appears (see Figure 7.17).

To Set Startup Parameters

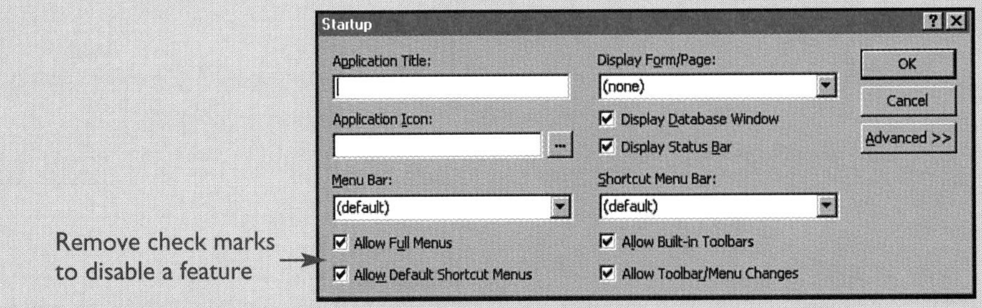

Figure 7.17
The Startup dialog box enables the designer to control the toolbars and menus to simplify them or to restrict the user's ability to change the design.

2 In the Display Form/Page drop-down list, select Switchboard.
This causes the Switchboard form to open automatically when the database is opened.

3 Click Display Database Window to deselect it.
When you close the switchboard form, the database window will not be available to the user; so, he or she cannot get into the design of the database.

4 Check the Display Status Bar check box to make sure it is selected.
This option could remove the status bar from the bottom of the screen to increase the available window space and simplify the screen. We will leave it turned on in this example.

5 Click Allow Built-in Toolbars to deselect it.
This option removes the toolbar from the top of the screen, increasing the available window space and simplifying the screen.

6 Click Allow Toolbar/Menu Changes to deselect it.
This prevents a user from adding the toolbars back to the screen.

7 Click Allow Full Menus to deselect it.
This changes the menu options from a full list of editing choices to a short list of choices that are appropriate for using the database rather than designing it.

8 Click Allow Default Shortcut Menus to deselect it.
This disables the shortcut menus options that are normally available by clicking with the right mouse button. Check to make sure that your dialog box looks like Figure 7.18.

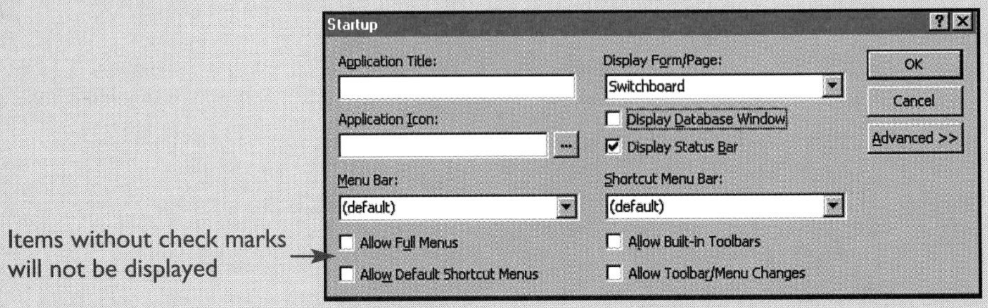

Figure 7.18
The Startup dialog box displays the new settings.

continues ▶

To Set Startup Parameters (continued)

Other Startup Options
The Startup dialog box can also help you design your own menu bars and shortcut menus. You can use this dialog box to create a special icon on the desktop that will run this version of the database. We will not use these options at this time.

9. **Click OK to close the Startup dialog box. Close the database.**
The next time the Customer with Switchboard database is opened, the start-up parameters will be used and the switchboard will open automatically.

10. **Open the Customer with Switchboard database again.**
The Switchboard form opens automatically. Notice that there are several differences. The menus have fewer choices; the right mouse button does not produce a shortcut menu, and the toolbar is not available (see Figure 7.19).

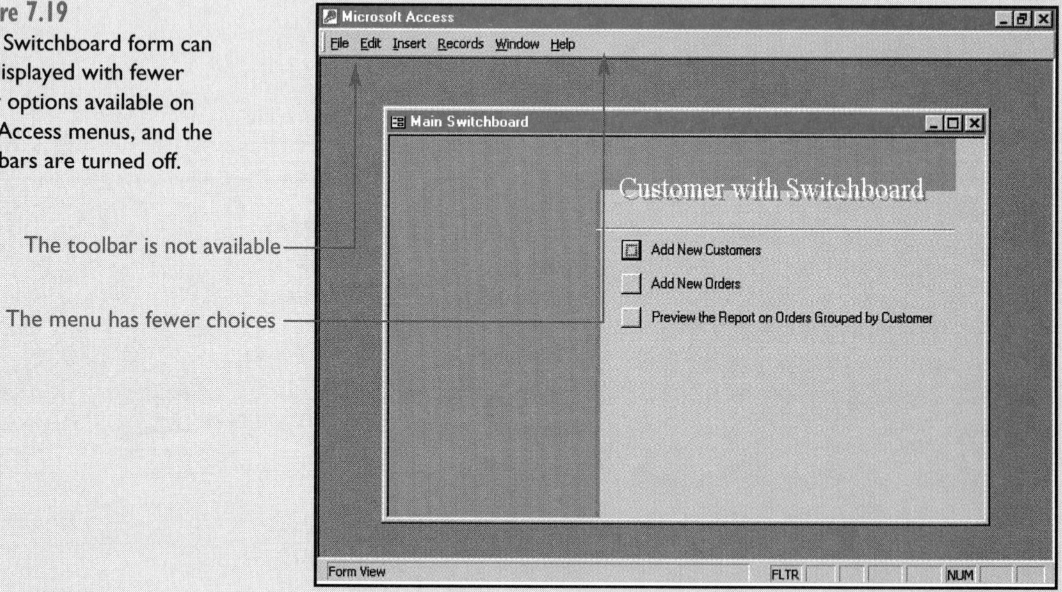

Figure 7.19
The Switchboard form can be displayed with fewer user options available on the Access menus, and the toolbars are turned off.

11. **Close the Switchboard form.**
The settings from the startup will stay in effect until Access is closed.

12. **Close Access.**
When you start Access again, the normal toolbars and menus will be displayed.

How to Override the Startup Parameters
If you choose to suppress the display of the toolbar and menu options used for design, you do not have a way to change the startup parameters. To open the database and bypass the startup parameters, hold down Shift when you open the database.

Lesson 6: Setting Access Defaults

Startups control the environment of a single database, whereas Access-based defaults control the environment for any Access database that is opened from your installed copy of Access.

In this lesson, you learn how to change some of the defaults that Access uses.

To Set Access Defaults

1. **Launch Access and open the Prices database from your floppy disk.**
   The Prices database opens. The normal menus and toolbars are visible.

2. **Choose Tools, Options from the menu.**
   The Options dialog box appears.

3. **Click the Keyboard tab.**
   The default settings are displayed for movement of the cursor after ↵Enter is pressed or when the arrow keys are used (see Figure 7.20).

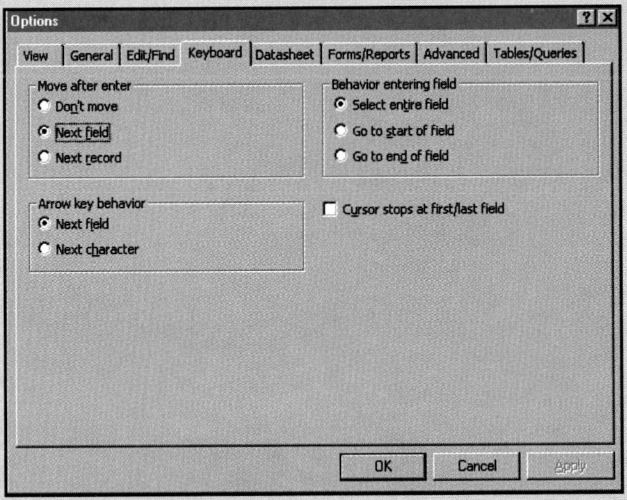

Figure 7.20
The Options dialog box can be used to set defaults for the Access program.

   After ↵Enter is pressed, the default setting for movement of the cursor is to move to the next field to the right in the current record. If you are entering or changing the data in one field, however, it is more convenient to move automatically to the next record.

4. **Click on Next record in the Move after Enter area.**

5. **Click the Apply button.**
   The cursor will now move down the column of data each time you press ↵Enter when you are in a datasheet view. If you are in a form, the view will page from one record to the next and remain in the same field when you press ↵Enter.

6. **Click the Datasheet tab.**
   The default options for the appearance of the datasheet are displayed (see Figure 7.21).

continues ▶

To Set Access Defaults (continued)

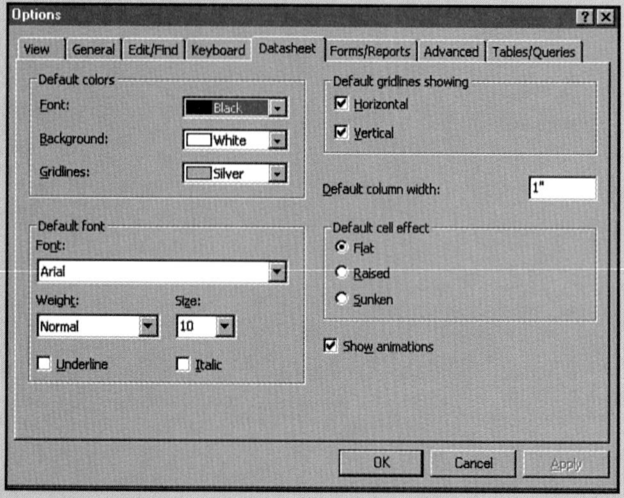

Figure 7.21
The default values for Datasheet View are displayed.

Changes on this form affect the appearance of any datasheet opened in Access.

7. **Change the default colors to White, Gray, and Aqua for the Font, Background, and Gridlines options, respectively. Click the Vertical option in the Default Gridlines Showing section to deselect it.**
Your Options Datasheet dialog box should look like Figure 7.22.

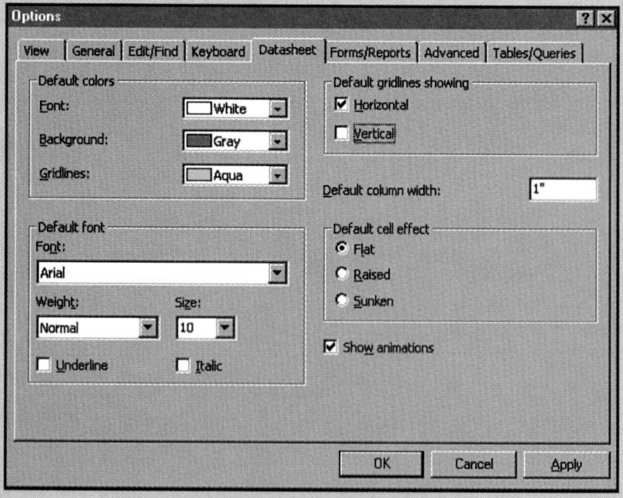

Figure 7.22
The Options Datasheet dialog box displays the new settings.

8. **Click OK to close the Options dialog box.**
These new settings are applied upon closing this dialog box.

9. **Open the Stock on Hand table in Datasheet View.**
The new default colors and gridlines settings will be displayed (see Figure 7.23).

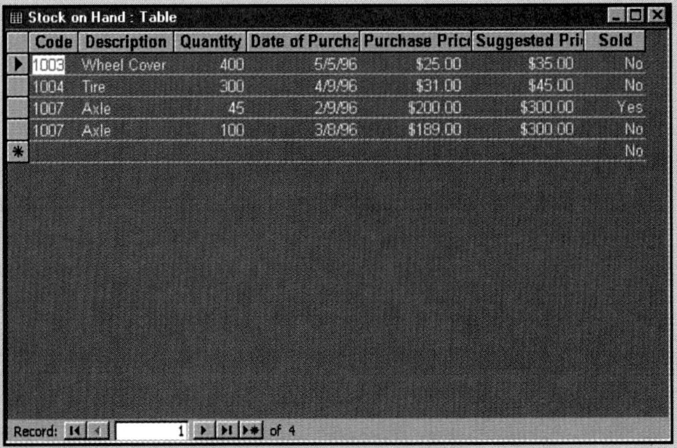

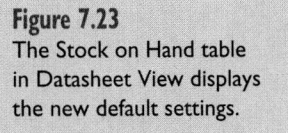

Figure 7.23
The Stock on Hand table in Datasheet View displays the new default settings.

10 Press ↵Enter several times.

Notice how the cursor moves down the column, from one record to the next, rather than across the fields.

11 Close the table.

12 Choose Tools, Options from the menu.

If you share your computer with others, it is important that you return the settings to their original values.

13 Click on the Datasheet tab. Change the default colors back to Black, White, and Silver for the Font, Background, and Gridlines options, respectively. Click the Vertical Default Gridlines check box to select it.

14 Click on the Keyboard tab. Change the Move After Enter option to Next field.

15 Click on OK to make the changes and restore the original settings.

16 Close the table and close the database. Close Access.

Default Settings Affect Other Databases

Use caution when changing the default Access settings, because they will affect all of your Access databases. If you share your computer with others in a laboratory setting, it would be discourteous to personalize the program without the consent of others who may not know how to change it back. Also, if you are using a copy of Access that is installed on a network server, the defaults will affect anyone else in your workgroup who uses the program. In the previous lesson, we only changed defaults that affected appearance. You could change operational defaults that could affect the function of the program, and you may not remember the original settings. Use this feature with care.

Summary

You can make it more difficult for unauthorized people to view your data by adding a password and encrypting the database.

If you are designing a database for use by others, you can provide a menu of options called a Switchboard. You can also restrict the use of editing features and change default settings for color and movement of the cursor.

Checking Concepts and Terms

True/False

For each of the following, check *T* or *F* to indicate whether the statement is true or false.

__T __F **1.** To add a password to a database, the first step is to open it by double-clicking on its name or icon. [L7]

__T __F **2.** To remove the password from a database, you must open the database. This implies that you know what the password is. [L7]

__T __F **3.** You can only use one switchboard with a database. [L7]

__T __F **4.** Encrypting a database prevents someone from reading data in the database by using a word processing program. [L7]

__T __F **5.** Default settings must be changed with no databases open because they affect all of the databases that are opened with that installation of Access. [L7]

__T __F **6.** The best passwords are the ones you do not forget. Keep it simple. Use something short, such as your birth date. [L7]

__T __F **7.** You can change the colors used to display tables using startup parameters. [L7]

__T __F **8.** Startup parameters may be used to disable certain toolbar and menu items normally used to edit the design of the database. [L7]

__T __F **9.** Switchboards are used to switch back and forth between Office applications, such as Word, Excel, PowerPoint, and Access. [L7]

__T __F **10.** Encrypting a database is a process of creating an archive copy for storage. [L7]

Multiple Choice

Circle the letter of the correct answer for each of the following questions.

1. Complete the following sentence. Startup parameters ______________. [L7]

a. are set with all of the databases closed

b. affect all databases opened by that installation of Access

c. are set after a database has been opened and only affect that database

d. are used to flash warning messages on the screen if there is too much traffic on the network

2. Which of the following is a Startup parameter setting that you could disable to simplify the appearance of the screen? [L7]

a. Display Status Bar

b. Display Headers/Footers

c. Display Database Names

d. Display Title Bar

3. If you wanted to limit the menu choices to those that would be useful for a user but not display those choices a designer would use, which of the following changes would you make to the Startup? [L7]
   a. De-select the Allow Built-in toolbars option.
   b. De-select the Allow Full Menus option.
   c. De-select the Allow Toolbar Changes option.
   d. De-select the Display Status Bar option.

4. A good password should have the following characteristics to make it hard to guess. [L7]
   a. It should be an easy to remember date.
   b. It should be an obscure word from the dictionary.
   c. It should include a symbol that is not a normal letter or number.
   d. It should be the same for all of your accounts.

5. If you have set the startup parameters so that they do not allow full menus, the Tools option does not appear. How do you change the startup parameters? [L7]
   a. Reinstall Access.
   b. Copy all of the data, forms, queries, and reports into a new database.
   c. Hold down Ctrl when you start Access.
   d. Close and reopen Access. Hold down Shift when you open the database.

6. Access uses the following term to describe data that has been scrambled and stored in coded form to prevent it from being read by someone who does not have the code. [L7]
   a. encrippled
   b. ciphered
   c. archived
   d. encrypted

7. Which of the following terms does Access use for a menu of choices represented by buttons on a form? [L5]
   a. main menu
   b. toolbox
   c. switchboard
   d. Connection Center

8. Which of the following is a setting that applies to all of the databases opened in Access? [L5]
   a. Default setting
   b. Startup setting
   c. Response setting
   d. Backup setting

9. Which of the following is a setting that applies to one database and is activated when that database is opened? [L6]
   a. Default setting
   b. Startup setting
   c. Response setting
   d. Backup setting

10. When you want to add or remove a password, the database must be opened in which of the following modes? [L7]
    a. Password mode
    b. Exclusive mode
    c. Read-only mode
    d. Archive mode

Discussion Questions

1. What are some methods of creating passwords that meet the guidelines provided in the first lesson but are still easy to remember?
2. Have you ever had anyone get into your files without permission? If the answer is no, how do you know?
3. Do you think you would ever design a database that someone else might use? If so, how important is it to you to restrict their ability to change the design either intentionally or unintentionally?
4. Do you share your computer with others? What would the ramifications be for others if you changed the default parameters of Access?
5. What is the proper role of the switchboard? When is it worth the extra time and effort to create one?

Skill Drill

Skill Drill exercises reinforce project skills. Each skill reinforced is the same, or nearly the same, as a skill presented in the project. Each exercise includes a brief narrative introduction, followed by detailed instructions in a step-by-step format.

1. Adding a Password to a Database

In the following exercise, you will add a password to protect a database named Books.

Insert an empty, formatted floppy disk in drive A before you start these exercises. The files that were created as part of the project will be used in the Challenge exercises, so keep the disk with those files for future use.

To add a password to a database, complete the following steps

1. Click the Open button. In the Open dialog box, locate AC3-0704 on your CD-ROM. Right-click the file, and select Send To, 3 1/2 Floppy (A) from the shortcut menu. Change the Look in box to 3 1/2 Floppy (A:).
2. Right-click AC3-0704, select Properties, and remove the Read-only property. Right-click AC3-0704 again, and select Rename. Change the name of the file to `Books`, and press Enter.
3. Select the Books file, click the drop-down arrow on the Open button, and open the Books database in Exclusive mode.
4. Choose Tools, Security, Set Database Password from the menu.
5. Type the password **`Books`**.
6. Verify the password by typing it again. Make sure to capitalize the first letter as shown.
7. Close the database and then reopen it. Try typing in the password as **`books`** to see if capitalization makes a difference. If that does not work, try **`Books`**.
8. Close the database.

2. Removing a Password from a Database

In this exercise, you remove a password from the Books database.

To remove a password from a database, complete the following steps

1. Click the Open button. In the Open dialog box, locate AC3-0705 on your CD-ROM. Right-click the file and select Send To, 3 1/2 Floppy (A) from the shortcut menu. Change the Look in box to 3 1/2 Floppy (A:).
2. Right-click AC3-0705, select Properties, and remove the Read-only property. Right-click AC3-0705 again, and select Rename. Change the name of the file to `Club` and press Enter.
3. Open the Club database in Exclusive mode. Use the password **`Club`**.
4. Choose Tools, Security, Unset Database Password from the menu.
5. Enter the password **`Club`**. Click OK.
6. Close the database and then reopen it. Confirm that the password is no longer required. Close the database.

3. Adding a Switchboard and Running It Automatically Whenever the Database Is Opened

In this exercise, you will set the startup parameters of a database to open a switchboard whenever the database is opened. In this way, you can create a database that a novice can use successfully without having to master the details of the Access program.

To add a switchboard and run it automatically whenever the database is opened, complete the following steps:

1. Click the Open button. In the Open dialog box, locate AC3-0706 on your CD-ROM. Right-click the file, and select Send To, 3 1/2 Floppy (A) from the shortcut menu. Change the Look in box to 3 1/2 Floppy (A:).
2. Right-click AC3-0706, select Properties, and remove the Read-only property. Right-click AC3-0706 again and select Rename. Change the name of the file to `Books with Switchboard`, and press Enter.
3. Open the Books with Switchboard database. Choose Tools, Database Utilities, Switchboard Manager to create a switchboard.
4. Click Edit. Add two new action items:
   - Add an item to open the Quick Entry form in Add mode. Use the text: `Add new books`.
   - Add an item to open the report, Book List. Use the following text: `Preview report on book status`.
5. Close the dialog boxes. Leave the database open to use in the next exercise.

4. Opening a Switchboard Automatically Whenever the Database Is Opened

In this exercise, you set the startup parameters of a database to open a switchboard whenever the database is opened. This way, you can create a database that a novice can use successfully without having to master the details of the Access program.

To run a switchboard automatically whenever the database is opened, complete the following steps:

1. Open the Startup parameters dialog box from the Tools menu.
2. Choose the switchboard form as the display form opened upon startup.
3. Click OK to close the Startup window. Close the database.
4. Open the Books with Switchboard database. The switchboard should appear automatically. Test both buttons.
5. Close the report preview form and the database, but leave Access open.

5. Encrypt a Database

In this exercise, you encrypt the Books with a Switchboard database.

To encrypt the database, complete the following steps:

1. Choose Tools, Security, Encrypt/Decrypt Database.
2. Locate the Books with Switchboard database on your floppy disk. Select it, and click OK.
3. Give the encrypted version a new name. Name it `Books with Encryption`, and click Save.
4. Open the database, and use the report to locate a key word for which you can search. Close the database.
5. Launch Word and open the encrypted file. Search for the name of a book that you know is in the file. It should not be found in the encrypted file. Close the file and close Word.

Challenge

Challenge exercises expand on or are somewhat related to skills presented in the lessons. Each exercise provides a brief narrative introduction followed by instructions in a numbered step or bulleted list format that are not as detailed as those in the Skill Drill section.

Before starting these exercises, insert an empty, formatted floppy disk in drive A. In the following exercises, you use a file that is similar to the one that was created in the first project.

1. Prevent Change to Data in One Field

There are various levels of security. In many cases, you just want to prevent accidental changes made by a well-meaning person. In such cases, it is sufficient to change the property of a field in a form to prevent accidental entries.

In the following exercise, a form named Update General Employee Information is used to make changes to nonsensitive data when people move or change their names. The Employee ID is displayed in this form, and you do not want a part-time employee who is unfamiliar with the database to change the employee number accidentally. A simple way to prevent that is to change the property of the field in that form.

To change the property of a field in a form to prevent changes:

1. Click the Open button. In the Open dialog box, locate AC3-0707 on your CD-ROM. Right-click the file, and select Send To, 3 1/2 Floppy (A) from the shortcut menu. Change the Look in box to 3 1/2 Floppy (A:).
2. Right-click AC3-0707, select Properties, and remove the Read-only property. Right-click AC3-0707 again and select Rename. Change the name of the file to `Projects` and press Enter.
3. Open the Projects database. Click the Forms button and select Update General Employee Information.
4. Open the form in Design view.
5. Right-click on the Employee ID text box (not the label box) and select Properties from the shortcut menu.
6. Click the Data tab. Change the Locked option from No to Yes. Close the Properties window.
7. Save the changes and switch to the Form view. Try to change the Employee ID number. It is not changeable. Close the form.
8. Open the Employee Information table. Attempt to edit one of the Employee ID numbers. You can still edit the table—locking the field in the form simply prevents accidents. Press Esc to restore the Employee ID number. Close the table.
9. Leave the database open to use in the next exercise.

2. Hide and Unhide Columns in a Table

Some information is not sensitive enough to warrant too much effort at concealment; however, it would be better if it were not displayed to everyone who looks at the table. An option that works well in this case is to hide the column or columns. Users who are not particularly familiar with Access will not think to look for hidden columns.

If you did not do the previous challenge exercise, perform steps 1 and 2, and open the Projects database before you start this exercise.

To hide the emergency contact information in the Employee Information table

1. Select the Employee Information table and open it in Datasheet view. Maximize the window.
2. Scroll to the right to display the Emergency Contact Number, Contact Person, and Relationship to Employee fields.
3. Choose Format, Unhide Columns. (Note: It is easier to use the Unhide option to hide columns than it is to select and hide them.)

4. Deselect the three fields mentioned in step 2 and click Close. The columns are not displayed.
5. Use this procedure to unhide the Emergency Contact Number.
6. Close the table, and save the changes.

3. Hide a Table, a Relationship, and a Form in a Database

It is also possible to hide database objects. This is a two-part process in which you first designate the object to be hidden, such as a table or form, and then change one of the Access options that displays hidden objects.

To hide a table and a form

1. Click the Tables button and locate the Private table.
2. Right-click on the Private table and select Properties from the shortcut menu.
3. Click the Hidden attribute to turn it on and hide the table. Click OK. The icon for the Private table is hidden.
4. Locate the Update Sensitive Information form. Repeat the previous two steps to turn on its Hidden attribute.
5. To unhide database objects, choose Tools, Options, and click the View tab, if necessary. Click the check box next to Hidden objects to select it. Click OK to apply and close the window. The icons for the table and form display but are dimmed.
6. Right-click on the Update Sensitive Information form and deselect its Hidden property. Leave the Hidden property selected for the Private table.
7. Set the option back to its original setting where it does not display hidden objects. The Update Sensitive Information form is visible but the Private table is not. (Normally, you would hide both, but one is restored to demonstrate that you know how to unhide a database object.) Close the database.

Discovery Zone

Discovery Zone exercises help you gain advanced knowledge of project topics and application of skills. These exercises focus on enhancing your problem-solving skills. Numbered steps are not provided, but you are given hints, reminders, screen shots, and references to help you reach your goal for each exercise.

You started this book by learning how to interview a manager to design a database. In that scenario, you were the expert. In the following exercises, you learn how to provide a network administrator with the information he or she needs to design a user-level security system for your Access databases. Network administrators are familiar with setting up user-level security, and you need to work with your network administrator to set up a similar system in Access.

1. Print Help Pages About Workgroups

A workgroup has an administrator who decides what groups exist in the workgroup and what those groups are allowed to do. He or she may then decide who is a member in each group.

There is plenty of information available from the Office Assistant about workgroups.

Goal: Print several reference pages concerning workgroups.

To print out some of the help pages that are most useful:

- Choose Help, Microsoft Access Help from the menu. Click the Office Assistant and search for the phrase, User-level security. Choose Protect a Microsoft Access database and its tables, queries, forms, reports, and macros with user-level security from the resulting list of topics.
- Click the Work with workgroup information files hyperlink.
- Click the Printer icon. The Print window opens. Click the check box labeled Print all linked documents. Click OK. The program will print a document for each of the links on this page—there are about 11 pages.
- Leave Help open.

2. Print Help Documents About User and Group Accounts

The next step is to learn something about user and group accounts.

Some terms are used that are very similar and often confused with one another. There is a high-level administrative group named Admins. Unfortunately, the program uses a very similar name, Admin, for an unknown user. Another opportunity for confusion is that there is a group named Users, but help messages often refer to two or more people as users.

Goal: Print several reference pages concerning user and group accounts.

To print out some of the help pages that are most useful

- Confirm that you are on the help page titled, Work with a workgroup information file. Click the Back button at the top of the Help screen to return to the Protect a Microsoft Access database and its tables, queries, forms, reports, and macros with user-level security page. Click on the Work with user and group accounts hyperlink.
- Click the Printer icon. The Print window opens. Click the check box labeled Print all linked documents. Click OK. The program will print a document for each of the links on this page—about 13 pages.
- Take some time to read these pages. Do not be surprised if you find them confusing; the following exercise will help you organize the material.
- Close Help.
- It is difficult to learn about this subject from these pages. Do not attempt to apply what you learn on these pages to a computer that is used on a network without consulting the network administrator. You can easily make a mistake that would result in locking people out of databases and causing a great deal of trouble. Even if you are working on your own computer that is not connected to a network, you could end up reinstalling Access and permanently locking yourself out of databases.

3. Planning to Implement User-Level Security

This time, you are on the user end of the interview. It is your job to describe what the workgroups, user groups, memberships and permissions should be. Refer to the case study that was used in Project 1, "Designing a Complex Database" and prepare a planning sheet that you can give to the network administrator.

Goal: Fill out a planning sheet that describes the workgroup, user groups, memberships, and permissions you plan to use.

To prepare for implementing user-level security

- Launch Word and open the file AC3-0708 from the CD-ROM. Save the form on your floppy disk using the name `Security Plan`.
- Choose a name for the workgroup and identify who will have the authority to administer it. Enter your name and make up a name for the network administrator.
- Fill in the appropriate boxes on the form to describe the following three user groups: Full Permissions, Enter Data, and Read-only. The Enter Data group has permission to enter data into all of the tables except the Private table. The Read-only group may look at any form or report but no tables or queries.
- Fill in the appropriate boxes on the form to describe the following four users: John, Paul, George, and Ringo.
- Assign the four people to the three groups.
- Print the form.

Task Guide

A book in the *Essentials* series is designed to be kept as a handy reference beside your computer even after you have completed all the projects and exercises. Any time you have difficulty recalling the sequence of steps or a shortcut needed to achieve a result, look up the general category in the alphabetized listing below, and then quickly home in on the task at hand. For your convenience, some tasks have been duplicated under more than one category. If you have difficulty performing a task, turn to the page number listed in the third column to locate the step-by-step exercise or other detailed description. For the greatest efficiency in using this Task Guide, take a few minutes to familiarize yourself with the main categories and keywords before you begin your search.

To Do This	Use This Command	Page Number
Application Management		
Database performance: analyze	Make a backup of your database. Choose Tools, Analyze; then select Performance. Select the object(s) you want to analyze; then click OK. Consider the ideas, recommendations, and suggestions, and make the appropriate changes.	[pg. 107]
Set Access defaults	Open a database. Choose Tools, Options from the menu. Make whatever changes are necessary using any of the numerous options. Write down original settings if you may want to reinstate them.	[pg. 201]
Toolbar buttons, add	Right-click on the toolbar; then choose Customize from the shortcut menu. Click the Commands tab and select the category containing the desired button(s). Drag the button to the toolbar and drop it.	[pg. 57]
Toolbar buttons, remove	Right-click on the toolbar; then choose Customize from the shortcut menu. To remove a button, drag it off the toolbar and let go. You can also hold down Alt and drag the button off the toolbar at any time.	[pg. 57]
Database Design		
Document the design	Choose Tools, Analyze; then select Documenter. Select the objects you want to document; then click OK. Click the Print button to print a record of the design.	[pg. 25]

continues ▶

To Do This	Use This Command	Page Number
Database Design		
Interview to determine design	Ask end users about the reports and forms they would like to see from the database. Determine what fields are necessary to produce these reports and forms and how they would be sorted, grouped, and filtered.	[pg. 3]
Organize fields into several tables	Group the fields into tables according to the item, event, person, or thing that they describe. Divide fields into the smallest possible units of information, if necessary. Determine the primary key field for each table.	[pg. 8]
Refine the design	Apply the rules of good database design to make sure that all fields in a table relate directly to the primary key field, that no one-to-many relationships exist between the primary key field and a non-key field (not a primary or foreign key field) within the same table, and that non-key fields do not appear in more than one table.	[pg. 16]
Test the design	Enter sample data into the tables. Determine which reports or forms will use criteria to restrict (filter) the output. Create a query for each report or form of this type to test the ability to filter the data according to the specified criteria.	[pg. 21]
Form		
Colors, change using buttons	In form Design view, select the text or label control you want to format. Use the Font/Fore Color button to change the foreground (usually text) color, the Fill/Back Color button to change the background color, or the Line/Border Color button to change the border color.	[pg. 43]
Colors, change using properties	In form Design view, right-click on the control or label you want to format. Choose Properties; then click the Format tab. In the Font/Fore Color, Fill/Back Color, or Line/Border Color area, click the Build button to choose a color.	[pg. 51]
ControlTips, add to controls	In form Design view, right-click on the control and choose Properties from the shortcut menu. Click the Other tab; then type in the desired ControlTip text in the ControlTip Text box. If the ControlTip is long, create multiple lines by pressing Shift+Enter at desired break points.	[pg. 55]

To Do This	Use This Command	Page Number
Form		
Filter, by filling in a form	Click the Filter by Form button on the toolbar. Enter the values to be matched in the empty form. The values entered in one form will be used with a logical AND function. Additional forms can be used to specify additional criteria by clicking the Or tab. These criteria will be used with those on the first form with the logical Or function.	[pg. 173]
Filter, by selecting contents of a field	Open a form and find a record that has a value you want to use as a filtering criterion for one of the fields. Click the value to place the cursor in that field box. Click the Filter by Selection button on the toolbar.	[pg. 172]
Filter, delete	Open Filter by Form and click the Clear Grid button. Click the Apply Filter button to apply the empty filter.	[pg. 173]
Filter, turn off	Click the Remove Filter button on the toolbar.	[pg. 172]
Format, copy between controls	In the form Design view, select the control or label formatted the way you want it. Click the Format Painter button; then click the control to which you want to copy the format. Double-clicking the Format Painter button keeps it active until you click the Format Painter button again.	[pg. 46]
Status bar, add instructions	In form Design view, right-click on the Control and choose Properties from the shortcut menu. Click the Other tab; then type in the desired Status bar text in the Status Bar Text box.	[pg. 53]
Subform, insert into form	Open an existing form in Design view. Click the Subform/Subreport button on the toolbox and draw a rectangle in the Form Design window where the subform will go. Select the subform from a list of existing forms, or create it using the wizard. The two forms must be based on tables that are joined one-to-many.	[pg. 139]
Query		
Crosstab, create simple	Create a query in Design view. Use the Query Type button to change to a crosstab query. Drag the necessary fields to the query design grid. Use the Crosstab box to choose which fields will be used as row header, column header, and cell value. Click the Total box in the column that will be used as the cell value and pick the desired function. Run the crosstab to see the query results.	[pg. 129]

continues ▶

To Do This	Use This Command	Page Number
Query		
Crosstab, create with conditions	Follow the previous directions to create a crosstab query. Drag any additional fields that may be necessary for setting conditions. Change the Total box in those fields to Expression or Where. Enter the condition(s) in the criteria box(es).	[pg. 132]
Crosstab, create with totals column	Create a query as previously described. Drag a field to the next empty column in the query design grid. Change the contents of the Crosstab box in that column to Row Heading. Change the contents of the Total box to Sum.	[pg. 133]
Parameters, use as Matching Criteria	Place a message that will prompt the user inside the Criteria box in the query design grid. Enclose the message within square brackets. Whenever the query is run, a dialog box appears displaying your message as the prompt and a box where the user may enter a value. The query will operate as if you had entered that value in the criteria box.	[pg. 175]
Parameters, use with Comparison Operators	Comparison operators such as greater than or between may be combined with parameters. Replace the values in the criterion with a parameter.	[pg. 176]
Parameters, use with Wildcards as Criteria	Precede the parameter with the Like operator. The user may enter the first few letters of the desired match followed by an asterisk.	[pg. 178]
Totals tool, use	Create a query in Design view. Add the fields and click the Totals button in the toolbar. Select the function from the Total box for each field you need to calculate. Place conditions in the Criteria row.	[pg. 126]
Report		
Chart Wizard, use	Create a new report. Choose a table or query; then select the Chart Wizard option. Choose the chart type; then add a title and decide whether to include a legend. Alternate between the Chart Wizard and report Design view to adjust the final appearance of the chart.	[pg. 147]
Subreport, insert into report	Open a report in Design view. Click the Subform/Subreport button in the toolbox and draw a rectangle in the Report Design window where the subreport will go. Select the subreport from a list of existing reports or create it using the wizard. The two reports must be based on tables that are joined one-to-many. Select the linking fields and run the query.	[pg. 143]

To Do This	Use This Command	Page Number
Table		
Analyze	Make a backup of your database. Choose Tools, Analyze, and select Table. Select the table you want to analyze. Choose whether to let the wizard decide how to break up the table(s). Move any fields that do not make sense. Rename the new tables. Correct any typos; then decide whether to create a query to duplicate the original table.	[pg. 103]
Link to a large table in another database	Open a database, then click File, Get External Data, Link Tables. Use the Link dialog box to find the desired database and click Link. Choose the desired table and click OK.	[pg. 167]
Relationship: create many-to-many	Create an intermediate table that contains fields that match each of the primary keys in the two tables. Create two, one-to-many relationships by dragging join lines from the appropriate field in the intermediate table to each of the primary key fields in the other two tables.	[pg. 14]
Relationship: create one-to-many	Add the tables to the Relationships window. Drag a join line between the primary key field of the "one" table and a matching field (foreign key) in the "many" table.	[pg. 12]
Relationship: create one-to-one	Add the tables to the Relationships window. Drag a join line between the primary key fields in two tables.	[pg. 10]
Update: based on values in another table	Create a new update query and select both tables. The tables must be joined by a one-to-many relationship. Drag the field to be updated and any other fields to be used with criteria from the target table into the query design. In the Update To box, specify the table and field name by enclosing them in square brackets and separating these by a period. For example: [Table].[Field]. Run the query.	[pg. 79]
Update: by substituting text	Create a query based on the table that needs to be updated. Drag the field to be updated and any other fields that may be used as limiting criteria to the design grid. Enter any necessary criteria. Click the Query Type button and select Update Query. Enter the new text in the Update To box. Click the Run button on the toolbar.	[pg. 71]

continues ▶

To Do This	Use This Command	Page Number
Tables		
Update: linked tables	Click the Relationships and Show Table buttons on the toolbar. If no relationship exists, add the two tables to the Relationships window and drag the primary key field from one table to its corresponding field in the other table. (If a relationship already exists, double-click the relationship line.) In the resulting dialog box, click Enforce Referential Integrity; then click Cascade Update Related Fields and Cascade Delete Related Records. Click Create and close the window.	[pg. 83]
Update: portions of fields	Create an update query. Use an expression such as Left([field name],#ofchars)= "characters" in the criteria box to find the appropriate records. Place an expression that combines new characters within quotation marks plus a portion of the existing field in the Update To box and run the query. [P3L2P8]	[pg. 74]
Update: with a calculated expression	Create an update query. In the Update To box, enter an expression that contains the field names within square brackets and uses mathematical operators. Run the query to update the table.	[pg. 77]
Tools		
Analyze a table	Make a backup of your database. Choose Tools, Analyze; then select Table. Select the table you want to analyze. Choose whether to let the wizard decide how to break up the table(s). Move any fields that do not make sense. Rename the new tables. Correct any typos; then decide whether to create a query to duplicate the original table.	[pg. 103]
Analyze data using Excel	Open the object you want to link; then choose Tools, Office Links, Analyze It with MS Excel. Use Excel to edit, modify, reformat, or analyze the information.	[pg. 112]
Analyze database performance	Make a backup of your database. Choose Tools, Analyze; then select Performance. Select the object(s) you want to analyze and click OK. Consider the ideas, recommendations, and suggestions, and make the appropriate changes.	[pg. 107]
AutoCorrect data entry	Choose Tools, AutoCorrect. Type a shortcut in the Replace box; then type the replacement in the With box. Click Add to add your shortcut to the AutoCorrect list.	[pg. 99]

To Do This	Use This Command	Page Number
Tools		
Encrypt a database	Start Access but do not open a database. Use the Tools, Security, Encrypt/Decrypt command from the menu. Select the database to be encrypted, and enter a new name for it. Click Save to encrypt and save the new version.	[pg. 193]
Name AutoCorrect	Choose Tools, Options; then click the General tab. If necessary, click the check box for the Track name AutoCorrect info option. Click the check box for the Perform name AutoCorrect option. Click OK; then make the field or object name changes.	[pg. 110]
Password, assign	Open the database by choosing the File, Open command and select the Open Exclusive option. Use the Tools, Security, Set Database Password command to display the Set Database Password dialog box. Enter the password. Enter the password again to verify it. Close the database.	[pg. 189]
Password, remove	Open the database in exclusive mode using the File, Open command and the Open Exclusive option. Enter the correct password. Choose Tools, Security, Unset Database Password from the menu. Type the current password and click OK.	[pg. 191]
Spelling, correct	Click the Tables object button and open the table you want to check. Select the column (field) or columns to check; then choose Tools, Spelling or click the Spell Check button. Make any necessary changes.	[pg. 97]
Startup, set parameters	Open the database and choose Tools, Startup from the menu. Select the desired form that will be opened when the database is opened, such as the Main Switchboard. Click any other check boxes to set startup parameters. Close the dialog box and the database. Open the database to test the startup parameters.	[pg. 198]

continues ▶

To Do This	Use This Command	Page Number
Form		
Switchboard, create	Select a database that already has several forms and reports. Choose Tools, Database Utilities, Switchboard Manager from the menu. Click Yes to create a new switchboard. Click Edit to add options to the main switchboard. Click New to add new action buttons. Fill in the resulting dialog box to determine the text to be shown on the switchboard, the action to be taken, and the report or form that is the object of that action. Repeat this process to add more action buttons to the switchboard form. Click the buttons to test them.	[pg. 194]

Glossary

All key terms appearing in this book (in bold italic) are listed alphabetically in this Glossary for easy reference. If you want to learn more about a feature or concept, turn to the page reference shown after its definition. You can also use the Index to find the term's other significant occurrences.

Add mode Enables users to enter new records into a form but does not allow them to view existing records. [pg. 196]

AutoCorrect A tool that enables you to enter shortcuts for longer words or phrases or to correct common typos. [pg. 96]

Cascade delete To delete related data in a second table by deleting a record in the first table. The tables must be joined to make this possible. [pg. 82]

Cascade update To change data in a second table by making a data change in the first table. The tables must be joined to make this possible. [pg. 82]

Comparison operators Used to determine a range of records that qualify to be included in the display. An example is the Between operator. [pg. 177]

Control A general term for objects on a form or report, such as text boxes, label boxes, buttons, and calculated fields. [pg. 42]

ControlTip A pop-up tip that can be added to a control; similar to a ScreenTip. [pg. 55]

Crosstab A query used for summarizing data from large databases; summarizes the relationship between two or more fields. [pg. 124]

Document a design Record a description of the database objects, their properties, and the relationships between them. [pg. 25]

Documenter A tool that looks at database objects and provides information on each object and control. [pg. 96]

Dynaset A subset of data in a database. [pg. 166]

Edit mode Mode that enables the user to make changes, add new records, and view existing records in a form. [pg. 196]

Encryption Using an encoding method to prevent unauthorized access to data. [pg. 193]

Equi-join Another name for an inner join. [pg. 13]

Excluding operators Used to display all of the records that do not match the criteria. [pg. 177]

Fifth Normal Form There are no duplicate non-key fields. [pg. 17]

Filter by Form A search feature that finds all the records matching values that you type into one or more fields on a blank form. [pg. 166]

Filter by Selection A search feature that finds all of the records matching a value in a field that you select. [pg. 166]

First Normal Form The cells in the table must hold a single value; there are no repeating groups or arrays. All entries in the same column are of the same kind, and each column has a unique name. The order of the columns is insignificant. No two rows are identical, and their order is also insignificant. [pg. 16]

Foreign key field The field on the many side of a one-to-many relationship. [pg. 12]

Format Painter A tool that enables you to copy the formatting of a control and paste the format on another control. [pg. 46]

Fourth Normal Form There are no one-to-many relationships between the primary key field and another non-key field in the same table. [pg. 17]

Inner join Only the records that match from both tables; also known as an equi-join. [pg. 13]

Intersection table A table that is used to join two other tables in a many-to-many relationship. It contains the key fields from both tables. [pg. 13]

Join The manner in which the common fields between two tables are associated. [pg. 11]

Key field A primary key field or a foreign key field. [pg. 4]

Left outer join All of the records in the table at the left, plus the matching records in the table on the right. In a one-to-many relationship, it is assumed that the "one" table is on the left. [pg. 13]

Many-to-many A type of relationship in which a record in one table may be related to more than one record in a second table, and a record in the second table may be related to more than one record in the first table. [pg. 13]

Name AutoCorrect A feature that automatically updates related parts of the database when an object or field is renamed. [pg. 96]

Normalization Applying design rules to table structure. [pg. 16]

Null The absence of data—an empty field. A null value is not the same as a zero or a space. [pg. 177]

Office Links A set of tools that enables you to create a mail merge, report data using Word, and analyze data using Excel. [pg. 96]

One-to-many A type of relationship in which a record in one table may be related to more than one record in a second table. [pg. 11]

One-to-one A type of relationship in which a record in one table may be related to one record in a second table. [pg. 10]

Parameter An entry that can be used as a filter or an argument in a formula. [pg. 166]

Password A word or string of characters that is required to gain full or partial access to a multi-user computer system or its data resources. [pg. 189]

Performance Analyzer A tool that looks at database objects and gives recommendations, suggestions, and ideas for improving their performance. [pg. 96]

PivotTable An interactive form that is similar to a crosstab query, showing the relationship between fields in a spreadsheet-like format. [pg. 124]

Property An attribute of a field that you can use to define characteristics of that field. [pg. 21]

Read-only mode Enables the user to view existing records but not change them or add new records. [pg. 196]

Referential integrity A matching field is required to exist in the joined table. [pg. 15]

Relationship The connection between two tables. [pg. 10]

Right outer join All of the records in the table at the right, plus the matching records in the table on the left. In a one-to-many relationship, it is assumed that the "many" table is on the right. [pg. 13]

Second Normal Form The table is in First Normal Form and all the non-key fields in the table relate to the primary key, which is made of a combination of two or more fields. [pg. 17]

Share level security A password is required to open the database. [pg. 189]

Spelling checker A tool that enables you to compare words in your database to words in a dictionary. [pg. 96]

Startup parameters The settings used to control the way a database is opened and what features are available to the user. [pg. 198]

Subform A form placed within another (main) form, showing data from another table related to the selected record from the main form. [pg. 139]

Subreport A report placed within another (main) report, showing data from another table related to the selected record from the main report. [pg. 143]

Switchboard A form that acts as a menu, with buttons that take you to forms or reports, or even other switchboards. [pg. 194]

Table Analyzer A tool that looks for duplications in fields and splits tables to make them more efficient. [pg. 96]

Third Normal Form The table is in Second Normal Form and has no transitive dependencies. [pg. 17]

Update query A query that enables you to replace all or part of a field, or to alter the contents of a numeric field by performing calculations. [pg. 70]

Wildcard An asterisk that may be used in place of text. [pg. 177]

Index

Symbols

*** (asterisks), Like operator, 184**
= (equal sign) comparison operators, 177
 # (pound symbols), complex criteria, 78

A

Add button, 10
Add mode, opening, 196
adding
  conditions (exercise), 159
  subforms, 139-142
    existing forms (exercise), 158
analysis tools
  Documenter (exercise), 120
  Office Links, 112-115
  Performance Analyzer, 107-109
    exercise, 118
  Table Analyzer, 102-106, 117
Analyze command (Tools menu), 25, 103
analyzing data, 135-138
  PivotTables (exercises), 156-161
Apply Filter button, 24, 174
applying Totals tool, 126-128
  queries (exercise), 154
asterisks (*), Like operator, 184
AutoCorrect, 96-102
  command (Tools menu), 100
  dialog box, 100
  exercise, 118
automatic updates, 82-85
AutoReport, 142

B

backgrounds, 62
  modifying with buttons, 43-46
Between operator, 183
borders, modifying with buttons, 43-46
Boyce-Codd Normal Form, 17
brackets, query messages, 175
Build button (Form Design toolbar), 51
buttons
  Add, 10
  Apply Filter, 24, 174
  backgrounds, 43-46
  borders, 43-46
  Clear Grid, 174
  Close, 171
  colors, 43-46
  Database window, 71
  Datasheet view, 78
  Design, 14, 178
  Filter by Form, 24, 173
  Filter by Selection, 172
  Form Design toolbar
    Build, 51
    Define Custom Colors, 51
    Design, 51
    Form Painter, 46-48
    View, 46
  Formatting toolbar, 43-46
    Design, 44
    Fill/Back Color, 45
    Font/Fore Color, 44-45
    Forms object, 43
    Line/Border, 47

Insert Rows, 8
Join Type, 12
Link, 168
Primary Key, 14
Queries, 22, 183
Queries Object, 171
Relationships, 10
Remove Filter, 25, 172-173
Run, 176
Save, 24
Select All, 25
text, 43-46
toolbars
adding to, 64-65
creating, 57-59
editing, 68
macros, 67-68
removing, 59
resetting, 60
View, 176

C

Calculated expressions, updating, 76-79
Calculated Update query, 79
calculations
PivotTables, 135-138
exercises, 156-161
user input (exercise), 183
cascade deletes, 82
exercise, 90
warning messages, 85
cascade updates, 82
creating (exercise), 89-90
character counts, expressions, 75
characters, Mid expressions, 76
Chart Wizard
creating, 147-150
exercise, 157-158
Chart Wizard dialog box, 147
charts
Excel (exercise), 162
reports
Chart Wizard, 147-150
Chart Wizard (exercise), 157-158
Clear Grid button, 174
Close button, 171
Close command (File menu), 150
Color dialog box, 51
colors
backgrounds, 43-46
controls (exercises), 62-63
modifying
exercise, 62
with properties, 50-52
text, 43-46
columns
crosstab queries
conditions (exercises), 155, 159
conditions/totals, 131-135
hiding, 208
combining reports, 143-146
commands
Data menu, Subtotals
Edit menu
Find, 192
Select All, 50
File menu
Close, 150
Get External Data, 167
Page Setup, 146
Print, 26
Help menu, Microsoft Access Help, 210
Tools menu
Analyze, 25, 103
AutoCorrect, 100
Database utilities, 194
Office Links, 113
Options, 201
Security, 189
Startup, 198
comparison operators, 177
queries, 176-177
complex criteria, pound symbols (#), 78
compound filters, creating (exercise), 185
concatenation operator (exercise), 185

conditions
- crosstab queries, 131-135
  - *exercises, 155, 159*

configuring toolbars, 66

controls
- colors, 62-63
- ControlTips, 42
  - *adding to, 54-57*
  - *creating, 52-54*
- formatting
  - *copying between, 46-48*
  - *multiple, 48-50*
- forms, 42
- hiding (exercise), 66
- modifying, 66

ControlTips, 42, 55
- controls, 54-57
- creating, 52-54
- fields
  - *adding to, 63-64*
  - *typing into multiple, 56*
- pointers, 57
- text, 55

copying
- ControlTips, 55
- formatting between controls, 46-48
- status bar text, 54

criteria
- pound symbol (#), 78
- Update queries, 90-91
- wildcards, 177-178

criteria box, 23

Criteria expressions, 79

crosstab queries. *See also* queries
- columns
  - *conditions (exercises), 155, 159*
  - *conditions/totals, 131-135*
- creating, 129-131
  - *exercises, 155, 160*

Crosstab Query Wizard, 129

Crosstab Wizard, exercise, 160

Customize dialog box, 57

D

Data menu commands, Subtotals, 114

data sharing, 188
- defaults, 203
- Help pages, 209-210
- passwords
  - *assigning, 188-190*
  - *exercise, 206*
  - *modifying, 190-191*
  - *removing, 190-191, 206*
- startup parameters
  - *overriding, 200*
  - *setting, 198-207*
- Switchboards, 194-198

Database Utilities command (Tools menu), 194

Database window, 43
- Tables object button, 71

databases
- encrypting, 191-194
  - *exercise, 207*
- passwords
  - *assigning, 188-190*
  - *exercise, 206*
  - *modifying, 190-191*
  - *removing, 190-191, 206*
- PivotTables, 135-138
  - *exercises, 156-157, 161*
- queries
  - *Totals tool, 126-128*
  - *Totals tool (exercise), 154*

Datasheet view, View button, 78

default field settings, modifying, 120

defaults, 201-203

Define Custom Colors button (Form Design toolbar), 51

defining fields, 3-5

deleting, 59

Design button, 14, 178
- Form Design toolbar, 51
- Formatting toolbar, 44

design grids, 22

Design view, 8

designing databases, 2-6
documenting, 25-26
summary reports, 35-38
testing, 21-25
dialog boxes
Chart Wizard, 147
Color, 51
Customize, 57
Edit Relationships, 83
Edit Switchboard Page, 195
Encrypt/Decrypt, 193
Enter Parameter Value, 177-178
Link, 167-168
Link Tables, 168
New Query, 71, 126
New Report, 147
Options, 201-202
Options Datasheet, 202
Password Required, 190-191
Paste Table As, 9
Relationships, 90
Set Database Password, 189
Show Table, 71, 126, 169
Simple Query Wizard, 171
Spelling, 98
Startup, 198-200
SubForm Wizard, 140
Subform/Subreport, 145
Subtotals, 114
Switchboard Manager, 195
Toolbar Properties, 67
Unset Database Password, 191
Zoom, 176
Documenter, 96
dialog box, 25
exercise, 120
window, 25
wizard, 25
documenting database designs, 25-26
Domain/Key Normal Form, 17
dynasets, 166

E

Edit menu commands
Find, 192
Select All, 50
Edit mode, opening, 196
Edit Relationships dialog box, 10, 83, 170
Edit Switchboard Page dialog box, 195
editing toolbar buttons (exercise), 68
Encrypt/Decrypt Database dialog box, 193
encrypting databases, 191-194
exercise, 207
Enter Parameter Value dialog box, 177-178
equal sign (=) comparison operators, 177
equi-joins, 13
Excel
charts (exercise), 162
data, analyzing, 112-119
excluding operators, 177
exclusion filters, creating (exercise), 185
executing queries, 128
existing forms. *See also* forms
adding, 139-142
exercise, 158
expressions
Calculated expressions, 76-79
character counts, 75
Criteria expressions, 79
Left character counts, 75
Mid characters, 76
Right character counts, 75
Update expressions, 79

F

fields
automatic removal of, 74
calculated fields, 92-93
ControlTip text, 56
ControlTips, 63-64
null value fields, 77
properties, 208
status bar messages, 63
text, 91-92

  Update queries, 74-76
    updating, 94
  visual cues, 63
Fifth Normal Form, 17
File menu commands
  Close, 150
  Get External Data, 167
  Page Setup, 146
  Print, 26
files, Read-only, 21
Fill/Back Color button (Formatting toolbar), 45
Filter by Form, 166, 178
  button, 24, 173
  records, 173-174
Filter by Selection, 166, 178
  button, 172
  exercise, 182
  records, 172
filters
  compound filters, creating, 185
  creating (exercise), 182
  exclusion filters, 185
  specific queries (exercise), 186
Find command (Edit menu), 192
First Normal Form, 16-17
Font/Fore Color button (Formatting toolbar), 44-45
foreign key fields, 12
Form Design toolbar
  Build button, 51
  colors, 50-52
  Define Custom Colors button, 51
  Design button, 51
  Form Painter button, 46-48
  Save, 46
  View button, 46
form letters, creating (exercise), 38-39
Form Painter button (Form Design toolbar), 46-48
Form view, creating, 52-54
formatting
  controls, 48-50
  copying between controls, 46-48
  reports, 146
  subforms, 142
Formatting toolbar
  colors, 43-46
  Design button, 44
  Fill/Back Color button, 45
  Font/Fore Color button, 44-45
  Forms object button, 43
  Line/Border Color button, 47
forms
  colors, 62
  controls, 42
    copying formatting between, 46-48
    hiding, 66
    modifying, 62-66
  ControlTips, 63-64
  existing
    adding, 139-142
    adding (exercise), 158
  hiding, 209
  messages, 65-66
  opening, 196
  PivotTables, 135-138
    exercises, 156-157, 161
  startup parameters
    overriding, 200
    setting, 198-207
  subforms
    adding, 139-142
    adding (exercise), 158
  Switchboards, 188
    creating, 194-198
    launching, 198
    linking, 198
  toolbars, 66
  Wizard, 139
Forms object button (Formatting toolbar), 43
Fourth Normal Form, 17
functions, creating (exercise), 160

G-H

Get External Data command (File menu), 167
group accounts, printing, 210

headers, crosstab queries (exercise), 160
Help menu commands, Microsoft Access Help, 210

Help pages
group accounts, 210
user accounts, 210
workgroups, 209
hiding
columns, 208
controls (exercise), 66
forms, 209
relationships, 209
tables, 209

I-K

inner joins, 13
input masks, 75
Insert Rows button, 8
inserting subreports, 142-146
irrelevant records, removing (exercise), 184
Is Not Null operators (exercise), 184
Is Not Null value fields, 177
Is Null value fields, 177
Join Type button, 12
joins, 11-13

L

label control boxes, modifying, 66
Left expressions, character counts, 75
left outer joins, 13
Like operator
matching fields (exercise), 184
queries, 182
Line/Border Color button (Formatting toolbar), 47
Link button, 168
Link dialog box, 167-168
Link Tables dialog box, 168
linked tables, Update queries, 82-85
linking tables, 166-172
links, ControlTips, 57

M

Macros, adding as, 67-68
Mail Merge, exercise, 121
many-to-many relationships, 13-17
matching criteria, parameters, queries, 175-176
menu bars, designing, 200
menu commands
Data menu, Subtotals
Edit menu
Find, 192
Select All, 50
File menu
Close, 150
Get External Data, 167
Page Setup, 146
Print, 26
Help menu, Microsoft Access Help, 210
Tools menu
Analyze, 25, 103
AutoCorrect, 100
Database utilities, 194
Office Links, 113
Options, 201
Security, 189
Startup, 198
messages
forms, 65-66
status bar, 52-54, 63
Microsoft Access Help command (Help menu), 210
Mid expressions, characters, 76
misspelled words, checking, 97-99

N

Name AutoCorrect, 96, 109-112
exercise, 119
New Query dialog box, 71, 126
New Report dialog box, 147
normalization, 16
null value fields, 77, 177

O

objects, summary reports, 120
Office Links, 96, 112-115
command (Tools menu), 113
Excel (exercise), 119
exercise, 119
Word, analyzing, 120

one-to-many relationship, 11-13
one-to-one relationship, 9-11
onscreen, databases, 4
operators
  concatenation operator (exercise), 185
  Like operator
    matching fields (exercise), 184
    queries, 182
Options command (Tools menu), 112, 201
Options Datasheet dialog box, 202
Options dialog box, 201

P

Page Setup command (File menu), 146
parameters, 176-183
parameter queries, 166
Password Required dialog box, 190-191
passwords, 189
  assigning, 188-190
    exercise, 206
  choosing, 190
  encryption, 191-194
    exercise, 207
  modifying, 190-191
  removing, 190-191
    exercise, 206
Paste Table As dialog box, 9
pasting
  ControlTips, 55
  status bar text, 54
Performance Analyzer, 96
  exercise, 118
Performance Analyzer Wizard, 107-109
PivotTables, 135-138
  exercises, 156-157, 161
  viewing, 137
  Wizard, 135
pointers, 57
pound symbols (#), 78
Primary Key button, 14
Print command (File menu), 26
printing
  Help pages (exercise), 209-210
  reports, 26
private tables, creating, 9
properties
  colors, 50-52
  of fields (exercise), 208
  toolbars, 67

Q

queries
  creating, 21-25, 171
  crosstab
    conditions columns (exercises), 155-159
    conditions/totals columns, 131-135
    creating, 129-131
    creating (exercises), 155, 160
  executing, 128
  exercise, 182-183
  form letters (exercise), 38-39
  operators, 176-177
  parameter queries, 166
  Totals feature (exercise), 159
  Totals tool, 126-128
    exercise, 154
  Update queries, 70
    backing up work, 82
    Calculated expressions, 76-79
    calculated fields, 92-93
    cascade deletes, 90
    cascade updates, 82, 89-90
    creating, 93-94
    data replacement, 70-74
    field data removal, 74-76
    field updates, 94
    fields, 91-92
    linked tables, 82-85
    multiple criteria, 90-91
    running multiple times, 79
    table updates, 79-82
  wildcards, 177-178
Queries button, 22, 183
Queries Object button, 171
query design grids, 74
Query Design window, 71, 80

R

read-only files, 21
read-only mode, opening, 196
records
- criteria, 6
- removing (exercise), 184
- selecting Filter by Form, 173-174
- sorting, 4
- tables, 11

redundant fields, eliminating, 16
referential integrity, 15
relationships
- hiding, 209
- join lines, 11
- many-to-many relationships, 13-21
- one-to-many, 11-13
- one-to-one, 9-11
- three tables, 13-21

Relationships button, 10
Relationships dialog box, 90
Relationships window, 10, 169
Remove Filter button, 25, 172-173
reports
- Chart Wizard, 147-150
  - *exercise, 157-158*
- combining, 143-146
- creating, 129-131
- crosstab queries (exercises), 155, 160
- formatting, 146
- pivot (exercises), 156-157, 161
- subreports, 142-146

resetting toolbars, 60
Right expressions, character counts, 75
right outer joins, 13
rows creating queries (exercise), 160
Run button, 176

S

Save button, 24
- Form Design toolbar, 46

screen, modifying, 122
Second Normal Form, 17
security
- encrypting databases, 191-194, 207
- passwords
  - *assigning, 188-190*
  - *exercise, 206*
  - *modifying, 190-191*
  - *removing, 190-191, 206*
- share-level security, 194
  - *exercise, 207*
  - *passwords, 189-191*
- user-level security, 194
  - *planning, 210*

Security command (Tools menu), 189
Select All button, 25
Select All command (Edit menu), 50
selecting
- fields (exercises), 30-34
- records, 173-174

serial numbers, analyzing based on, 89
Set Database Password dialog box, 189
share-level security, 194
- exercise, 207
- passwords, 189-191

shortcut menus, designing, 200
Show Table dialog box, 71, 126, 169
Show Table window, 83
Simple Query Wizard dialog box, 171
sorting records, 4
specific queries (exercise), 186
Spelling checker, 96-99
- exercise, 118

Spelling dialog box, 98
square brackets, query message, 175
Startup command (Tools menu), 198
Startup dialog box, 198-200
startup parameters
- overriding, 200
- setting, 198-200
  - *exercise, 206-207*

status bar, 52-54
- modifying (exercise), 63

SubForm Wizard dialog box, 140
Subform/Subreport Wizard, 142-146

Subform/Subreport Wizard dialog box, 145
subforms, 21
adding, 139-142
exercise, 158
formatting, 142
subreports, inserting, 142-146
Subtotals command (Data menu), 114
Subtotals dialog box, 114
summaries, fields, 4
summary reports
design support (exercises), 35-38
objects, 120
Switchboard Manager dialog box, 195
Switchboards, 188
creating, 194-198
forms, 196
launching, 198
linking, 198
startup parameters
overriding, 200
setting, 198-207

T

Table Analyzer, 96
exercise, 117
Table Analyzer Wizard, 102-106
tables
columns (exercise), 208
fields, organizing, 6-9
First Normal Form, 17
Fourth Normal Form, 17
hiding (exercise), 209
input masks, 75
joins, 11
linked table, 82-85
linking, 166-172
Mail Merge documents, 121
PivotTables, 135-138
exercises, 156-157, 161
private tables, 9
relationships, 9-13
Second Normal Form, 17
Update queries, 70
creating (exercise), 93-94
data replacement, 70-74
updating
Calculated expressions, 76-79
exercise, 88-89
with other table values, 79-82
Tables object button (Database window), 71
testing database designs, 21-25
text
colors, 43-46
fields, 91-92
text control boxes, modifying (exercise), 66
text fields, Update queries, 70
title box, modifying (exercise), 62
titling databases, 3
Toolbar Properties dialog box, 67
toolbars
buttons
adding to (exercise), 64-65
editing (exercise), 68
macros (exercise), 67-68
removing, 59
configuring (exercise), 66
creating, 57-59
customizing, 43
Form Design toolbar, Save, 46
Formatting toolbar, 43-46
properties (exercise), 67
resetting, 60
tools, 126-128
exercise, 154
Tools menu commands
Analyze, 25, 103
AutoCorrect, 100
Database utilities, 194
Office Links, 113
Options, 201
Security, 189
Startup, 198

tools
- AutoCorrect, 99-102
  - *exercise, 118*
- Documenter (exercise), 120
- Mail Merge (exercise), 121
- Name AutoCorrect, 109-112
  - *exercise, 119*
- Office Links, 112-115
  - *exercises, 119-120*
- Performance Analyzer, 107-109
  - *exercise, 118*
- Spelling checker, 97-99
  - *exercise, 118*
- Table Analyzer, 102-106
  - *exercise, 117*

Totals
- conditions (exercise), 159
- tool, 126-128
  - *exercise, 154*

U

Unset Database Password dialog box, 191
Update expressions, 79
Update queries, 70
- backing up work, 82
- calculated expressions, 76-79
- calculated fields, 92-93
- cascade deletes, 90
- cascade updates, 82
  - *creating, 89-90*
- creating (exercise), 93-94
- criteria, 90-91
- fields
  - *adding text to, 91-92*
  - *partial removal of, 74-76*
  - *updating, 94*
- linked tables, 82-85
- running multiple times, 79
- serial numbers, 89
- table data replacement, 70-74
- tables, 79-82, 88-89

updating databases, Name AutoCorrect, 109-112
user accounts, printing, 210
user input, calculations (exercise), 183
user-level security, 194
- planning (exercise), 210

V

view, Design, 8
View button, 176
- Datasheet view, 78
- Form Design toolbar, 46

viewing
- databases, 4
- PivotTables, 137

visual cues, creating (exercise), 63

W-Z

warning messages, cascade deletes, 85
wildcards, 177
windows
- Access, 122
- Database, 43
- Documenter, 25
- Edit Relationships, 15
- Filter by Selection, 172
- Query Design, 71, 80
- Relationships, 10, 169
- Show Table, 83

wizards
- Chart
  - *creating reports, 147-150*
  - *creating reports (exercise), 157-158*
- Crosstab (exercise), 160
- Crosstab Query, 129
- Documenter, 25
- Form, 139
- Performance Analyzer Wizard, 107-109
- PivotTable, 135
- Simple Query, 171
- Subform/Subreport, 142-146
- Table Analyzer Wizard, 102-106, 117

Word, analyzing, Office Links, 120
workgroups, 209

Zoom dialog box, 176